Da!

A Practical Guide to
Russian Grammar

Da!

A Practical Guide to
Russian Grammar

Tatiana Filosofova
and Marion Spöring

HODDER
EDUCATION
AN HACHETTE UK COMPANY

Orders: please contact Bookpoint Ltd, 130 Milton Park, Abingdon, Oxon OX14 4SB. Telephone: (44) 01235 827720. Fax: (44) 01235 400454. Lines are open from 9.00am to 5.00pm, Monday to Saturday, with a 24-hour message-answering service. You can also order through our website www.hoddereducation.co.uk

If you have any comments to make about this, or any of our other titles, please send them to educationenquiries@hodder.co.uk

British Library Cataloguing in Publication Data
A catalogue record for this title is available from the British Library

ISBN: 978 1 444 14878 7

First Edition Published 2012
Impression number   10 9 8 7 6 5 4 3 2 1
Year   2015, 2014, 2013, 2012

Cover photo: Russian dolls © minimo – Fotolia
Typeset by Integra, India.
Printed in Great Britain for Hodder Education, part of Hachette UK, 338 Euston Road, London NW1 3BH.

Contents

Acknowledgements

We would like to thank all our colleagues and students who made valuable inputs to the book. Especially warm thanks are due to the many generations of students at the universities of Glasgow, Dundee, Edinburgh and St Andrews whose linguistic curiosity and determination to learn Russian inspired us to produce this practical grammar book. Special thanks go to John Spink, Anna Darmody and Jeremy Burnell, who read some selected chapters of the book and made their valuable comments.

We would like to express our appreciation to our editors at Hodder Education, Bianca Knights, Lavinia Porter and Virginia Catmur, for their professional advice, help and support throughout all stages of the project.

How to use this book

Добро́ пожа́ловать! We hope you will enjoy using *Да!* This reference grammar and practice book is intended for Basic and Intermediate learners of Russian. All essentials are covered as well as more complex areas of the Russian language.

Read the following information carefully before you start, as it will give you tips on how to get the most out of the book.

Да! can be used in different ways, depending on your purpose.

It can be used to complement textbooks and course materials provided by your tutor or those you use for self-study, to support the understanding and practice of grammar.

There is no particular order in which you have to work through this book. All chapters are self-contained units and can be used in any order. In each chapter you will find cross-reference symbols to help you to look up any relevant topic.

If you wish to find out more about a specific grammatical area, look up the appropriate chapter.

If you would like to revise grammar more systematically, work through the book in sequence.

Features of *Да!*

- A glossary of grammatical terms with quick reference explanations.
- Grammar explanations with summary tables and examples.
- Exercises to practise and consolidate the grammar covered in each chapter and a key with answers.
- Free web resource exercises with the audio answers: to access these, go to www.hodderplus/languages
- Examples are taken from many different, authentic sources, such as business, literary, journalistic, academic and everyday language.
- Indications of level of difficulty in the grammar explanations and in the exercises so that you can choose the most relevant sections for yourself.
- A grammatical index to help you to find the answers to all your queries on Russian grammar.
- Summary tables for quick overview.
- Cross-referencing to related points of grammar, sign-posted by ☞.
- Coverage of points of special difficulty for the English-speaking learner, indicated by .

- Mr Smirnoff, the friendly face of Russian grammar, guiding you through the book

- Stress indicator. Russian stress is unpredictable, except for a small number of patterns that are explained in the book. The acute accent ´ indicates the stressed vowel in each word. The acute accent is omitted as unnecessary in two cases:
  (i) In monosyllabic words.
  (ii) If a word contains the letter Ё(ё), as it is always stressed. In authentic Russian texts the acute accent is not used and the letter Ё(ё) is replaced by the letter Е(е).
- Level indicator icons

Who is *Да!* for?

You need very little previous knowledge of formal Russian grammar in order to use this book. It is assumed, however, that you can read the Cyrillic (Russian) alphabet already so that you can understand the examples. Grammatical terms are explained in English and their Russian counterpart terms are given in the glossary. This way you will be able to use Russian reference textbooks later when you are ready to do so. If you are not yet ready for this, just use the equivalent English terms.

All the basic grammar areas are covered that are essential for Basic to Lower Intermediate level learners who may have just started to learn Russian or need to brush up on the beginnings of more advanced grammar. They are referred to as **Level 1**. If you feel that you are ready to deal with more challenging language concepts, vocabulary and examples, use the examples for **Levels 2** and **3**. See the quick reference guide (below) for descriptions of the levels. On occasion, there will be some overlap between levels.

Most importantly, this book is here to help you to use Russian with greater confidence in speaking and writing by complementing whichever way you have started to learn, in classes or on your own, with a textbook or without, with friends or family, in a Russian-speaking country or with Russian speakers in your home environment.

Да! is recommended for adult learners, but will also appeal to younger age groups. It can be used in schools, colleges and universities, as well as in evening classes, in English-speaking countries.

Quick reference guide to levels

Levels of progression and difficulty generally take into account language level indicators such as those of the CEF (Common European Framework, Council of Europe), and the Russian as a Foreign Language Standards set by the MGU (Moscow State University). Approximate equivalents of levels:

Level 1 up to CEF B1 or MGU Basic
Level 2 CEF B1/B2 or MGU Second Certificate
Level 3 CEF C1/C2 or MGU Third Certificate

Level 1 – Elementary, for beginners and post-beginners, covers essentials such as: basic concepts and vocabulary, basic spelling rules, essential characteristics of nouns, adjectives, pronouns and verbs, with a minimum inclusion of exceptions to rules. There is some overlap with **Level 2** on occasion.

Level 2 – Lower Intermediate, covers more advanced grammar. Vocabulary and concepts at this level have been expanded with the focus on areas that tend to be more challenging for the English-speaking learner, such as use of verbal aspects, verbs of motion and the highly inflected case system. Gerunds and the basic use of participles that are essential for writing are also introduced. There is some overlap with **Levels 1** and **3** on occasion.

Level 3 – Upper Intermediate. Learners are introduced to more complex sentence structures, passive constructions, figurative meanings of the verbs of motion and a more advanced vocabulary. Examples are drawn from more complex authentic texts such as literary extracts and newspapers. There may be some overlap with **Level 2** on occasion.

Most importantly, remember that language learning is about communicating and enjoying working with the language and the experiences it opens up for you.

Enjoy and good luck! Желáем успéха и всегó дóброго! В дóбрый путь!

Tanya Filosofova
Marion Spöring

Glossary of grammatical terms

Adjectives/прилага́тельные are declinable words that describe a noun and agree with a noun they describe in gender, number and case. They can also be used as predicates.

Adverbs/наре́чия are indeclinable words. Adverbs mainly qualify verbs, but also adjectives and other adverbs.

Agreement/согласова́ние is based on the principle that words that provide additional information about a main word must agree grammatically with it.

Articles are defining words before a noun to express whether it is definite (the) or indefinite (a). There are no articles in Russian.

Cases/падежи́ are word forms. Russian has a six-case system. This means that nouns, pronouns, adjectives and numbers have different endings depending on their role in a sentence. The choice of ending depends on that grammatical role, i.e. whether the word acts as a subject or object, or describes location, timing etc.

Clause/гла́вное и́ли прида́точное предложе́ние is a part of a compound or complex sentence that contains a verb.

Conjugation/спряже́ние is a set of verb endings that reflects the person and number they are used in.

Conjunctions/сою́зы are indeclinable link words. They link individual words within a sentence or clauses in compound and complex sentences.

Declension/склоне́ние is a set of endings for nouns, adjectives, pronouns and numerals that reflects the case they are used in.

Gender/род is a grammatical category that divides nouns into masculine, feminine and neuter.

Gerunds/дееприча́стия are a verbal form that combines characteristics of verbs and adverbs.

Infinitive/инфинити́в is the basic (dictionary) form of a verb.

Mood/наклоне́ние is a verbal category that defines the speaker's attitude towards the action.

Nouns/существи́тельные denote material objects, living things, events or ideas.

Numbers (numerals) /числи́тельные are words that denote quantity.

Objects/дополне́ния are nouns, pronouns or phrases at which an action is aimed.

Participles/причáстия	are verbal forms that combine characteristics of verbs and adjectives.
Predicates/сказýемые	are one of the core-elements of a sentence. The predicate explains the actions of the subject or denotes its status or quality. The predicate can appear in a one-word form (verb) or in a compound form consisting of a verbal link with a noun, adjective, participle or infinitive.
Prefixes/пристáвки	consist of one or more syllables added to the beginning of the word, which alter its meaning.
Prepositions/предлóги	clarify the various relationships between a noun, pronoun or a noun phrase and other words in a sentence. Prepositions are mainly used when talking about time, location, start and end points of movement, when indicating ownership, reasons and consequences of an action. Prepositions play an important role in governing nouns or pronouns. Some prepositions can be used in several cases and their use depends on the context.
Pronouns/местоимéния	are words that qualify or replace a noun.
Stems/оснóвы	are a core-part of the word from which different word forms are formed. Stems may consist of a root, prefix and suffix. The ending is not a part of the stem.
Subjects/подлежáщие	are one of the core-elements of a sentence. In active constructions the subject indicates the person or thing who carries out the action. In passive constructions the subject is a person or a thing at whom the action is directed.
Suffixes/сýффиксы	consist of one or more syllables added to the end of the word, which alter its meaning.
Tense/врéмя	indicates the time of an action: present, past or future.
Transitivity/перехóдность	clarifies the relationship between a verb and object. It establishes whether the verb must take a direct object to convey the message correctly (transitive verb) or whether it cannot have an object (intransitive verb).
Verbs/глагóлы	are words that define an action or a state.
Verbal aspect/вид глагóла	is a grammatical category that describes how the action is carried out. There are two verbal aspects. Perfective aspect (**совершéнный вид**) describes a complete, single action. Imperfective aspect (**несовершéнный вид**) describes an ongoing or repeated action or denotes the fact that an action had occurred.
Voice/залóг	is a grammatical category that clarifies the relationship between a verb and subject in a sentence. The verb describes what the subject does itself (active voice), or what is done to the subject by someone or something else (passive voice).

1 Introduction

1.1 About the language

Russian is a widely used language, spoken not only in Russia but across the world by first language (native) speakers, and also by many people who use it as their second language. Estimates vary between 160 and 250 million speakers worldwide.

Russian belongs to the Indo-European family of languages and is one of the East Slavonic languages of the Slavonic languages branch. It shares this Eastern Slavonic grouping with Belarusian and Ukrainian. Other Slavonic language groups are South Slavonic (Bulgarian, Serbian, Croatian, Macedonian and Slovene) and West Slavonic (Polish, Czech and Slovak).

There are 33 letters in the alphabet (21 consonants, 10 vowels, a soft and a hard sign). The name used for the Russian alphabet, Cyrillic, is derived from the initial development of a writing system for Church Slavonic by the Byzantine saint Cyril.

Level 1, 2

1.2 Transliteration

1.2.1 Transliteration of Russian letters into English

Phonetic transcriptions of the sounds of Russian letters are sometimes used by English speakers. However, the current standard transliteration of (written) Russian letters into English is that of the Library of Congress (LOC), Washington, DC. The LOC transliteration is used worldwide. There are also some other transliteration conventions, such as the British Standard transliteration (BS2979:1958) used by Oxford University Press.

Russian printed letter (capital, lower case)	Transliteration (spelling in Latin alphabet), LOC standard	Russian printed letter (capital, lower case)	Transliteration (spelling in Latin alphabet), LOC standard
Й, й	I, i (ĭ)	Щ, щ	Shch, shch
А, а	A, a	Р, р	R, r
Б, б	B, b	С, с	S, s
В, в	V, v	Т, т	T, t
Г, г	G, g	У, у	U, u
Д, д	D, d	Ф, ф	F, f
Е, е Ё, ё	E, e Ë, ë	Х, х	Kh, kh
Ж, ж	Zh, zh	Ц, ц	Ts, ts
З, з	Z, z	Ч, ч	Ch, ch
И, и	I, i	Ш, ш	Sh, sh

Russian printed letter (capital, lower case)	Transliteration (spelling in Latin alphabet), LOC standard	Russian printed letter (capital, lower case)	Transliteration (spelling in Latin alphabet), LOC standard
К, к	K, k	ъ	”
Л, л	L, l	Ы, ы	Y, y
М, м	M, m	ь	’
Н, н	N, n	Э, э	Ė, ė
О, о	O, o	Ю, ю	Iu, iu
П, п	P, p	Я, я	Ia, ia

Comments on the table

- The letter Ë, ë is not used in authentic Russian texts. It appears only in texts especially designed for foreign learners, in order to indicate pronunciation. When transliterating Ë, ë, the letter E, e is often used.
- Some Russian proper names are still transliterated using a nineteenth-century French system of transliteration. For example, the name of the famous Russian composer Чайко́вский is spelt Tchaikovsky, the name of the Russian entrepreneur Смирно́в is spelt Smirnoff.

1.2.2 Transliteration of some English words into Russian

Spelling of foreign names is based on an approximation of the word to Russian phonetic (pronunciation) rules. For example, Шекспи́р – Shakespeare.

The letter *h* (when it has a 'breathy' sound at the beginning of a word or syllable) is expressed by either **г** or **х**	**Г**а́мбург (Hamburg), **Г**ава́йи (Hawaii), **Г**олливу́д (Hollywood), **Х**э́мптон Корт (Hampton Court) Exception: **ю**мор (humour)
The letter *j* is expressed by two letters, **дж**	**Дж**он (John)
The letter *w*, when used as a consonant, is expressed by either **в** or **у**	**В**и́льям, **У**и́льям (William)
English *th* is often expressed by **т**	Пер**т** (Perth)

Level 1, 2 ## 1.3 Spelling rules

There are some basic spelling rules in Russian that are important for word formation and declension. The general concept of the spelling rules is as follows:

Certain vowels cannot be written after certain consonants in any position within a word (prefix, root, suffix, ending). These rules affect the declension of nouns, adjectives, pronouns and numerals, verb conjugations and the formation of various verbal forms.

The most important rules are listed here.

1.3.1 Spelling rule 1

After	Never write	Always write
г, к, х, ж, ш, щ, ч, ц	я	а
г, к, х, ж, ш, щ, ч, ц	ю	у

For example, маши́на, ре́ки, крича́т, чу́до, высо́кий, больши́е, ти́хий, лежу́.

Exceptions: **Цю́рих** (Zurich), пара**шю́**т.

1.3.2 Spelling rule 2

After	Never write	Always write
г, к, х, ж, ш, щ, ч	ы	и

For example, пла**щи́**, вра**чи́.**

1.3.3 Spelling rule 3

To follow this rule it is necessary to know where the stress falls.

After	Write	Write
ж, ш, щ, ч, ц	о (if stressed)	е (if unstressed)

For example, хоро́**ш**его, большо́го.

1.4 Hard and soft stems and endings

Russian makes a distinction between *hard* and *soft* stems and endings. This influences the *declension* and *formation* of the words, as the *stem* and *ending* of a word indicate whether the word follows the hard or soft ending pattern. If the dictionary form of a word has a hard ending, it follows the hard ending pattern when it declines. If the dictionary form of a word has a soft ending, it follows the soft ending pattern when it declines.

The dictionary form of a noun **has a hard ending if it ends with:**

- Vowels **а, о, у, ы** or **э**
- Any consonant except **й, ч** or **щ**

The dictionary form of a noun **has a soft ending if it ends with:**

- Vowels **я, ё, ю, и** or **е**
- Consonants **й, ч** or **щ**
- The soft sign **ь**

Examples of nouns with hard endings	Examples of nouns with soft endings
у́гол (corner), брат (brother), оте́ц (father), каранда́ш (pencil), дом (house), хулига́н (hooligan)	автомоби́ль (car), у́голь (coal)
сестра́ (sister)	земля́ (earth)

👁 The consonants **г, к, х, ж, ш, ч, щ** and **ц** are affected by spelling rules (☞ 1.3). The spelling rules do not change the hardness or softness of the stem or ending, but modify the pattern that the word follows when it is declined.

Adjectival endings contain two letters. The first letter of the ending indicates its hardness or softness. The dictionary form of an adjective **has a hard ending if it ends with -ый or -ой**. The dictionary form of an adjective **has a soft ending if it ends with -ий**. The verb conjugation and formation of the verbal forms are not affected by the hardness or softness of their stems and endings.

1.5 Use of lower-case (small) and upper-case (capital) letters

The use of small and capital letters does not always correspond in Russian and English. In Russian, capital letters are used:

- At the beginning of a sentence: **У** нас есть до́мик в дере́вне. (We have a small house in the country.)
- For proper names: **Л**о́ндон (London), **С**мит (Smith). However, if names of inanimate objects, such as institutions, official titles, names of holidays etc. consist of several words, usually only the first word is written with a capital letter: **Н**о́вый **г**од (New Year), **Б**ольшо́й **т**еа́тр (the Bolshoi Theatre), **Н**о́белевская **п**ре́мия (the Nobel Prize).
- If a geographical name consists of a proper name and a word that indicates generic type, only the proper name is written with a capital letter: **М**осква́-**р**ека́ (river Moskva), **С**е́верный **п**о́люс (North Pole).
- Governmental and international organisations are usually spelt with capital letters throughout: **С**ою́з **С**ове́тских **С**оциалисти́ческих **Р**еспу́блик (USSR), **С**оединённые **Ш**та́ты **А**ме́рики (USA).
- To indicate the formal 'you' (**Вы**) in all its forms: **Б**лагодарю́ **В**ас. (I thank you.)

Unlike in English, the following words are written with small (lower-case) letters:

- Nouns and adjectives describing nationality or inhabitants of cities and towns: Он – **а**мерика́нец. (He is American.) Они́ **п**етербу́ржцы. (They are from St Petersburg.)
- Nouns and adjectives describing country of origin of people or objects: Мы пьём **и**нди́йский чай. (We drink Indian tea.)
- Days of the week and months: Он прие́хал в **с**убббо́ту. (He arrived on Saturday.) У них о́тпуск в **с**ентябре́. (They will take a holiday in September.)
- The pronoun **я** (I): Вчера́ **я** был до́ма. (Yesterday I stayed at home.)

Level
1, 2

Упражне́ния

1. Insert the appropriate letter:

1. Мой кни́г… (и/ы) 2. В сле́дующ…м (о/е) году́ 3. Где леж…т (а/я) игру́шк… (и/ы)? 4. Они́ испа́нц… (и/ы). 5. Говори́ть о Больш…м (о/е) те́атре.

2. Divide the nouns into two columns. Put the nouns with a hard ending into the first column and those with a soft ending into the second:

стул, слова́рь, окно́, Австра́лия, собра́ние, чай, врач, пого́да, психоло́гия, пло́щадь

2 Nouns: animate and inanimate nouns, and gender

Nouns define and name material objects, living things, events and abstract concepts, for example, дом (house), добро́ (kindness), вы́боры (elections), челове́к (person). Nouns fall into two categories:

- Proper nouns (names): Москва́ (Moscow), Мари́я (Maria).
- Common nouns such as type or class: го́род (city), фами́лия (last name/surname).

Russian nouns have the following characteristics. For detailed information about these characteristics, see the sections indicated:

- Nouns do not take an article (☞ 2.1).
- Nouns can be animate or inanimate (☞ 2.2).
- Nouns are divided into three genders: masculine, feminine and neuter (☞ 2.3).
- Most nouns have two number forms – singular and plural. A small group of nouns can be used only in either the singular or plural but not both (☞ 3.1–3.6).
- All nouns, apart from a few exceptions, are declinable. This means nouns change their ending according to their grammatical role in the sentence, such as subject, object, description of location, expression of time etc. Nouns can be presented in six grammatical forms, called cases. The six-case system is one of the core elements of Russian grammar. For the meaning and function of the six-case system and the principles of case formation (declension), ☞ 4. For individual cases ☞ 5–10.

2.1 Absence of articles

Unlike English, Russian has neither definite (*the*) nor indefinite (*a*) articles. When translating from English into Russian the articles are omitted. For example:

This is **a** book.   Это кни́га.
The/a book is on the table.   Кни́га на столе́.

2.2 Animate and inanimate nouns

The grammatical division of nouns into animate and inanimate categories is different in Russian when compared with English. It is important to understand this division for two practical reasons:

- The concept of animate/inanimate nouns affects the form of the direct object of the sentence, which is expressed by the accusative case (☞ 6.2.1). In the accusative case, masculine animate and inanimate singular nouns take different endings (☞ 4.2.1.1); and all animate and inanimate nouns in the plural take different endings (☞ 4.3.1).
- The choice between **кто?** (who?) and **что?** (what?) depends on whether the noun is animate or inanimate. It is necessary to use **кто?** (who?) when asking about animate nouns and **что?** (what?) when asking about inanimate nouns.

In Russian, the following nouns are animate:

- People, except some collective nouns such as толпа (crowd), народ (people), молодёжь (youth), áрмия (army).
- All types of animals, general or individual, except micro-organisms: микроб (microbe), вирус (virus), бактéрия (bacterium), and some collective nouns that describe animals: скот (cattle), стáя (flock).
- Fictitious creatures, if they can act as 'a human', such as вампир (vampire), чудовище (monster), зóмби (zombie), русáлка (mermaid).

The remaining nouns are inanimate.

Level 3

👁 Curiously, the nouns покойник and мертвéц (dead person) are animate, but the noun труп (corpse) is inanimate. Some nouns that can 'imitate' human activity, such as рóбот (robot), кýкла (puppet/doll), ферзь ('queen' in chess, or any other chess figure), change their endings as animate nouns. However, they respond to the question of an inanimate noun **что?** (what?). In the case of animals, if they are considered as 'food' and not living beings, they decline as inanimate nouns. Sometimes both forms, animate and inanimate, are acceptable. For example:

Из рецéпта (an extract from a recipe):

Кальмáры (accusative, inanimate) отварить, нарéзать.	Boil the squid and then slice them.
Кальмáров (accusative, animate) вáрят в солёной водé.	Boil the squid in salt water.

2.3 Gender

Gender is one of the key points of Russian grammar, as noun declension and formation of plural nouns are determined by the noun gender. There are some additional factors that contribute to the formation of various grammatical noun forms: softness or hardness of the noun stem and some spelling rules (☞ 1.3–1.4).

In a sentence, all the words that describe a noun agree in gender with the noun that they qualify (☞ 11, 14, 15, 16.2.3).

Level 1, 2

2.3.1 Natural (biological) and grammatical gender

Russian nouns are divided into three genders: masculine, feminine and neuter. The gender of all Russian nouns describing people and animals is determined by their *natural* (biological) gender. The majority of these nouns have male/female gender pairs: брат (brother) – сестрá (sister); муж (husband) – женá (wife); кот (tomcat) – кошка (female cat); бык (bull) – корóва (cow) etc. The gender of all other nouns is considered as *grammatical* gender as opposed to *natural* (biological) gender. It is determined purely by the noun ending in the dictionary form. For example, nouns ending in a consonant in their dictionary form fall into the category of masculine grammatical gender. Nouns ending in the vowels -а/-я in their dictionary form fall into the category of feminine grammatical gender. As the examples above show, the *biological* and *grammatical* gender of the majority of nouns coincide. However, there are some exceptions.

- 👁 Note that the natural and grammatical genders of a noun do not always coincide. If this is the case, the **natural (biological) gender of the noun prevails**. In Russian, several nouns denoting a male person, including Russian shortened male names and diminutive male names, have feminine endings -а/-я. These nouns fall into the category of masculine nouns, and agree with the masculine form of the adjective (☞ 11), but follow the pattern of feminine nouns when declined (☞ 4.2.2).

Male persons	Shortened male names	Diminutive male names
па́па (daddy)	Пе́тя (Petya)	Пе́тенька (Peten'ka)
де́душка (granddad) дя́дя (uncle)	Са́ша (Sasha)	Са́шенька (Sashen'ka)
ю́ноша (youth) *young man*	Ми́ша (Misha)	Ми́шенька (Mishen'ka)
мужчи́на (man)	Во́ва (Vova)	Во́вочка (Vovochka)

ю́ность noonisch as collectiv

- Some indeclinable nouns of foreign origin ending with **-e, -o, -y** are masculine, if they are animate and describe animals (☞ 2.3.7).

Level 3
The majority of nouns denoting animals have two different forms, male and female. Curiously, two commonly used nouns have only a feminine form: соба́ка (dog) *sabaka* and обезья́на (monkey) *abezyana*. The masculine word пёс (dog) *pyos* is used mainly in idioms and when talking about a pet in popular speech. All nouns denoting young animals are masculine: котёнок (kitten) *katyonak*, щено́к (puppy) *shchynok* etc. If it is necessary to indicate the gender of an animal, two additional words, саме́ц (male) or са́мка (female) are used. In popular speech, Russians often use the words ма́льчик (boy) or де́вочка (girl) when indicating the gender of pets.

Level 2

2.3.2 Gender of nouns denoting occupation

- Most nouns denoting occupations have **only a masculine form**:

  стро́итель *straiciel*   builder   профе́ссор   professor
  пло́тник   carpenter   врач *vrach*   doctor

- A few nouns denoting occupations have **only a feminine form**:

  домохозя́йка *damacha zyayka*   housewife   ня́ня/сиде́лка   nanny/nurse

In these cases, the same noun is used to describe both male and female persons who hold these occupations. An adjective used in this construction must agree with the noun that names an occupation:

  Он изве́ст**ный** профе́ссор. *izvyestnyey*   He is a famous professor.
  Она́ изве́ст**ный** профе́ссор.   She is a famous professor.

- Several nouns denoting occupations use suffixes to make the feminine noun of the pair. The most common suffixes are **-к-, -анк-, -ниц-/-иц-, -чиц-, -щиц-, -ис-/-есс-**.

Male	Female
студе́нт (student)	студе́нт**к**а
учи́тель (teacher)	учи́тель**ниц**а
царь (tsar)	цар**и́ц**а
перево́дчик (translator)	перево́д**чиц**а *perevodchitsa / perevotcheek*
продаве́ц (a shop assistant)	продав**щи́ц**а *prodavshitza*
актёр (actor) *aktyor*	актр**и́с**а
поэ́т (poet)	поэт**е́сс**а

перево́д = translation

2.3.3 Inanimate masculine nouns

In Russian, the following inanimate nouns are considered masculine:

- All nouns that end with a consonant, for example:

стол	table
чай	tea
дом	house

- Some nouns ending in **-ь**. Note that in Russian there are many nouns ending in **-ь** that are feminine nouns. Therefore, the gender of nouns ending with **-ь** must be checked in a dictionary. Here are some frequently occurring masculine nouns ending with **-ь**:
  - Months ending in **-ь**
  - A number of occupations (☞ 2.3.2)
  - Other commonly occurring nouns ending with **-ь** include путь (way), портфе́ль (briefcase), слова́рь (dictionary), день (day), ого́нь (fire), у́голь (coal), календа́рь (calendar), рубль (rouble), дождь (rain), кора́бль (ship).

2.3.4 Inanimate feminine nouns

In Russian, the following inanimate nouns are considered feminine:

- All inanimate nouns that end with vowels **-а/-я**, if they are not masculine (☞ 2.3.1):

кни́га	book
дере́вня	village
Росси́я	Russia

- Many nouns with the soft sign **-ь** (the gender of nouns ending with **-ь** must be checked in a dictionary):

пло́щадь	square
о́бласть	district

2.3.5 Inanimate and animate neuter nouns

In Russian, the following inanimate nouns are considered neuter:

- All inanimate nouns that end with the vowels **-о, -е, -ё**:

окно́	window
по́ле	field
общежи́тие	hall of residence
ружьё	gun

- Some indeclinable nouns of foreign origin ending with **-и, -у, -ю** (☞ 2.3.7)
- Nouns that end with **-мя**:

вре́мя	time		стре́мя	stirrup
се́мя	seed		и́мя	name
бре́мя	burden		зна́мя	banner
пле́мя	tribe		те́мя	crown (of head)
вы́мя	udder		пла́мя	flame

Most Russian neuter nouns are inanimate. A few animate nouns ending with **-о**, **-ое**, or **-ее** denote a type or class of living beings. These are also considered neuter: живо́тное (animal), насеко́мое (insect), млекопита́ющее (mammal), лицо́ (person), существо́ (creature). The noun дитя́ (baby) is also considered neuter.

Level 3

2.3.6 Nouns of common gender

In Russian, there are several nouns ending in -а/-я that can function as masculine or feminine nouns. Usually they indicate personal characteristics or status: ýмница (clever person), неряха (untidy person). For example:

Какóй **он ýмница**!	What a clever man he is!
Какáя **онá ýмница**!	What a clever woman she is!
Он прекрáсный **коллéга**.	He is a great colleague.
Онá прекрáсная **коллéга**.	She is a great colleague.

Level 2, 3

2.3.7 Gender of indeclinable nouns of foreign origin and abbreviations

The majority of indeclinable nouns of foreign origin, including names, are:

- Masculine, if they are animate and describe animals: кенгурý (kangaroo), шимпанзé (chimpanzee). If it is necessary to indicate the gender of the individual animal, the additional word for male or female is used in this context: самéц кенгурý (male kangaroo), сáмка шимпанзé (female chimpanzee).
- Neuter, if they are inanimate: метрó (metro), таксú (taxi), интервью (interview), меню (menu). There are some exceptions. For example, кóфе (coffee), пенáльти (penalty) and торнáдо (tornado) are masculine nouns and салями (salami) and авеню (avenue) are feminine.
- Masculine or feminine, if they are animate, describing people. Their grammatical gender coincides with the natural (biological) gender of the person, regardless of the noun ending: стáрая лéди (old lady) – feminine, велúкий **Вéрди** (Great Verdi) – masculine.

However, indeclinable nouns of foreign origin that name a geographical location (including rivers, mountains, cities etc.), titles of published materials (books, newspapers etc.) and some names of insects, birds or animals follow different rules. Their gender coincides with the gender of the Russian noun that describes the relevant class/type: большóй **гóрод** Тбилúси (masculine, because of the masculine gender of the noun **гóрод**) – the big **city** of Tbilisi; газéта «Таймс» (feminine, because of the feminine gender of the noun **газéта**) – the 'Times' **newspaper**; мýха цецé (feminine, because of the feminine gender of the noun **мýха**) – tsetse fly.

The grammatical gender of abbreviations is determined by the grammatical gender of the principal noun in the abbreviation. For example, АЭС – áтомная электростáнция (nuclear power station) is a feminine noun because the principal noun of this abbreviation, **электростáнция** (power station), is feminine.

Level 1

Упражнéния

1. Identify the nouns as either A (animate) or I (inanimate):
кот, семья, человéк, я́блоко, лóшадь, вúрус, окнó, милиционéр, пáпа, нарóд, чудóвище, рóбот.

2. Divide the nouns into three columns, masculine, feminine and neuter:
окнó, упражнéние, Москвá, Урáл, кóмната, чай, врéмя, человéк, я́рмарка, план, дéло, янвáрь, плóщадь, живóтное.

Обобщáющее упражнéние

Level 1, 2

For adjectives, ☞ 11.1.

3. Identify the gender of each noun. Form phrases by combining the adjectives provided and the nouns.

Модель: трамва́й – m, но́вый трамва́й.

А. молодо́й: ю́ноша, де́вушка, маэ́стро, млекопита́ющее, водопрово́дчик.

В. большо́й: Онта́рио (о́зеро), такси́, ООН (Организа́ция Объединённых На́ций).

С. интере́сный: хо́бби, конце́рт, заявле́ние.

3 Nouns: number

Level 1, 2, 3

As in English, Russian nouns have two numbers: singular and plural.

The plural noun is formed by adding the appropriate ending to the singular form. The plural noun ending is determined by **the noun gender, hardness or softness of the noun's stem and the spelling rules.**

To form any plural noun, take the following steps:

- If a noun ends with **a consonant other than й,** remove nothing. Such a singular noun has no ending.
- If a noun ends with **a vowel, ь** or **й,** remove it.
- What is left after removing the ending is **the stem** of the word.
- Decide whether the stem is **hard** or **soft** (☞ 1.4).
- Check whether any **spelling rules** apply (☞ 1.3).
- Add the appropriate ending.
- Note that some nouns are irregular and follow a special pattern.

Level 1, 2

3.1 Plural masculine and feminine nouns

Masculine and feminine nouns follow the same pattern:

	Masculine nouns with hard stem	Feminine nouns with hard stem	Masculine nouns with soft stem	Feminine nouns with soft stem	Masculine and feminine nouns that are affected by spelling rules
Singular	Noun ends in a consonant that is not affected by the spelling rules	Noun ends in **-a** and the stem of a noun ends in a consonant that is not affected by the spelling rules	Noun ends in **-ь** or **-й**	Noun ends in **-я** or **-ь**	Stem of the noun ends in **-г, -к, -х, -ж, -ш,-ч,** or **-щ** and therefore is affected by a spelling rule (☞ 1.3)
	стол	газе́та	слова́рь	дере́вня	каранда́ш/ кни́га
Plural	**-ы**	**-ы**	**-и**	**-и**	**-и**
	столы́	газе́ты	словари́	дере́вни	карандаши́ / кни́ги

Level 1, 2

3.2 Plural neuter nouns

Neuter nouns follow a pattern which differs from that of masculine and feminine nouns:

	Neuter nouns with hard stem	Neuter nouns with soft stem	Neuter nouns with soft stem
Singular	Noun ends in **-o**	Noun ends in **-e**	Noun ends in **-ё**
	окно́	*sea* мо́ре/общежи́тие	ружьё
Plural	**-а**	**-я**	**-я**
	о́кна	моря́/общежи́тия	ру́жья

Level 2
3.3 Irregular plural nouns

👁 In Russian, there are many irregular plural nouns. Note that the list below is not exhaustive, but it does include some frequently occurring nouns.

- Some masculine nouns have plural ending **-а/-я** instead of **-ы/-и**. Note that the stress moves to the last syllable in the plural:

лес (forest) – леса́
дом (house) – дома́
глаз (eye) – глаза́
век (century) – века́
но́мер (number/hotel room) – номера́
профе́ссор (professor) – профессора́
па́спорт (passport) – паспорта́
дире́ктор (director) – директора́

бе́рег (shore) – берега́ *На берегу́.*
го́род (city) – города́
по́езд (train) – поезда́ *poyezd.*
о́стров (island) – острова́ *ostraf -*
ве́чер (evening) – вечера́
учи́тель (teacher) – учителя́
а́дрес (address) – адреса́
го́лос (voice) – голоса́

- Some neuter nouns have plural ending **-и** instead of **-а/-я**:

у́хо (ear) – у́ши
ве́ко (eyelid) – ве́ки
плечо́ (shoulder) – пле́чи

коле́но (knee) – коле́ни
я́блоко (apple) – я́блоки

- Some masculine and neuter plural nouns end in **-ья** instead of **-ы/-и**:

друг (friend) – друзья́ *zdrook*
брат (brother) – бра́тья *brasia*
стул (chair) – сту́лья
де́рево (tree) – дере́вья

перо́ (feather) – пе́рья
крыло́ (wing) – кры́лья
лист (leaf) – ли́стья
сын (son) – сыновья́

- Some masculine nouns have a different word altogether as their plural form:

челове́к (person) – **лю́ди** (people)   **ребёнок** (child) – **де́ти** (children)
ribyonik *anglichanin*

Level 2, 3
3.4 Plural nouns that follow special patterns

👁 Some nouns follow special patterns in plural. Note that the list below is not exhaustive, but it does include some frequently occurring nouns:

- Nouns in **-ин** that indicate a status or nationality lose the suffix **-ин** and can have various endings, **-е**, **-ы** or **-а**: *anglichanyen*

крестья́нин (peasant) – крестья́не *Christianeen*
граждани́н (citizen) – гра́ждане *grazdanyeen*
тата́рин (Tatar man) – тата́ры *Hozyayeen*
хозя́ин (owner/master) – хозя́ева

англича́нин (Englishman) – англича́не
болга́рин (Bulgarian man) – болга́ры
грузи́н (Georgian) – грузи́ны
господи́н (Mr, Sir) – господа́ *gaspadeen*

- Nouns in **-онок/-ок/-ёнок** that indicate young animals lose the suffixes **-онок/-ок/-ёнок** and replace them with the suffixes **-ат/-ят.** They usually have the ending **-а**:

волчо́нок (wolf-cub) – волча́та *Valchyonok*
котёнок (kitten) – котя́та

щено́к (puppy) – щеня́та/щенки́
поросёнок (piglet) – порося́та

- The nouns мать (mother) and дочь (daughter) have the suffix -ер- added to the stem before the feminine soft ending -и:

  мать (mother) – ма́тери   дочь (daughter) – до́чери

- Neuter nouns ending in -мя (☞ 2.3.5) have the suffix -ен- added to the stem before the ending:

  вре́мя (time) – времена́   и́мя (first name) – имена́

3.5 Nouns that have only a plural form

Level 2, 3

- Several nouns have only a plural form. Some of them indicate a pair (for example, 'a pair of trousers'). Note that the list below is not exhaustive, but it does include some frequently occurring nouns:

брю́ки	trousers	джи́нсы	jeans
очки́	spectacles	но́жницы	scissors
роди́тели	parents		

- Other nouns that are used only in the plural:

де́ньги	money	по́хороны	funeral
весы́	scales	часы́	clock/watch
вы́боры	elections	су́тки	twenty-four hours
сли́вки	cream	ро́ды	childbirth
кани́кулы	student vacation	макаро́ны	pasta

3.6 Nouns that only have a singular form

Level 2, 3

Some nouns have only a singular form. Among them are:

Collective nouns	Abstract nouns
молодёжь (youth)	любо́вь (love)
ме́бель (furniture)	внима́ние (attention)
посу́да (crockery)	вес (weight)
оде́жда (clothes)	длина́ (length)
Substances/Liquids:	**Food (vegetables, berries)**
желе́зо (iron)	лук (onions)
нефть (oil)	карто́фель (potatoes)
вода́ (water)	мали́на (raspberries)

The list above is not exhaustive, but it does include some frequently occurring nouns.

3.7 Stress change

Level 2, 3

The position of the stress changes in the following plural nouns:

- In **two-syllable** plural neuter nouns the stress moves to the opposite syllable from its original position in the singular form:

  окно́ (window) – о́кна   мо́ре (sea) – моря́
  де́ло (business/matter) – дела́

- In **one-** or **two-syllable** plural masculine nouns, the stress usually moves from the stem to the ending:

сад (garden) – сады́

вéчер (evening) – вечерá

язы́к (tongue/language) – языки́

Упражнéние

Level 1, 2

1. Give the plural of the following singular nouns:

ло́шадь, сад, кни́га, сестра́, брат, маши́на, соба́ка, преподава́тель, мо́ре, окно́, каранда́ш, англича́нин, го́род, упражнéние, край.

Level 2

2. Replace:

A. The singular nouns by plural.

B. The plural nouns by singular.

A. Моде́ль: го́род – города́

дом, глаз, у́хо, я́блоко, ребёнок, граждани́н, щено́к, мать, вре́мя.

B. Моде́ль: де́ти – ребёнок

друзья́, англича́не, порося́та, паспорта́, до́чери, пле́чи, учителя́, дере́вья, имена́.

Level 1, 2

Обобща́ющее упражнéние

3. Replace the English plural nouns by Russian equivalents in the correct form.

Познако́мьтесь с господи́ном Смирно́вым

Господи́н Смирно́в пока́зывает фотогра́фию свое́й семьи́ и объясня́ет, кто есть кто:

1. Вот сидя́т мои́ (**parents**), (**uncles, aunts**) и (**twin nephews**). 2. У них (**kittens**). 3. Ря́дом с ни́ми – мои́ (**nieces**). 4. Сле́ва стоя́т мои́ (**female cousins**). 5. Ря́дом с ни́ми – их (**husbands**). 6. Они́ о́ба (**Englishmen**) и у них одина́ковые (**names**). 7. Спра́ва – мои́ родны́е (**brothers**) и их (**wives**). 8. А сза́ди стоя́т мои́ (**colleagues**) и (**friends**).

4 Nouns: the concept of cases and the principle of noun declension

4.1 Concept of cases

Russian belongs to a group of languages that have a well-developed system of declension of nouns, pronouns, adjectives and numerals. Other languages that have well-developed systems of declension include Latin, Greek, Finnish, German, Dutch and other Slavic languages.

Unlike English, word order in a Russian sentence is flexible and does not determine a word's function in a sentence (☞ 31.2). In Russian, the form of the word, in particular its ending, is essential for the definition of the word's role in the sentence. There may also be prepositions governing nouns in a sentence. Prepositions are also important for helping us to understand the functions words play in a sentence.

The choice of ending depends on what grammatical role the word plays in a sentence: whether it acts as subject or object, or describes location, destination, timing, ownership etc. The endings help us to understand the relationship between the words in the sentence. In contemporary Russian, each noun, pronoun, adjective and numeral can have six different grammatical forms called cases. (There is a small number of indeclinable nouns, mainly of foreign origin; ☞ 2.3.7.) Each case has various possible endings. The names of the Russian cases are as follows:

- Nominative
- Accusative
- Genitive
- Dative
- Instrumental
- Prepositional

The verb in a Russian sentence agrees with the subject of the sentence and changes its endings to agree with the subject. The subject of the sentence is usually a noun, personal pronoun or noun phrase. For discussion of the verb and its forms, ☞ 16–25.

The examples below show how different cases (forms) of the noun **Москва́** (Moscow) convey the different grammatical roles of the noun **Москва́** in the sentence:

Москва́ – столи́ца России.	**Moscow** is the capital of Russia.	The nominative case indicates the subject of the sentence.
Я люблю́ **Москву́**.	I love **Moscow.**	The accusative case indicates the direct object of the sentence.
Это музе́и **Москвы́**.	Here are the museums **of Moscow.**	The genitive case indicates the origin of the museums.
Мы гуля́ем **по Москве́**.	We are **walking around Moscow.**	The dative case here indicates the route of the journey.

| Россияне гордя́тся **Москвóй**. | Russians are **proud of Moscow.** | The verb 'to be proud of' requires the instrumental case without a preposition. |
| Они́ живу́т **в Москвé**. | They live **in Moscow.** | The prepositional case used with the preposition **в** (in) indicates location. |

4.1.1 Nominative case

The nominative case is that given as the dictionary form of nouns, pronouns, adjectives and numerals (☞ 5).

4.1.2 Five *oblique* cases

The five cases (other than the nominative) are called the *oblique* cases. The accusative, genitive, dative and instrumental cases can be used with or without prepositions. The prepositional case must be used with a preposition. Each of the *oblique* cases can have several grammatical roles in a sentence. The *oblique* cases can denote:

- The object of a sentence (direct and indirect)
- Location (where)
- The start and end points of a movement (going to and coming from)
- The route of a journey (moving around, across, along etc.) and the distance
- Time (when, frequency and duration)
- Ownership and relationship (whose?)
- Quantity (how many? how much?)
- Size, shape, weight, length, age, cost
- Instrument of an action (by what, with what)

Additionally, each of the *oblique* cases can have:

- Several verbs that require the particular case
- Several prepositions that are used with the particular case

All five cases can also be used in many idioms.

The summary table shows that some grammatical roles of the *oblique* cases are unique and are served only by one case. Other roles, in particular those of indirect object, time, destination and location, can be expressed by more than one case, even by all five *oblique* cases. To choose the right case it is necessary to understand the context and to consider the use of the appropriate prepositions and verbs that might govern a noun in this context. The grammatical roles of each case are dealt with in the appropriate chapter. This summary table gives an overview of the function of all five *oblique* cases:

Case's role in a sentence	Oblique case				
	Accusative	Genitive	Dative	Instrumental	Prepositional
Direct object (clarifies transitive verbs, ☞ 21.1.1)	√	√			
Indirect object (indicates 'a recipient', to whom an action is directed)			√		
Prepositional constructions (with various prepositions)	√	√	√	√	√
Location		√		√	√

Level 1, 2

Case's role in a sentence	Oblique case				
	Accusative	Genitive	Dative	Instrumental	Prepositional
The start and end points of a movement	√	√	√		
Movement along a surface		√	√		
Time	√	√	√	√	√
Ownership and relationship		√			
Quantity		√	√		
Weight, length, cost	√	√			
Age			√		
Instrument				√	
Impersonal sentences (☞ 30)			√		
Uses after certain verbs	√	√	√	√	√
Uses as a part of an idiom	√	√	√	√	√

Level 1, 2

4.2 Declension of nouns

This section explains the principles of the declension of nouns. Declension of adjectives, pronouns and numerals is explained in the following sections:

Declension of adjectives, ☞ 11.
Declension of pronouns, ☞ 14.
Declension of numerals, ☞ 15.

This section aims to cover the principles of noun declension and to give an overview of the sets of endings for all six cases. Each section that covers a particular case also provides a summary table of the case endings.

To decline any noun, take the following steps:

- If the dictionary form of a noun ends with **a vowel, -й**, or **-ь**, remove it.
- If a noun ends with **a consonant other than й**, remove nothing. Such a noun has no ending in the nominative.
- What is left after removing the ending is **the stem** of the word.
- Decide whether the stem is **hard or soft** (☞ 1.4).
- Finally, check whether any **spelling rules** apply (☞ 1.3).
- Add the appropriate ending according to the pattern that the noun follows.

Singular nouns follow **three declensions** (patterns), explained in the appropriate subsection: ☞ 4.2.1, 4.2.2 or 4.2.3. Each declension is determined by the noun gender and the dictionary form. Ending variants are determined by the noun gender, whether the stem is hard or soft, and the spelling rules. Each declension has:

- A set of hard endings
- A set of soft endings
- Soft ending variants for nouns that end in **-ий/-ие/-ия**

- A set of endings that is affected by spelling rules
- Several exceptions

4.2.1 The first declension: singular nouns

The first declension covers:

- All masculine nouns that end with **a consonant** and **-ь,** except the noun **путь** (road/way).
- All neuter nouns, except nouns ending in **-мя** and the noun **дитя́** (baby).

4.2.1.1 Sample patterns for masculine singular nouns

Case	Hard endings: nouns ending with hard consonants that are not affected by the spelling rules	Soft endings: nouns ending with **-ь** or **-й**	Soft ending variant: nouns ending with **-ий**	Endings affected by the spelling rules: nouns ending with **-г, -к, -х, -ж, -ш, -ч, -щ, -ц**
N	стол/брат	слова́рь/геро́й	санато́рий/ Мефо́дий	ме́сяц /врач
A (an.)	бра́та (as genitive)	геро́я (as genitive)	Мефо́дия (as genitive)	врача́ (as genitive)
A (inan.)	**стол** (as nominative)	**слова́рь** (as nominative)	**санато́рий** (as nominative)	**ме́сяц** (as nominative)
G	**-а** стола́/бра́та	**-я** словаря́/геро́я	**-я** санато́рия/ Мефо́дия	**-а** ме́сяца/врача́
D	**-у** столу́/бра́ту	**-ю** словарю́/геро́ю	**-ю** санато́рию/ Мефо́дию	**-у** ме́сяцу/врачу́
I	**-ом** столо́м/бра́том	**-ем** (if unstressed), **-ём** (if stressed): словарём/геро́ем	**-ем** санато́рием/ Мефо́дием	**-ом** (if stressed), **-ем** (if unstressed after **-ж, -ш, -щ, -ч, -ц**): ме́сяцем/врачо́м
P	**-е** столе́/бра́те	**-е** словаре́/геро́е	**-и** санато́рии/ Мефо́дии	**-е** ме́сяце/враче́

Comments on the table

- 👁 Masculine nouns in the accusative case follow two different patterns, one for animate and another for inanimate nouns. This rule does not apply to feminine or neuter nouns.
- 👁 Several masculine nouns in the prepositional case have additional endings **-у/-ю.** The ending **-у** is used only when describing location (☞ 10.1.1).
- 👁 Several masculine nouns have alternative endings **-у/-ю** in the genitive case when describing the 'partitive' meaning (☞ 7.2.2.4).

4.2.1.2 Sample patterns for neuter singular nouns

Note that the set of neuter noun endings is identical to the set of masculine nouns. Neuter nouns are not affected by the spelling rules:

Case	Hard endings: nouns ending with -о	Soft endings: nouns ending with -е/-ё	Soft ending variant: nouns ending with -ие
N	окно́	мо́ре/ружьё	упражне́ние
A	**окно́** (as nominative)	**мо́ре/ружьё** (as nominative)	**упражне́ние** (as nominative)
G	-а окна́	-я мо́ря/ружья́	-я упражне́ния
D	-у окну́	-ю мо́рю/ружью́	-ю упражне́нию
I	-ом окно́м	-ем (if unstressed), -ём (if stressed): мо́рем/ружьём	-ем упражне́нием
P	-е окне́	-е мо́ре/ружье́	-и упражне́нии

Level 1, 2

4.2.2 The second declension: singular nouns

The second declension covers:

- All feminine nouns that end in -а/-я/-ия
- All masculine nouns that end in -а/-я
- All nouns of common gender

Sample patterns for **feminine, masculine** and **common gender** nouns ending with -а/-я:

Case	Hard endings: nouns ending with -а; the stem of the noun ends in a consonant that is not affected by the spelling rules	Soft endings: nouns ending with -я	Soft ending variant: nouns ending with -ия	Endings affected by the spelling rules: nouns whose stem ends with -г, -к, -х, -ж, -ш, -ч,-щ, -ц
N	-а па́па/ма́ма/сирота́	-я дере́вня/ дя́дя	-ия Росси́я	-а кни́га
A	-у па́пу/ма́му/сироту́	-ю дере́вню/ дя́дю	-ю Росси́ю	-у кни́гу
G	-ы па́пы/ма́мы/сироты́	-и дере́вни/ дя́ди	-и Росси́и	и кни́ги -ы (only after -ц)
D	-е па́пе/ма́ме/сироте́	-е дере́вне/дя́де	-и Росси́и	-е кни́ге
I	-ой па́пой/ма́мой/ сирото́й	-ей дере́вней/ дя́дей	-ей Росси́ей	-ой кни́гой -ей (only if unstressed after -ж, -ш, -ч, -щ and -ц)
P	-е па́пе/ма́ме/сироте́	-е дере́вне/дя́де	-и Росси́и	-е кни́ге

4.2.3 The third declension: singular nouns

The third declension covers

- all feminine nouns that end with **-ь**

Sample patterns for **feminine nouns** ending in **-ь**. These nouns follow the pattern of nouns with soft endings:

Case	Soft endings: nouns ending with -ь
N	пло́щадь/мать/дочь
A	пло́щадь/мать/дочь (as nominative)
G	пло́щади/ма́тери/до́чери
D	пло́щади/ма́тери/до́чери
I	пло́щадью/ма́терью/до́черью
P	пло́щади/ма́тери/до́чери

Comments on the table

 The two feminine nouns мать (mother) and дочь (daughter) have the suffix **-ер-** added to the stem throughout the declension.

 Neuter nouns ending in **-мя** (☞ 2.3.5), the neuter noun **дитя́** (baby) and the masculine noun **путь** (road, way) follow their own patterns, which are similar to the third declension, except for the variations in the instrumental case:

Case	Neuter nouns ending in -мя	The noun путь	The noun дитя
N	вре́мя	путь	дитя́
A	вре́мя (as nominative)	путь (as nominative)	дитя́ (as nominative)
G	вре́мени	пути́	дитя́ти
D	вре́мени	пути́	дитя́ти
I	вре́менем	путём	дитя́тей
P	вре́мени	пути́	дитя́ти

4.3 Declension of plural nouns

For the formation of plural nouns, ☞ 3.

4.3.1 Overview

All plural nouns follow the same pattern in the dative, instrumental and prepositional cases. In the genitive case, feminine and neuter nouns follow similar patterns and masculine nouns follow a different pattern. Plural animate nouns in the accusative case follow the pattern of the genitive case. Plural inanimate nouns in the accusative case follow the pattern of the nominative case.

Sample patterns for **plural nouns** in all cases except the genitive:

Case	Hard endings	Soft endings	Endings affected by the spelling rules
	Masculine nouns ending with a hard consonant except **-г**, **-к**, **-х**, **-ж**, **-ш**, **-ч** and **-щ**. Feminine and masculine nouns ending with **-а**. Neuter nouns ending with **-о**.	Masculine nouns ending with **-й** or **-ь**. Feminine nouns ending with **-я** or **-ь**. Neuter nouns ending with **-е/-ё**.	All nouns whose **stem** ends with **-г**, **-к**, **-х**, **-ж**, **-ш**, **-ч** and **-щ** (mainly masculine and feminine nouns).
N	**-ы** сто́лы/студе́нты/ко́мнаты/племя́нницы/слова́	**-и** словари́/геро́и/дере́вни/тёти/моря́	**-и** врачи́/кни́ги
A (an.)	студе́нтов (as genitive) племя́нниц (as genitive)	геро́ев (as genitive) тётей/тёть (as genitive)	враче́й (as genitive)
A (inan.)	**столы́** (as nominative) **ко́мнаты** (as nominative) **слова́** (as nominative)	**словари́** (as nominative) **дере́вни** (as nominative)	**кни́ги** (as nominative)
D	**-ам** стола́м/студе́нтам/ко́мнатам/племя́нницам/слова́м	**-ям** словаря́м/геро́ям/деревня́м/тётям/моря́м	**-ам** врача́м/кни́гам
I	**-ами** стола́ми/студе́нтами/ко́мнатами/племя́нницами/слова́ми	**-ями** словаря́ми/геро́ями/деревня́ми/тётями/моря́ми	**-ами** врача́ми/кни́гами
P	**-ах** стола́х/студе́нтах/ко́мнатах/племя́нницах/слова́х	**-ях** словаря́х/геро́ях/деревня́х/тётях/моря́х	**-ах** врача́х/кни́гах

Level 2, 3

4.3.2 Formation of plural genitive nouns

👁 4.3.2.1 Formation of masculine plural genitive nouns

Plural masculine nouns in the genitive case, except those that end with -а/-я, can have the following endings: -ов/-ев/-ёв/-ей. These variations are determined by the nouns' dictionary forms.

Soft endings		Special ending	Hard endings
Nouns ending in **-ж**, **-ш**, **-ч**, **-щ**, or **-ь**	Nouns ending in **-й/-ий**	Nouns ending in **-ц**	Nouns ending in any consonants, except **-ж**, **-ш**, **-ч**, **-щ**, **-ц**, **-й** or **-ь**
врач/каранда́ш/слова́рь	геро́й/слой/санато́рий	ме́сяц/молоде́ц	стол/дом
-ей враче́й/карандаше́й/словаре́й	**-ев** (if unstressed): геро́ев/санато́риев **-ёв** (if stressed): слоёв	**-ев** (if unstressed): ме́сяцев **-ов** (if stressed): молодцо́в	**-ов** столо́в/домо́в

👁 **There are some exceptions to the pattern above.** Note that the list below is not exhaustive, but it does include some frequently occurring nouns:

Nominative singular	Genitive plural
брат (brother)	бра́т**ьев**
стул (chair)	сту́л**ьев**
лист (leaf)	ли́ст**ьев**
друг (friend)	друз**е́й**
сын (son)	сынов**е́й**
ребёнок (child)	**дет**е́й
челове́к (person)	**челове́к/люде́й**
раз (one time)	**раз**
сапо́г (boot)	**сапо́г**
солда́т (soldier)	**солда́т**
глаз (eye)	**глаз**

👁 The noun **челове́к** (person) has two forms in the genitive plural (☞ 7.2.2.1).

👁 4.3.2.2 Formation of genitive plural of feminine, neuter and masculine nouns ending in -*а*/*я*

All plural feminine and neuter nouns, masculine nouns that end with -**а**/-**я** and common gender nouns in the genitive case can have the following endings: 'zero' ending or -**ей**:

Hard endings	Soft endings		
Masculine nouns ending with -**а**. Feminine nouns ending with -**а**. Neuter nouns ending with -**о**. Common gender nouns ending with -**а**.	Feminine nouns ending with -**ия** and -**ья** (if unstressed). Neuter nouns ending with -**ие** and -**ье**.	Feminine nouns ending with -**я**.	Neuter nouns ending with -**е**/-**ё**. Feminine nouns ending with -**ь** and -**ья** (if stressed).
де́душка/газе́та/сло́во/ колле́га	а́рмия/колду́нья (witch)/ упражне́ние/ожере́лье (necklace)	спа́льня/ва́фля	по́ле/ружьё/ пло́щадь/семья́
'zero' ending: де́душек/ газе́т/слов/колле́г	'zero' endings but the end of the stem changes to -**ий**: а́рмий/ колду́ний/упражне́ний/ ожере́лий	'zero' ending: спа́лен. Some nouns have -**ь** added to the ending: ва́фель	-**ей** поле́й/ру́жей/ площаде́й/семе́й

Comments on the table

- 'Zero' endings mean that nouns lose the ending of their dictionary form.
- If the noun stem ends in **two or more consonants**, so-called '*fleeting*' vowels (-**о** or -**е**) are inserted between those consonants to ease pronunciation. For more information, ☞ 4.5.

👁 Although it is possible to advise on how to choose between the two 'fleeting' vowels, there are many exceptions that do not fit into the following rule:

- The letter -o- is usually inserted between a consonant (except ж, ш, ч, й) and the consonant к: ошибка – ошибок (mistakes), марка – марок (stamp). Exceptions: искра – искр (spark), буква – букв (letters).
- The letter -e- is usually inserted between ж, ш, ч and the consonant к: ложка – ложек (spoons), девушка –девушек (girls), палочка – палочек (diminutive of stick).
- The letter -e- is usually inserted between the consonants -сл-, -фл-, -сн-, -вн-: число – чисел (numbers, dates), десна – дёсен (gums).
- The letter -e- usually replaces the letters -ь- and -й-: письмо – писем; свадьба – свадеб (wedding), лейка – леек (watering-can). Exceptions: просьба – просьб (request), война – войн (war).
- The letter -e- is usually inserted between the two last consonants in many feminine nouns ending with -я: вишня – вишен (cherry), земля – земель (land). Exception: кухня – кухонь (kitchen).
- The letter -ё- is inserted in some nouns before or after the consonant -p-: озеро – озёр (lake), сестра– сестёр (sister), серьга – серёг (ear-rings), кочерга/кочерёг (poker).
- The fleeting vowels are not usually inserted between two consonants, if the stem of a noun ends in the pairs formed from the consonants: б, в, л, м, н, п, р, ж, з: баржа – барж (barge), волна – волн (waves), изба – изб (peasant hut) etc.

👁 The following nouns have genitive plural endings that differ from the common pattern:

- Masculine nouns юноша (youth) and дядя (uncle), feminine nouns тётя (aunt), доля (part, share), свеча (candle) have the ending -ей instead of the 'zero' ending: юношей, дядей, тётей, долей, свечей. Note the alternative form of the noun тётя–тёть is common.
- Feminine nouns ending with -ня do not usually have ь in the genitive plural except барышня – барышень (old-fashioned word for 'young lady'), деревня – деревень (village), кухня – кухонь (kitchen), яблоня – яблонь (apple-tree), няня – нянь (nurse/child minder).
- Neuter nouns низовье (lower reaches of a river), платье (dress), устье (mouth of a river) end in -eв: низовьев, платьев, устьев.

👁 4.3.3 Genitive plural of nouns that have only a plural form

Nouns that have only a plural form follow various patterns. The list below is not exhaustive, but it does include some frequently occurring nouns.

- Some of them have the 'zero' ending:

Nominative plural	Genitive plural
брюки (trousers)	брюк
ножницы (scissors)	ножниц
деньги (money)	денег
сутки (twenty-four hours)	суток
сливки (cream)	сливок
каникулы (student vacation)	каникул
похороны (funeral)	похорон
макароны (pasta)	макарон

- Some have the hard ending -**ов**:

Nominative plural	Genitive plural
джи́нсы (jeans)	джи́нсов
очки́ (spectacles)	очко́в
весы́ (scales)	весо́в
часы́ (clock/watch)	часо́в
вы́боры (election/s)	вы́боров

- Some have the soft ending -**ей**:

Nominative plural	Genitive plural
роди́тели	роди́телей

<table>
<tr><td>Level
3</td><td></td></tr>
</table>

4.3.4 Nouns that follow special patterns in plurals

For the declension of regular plural nouns, ☞ 4.3.1.

👁 There are some plural nouns that follow special patterns:

- Nouns ending in -**ин** that indicate a status or nationality: тата́рин
- Nouns ending in -**онок**/-**ёнок** that indicate young animals: котёнок

They have irregular plural nominative (☞ 3.4), accusative and genitive forms. For example:

Case	Plural nouns ending in -ин: тата́рин – тата́ры, англича́нин – англича́не	Plural nouns ending in -онок/-ёнок: щено́к – щеня́та	Noun хозя́ин – хозя́ева	Noun господи́н – господа́
N	тата́ры/англича́не	щеня́та	хозя́ева	господа́
A	тата́р/англича́н	щеня́т	хозя́ев	госпо́д
G	тата́р/англича́н	щеня́т	хозя́ев	госпо́д
D	тата́рам/англича́нам	щеня́там	хозя́евам	господа́м
I	тата́рами/англича́нами	щеня́тами	хозя́евами	господа́ми
P	тата́рах/англича́нах	щеня́тах	хозя́евах	господа́х

Other nouns that follow special patterns include:

- The masculine nouns **чёрт** (devil), **сосе́д** (neighbour), **у́хо** (ear) and **о́ко** (old word for eye) have **hard singular endings** and follow the regular pattern of first declension masculine and neuter nouns with hard endings (☞ 4.2.1.1). However, they have **soft plural endings**.
- The nouns **чу́до** (miracle) and **не́бо** (sky/heaven) have the additional suffix -**ес**- in the plural and keep it throughout the declension.
- The nouns **роди́тели** (parents), **де́ти** (children) and **лю́ди** (people) are plural nouns and follow the soft plural pattern. Note the ending -**ьми** in the instrumental case of the nouns **де́ти** and **лю́ди**.

Case	Examples of plural nouns that follow special patterns							
N	че́рти	сосе́ди	у́ши	о́чи	чудеса́	роди́тели	де́ти	лю́ди
A	чертей	сосе́дей	у́ши	о́чи	чудеса́	роди́телей	детей	людей
G	чертей	сосе́дей	ушей	очей	чуде́с	роди́телей	детей	людей
D	чертя́м	сосе́дям	уша́м	оча́м	чудеса́м	роди́телям	де́тям	людям
I	чертя́ми	сосе́дями	уша́ми	оча́ми	чудеса́ми	роди́телями	детьми́	людьми́
P	чертя́х	сосе́дях	уша́х	оча́х	чудеса́х	роди́телях	де́тях	людях

<table>
<tr><td>Level
2, 3</td></tr>
</table>

4.4 Declension of proper names

4.4.1 Declension of Russian first names, patronymics and place names

Russian first names (full form), patronymics and place names are declined as other nouns. They follow the noun patterns described above: ☞ 4.2.1–4.2.3 and 4.3.

Case	Masculine first name/ place name	Feminine first name/place name	Masculine patronymic	Feminine patronymic
N	Бори́с/Андре́й/Но́вгород	Варва́ра/Мари́я/ Москва́	Петро́вич	Петро́вна
A	Бори́са/Андре́я (animate, as genitive) Но́вгород (inanimate, as nominative)	-у/-ю Варва́ру/Мари́ю/ Москву́	-а Петро́вича	-у Петро́вну
G	-а/-я Бори́са/Андре́я/ Но́вгорода	-ы/-и Варва́ры/Мари́и/ Москвы́	-а Петро́вича	-ы Петро́вны
D	-у/-ю Бори́су/Андре́ю/ Но́вгороду	-е/-и Варва́ре/Мари́и/ Москве́	-у Петро́вичу	-е Петро́вне
I	-ом/-ем Бори́сом/Андре́ем/ Но́вгородом	-ой/-ей Варва́рой/Мари́ей/ Москво́й	-ем Петро́вичем	-ой Петро́вной
P	-е Бори́се/Андре́е/ Но́вгороде	-е/-и Варва́ре/Мари́и/ Москве́	-е Петро́виче	-е Петро́вне

4.4.2 Declension of Russian surnames

- Russian singular masculine surnames ending with **-ов/-ев/-ин/-ич** decline like first declension nouns. The form of the instrumental case is an exception to the rule and has an adjective ending.
- Russian singular masculine surnames ending with **-ский**, singular feminine surnames ending with **-ова/-ева/-ина/-ая/-ская** and the surnames in plural ending with **-вы/-ые/ -ские** decline like adjectives. The feminine surname in the accusative case is an exception to the rule and has a noun ending.

Case	Example of masculine surname ending with -ов/-ев/-ин/-ич	Example of masculine surname ending with -ский	Example of feminine surname ending with -ова/-ева/-ина/-ая/-ская	Example of surnames in plural ending with -вы/-ые/-ские
N	Лéрмонтов	Достоéвский	Панóва	Некрáсовы
A	-а Лéрмонтова (animate, as genitive)	-ого Достоéвского	-у Панóву	-ых Некрáсовых
G	-а Лéрмонтова	-ого Достоéвского	-ой Панóвой	-ых Некрáсовых
D	-у Лéрмонтову	-ому Достоéвскому	-ой Панóвой	-ым Некрáсовым
I	-ым Лéрмонтовым	-им Достоéвским	-ой Панóвой	-ыми Некрáсовыми
P	-е Лéрмонтове	-ом Достоéвском	-ой Панóвой	-ых Некрáсовых

Russian surnames ending in -ских or -о do not decline: Пóльских, Шевчéнко, Петрéнко etc.

4.4.3 Declension of foreign proper names

Foreign names, place names and names of the books, films etc. are declined as in Russian, if they fit the Russian gender system. However, if they do not fit the pattern they do not decline.

For information on noun gender, including names, ☞ 2.3.

For example, the name Sherlock Holmes (**Шéрлок Хóлмс**) is declinable because both the first name and the surname fit the pattern of Russian male names: читáть о Шéрлоке Хóлмсе (to read about Sherlock Holmes). Contrast this with Jane Eyre (**Джейн Эйр**): читáть о Джейн Эйр (to read about Jane Eyre). This feminine name ends in a consonant and therefore does not fit the pattern of Russian female names.

4.4.4 Declension of abbreviations

For information on abbreviation gender, ☞ 2.3.7.

The grammatical gender of abbreviations is determined by the grammatical gender of the principal noun in the abbreviation. Usually only masculine gender abbreviations ending in a consonant decline. They follow the pattern of the first declension. For example:

- СПИД (AIDS) – болéть СПИДом (to have AIDS)
- Газпрóм (Gazprom – Russian energy company) – дохóды Газпрóма (Gazprom's profit)

4.5 The 'fleeting' vowels

👁 Some words have so-called '*fleeting*' vowels in their stems. The term '*fleeting*' describes the phenomenon whereby a vowel is not present in all forms of the word. The fleeting vowels can appear in nouns, adjectives and verbs. However, they are especially common in nouns. For example:

- Some masculine nouns contain the fleeting vowels -**о** or -**е/-ё** in the final syllable. The fleeting vowel is dropped in all cases except the nominative, if the noun is animate.

Inanimate nouns lose their fleeting vowels in the four cases other than the nominative and accusative (for the declension of masculine animate and inanimate nouns, ☞ 4.2.1). This rule affects in particular the majority of masculine nouns ending with **-ец** and **-ок/-ёк** and several nouns ending with **-ор/-ёр**, **-ол/-ёл**, **-ей** and **-ь.**

- Some monosyllabic masculine nouns – **лёд** (ice), **рот** (mouth), **сон** (sleep), **день** (day), **пень** (stump) – have the fleeting vowels **-o/-e/-ё** in their root. The fleeting vowels **-o/-e/-ё** are dropped in all cases other than nominative and accusative. Note that the letter **ё** changes into the letter **ь** in the root of the noun **лёд** in all cases except the nominative and accusative.
- Some feminine nouns ending with **-ошь**, **-ожь** or **-овь** have the fleeting vowel **-o** in the final syllable. The vowel **-o** is dropped in all cases except the nominative and accusative.
- Some nouns have the fleeting vowels **-o** or **-e** only in the genitive plural case. If the stem of a noun ends in **two or more consonants**, **-o** or **-e** are inserted between them to ease pronunciation. For an explanation, ☞ 4.3.2.
- The plurals of the nouns mentioned in these bullet points lose their fleeting vowels in all six cases, including the nominative case.

Examples of declension of nouns with fleeting vowels:

Case	Singular nouns		
	Examples of stems with a fleeting vowel in the final syllable	Examples of stems with a fleeting vowel in the noun root	Examples of some feminine nouns ending in **-ошь**, **-ожь** or **-овь** with the fleeting vowel **-o**
N	отéц/ры́нок	лёд/день/рот	ложь/цéрковь
A	отцá/ры́нок	лёд/день/рот	ложь/цéрковь
G	отцá/ры́нка	льда/дня/рта	лжи/цéркви
D	отцý/ры́нку	льду/дню/рту	лжи/цéркви
I	отцóм/ры́нком	льдом/днём/ртом	лóжью/цéрковью
P	отцé/ры́нке	льде/дне/рте	лжи/цéркви

Case	Plural nouns
N	отцы́/ры́нки/льды/дни/рты/цéркви
A	отцóв/ры́нки/льды/дни/рты/цéркви
G	отцóв/ры́нков/льдов/дней/ртов/церквéй
D	отцáм/ры́нкам/льдам/дням/ртам/церквáм
I	отцáми/ры́нками/льдáми/дня́ми/ртáми/церквáми
P	отцáх/ры́нках/льдах/днях/ртах/церквáх

Level
2, 3

Обобщающее упражнение

Identify the number and case of the nouns in bold: put the letters S or Pl to indicate the number and the letters N, A, G, D, I or P to indicate the case.

1. **Господин Смирнов** расскáзывает о **Москвé**.

2. **Господин Смирнóв** родился и вы́рос в **Москвé**. 3. Сегóдня он с **удовóльствием** покáзывает свóим зарубéжным **коллéгам Москвý**. 4. Начинáют они **знакóмство с гóродом с Кремля́**. 5. **Господин Смирнóв** расскáзывает свóим **гостя́м истóрию гóрода**. 6. Он говори́т, что **Кремль** был надёжной **крéпостью** на **холмáх**, недалекó от **реки и дорóг**. 7. К 15-ому **вéку Москвá** стáла **столи́цей** рýсского **государства**. 8. До 1917-ого **гóда** в **Москвé** бы́ло 450 **церквéй**. 9. К **счáстью**, нéкоторые из э́тих **церквéй** сохрани́лись. 10. **Гóсти господи́на Смирнóва** интересýются **истóрией и искýсством** и хотя́т обойти́ все **музéи гóрода**. 11. К **сожалéнию**, э́то невозмóжно! 12. Они́ согласи́лись с **предложéнием господи́на Смирнóва** пообéдать в егó люби́мом **кафé «Ёлки-Пáлки»** и за **обéдом и крýжкой пи́ва** обсуди́ть, каки́е **достопримечáтельности** они́ смóгут посмотрéть за оди́н **день.**

5 Nouns: nominative case

For the concept of the six-case system and the principles of noun declension, ☞ 4.

The singular nominative case is the *dictionary form* of all declinable parts of speech: nouns, pronouns, adjectives and numerals. The nominative case is not governed by any prepositions. However, in a very few idioms, nouns in the nominative case can appear after the preposition **в** (to) or the particle **за** (such) (☞ 5.3.1).

The nominative case can have singular and plural numbers. For information on the plural nominative case of nouns, ☞ 3.

The nominative case has several roles in a sentence. It can indicate the core elements of the sentence, i.e. the subject or the predicate. The nominative case can also be used as part of some idioms, when making lists, giving names or addressing a person directly. This chapter discusses these roles.

5.1 Using the nominative case as the subject of a sentence

The main grammatical role of the nominative case is to indicate the subject of the sentence. The subject is one of the core elements of a sentence; it explains whom/what the sentence is about. The subject answers the questions **кто?** (who?) or **что?** (what?). For example:

- **Господи́н Смирно́в** (subject) **рабо́тает** (predicate). **Mr Smirnoff** is working.
- **Пенсионе́ры** (subject) **не рабо́тают** (predicate). **Retired people** do not work.
- **Це́ны** (subject) бы́ли **сни́жены** (predicate). **Prices** were reduced.
- **Сто́лик** (subject) **свобо́ден** (predicate). **The table** is free.

The second core element of a sentence is the predicate (verb or verbal phrase).

The predicate can describe what the subject does (the first two examples given above) or what is done to the subject by someone or something (the third and the fourth examples given above). In a sentence, the predicate must agree with the subject. Present and future tense verbs agree with the subject in person and number. Past tense verbs, short-form participles and short-form adjectives agree with the subject in number and gender (if in the singular form).

👁 5.1.1 Using the nominative case as subject in constructions describing possession, ownership, absence or presence

Some English and Russian sentence structures do not fully correspond. In particular, constructions that describe possession, ownership, absence or presence are different. Their word order and position of the subject of the sentence in the nominative case differ. Translation into/from English can convey the meaning of the sentence, but not its structure:

- **Constructions that describe possession or ownership**: У Мари́и есть **маши́на** (subject in the nominative case). Maria has **a car.** У дете́й есть **игру́шки** (subject in the nominative case). The children have **some toys**. These Russian sentences are equivalents of the English constructions '*one has got something/someone*'. In a Russian sentence, the indicated '*possession*' is the subject of the sentence and in the nominative case, and the '*owner*' is in the genitive case (☞ 7.3.1).

- **Constructions that describe the presence of someone or something:** В но́мере есть все удо́бства (subject in the nominative case). All facilities are there in the hotel room. Извини́те, где здесь **па́спортный контро́ль** (subject in the nominative case)? Excuse me, where is the passport control here? These Russian sentences are equivalent to the English constructions '*there are/is someone/something/somewhere*'. In Russian, the usual position of the subject in this type of sentence is at the end of the sentence. The special form of **есть** (to be) is the Russian equivalent of the English expression '*there is/there are*'.

Level 2 ### 👁 5.1.2 Using the nominative case as the subject in sentences describing likes, dislikes or necessity

Russian sentences that describe likes, dislikes or necessity may cause some difficulties when translating from/into English. This type of Russian sentence is equivalent to the English constructions '*one likes someone/something*' or '*one needs someone/something*'. However, English and Russian sentence structures do not correspond. In Russian, in this type of sentence, the described '*person*' who '*likes or needs*' something is not the grammatical subject of the sentence, but an indirect object in the dative case. The '*subject*' of his/her '*likes or needs*' is the grammatical subject of the sentence in the nominative case (☞ 8.2.3 and 30). For example:

Russian sentence	English sentence	Literal translation into English
Мари́и (indirect object in the dative case) нра́вится **фильм** (subject in the nominative case).	Maria likes **the film**.	'**The film** pleases Maria/ appeals to Maria.'
Господи́ну Смирно́ву (indirect object in the dative case) не понра́вилось **Ва́ше замеча́ние** (subject in the nominative case).	Mr Smirnoff did not like **your comment**.	'**Your comment** displeased Mr Smirnoff / did not appeal to Mr Smirnoff.'
Ме́стному сове́ту (indirect object in the dative case) нужны́ **де́ньги** (subject in the nominative case).	The local council needs **money**.	'**Money** is needed to the local council.'
Господи́ну Смирно́ву (indirect object in the dative case) не ну́жен **но́вый ноутбу́к** (subject in the nominative case).	Mr Smirnoff does not need **a new laptop**.	'**A new laptop** is not needed to Mr Smirnoff.'

If the like or need takes the form of '*doing something*', an impersonal sentence is used. An impersonal sentence has no grammatical subject in the nominative case. The core element of an impersonal sentence is a verb **нра́виться/понра́виться** (like) or an adverb **на́до/ну́жно** (need), followed by an infinitive. The described '*person*' who '*likes or needs to do something*' is the indirect object of the sentence in the dative case (for impersonal sentences, ☞ 30). For example:

Russian sentence	English sentence	Literal translation into English
Студе́нтам (indirect object in the dative case) нра́вится говори́ть по-ру́сски.	Students like speaking Russian.	'Speaking Russian pleases **students**.'

Russian sentence	English sentence	Literal translation into English
Бизнесме́ну (indirect object in the dative case) на́до подписа́ть контра́кт.	The businessman needs to sign a contact.	'It is necessary **to a businessman** to sign a contract.'

5.1.3 Using the nominative as the subject of a sentence without a predicate

Level 2

There is one fundamental difference between English and Russian sentences. A Russian sentence does not need to have both core elements of a sentence – subject and predicate. A sentence can have either just a subject or just a predicate to be considered and function as a proper sentence and not a fragment (☞ 31.1).

Sentences that contain just a subject are frequently used in poetry and lists. For example:

Ночь. У́лица. Фона́рь. Апте́ка. Бессмы́сленный и ту́склый **свет**. (Блок)	Night, street, lamp, drugstore, A dull and meaningless light.
Шёпот, ро́бкое дыха́нье, **Тре́ли** соловья́, **Серебро́ и колыха́нье** Со́нного ручья́. (Фет)	Whispers, timid breathing, Trill of the nightingale, Silver and swaying Of the sleepy creek.
Телевизио́нная програ́мма переда́ч: 18.00 «**Челове́к и зако́н**» 19.30 «**Брат**», фильм 21.00 **Информацио́нная програ́мма «Вре́мя»**	TV schedule: 'Man and the Law' 'Brother' (film) News programme 'Time'

5.2 Using the nominative case as the predicate

Level 1, 2

The nominative case can be used as an essential part of the compound predicate (verbal phrase) that contains the verbal link **быть** (to be) and a noun in the nominative case. The noun of the predicate usually denotes quality, status, type or class of the subject of the sentence. In Russian, **быть** (to be) is normally omitted in the present tense. In the present tense, both the subject and predicate, in this type of sentence, are in the nominative case. If both the subject and part of the predicate are nouns, a dash takes the place of the omitted **быть** (to be):

Господи́н Смирно́в (subject) – **бизнесме́н** (predicate).	Mr Smirnoff **is a businessman**.
Его́ жена́ (subject) – **краса́вица и у́мница** (predicate).	His wife **is beautiful and clever**.
Глоба́льное потепле́ние (subject) – нау́чный **факт** (predicate).	Global warming **is a scientific fact**.
Э́то **ро́бот** (predicate).	This **is a robot**.

For **быть** (to be), ☞ 16.2.

In the past and future tenses, **быть** (to be) cannot be omitted as the verbal link of the compound predicate. **Быть** (to be) is present in sentences and agrees with the subject of the sentence in number and gender:

Его́ жена́ (subject) **была́** (feminine singular form, past tense) **краса́вица и у́мница** (predicate).	His wife **was a beautiful and clever person**.

However, in the future tense, the noun that forms the essential part of the predicate is usually used in the instrumental case:

> Господи́н Смирно́в (subj.) **бу́дет бизнесме́ном**   Mr Smirnoff **will be/will become**
> (predic.; the noun is in the instrumental case).   a **businessman**.

Level 2, 3

In the past tense, the noun that forms the essential part of the predicate can be used either in the nominative case or instrumental case to convey two different ideas.

- The noun in the nominative case indicates the permanent nature of the described quality, status, type, group etc.
- The noun in the instrumental case indicates the temporary nature of the described quality, status, type, group etc.

Often the choice of the case depends on a speaker's interpretation. For example:

> Лев Толсто́й **был вели́кий писа́тель**   Leo Tolstoy was a great writer (meaning
> (noun in nominative case emphasises   'of all time').
> permanent quality).
>
> Лев Толсто́й **был вели́ким писа́телем**   Leo Tolstoy was a great writer (meaning
> (noun in instrumental case emphasises   'of his time').
> temporary quality).

For the instrumental case, ☞ 9.2.4.

Level 1

5.3 Other uses of the nominative case

In a sentence, the nominative case can have roles other than indicating the subject or predicate of a sentence. The nominative case can be used:

- To indicate the proper name of people or animals in the constructions **Как Вас зову́т?/ Меня́ зову́т...** (What is your name?/My name is...):

> Меня́ зову́т **Мари́я**.   My name is **Maria**.
> Студе́нта зову́т **Ива́н**.   The student's name is/the student is
>   called **Ivan**.
> Кота́ зову́т **Ба́рсик**.   The cat's name is/the cat is called **Barsik**.

- To indicate the proper name of an inanimate object (city, street, shop) in the construction **Как называ́ется ...?** (What is it called?):

> Как называ́ется э́тот **го́род**?   What is this **city** called?
> **Го́род** называ́ется **Но́вгород**.   **The city** is called **Novgorod**.

For more on these constructions, ☞ 6.2.2.

Level 2, 3

- 🔊 To indicate apposition to a name within a generic class:

> Тури́сты слу́шали о́перу (generic class)   The tourists listened to the opera
> «**Снегу́рочка**» (apposition to a name of a   **'The Snow-Maiden'**.
> generic class in the nominative case).
>
> Дава́й встре́тимся на ста́нции метро́   Let's meet at **'Lubianka'** station.
> (generic class) «**Лубя́нка**» (apposition to a
> name of a generic class in the nominative case).

- However, if the noun that indicates the generic class is omitted, the apposition to this noun becomes an independent part of the sentence, and declines according to its grammatical role in the sentence:

> Тури́сты слу́шали «**Снегу́рочку**»   The tourists listened to **'The Snow-Maiden'**.
> (direct object in the accusative case).
>
> Дава́й встре́тимся на «**Лубя́нке**»   Let's meet at **'Lubianka'**.
> (location, prepositional case).

- As a direct address to someone or something:

Дорога́я **Ната́лия Серге́евна!**	Dear Natalia Sergeevna!
Ой, **Вань**, смотри́, каки́е кло́уны! (Высо́цкий)	Oh, **Van'**, look, what clowns!
О вели́кий и могу́чий, **ру́сский язы́к!** (Турге́нев)	O great and powerful **Russian tongue!**

- In the comparative construction introduced by the conjunction **чем** (than) (☞ 12.3):

Фру́кты и о́вощи поле́знее, **чем торты́** и **пече́нье** (nominative).	Fruit and vegetables are healthier than cakes and cookies.

If **чем** (than) is omitted, the noun in the comparative construction is used in the genitive case (for more on these constructions, ☞ 7.2.4):

Фру́кты и о́вощи поле́знее торто́в и пече́нья (genitive).	Fruit and vegetables are healthier than cakes and cookies.

- In the generalizing construction introduced by the conjunction **как** (such as):

Таки́е живо́тные, **как сиби́рский тигр и сне́жный леопа́рд**, нахо́дятся под угро́зой вымира́ния.	Animals **such as Siberian tigers and snow leopards** are under the threat of extinction.

- The nominative case is used after the cardinal numbers **оди́н/одна́/одно́** (one) and after any compound cardinal numbers that end in **оди́н/одна́/одно́** (one): **оди́н рубль** (one rouble), **два́дцать оди́н год** (twenty-one years), **три́дцать одна́** кни́га (thirty-one books).

For numbers, including the gender of 'one', ☞ 15.

For the use of cases after different cardinal numbers, ☞ 7.2.2.3.

5.3.1 Using the nominative case in idioms

Level 3

Exclamations that are introduced by the particle **что** (what) and the particle **за** (such) are common. They are followed by a noun in the nominative case:

Что за **невезу́ха**!	Such (what) a misfortune!
Что э́то за **чепуха́**!	Such (what) nonsense!
Что он за **сотру́дник**!	What kind of a worker is he!

In the examples, 'за' is a part of the exclamation '**что за**!' (such/what) and does not govern the following noun in the nominative case.

The plural form of an animate noun can appear in a form that is identical to the nominative case governed by the preposition **в** (to). These idioms convey the meaning of joining a group or class of people. The most frequently occurring idioms of this type are:

- идти́/ходи́ть **в го́сти** (to visit someone): Вчера́ мы ходи́ли **в го́сти** к на́шим друзья́м. (Yesterday we visited our friends.)
- баллоти́роваться **в депута́ты** (standing as MPs): Пять кандида́тов баллоти́руются **в депута́ты** Госду́мы от па́ртии «Зелёных». (Five candidates from the Green party are standing as MPs.)

Упражне́ния

Level 1

1. Translate into Russian:

1. Vera is a teacher.
2. *Harry Potter* is a book.
3. The newspaper is on the table.
4. My father is called Sasha.
5. The airport is called Pulkovo.

2. Translate into Russian:

1. 21 windows, 101 flats.
2. Computers are more expensive than books.
3. Animals such as tigers and leopards are on the brink of extinction.
4. We saw the opera *Tosca*.

Обобща́ющее упражне́ние

3. Something has gone wrong with Mr Smirnoff's application form. Match the answers to the questions.

Господи́н Смирно́в заполня́ет анке́ту: пе́рвая часть – ли́чные да́нные

Вопро́сы	Отве́ты
1. Фами́лия, и́мя, о́тчество	1. Не жена́т
2. Год, число́ и ме́сто рожде́ния	2. Кроссво́рды, лы́жи, волейбо́л
3. Национа́льность	3. Смирно́в Алекса́ндр Дми́триевич
4. Образова́ние, специа́льность	4. Ло́ндонская шко́ла эконо́мики, Магистрату́ра 2004–2005
5. Учёная сте́пень	5. 03.12.1982. Москва́
6. Стажиро́вки. Повыше́ние квалифика́ции	6. Моско́вский госуда́рственный университе́т: 1999–2004, специа́льность: инжене́р-программи́ст
7. Семе́йное положе́ние	7. Англи́йский, неме́цкий
8. Зна́ние иностра́нных языко́в	8. Ру́сский
9. Интере́сы, увлече́ния	9. Не име́ю

6 Nouns: accusative case

For the concept of the six-case system and the principles of noun declension, ☞ 4.

The accusative case is one of the six Russian cases. In a sentence or phrase, the accusative case has several roles. It can be used with or without a preposition. This chapter provides a summary of noun endings in the accusative case and explains its grammatical roles.

Level 1, 2

6.1 Summary table of noun endings in the accusative case

Masculine animate nouns	Hard endings (ending in a consonant, except **-й**) and endings affected by a spelling rule (☞ 1.3)	**-a** Same as genitive (☞ 7.1)
	Soft endings	**-я** Same as genitive (☞ 7.1)
All masculine inanimate nouns	Same as nominative (no change)	
All neuter nouns	Same as nominative (no change)	
Feminine nouns	Hard endings: nouns ending in **-a**	**-y**
	Soft endings: nouns ending in **-я**	**-ю**
	Soft endings: nouns ending in **-ь**	Same as nominative (no change)
All plural nouns	Animate	Same as genitive (☞ 7.1)
	Inanimate	Same as nominative (no change)

Comments on the table

- 👁 The accusative case is the only case in which endings are affected by the concept of animate/inanimate nouns (☞ 2.2). Animate singular masculine nouns take the same endings as masculine singular nouns in the genitive case. Inanimate singular masculine nouns do not change. Singular neuter and feminine nouns are not affected by the concept of animate/inanimate nouns.
- All plural animate nouns take the same endings as the genitive case. All rules and ending variations applied to the genitive case are valid for the accusative case. Plural inanimate nouns are the same as the nominative plural.
- 👁 Some nouns have so-called 'fleeting' vowels **-o/-e/-ё** in the final syllable in any case other than nominative singular: accusative отéц – отцá (father) (☞ 4.5).
- For hard and soft endings and the spelling rules, ☞ 1.3–1.4.

6.2 Using the accusative case without a preposition

6.2.1 The main role of the accusative case without a preposition

In a sentence, a noun or pronoun in the accusative case indicates the direct object of the sentence. The direct object explains the aim of the action. For example:

- Cа́ша **лю́бит рок-му́зыку** (direct object). (Sasha **loves rock-music**.) The direct object of the sentence, **рок-му́зыку** (rock-music), explains the aim of the action **лю́бит** (loves): **Что** лю́бит Саша? **What** does Sasha love?
- Де́ти **едя́т моро́женое** (direct object). (The children **are eating ice-cream**.) The direct object of the sentence, **моро́женое** (ice-cream), explains the aim of the action **едя́т** (eat): **Что едя́т** де́ти? **What are** the children **eating**?

A direct object follows a verb that does not require a preposition to govern the following noun (a transitive verb) (☞ 21). The question words used to describe a direct object are: **что?** (what?) for inanimate nouns, and **кого́?** (whom?) for animate nouns.

👁 Russian and English verbs do not fully correspond on either transitivity or the use of prepositions that govern nouns. For example:

игра́ть в футбо́л	to **play football**
слу́шать ра́дио	to **listen to** the radio

👁 Russian sentence word order is flexible (☞ 31.2). The subject of the sentence can appear at the end of the sentence and the object at the beginning of the sentence before the verb:

Профе́ссор (subject) пи́шет **статью́** (object).	The professor writes an article.
Статью́ (object) пи́шет профе́ссор (subject).	It is a professor who is writing an article.

6.2.2 Using the accusative case without a preposition when giving a proper name

The accusative case without a preposition is used to give a proper name to a person or animal:

Russian expression	English equivalent	Literal translation into English
Как **зову́т ребёнка?**	What is the child's name?/ What is the child called?	How (do they) call child?
Ребёнка зову́т Ма́ша.	The child's name is/the child is called Masha.	Child they call Masha.
Как **зову́т кота́?**	What is the cat's name?/ What is the cat called?	How (do they) call cat?
Кота́ зову́т Барси́к.	The cat's name is/the cat is called Barsik.	Cat they call Barsik.
Как **Вас зову́т?** (For the personal pronoun forms in the six cases, ☞ 14.)	What is your name?/What are you called?	How (do they) call you?
Меня́ зову́т Та́ня.	My name is /I am called Tanya.	Me they call Tanya.

6.2.3 Using the accusative case without a preposition in time expressions

The accusative case without a preposition is used in some time expressions:

- To emphasise the length of an action after the pronoun **весь** (whole) and the adjective **це́лый** (whole). For example:

Как до́лго/Ско́лько вре́мени он боле́л?	**For how long** was he ill?
Он боле́л **всю неде́лю/це́лую неде́лю**.	He was ill **for a whole week.**
Как до́лго/Ско́лько вре́мени они́ рабо́тают?	**For how long** are they working?
Они́ рабо́тают **це́лый ве́чер**.	They are working **for the whole evening.**

👁 Note the absence of the preposition in these Russian time expressions.

👁 If the adjective **це́лый** (whole) is used in the plural, in an expression of time, both the adjective and the following noun are used in the instrumental case without a preposition: це́лыми вечера́ми (for entire evenings), це́лыми дня́ми (for entire days).

For forms of the pronoun **весь** (whole), ☞ 14.6; for adjectives, ☞ 11.

- To indicate the precise duration of an action: **Ско́лько вре́мени?/Как до́лго?** (How long for). For example:

Как до́лго/Ско́лько вре́мени они́ изуча́ли грамма́тику?	**For how long** did they study grammar?
Они́ изуча́ли грамма́тику **год**.	They studied grammar **for a year**.
Как до́лго/Ско́лько вре́мени де́ти игра́ли?	**For how long** did the children play?
Де́ти игра́ли **два часа́**.	The children played **for two hours**.

👁 Only imperfective verbs are used in this construction: ☞ 20.4.2. For the concept of verbal aspect, ☞ 20. For the use of these constructions in the future tense, ☞ 20.5.1.

👁 If the expression of time contains a number, the number is in the accusative case. The noun that follows is used in the nominative singular, genitive singular or genitive plural, depending on the number (☞ 7.2.2.3)

- To emphasise the frequency of an action after the adjective **ка́ждый** (every). For example:

Как ча́сто они́ смо́трят телеви́зор?	**How often** do they watch TV?
Они́ смо́трят телеви́зор **ка́ждый ве́чер**.	They watch TV every evening.

The expression of time with **ка́ждый** can be replaced with a noun in the dative plural with the preposition **по** (on) when describing days of the week and parts of the day:

ка́ждый четве́рг	every Thursday
по четверга́м	on Thursdays
ка́ждый ве́чер	every evening
по вечера́м	in the evenings

The noun **день** (day) is an exception to this rule and is not used in the plural dative case.

- With the word **наза́д** (ago)/**тому́ наза́д** (ago)

неде́лю **тому́ наза́д**/неде́лю **наза́д**	a week ago
год **тому́ наза́д**/год **наза́д**	a year ago

Упражне́ния

1. Put the nouns in brackets into the appropriate form:

1. Ва́ня слу́шает (о́пера).
2. На ры́нке мо́жно купи́ть (ры́ба, хлеб, фру́кты).
3. Они́ давно́ не ви́дели (друг).
4. Гид встреча́ет (тури́сты).
5. Как зову́т (соба́ка)?

2. Answer the questions using the following time expressions: неде́лю наза́д, весь ме́сяц, це́лое у́тро, ка́ждый день.

1. Как ча́сто ты гуля́ешь в па́рке?
2. Когда́ Вы прилете́ли в Москву́?
3. Как до́лго Андре́й ждал повыше́ния зарпла́ты?
4. Как до́лго хиру́рги опери́ровали больно́го?

6.3 Using the accusative case with a preposition

The accusative case can be used with several prepositions. The table summarises the prepositions that can govern the accusative case and explains the context in which the accusative case with a preposition is used:

Context	Question asked	Preposition used	Examples
To indicate the end point of the movement (destination)	куда́? (where to?)	в (to/into) на (to/on to) под (under) за (beyond/behind)	6.3.1
To indicate the route of a journey, a movement against something or through some obstruction	как (how?)	че́рез (across/over/through) о (against) сквозь (through)	6.3.1
In time expressions	когда́? (when?)	в (at/on) на (at/on/for) че́рез (within/in/every other day etc.) спустя́ (after) по (up to)	6.2.3
In prepositional constructions after a number of verbs, in some idioms and phrases	various	на (for/at/on) за (for) про (about) в (in) че́рез (by some means)	6.3.3

6.3.1 Using the accusative case with verbs of motion and other verbs describing movements

Nouns in all cases, except the nominative case, can describe various movements. However, the accusative case is used most frequently in this context. The accusative case, with the prepositions listed in the table above, indicate:

- The end point of the movement: **в** (to), **на** (to), **под** (under), **за** (behind)

- The route of a journey: **че́рез** (across, over, through)
- Movement against something: **о** (against)
- Movement through some obstructions: **сквозь** (through)

The fourteen *verbs of motion* are mainly used with the accusative case when describing the end point of the movement (destination) or the route of a journey:

идти́ **в магази́н**	to go to a shop
е́хать **на рабо́ту**	to go to work
лезть **под стол**	to get under the table

заéхать **зá угол**   to go round the corner

перейтú **чéрез ýлицу**   to cross the street

For the verbs of motion, ☞ 24 and 25.

In Russian, there are many verbs, other than the fourteen verbs of motion, which describe movement. If the verb describes the end point of the movement, movement against something or movement through obstructions it requires the accusative case. The most frequently occurring verbs that describe movement (other than verbs of motion) are listed below:

класть/положúть (**в, на, под, за**)	to put
стáвить/постáвить (**в, на, под, за**)	to place (in a standing position)
вéшать/повéсить (**в, на, под, за**)	to hang
поднимáться/поднят́ься (**в, на, под, за**)	to go up
спускáться/спустúться (**в, на, под, за**)	to go down
бросáть/брóсить (**в, на, под, за, через**)	to throw
ударят́ь(ся)/удáрить(ся) (**о**)	to knock/to hit/to strike
пробирáться/пробрáться (**через, сквозь**)	to force one's way
садúться/сесть (**в, на, под, за**)	to sit down/to take a train, bus (any means of transport)

<table>
<tr><td>Level
1, 2</td><td>

6.3.1.1 Using the prepositions **в** and **на** with the accusative case when describing various movements

</td></tr>
</table>

👁 The two Russian prepositions **в** and **на** are translated into English as the preposition *to*. The use of the prepositions **в** and **на** in the accusative case is based on the same principle as the use of the same prepositions in the prepositional case (☞ 10.2.1).

The vowel **о** is added to the preposition **в** to ease pronunciation if the preposition is attached to a noun starting with two or more consonants and one of these consonants is **в** or **ф**. For example, **во двор** (to a yard/quad). The vowel **о** is added to the preposition **в** to ease pronunciation if the preposition is attached to a noun starting with consonant **в** or **ф** followed by the soft sign. For example, **во Вьетнам** (to Vietnam), **во фьорд** (to a fiord/fjord).

The summary table explains the use of **в** and **на** with the accusative case when describing various movements:

The preposition **в** (to/into) is used to indicate:	The preposition **на** (on/on to) is used to indicate:
Moving inside: положúть рýчку **в** сýмку (to put a pen into a bag), входúть **в** лифт (to enter a lift).	Moving on to a surface: положúть рýчку **на** стол (to put a pen onto the table), спустúться **на** зéмлю (to climb down on to the land).
Moving into a building or into any enclosed space, such as woods, a park, a yard: войтú **в** здáние (to enter the building), éхать **в** лес (to go to the woods), прийтú **в** парк (to arrive at the park).	Moving to the outdoors, to places such as the street, square, avenue, junction, field, road, path, motorway: вы́йти **на** ýлицу (to go out on to the street), вы́ехать **на** шоссé (to enter the motorway).
Moving to places that denote geographical locations such as а континéнт (continent), гóрод (city/town), дерéвня (village), райóн (district): прилетéть **в** Москвý (to arrive in Moscow), приплы́ть **в** Áфрику (to arrive by ship in Africa).	Moving to places that are located on the shore/bank of the river, lake, sea, ocean: прийтú **на** бéрег (to arrive at the shore), прилетéть **на** Байкáл (to arrive by plane at Lake Baikal).

Joining a group: вступа́ть **в** па́ртию (to join the party), поступа́ть **в** университе́т/**в** шко́лу (to start at university/to start at school).	Moving to places denoting the points of the compass: **на** се́вер (to the north), **на** юг (to the south), **на** восто́к (to the east), **на** за́пад (to the west).
Also: поднима́ться **в** го́ры (to climb the mountains/to go up into the mountains), выходи́ть **в** мо́ре (to go to the sea).	Attending an event: идти́ **на** о́перу (to go to the opera), е́хать **на** вы́ставку (to go to an exhibition).
◉ **Exceptions (moving to the following destinations): на** вокза́л (to the railway station), **на** ста́нцию (to the station), **на** по́чту (to the post office), **на** фа́брику/**на** заво́д (to the factory), **на** стадио́н (to the stadium), **на** ры́нок (to the market), **на** да́чу (to the country house), **на/в** ку́хню (to the kitchen), **на** эта́ж (to a floor), **на** флот (to the navy), **на** Ура́л (to the Urals), **на** Кавка́з (to the Caucasus), **на** Ро́дину (to the Motherland).	

◉ Use of the prepositions **в** and **на** follows the same principles in the accusative and prepositional cases: ☞ 10.2.1.

For prepositions used with verbs of motion, ☞ 25.7.

Level 1,2,3

Summarising text

Господи́н Смирно́в е́дет в Сама́ру	Mr Smirnoff is going to Samara
Господи́н Смирно́в **е́дет на конфере́нцию в Сама́ру**. Он **прие́хал на вокза́л, перешёл че́рез пло́щадь** и **вы́шел на платфо́рму**. Был час пик, и он до́лго **пробира́лся сквозь толпу́** на платфо́рме. Наконе́ц, он **сел в по́езд, вошёл в купе́, положи́л** ноутбу́к **на сто́лик, поста́вил** чемода́н **под сто́лик,** и **пове́сил** пальто́ **на крючо́к**. В купе́ бы́ло о́чень тесно́, и господи́н Смирно́в **уда́рился** голово́й **о по́лку**. Ну, ничего́! Могло́ быть и ху́же! Наконе́ц, он **сел за сто́лик** и включи́л свой ноутбу́к. По́езд **отпра́вился в Сама́ру**, а господи́н Смирно́в на́чал рабо́тать.	Mr Smirnoff **is going to Samara for a conference.** He arrived at the train station, crossed the square and went on to the platform. It was rush-hour and for a long time he was forcing his way through the crowd on the platform. Finally, he got on the train, entered a compartment, put his laptop on the table, put his suitcase under the table, and hung his coat on a hook. The compartment was very cramped and he knocked his head against a shelf. Never mind! It could have been worse! Finally, he sat down at the table and turned on his laptop. The train departed for Samara, and Mr Smirnoff began working.

Level 1, 2

6.3.2 Using the accusative case in time expressions

Nouns in all cases except the nominative can be used in time expressions. The choice of the case depends on the noun's meaning and the preposition that governs the noun. The accusative case is used to indicate days of the week. The preposition **в** (on) governs nouns in the accusative case:

Дни неде́ли (Days of the week)	Когда́? (When?)
понеде́льник	в понеде́льник
вто́рник	во вто́рник

Дни неде́ли (Days of the week)	Когда́? (When?)
среда́	в сре́ду
четве́рг	в четве́рг
пя́тница	в пя́тницу
суббо́та	в суббо́ту
воскресе́нье	в воскресе́нье

The accusative case is also used in the following time expressions:

- To point to a part of the day, or a particular day, month or year (with the preposition **в**):

в ту ночь	that night
в тот год	that year
в по́лночь	at midnight
в по́лдень	at midday
в нового́днюю ночь	on New Year's Eve
в то зи́мнее у́тро	on that winter morning

- To indicate a holiday or an event (with the preposition **на**):

на Но́вый год	at New Year
на Рождество́	at Christmas
на мой день рожде́ния	on my birthday
на пра́здник	on a public holiday

- After the prepositions **че́рез** (within/in/every other day, week etc.) and **спустя́** (after):

че́рез неде́лю	in a week
че́рез день	every other day
спустя́ год	after a year

- After the preposition **по** (up to):

с четверга́ **по суббо́ту**	from Thursday up to Saturday

- To indicate the precise duration of an action: **За ско́лько вре́мени?** (How long?). The shorter question, **За ско́лько?**, is used in popular speech. For example:

За ско́лько вре́мени они́ постро́или дом?	**How long** did it take them to build the house?
Они́ постро́или дом **за ме́сяц**.	It took them **a month** to build the house.
За ско́лько вре́мени учёный написа́л докла́д?	**How long** did it take the scientist to write the paper?
Учёный написа́л докла́д **за пять часо́в.**	It took the scientist **five hours** to write the paper.

✎ Note that usually perfective verbs are used in this time construction with the preposition **за** (for). For a detailed explanation, ☞ 20.4.2; for verbal aspect, ☞ 20.

✎ If the time expression contains a number, the number is used in the accusative case. However, the noun that follows is used in the nominative singular, genitive singular or genitive plural, depending on the number (☞ 7.2.2.3): **Пять** (accusative) часо́в. **Два** (accusative) часа́.

- ✎ To indicate the precise duration of an action in which the result of the action can be reversed: **На ско́лько вре́мени?** (How long for?). The shorter question, **На ско́лько?**, is used in popular speech. (For a detailed explanation, ☞ 20.4.2; for verbal aspect, ☞ 20.) For example:

На ско́лько вре́мени/На ско́лько студе́нты бра́ли кни́ги в библиоте́ке?	**For how long** did the students borrow the books from the library?

Студе́нты бра́ли кни́ги в библиоте́ке **на ме́сяц**.	The students borrowed the books from the library **for a month.**
На ско́лько вре́мени/На ско́лько они́ вы́шли из до́ма?	**For how long** did they leave the house?
Они́ вы́шли из до́ма **на де́сять мину́т**.	They left the house **for ten minutes.**

👁 If the time expression contains a number, the number is used in the accusative case. However, the noun that follows is used in the nominative singular, genitive singular or genitive plural, depending on the number (☞ 7.2.2.3).

6.3.3 Using the accusative case in prepositional constructions

The accusative case of a noun can be used with the following prepositions:

- **Про** (about): **про кого́?** (about whom?), **про что?** (about what?). The preposition **про** is common in popular speech and poetry. The verbs **говори́ть** (to speak), **мечта́ть** (to dream), **ду́мать** (to think), **петь** (to sing) etc. often take a noun in the accusative case with the preposition **про**. For example:

Спой нам, ве́тер, **про ди́кие го́ры**,	Sing to us, the wind, about the wild mountains,
Про глубо́кие та́йны море́й,	About the deep mysteries of the seas,
Про пти́чьи разгово́ры,	About bird calls,
Про си́ние просто́ры	About the blue expanse
Про сме́лых и больши́х люде́й!	About brave and great people!
(Ле́бедев-Кума́ч)	

The preposition **о** (about) is equivalent to the preposition **про**. The preposition **о** is more commonly used than the preposition **про** and is used with a noun or pronoun in the prepositional case.

For the prepositional case and the use of the preposition **о**, ☞ 10 and 10.3.

- **За** (for): **за кого́?** (for whom?) **за что?** (for what?). The preposition **за** is an essential part of many popular Russian toasts:

За здоро́вье!	(To) your health!
За мир и дру́жбу!	(To) peace and friendship!
За хозя́йку!	(To) the hostess!
За гостеприи́мных хозя́ев!	(To) the hospitable hosts!

- **За** (on behalf of someone): **де́лать что́-то за кого́?** (to do something on behalf of whom?): Господи́н Смирно́в согласи́лся рабо́тать **за больно́го колле́гу**. (Mr Smirnoff has agreed to work for his sick colleague.)

- **На** (for): на кого́? (for whom?), на что? (for what?):

сто́лик на двои́х	a table for two
копи́ть де́ньги на пое́здку	to save up for a trip
на до́брую па́мять	for good memories

- **Че́рез** (by some means):

Как они́ обща́ются? –	How do they communicate? –
Они́ обща́ются **че́рез перево́дчика**.	They communicate **through an interpreter**.
Как он нашёл рабо́ту? – Он нашёл рабо́ту **че́рез интерне́т**.	How did he find a job? – He found a job **through the Internet**.

6.4 Verbs that require the accusative case with a preposition

In Russian, several verbs require the accusative case with a preposition.

👁 As Russian sentences have flexible word order, a noun or pronoun in the accusative case does not always appear immediately after the verb that requires that case. Furthermore, the same verb can take several different cases. Also, note that the use of prepositions may differ in

Russian and English. A (non-exhaustive) list of the most frequently occurring verbs that take the accusative case is given below, and should be memorised. In the list, both verbal aspects are provided, if both aspects are used in this context; the imperfective aspect appears first, and then the perfective. Note that all words derived or formed from the listed verbs (nouns, participles, gerunds) normally require the same preposition and case: for example, игра́ть в футбо́л (to play football), игра́ в футбо́л (the game of football), игра́я в футбо́л (playing football).

- Verbs followed by the preposition **в**. The majority of the verbs suggest involvement:

Verbs	Examples
ве́рить/пове́рить во что?/в кого́? (to believe in what/in whom?)	ве́рить в чу́до (to believe in miracles)
влюбля́ться/влюби́ться во что?/в кого́? (to fall in love with what/with whom?)	влюби́ться в при́нца (to fall in love with a prince)
игра́ть/сыгра́ть во что? (в игру́) (to play what?) (a game)	игра́ть в футбо́л (to play football), игра́ть в би́нго (to play bingo), игра́ть в лотере́ю (to play the Lottery), игра́ть в ку́клы (to play with dolls), игра́ть в игру́шки (to play with toys)
вступа́ть/вступи́ть во что? (в организа́цию) (to enter what?) (an organisation)	вступи́ть в па́ртию «Зелёная Росси́я» (to enter the Russian Green party)
поступа́ть/поступи́ть куда́? (в образова́тельное учрежде́ние) (to enter/to start what?) (an educational institution)	поступи́ть в университе́т (to start at university), поступи́ть в шко́лу (to start at school)
одева́ться/оде́ться/быть оде́тым во что? (to get dressed in what?)	оде́ться в джи́нсы и ку́ртку (to get dressed in jeans and a jacket)
вме́шиваться/вмеша́ться во что? (to get involved in what?)	вмеша́ться в разгово́р (to get involved in (interrupt) the conversation), вмеша́ться в дра́ку (to get involved in a fight)
идти́/ходи́ть (and any verbal forms derived from the verbs of motion meaning 'moving to') куда́? (to go where?) идти́ в го́сти к кому́? (to visit whom?)	прие́хать в го́сти к роди́телям (to visit parents), идти́ в го́сти к дру́гу (to visit a friend)

- Verbs followed by the preposition **на**. These verbs have various meanings:

Verbs	Examples
наде́яться/понаде́яться на кого́? на что? (to hope for, to rely on whom? on what?)	наде́яться на дру́га (to rely on a friend), наде́яться на везе́ние и уда́чу (to hope for luck and success)
рассчи́тывать на кого́? на что? (to rely on whom? on what?)	рассчи́тывать на колле́гу (to rely on a colleague)
жа́ловаться/пожа́ловаться на кого́? на что? кому́? куда́? (to complain about what? about whom? to whom? where?)	пожа́ловаться на сосе́да в поли́цию (to complain to the police about a neighbour), пожа́ловаться на боль врачу́ (complain about the pain to a doctor)
влия́ть/повлия́ть на кого́? на что? (to influence whom? what?)	влия́ть на сы́на (influence a son), повлия́ть на реше́ние (influence the decision)

..rbs	Examples
смотре́ть/посмотре́ть на кого́? на что? (to look at whom? at what?)	смотре́ть на карти́ну (to look at the picture)
серди́ться/рассерди́ться на кого́? на что? (to be angry/to get cross at/with whom? at/with what?)	рассерди́ться на нача́льника (to get cross with the boss)

- Verbs followed by the preposition **за**. The majority of the verbs suggest the meaning of reaction to one's actions:

Verbs	Examples
благодари́ть/поблагодари́ть кого́? за что? (to thank whom? for what?)	поблагодари́ть сотру́дников за рабо́ту (to thank the staff for their work)
нака́зывать/наказа́ть кого́? за что? (to punish/to penalise whom? for what?)	наказа́ть престу́пника за преступле́ние (to punish the criminal for the crime)
хвали́ть/похвали́ть кого́? за что? (to praise whom? for what?)	хвали́ть дете́й за хоро́шее поведе́ние (to praise children for good behaviour)
награжда́ть/награди́ть кого́? за что? чем? (to decorate/to reward/to award whom? with what?)	награди́ть солда́та меда́лью (to decorate a soldier with a medal), награди́ть сотру́дников пре́мией (to reward the staff with a bonus)
руга́ть/отруга́ть кого́? за что? (to scold whom? for what?)	руга́ть подро́стка за прогу́лы (to scold a teenager for truancy)
критикова́ть/раскритикова́ть кого́? за что? (to criticise whom? for what?)	критикова́ть прави́тельство за рефо́рму (to criticise the government for the reform)
выходи́ть/вы́йти за́муж за кого́? (to get married to whom? [female only]); ☞ the comments below	вы́йти за́муж за кинозвезду́ (to get married to a movie star)

Comments on the table

👁 In Russian, there are two expressions that mean *to get married*, one for a man and the other for a woman. The expression **выходи́ть/вы́йти за́муж за кого́?** (followed by the accusative case) indicates that it is a woman who gets married. The expression **жени́ться на ком?** (followed by the prepositional case) indicates that it is a man who gets married.

Level 3

6.5 Using the accusative case with a preposition in idioms

There are several idioms where a noun in the accusative case with a preposition is its core element. For example:

О́ко **за о́ко**, зуб **за зуб**.	An eye for an eye (tooth for a tooth).
Сыт **по го́рло**.	I am full up (stuffed to the gills).
Влюби́ться **по́ уши**.	To fall in love (to be head over heels in love).
Как бог **на́ душу** поло́жит.	To do something without a proper plan or preparation.
Жить душа́ **в ду́шу**.	To live in perfect harmony.
Нашла́ коса́ **на ка́мень**.	A clash of conflicting personalities.
Как **в во́ду** гляде́л.	To predict something with a high level of accuracy.
Как **об сте́нку** горо́х.	It is impossible to get through to someone.
Не **в бровь**, а **в глаз**.	Spot on.

| Не уда́рить па́лец **о па́лец.** | To do nothing. |
| Не уда́рить лицо́м **в грязь.** | Not to get bogged down. |

Упражне́ния

Level 1, 2

1. Insert **в** or **на** as appropriate.

1. Положи́те журна́лы ... стол, поста́вьте кни́ги ... по́лку.
2. Моя́ сестра́ поступи́ла ... университе́т.
3. Рабо́чие иду́т ... рабо́ту.
4. Ле́том семья́ е́дет ... дере́вню.
5. Пётр вошёл ... лифт.

Level 2, 3

2. Insert the appropriate preposition.

1. Кот спря́тался ... угол.
2. Нача́льник поблагодари́л сотру́дников ... рабо́ту.
3. Мари́я наде́ется ... по́мощь дру́га.
4. Дава́йте вы́пьем ... хозя́йку до́ма!
5. Свет не прохо́дит ... стекло́.
6. Почему́ ку́рица перешла́ ... доро́гу?
7. Предпринима́тель взял креди́т в ба́нке ... год.
8. Са́ша лю́бит игра́ть ... гольф.
9. Спортсме́н вмеша́лся ... дра́ку.
10. ... по́лночь начина́ется фейерве́рк.

Level 2, 3

Обобща́ющее упражне́ние

3. Put the words in brackets into the correct form.

Воскре́сный обе́д

1. Сего́дня воскресе́нье. Господи́н Смирно́в и его́ подру́га Ири́на реши́ли пригото́вить вку́сный (обе́д), но они́ не хотя́т тра́тить мно́го вре́мени на (приготовле́ние) блюд. 2. Вот каки́е (реце́пты) им удало́сь найти́ на са́йте «Вку́сно и бы́стро».

Борщ

3. Отвари́ть (говя́дина) и́ли (свини́на), наре́зать и отвари́ть (карто́шка).
4. Наре́зать и потуши́ть (свёкла, морко́вь, капу́ста, лук).
5. Доба́вить тома́тную (па́ста), (соль, пе́рец) по вку́су. Вари́ть 10–15 мину́т.

Сала́т «Оливье́»

6. (Карто́фель), (морко́вь) и (я́йца) отвари́ть, наре́зать.
7. (Огурцы́) и (лук) наре́зать.
8. Доба́вить зелёный (горо́шек).
9. Соедини́ть все (ингредие́нты), доба́вить (майоне́з и соль) по вку́су.

Прия́тного аппети́та!

7 Nouns: genitive case

For the concept of the six-case system and the principles of noun declension, ☞ 4.

The genitive case is one of the six Russian cases. In a sentence or a phrase, the genitive has several roles. It can be used with or without a preposition. This chapter provides a summary of noun endings in the genitive case and explains its grammatical roles.

Level 1, 2

7.1 Summary tables of noun endings in the genitive case

7.1.1 Singular nouns

Masculine and neuter nouns	Hard stem (masculine nouns ending in a hard consonant, neuter nouns ending in **-о**) and stem ending with **-г, -к, -х, -ж, -ш, -щ, -ц**	**-а**
	Soft stem (masculine nouns ending in **-й** and **-ь**, neuter nouns ending in **-е/ё**)	**-я**
Feminine nouns	Hard stem (feminine nouns ending in **-а**)	**-ы**
	Soft stem (feminine nouns ending in **-я** and **-ь**) and stem ending in **-г, -к, -х, -ж, -ш, -щ, -ч**	**-и**

Level 2, 3

7.1.2 Plural nouns

👁 The genitive case is the only case that has several different endings and several exceptions.

For information on the formation of plural nouns in the genitive case and the list of exceptions, ☞ 4.3.2.

Masculine nouns	All nouns except those ending with **-ж, -ш, -ч, -щ, -й, -ь**, and stressed ending after **-ц**	**-ов**
	Nouns ending with **-ж, -ш, -ч, -щ, -ь**	**-ей**
	Nouns ending with **-й**	**-ев** (if unstressed) **-ёв** (if stressed)
	Nouns with unstressed ending after **-ц**	**-ев**
Neuter nouns	Nouns ending with **-о**	'zero' ending
	Nouns ending with **-ие**	'zero' ending (stem changes to **-ий**)
	Nouns ending with **-е/ё**	**-ей**
Feminine nouns	All nouns except those ending with **-ь**	'zero' ending
	Nouns ending with **-ь**	**-ей**
	Nouns ending with **-ия**	'zero' ending (stem changes to **-ий**)

Comments on the tables

- ● 👁 Some nouns have so-called '*fleeting*' vowels -**o**/-**e**/-**ë** in the final syllable of any case other than nominative singular: от**é**ц – отц**á** (father), пирож**ó**к – пирожк**á** (pie) etc. For the fleeting vowels, 🖝 4.5.
- ● For hard and soft endings and the spelling rules, 🖝 1.3 and 1.4.

7.2 Using the genitive case without a preposition

7.2.1 The main role of the genitive case without a preposition

vel
2, 3

In Russian, a noun in the genitive case is used after another noun in possessive constructions or constructions that describe the relationship between two objects. Genitive case constructions are the Russian equivalent of English possessive constructions such as ***one's*** *book* or *a cup **of** tea*. For example:

English possessive construction	Russian equivalent (the second noun in each phrase is in the genitive case)
a bowl of soup	таре́лка су́п**а**
a glass of wine	бока́л вин**á**
a mug of milk	кружк**á** молок**á**
a group of students	гру́ппа студе́нт**ов**
a student's room	ко́мната студе́нт**а**
a neighbour's house	дом сосе́д**а**

👁 The Russian genitive construction and the English possessive constructions do not fully correspond. Word order differs in Russian and English for possessive constructions. In Russian, the noun in the genitive case always **follows the noun that it describes**. Some Russian genitive constructions can be translated into English by using an adjective.

A noun in the genitive case can indicate different types of relationship between two nouns. A noun in the genitive case can indicate:

Level
1, 2

- **Ownership:** ку́ртка Ми́ши (Misha's jacket), маши́на отц**á** (father's car), слова́рь шко́льника (pupil's dictionary) etc. The noun in the genitive case answers the question **чей?/чья?/чьё?/чьи?** (whose?).
- **Relationships between members of a group** (family relations, relations inside a group of people or animals):

сестра́ Ви́ктора	Victor's sister
мать ма́льчика	the boy's mother
ли́дер гру́ппы	leader of the group
секрета́рь па́ртии	secretary of the party
отря́ды прима́тов	groups of primates

Level
2, 3

- **Relationships between the whole and the part:**

обло́жка кни́ги	the cover of the book/the book cover
ру́чка две́ри	the door's handle/the door handle
экра́н компью́тера	the computer's screen/the computer screen
мото́р маши́ны	the car's engine/the car engine

- **Content:**

буты́лка кока-ко́лы	bottle of coca-cola
коро́бка конфе́т	box of candy
буке́т цвето́в	bouquet of flowers
стака́н воды́	glass of water

- **An animate or inanimate object whose quality or property is described:**

свет луны́	moonlight
шум мо́ря	noise of the sea
бога́тства Сиби́ри	richness of Siberia
любо́вь ма́тери	mother's love
подде́ржка друзе́й	friends' support
наро́ды Росси́и	peoples of Russia
расти́тельность ту́ндры	flora of the tundra

- **Objectives of an action:**

изуче́ние ру́сского языка́	study of the Russian language
закры́тие фестива́ля	closure of the festival
проведе́ние репети́ции	conducting of a rehearsal
уро́к му́зыки	music lesson

- **The agent of an action:**

вы́ступление юмори́ста	performance by a comedian
аплодисме́нты зри́телей	audience applause
заявле́ние прави́тельства	announcement by the government

- **The person or event in whose honour a place or establishment was named:**

ста́нция «Пло́щадь Револю́ции»	Revolution Square station
парк и́мени М. Го́рького	Gorky park, literally 'the park named after Gorky'
Моско́вский госуда́рственный университе́т и́мени М. В. Ломоно́сова	Moscow M. V. Lomonosov State University, literally 'the Moscow State University named after Lomonosov'
музе́й-кварти́ра Ф. М. Достое́вского	the Dostoevsky museum
пло́щадь Льва Толсто́го	Tolstoy Square

👁 The dative case is used when describing monuments erected in someone's honour(☞ 8.2.1).

Level 1, 2, 3

Other constructions can express the idea of 'possession'. These constructions can contain:

Level 1, 2

- A noun and a possessive pronoun that describes the noun: моя́ соба́ка (my dog), его́ дом (his house), её друг (her friend), наш нача́льник (our boss). For possessive pronouns, ☞ 14.4.

Level 3

- A noun and a possessive adjective that describes the noun. Possessive adjectives are formed by using the suffixes **-ин, -ов** or **-ий**. For example:

ба́бушка	ба́бушк**ин**	ба́бушк**ины** ска́зки	granny's tales
оте́ц	отцо́в	отц**о́в** нака́з	father's instruction
медве́дь	медве́жий	медве́**жья** берло́га	the bear's den
телёнок	теля́чий	теля́**чья** ко́жа	calf skin

👁 The use of the suffix **-ий** is often complicated by internal changes in the stem and by the replacement of **и** by **ь** in all forms other than the masculine.

Level 3

Possessive adjectives are formed from only a limited number of nouns. The possessive adjectives can be replaced by nouns in the genitive case, if they are derived from the same root:

Possessive adjectives	Genitive case constructions	English
ба́бушкины ска́зки	ска́зки ба́бушки	granny's tales
отцо́в нака́з	нака́з отца́	father's instruction
медве́жья берло́га	берло́га медве́дя	the bear's den
ли́сий след	след лисы́	the fox's footprint

Some possessive adjectives become proverbs and are used in figures of speech. For example:

ахилле́сова пята́	Achilles' heel
дамо́клов меч	the Sword of Damocles
крокоди́ловы слёзы	crocodile tears
медве́жий у́гол	godforsaken place
медве́жья услу́га	well-meant action having the opposite effect

Level 2, 3

7.2.2 Other roles of the genitive case without a preposition: the genitive of quantity

The genitive case can describe quantity, both precise and indefinite.

7.2.2.1 Using the genitive case to indicate an indefinite quantity

To indicate an indefinite quantity, a noun in the genitive case follows the words:

- **мно́го** (many/much/a lot)
- **немно́го** (not many/not much)
- **ма́ло** (a few/little)
- **нема́ло** (not a few/not a little/considerable)
- **ско́лько** (how much/how many)
- **сто́лько** (so many/so much)
- **не́сколько** (a few/several).

These words are usually described as indefinite numerals (☞ 15).

Ско́лько **люде́й** (genitive case),	As many opinions as people.
сто́лько и **мне́ний** (genitive case)	

The question word **ско́лько** is used in dative case constructions to indicate age: **Ско́лько Вам лет? Ско́лько лет ребёнку?** ☞ 8.2.2.

If the noun in the genitive case is a countable noun, it is always used in the plural after the words listed above. For example:

- мно́го книг (a lot of books)
- не́сколько музе́ев (several museums)
- сто́лько пра́вил (so many rules).

If the noun in the genitive case is an uncountable abstract noun or a noun that does not have a plural number, it is always used in the singular after the words listed above. For example:

- **ма́ло** внима́ния (little attention)
- **сто́лько** интере́са (so much interest)
- **мно́го** любви́ (a lot of love)
- «**Мно́го** шу́ма из ничего́» ('Much Ado About Nothing').

For nouns that do not have a plural form, ☞ 3.6.

◉ The nouns **челове́к** (person)/**лю́ди** (persons/people)/**челове́к** (persons, irregular form of the genitive plural) are used after numerals in the following way:

- The noun **челове́к** is a countable noun. **Челове́к** is used after **ско́лько?** (how many?), the indefinite numeral **не́сколько** (several) or any precise number. Note that **челове́к** is used in the nominative singular after 'one' or any compound number ending with 'one'. **Челове́к** is used in the genitive singular after numbers 'two', 'three' or 'four' or any compound number ending with 'two', 'three' or 'four'.

ско́лько здесь **челове́к?**	How many people are here?
не́сколько челове́к	several persons
пять челове́к	five people
оди́н челове́к	one person
два челове́ка	two persons

- The noun **лю́ди** (persons/people) is uncountable. The regular genitive plural of the noun **лю́ди** is used after **мно́го** (many/much/a lot), **немно́го** (not many/not much), **ма́ло** (a few/little), **нема́ло** (not a few/not a little/considerable):

мно́го люде́й	a lot of people
ма́ло люде́й	few people.

- In popular speech, the noun **наро́д** (people/folk) in the singular genitive form often replaces the noun **лю́ди** (people).

мно́го **наро́ду**	a lot of people/a lot of folk
ма́ло **наро́ду**	a few people/a few folk
немно́го **наро́ду**	a few people/a few folk

- Note the special ending **-у** in **наро́ду**.

Level 2, 3

7.2.2.2 Using the genitive case after words indicating measurement

The singular genitive case is used to indicate a part of the whole object after words indicating measurement, such as че́тверть (quarter), полови́на (half), треть (third part), часть (part), кусо́к (a piece):

че́тверть буты́лки	quarter of a bottle
полови́на я́блока	half an apple
треть кру́га	a third of the circle
часть уро́ка	part of the lesson
кусо́к то́рта	piece of cake

◉ The prefix **пол-** is the shorter form of **полови́на** and is common in popular speech: **полкило́** (half a kilogram), **полме́тра** (half a metre), **полчаса́** (half an hour), **полго́да** (half a year), **поллитра** (half a litre), **пол-Росси́и** (half of Russia), **пол-я́блока** (half an apple). If the noun starts with the consonant **л**, a capital letter or a vowel, the prefix **пол-** and the following noun are separated by a hyphen. The spelling of the word **поллитра** is an exception to the rule. The prefix **пол-** can be attached only to a noun in the singular genitive form.

Без поллитры не разберёшься! (Without a pint I cannot tell) – a popular Russian proverb/ joke that means 'a person cannot understand something really difficult unless they consume half a litre of vodka'.

Level 2, 3

◉ 7.2.2.3 Using the genitive case after numbers

For numerals, their types and declension and gender of the numbers 'one' and 'two', ☞ 15; **15.3.1,** for the nominative case, ☞ 5.

The genitive singular is used after the cardinal numbers 'two', 'three' and 'four', after any compound cardinal numbers that ends in any of these numbers and after the word о́ба/о́бе (both). For example:

два бутербро́да	two sandwiches
три ле́кции	three lectures
четы́ре у́лицы	four streets
óба гла́за	both eyes
два́дцать **две** неде́ли	twenty-two weeks
сто **три** рубля́	one hundred and three roubles
шестьдеся́т **четы́ре** го́да	sixty-four years
óбе руки́	both hands

The genitive plural is used after all the cardinal numbers except 'one', 'two', 'three' and 'four' or compound numbers that end in 'one' 'two', 'three' or 'four'. The genitive plural is also used after the collective numbers дво́е ('group of' two), тро́е ('group of' three), че́тверо ('group of' four), пя́теро ('group of' five). For example:

пять домо́в	five houses
двена́дцать яи́ц	twelve eggs
три́дцать я́блок	thirty apples
дво́е бра́тьев	two ('group of' two) brothers
сто лет	hundred years
ты́сяча рубле́й	thousand roubles
два́дцать пять до́лларов	twenty-five dollars
се́меро котя́т	seven ('group of' seven) kittens

The nominative case is used after **оди́н/одна́/одно́** (one) and after any compound numbers that end in **оди́н/одна́/одно́** (one): **оди́н рубль** (one rouble), **два́дцать оди́н год** (twenty-one years), **три́дцать одна́ кни́га** (thirty-one books).

<table><tr><td>Level
3</td></tr></table>

7.2.2.4 Other roles of the genitive case without a preposition: the 'partitive' genitive

The singular genitive case can indicate part of a whole substance or liquid. The Russian constructions, where the genitive case is used to describe part of the whole, are equivalent to English constructions with the words *some, more of something, a bit of something*. For example:

Хоти́те **воды́**?	Would you like **some water**?
Нале́йте **вина́**, пожа́луйста.	Pour **some wine**, please.
Мо́жно ещё **ча́ю**?	May I have **more tea**?
Отре́жьте **пирога́**, пожа́луйста.	Could you please cut me **some cake?**
Они́ купи́ли **хле́ба** и **сы́ра**.	They bought **some bread** and **cheese.**

Conversely, the accusative case is used to describe the whole substance or liquid. For example:

Мы лю́бим **шокола́д**.	We love chocolate.
Переда́йте **соль**, пожа́луйста.	Please pass me the salt.

Some masculine nouns that denote a substance or liquid have alternative genitive singular endings **-у/-ю** instead of the regular endings **-а/-я** when they are used to indicate part of the whole. They are usually used after the following verbs:

налива́ть/нали́ть	to pour	покупа́ть/купи́ть	to buy
ре́зать/наре́зать	to cut/to slice	дава́ть/дать	to give
пить/вы́пить	to drink	хоте́ть/захоте́ть	to want
есть/съесть	to eat	брать/взять	to take

Some common nouns that are used to convey the 'partitive' meaning with **-у/-ю** are:

са́хар – са́хар**у**	sugar	суп – су́п**у**	soup
мёд – мёд**у**	honey	чай – ча́**ю**	tea
конья́к – конья́к**у**	cognac	сыр – сы́р**у**	cheese

шокола́д – шокола́ду	chocolate	виногра́д – виногра́ду	grapes
лук – лу́ку	onions	пе́рец – пе́рцу	pepper
творо́г – творогу́	cottage cheese	кипято́к – кипятку́	boiled water
рис – ри́су	rice	шёлк – шёлку	silk
бензи́н – бензи́ну	petrol	кероси́н – кероси́ну	paraffin

The masculine nouns listed above have the same alternative endings **-у/-ю**:

- When indicating precise quantity rather than content, such as буты́лка (bottle), коро́бка (box), па́чка (package), ба́нка (jar), ми́ска (bowl), таре́лка (plate), кру́жка (mug), стака́н (glass), ча́шка (cup) of something: коро́бка шокола́ду, па́чка творогу́, па́чка ри́су, кру́жка кипятку́. For the use of the genitive case to indicate content, ☞ 7.2.1.

- In some idioms, usually with a preposition.

7.2.3 Other roles of the genitive case without a preposition: the genitive in time expressions

For the ordinal numerals, their declension and the principle of agreement with the nouns that they qualify, ☞ 15, **15.3.1.**

7.2.3.1 The date

The genitive case without a preposition is used to indicate the precise date:

Како́е сего́дня число́?	What is the date today?
Сего́дня седьмо́е **января́**.	Today is the seventh of January.
Когда́ ру́сские отмеча́ют Рождество́?	When do Russians celebrate Christmas?
Ру́сские отмеча́ют Рождество́ **седьмо́го января́**.	Russians celebrate Christmas on the seventh of January.
Како́го числа́ Вы е́дете в Москву́?	On what date are you going to Moscow?
Я е́ду в Москву́ **пя́того ию́ля**.	I am going to Moscow on the 5th of July.

Comments on the examples above:

- To answer the question **Како́е сего́дня число́?** (What is the date today?) in the present, past or future the following construction is used. There is no preposition. The date itself is expressed by the ordinal number in the neuter singular form in the nominative case. The ordinal numbers function as adjectives and, therefore, agree in gender, number and case with the noun that they qualify. When an ordinal number indicates the date, it agrees in gender, number and case with the singular neuter noun **число́** (date) in the nominative case. The following nouns that indicate the month and the year are in the singular genitive case.

Како́е сего́дня число́?	What is the date today?
Сего́дня второ́е **сентября́ две ты́сячи оди́ннадцатого го́да**.	Today is the 2nd of September 2011.
Како́е вчера́ бы́ло число́?	What was the date yesterday?
Вчера́ бы́ло пе́рвое **сентября́ две ты́сячи оди́ннадцатого го́да**.	Yesterday was the 1st of September 2011.
Како́е за́втра бу́дет число́?	What will the date be tomorrow?
За́втра бу́дет тре́тье **сентября́ две ты́сячи оди́ннадцатого го́да**.	Tomorrow will be the 3rd of September 2011.

- To indicate the date of an event and to answer the question **Когда́?/Како́го числа́?** (When?/ On what date?) a different construction is used. There is no preposition and the ordinal number that denotes the date and the following month and year are all in the genitive singular.

- 👁 The month and year are used in the genitive singular only if they form part of the date. If the month or year is used independently, it is in the prepositional case: ☞ 10.3.1.

7.2.3.2 Clock time

In popular speech, the genitive case without a preposition is used when telling the time. The following rule applies when indicating '*minutes past the hour*' in the first half of the clock:

де́сять мину́т пе́рвого	ten past twelve
два́дцать пять мину́т девя́того	twenty-five past eight
че́тверть двена́дцатого	quarter past eleven
полови́на второ́го	half past one

The first two examples above have the following structure: the cardinal numeral in the nominative case is followed by the noun **мину́та** in the genitive plural. The number indicates the minutes. The ordinal numeral in the genitive singular masculine concludes the phrase. Literally, the Russian phrase means 'how many minutes from out of the following hour have passed'. The ordinal number qualifies the noun **час** (hour) and agrees with it in gender, number and case. The last two examples show that when the words че́тверть (quarter) and полови́на (half) are used in a time expression, they are also followed by the ordinal number in the genitive singular masculine form.

For the declension of cardinal and ordinal numbers, ☞ 15.1.3, 15.2.2; for more on time expressions, and for the exact hours, ☞ 15.4.

Level 2, 3

7.2.4 Other roles of the genitive case without a preposition: genitive of comparison

The genitive case without a preposition is used in comparative constructions when comparing quality, quantity or measurement of two objects. A comparative adjective or adverb describes how two objects differ. The noun or personal pronoun with which the subject of the sentence is compared is used in the genitive case. The conjunction **чем (than)** is omitted in this construction. For example:

Ви́ктор моло́же **Петра́** (genitive).	Victor is younger than Peter.
Тигр сильне́е **ко́шки** (genitive).	A tiger is stronger than a cat.
Маши́на доро́же **велосипе́да** (genitive).	A car is more expensive than a bicycle.
Тест бу́дет ле́гче **экза́мена** (genitive).	The test will be easier than the exam.
Я́блоки бы́ли деше́вле **апельси́нов** (genitive).	The apples were cheaper than the oranges.

Быть (to be) is omitted in the present tense, but is used in the past and future tenses.

For comparative adjectives and adverbs, ☞ 12 and 13 respectively; for the use of **быть** (to be), ☞ 16.2.

Note, if the conjunction **чем (than)** is not omitted from the comparative construction, the noun or personal pronoun with which the subject of the sentence is compared is used in the nominative case (☞ 5.3):

Ви́ктор моло́же, чем **Пётр**.	Victor is younger than Peter.
Тигр сильне́е, чем **ко́шка**.	A tiger is stronger than a cat.
Маши́на доро́же, чем **велосипе́д**.	A car is more expensive than a bicycle.
Тест бу́дет ле́гче, чем **экза́мен**.	The test will be easier than the exam.
Я́блоки бы́ли деше́вле, чем **апельси́ны**.	The apples were cheaper than the oranges.

Level 2, 3

7.2.5 Other roles of the genitive case without a preposition: the genitive in negative constructions

Level 1, 2

The genitive case is used in constructions that describe the absence of someone or something in the present, past or future:

В го́роде нет **музе́ев**.	There are no museums in the city.

Level
2, 3

Дире́ктора не́ было на рабо́те.   The director was not at work.
В меню́ не бу́дет **ры́бы**.   There will be no fish on the menu.

Level
1, 2, 3

These Russian sentences are equivalent to the English constructions '*there are no/there is no someone/something somewhere*'. Note that these negative Russian constructions have no subject and are classified as *impersonal sentences*. For impersonal sentences and the negative construction with the genitive case, ☞ 30 and 30.5 respectively.

In a Russian negative construction, the noun that indicates the absent object is in the genitive case. It can be used in both the singular and plural.

Negative genitive constructions have no subject; therefore, the predicate of the sentence (the verb) does not have a subject with which it can agree. Unchangeable verbal forms therefore express the predicate of the sentence. They are the negative word **нет** (there is no/there are no) in the present tense and the negative forms of the verb **быть** (to be) in the past and the future tenses. In the past tense, the singular neuter form **не́ было** (there was no/there were no) is used. In the future tense the 3rd person singular form **не бу́дет** (there will be no) is used. Note that **нет, не́ было** and **не бу́дет** are the Russian equivalents of the English expressions *there is no/there was no/there will be no*.

For the affirmative construction that describes the presence of someone or something, ☞ 5.1.1.

 The construction that describes an object's absence is similar to the negative possessive construction: ☞ 7.3.1.2.

Level
2, 3

7.2.6 Verbs that require the genitive case without a preposition

Several verbs require the genitive case without a preposition.

 As Russian sentences have flexible word order, a noun or pronoun in the genitive case does not always appear immediately after the verb that requires that case. Furthermore, the same verb can take several different cases. A (non-exhaustive) list of the most frequently occurring verbs that take the genitive case is given below, and should be memorised. In the list, both verbal aspects are provided, if both aspects are used in this context; the imperfective aspect appears first, and then the perfective. Note that all words derived or formed from the listed verbs (nouns, participles, gerunds) normally require the same case: for example

жела́ть сча́стья	to wish happiness
жела́ние сча́стья	desire for happiness
жела́я сча́стья	wishing happiness
пожела́вший сча́стья	who wished happiness
жела́ющий сча́стья	who wishes happiness

Verbs	Examples
жела́ть/пожела́ть кому́? чего́? (to wish to whom? what?)	жела́ть роди́телям здоро́вья и сча́стья (to wish one's parents health and happiness)
достига́ть/дости́гнуть/дости́чь чего́? (to achieve what?)	дости́гнуть це́ли (to achieve the goal)
добива́ться/доби́ться чего́? (to strive for what?)	доби́ться успе́ха (to strive for success)
заслу́живать/заслужи́ть чего́? (to deserve what?)	заслужи́ть награ́ды (to deserve the reward/award/prize)
жа́ждать чего́? (to crave for what?)	жа́ждать сла́вы (to crave for glory)

Verbs	Examples
боя́ться чего́? (to be afraid of what?)	боя́ться высоты́ (to be afraid of heights)
пуга́ться/испуга́ться чего́? (to be frightened of what?)	испуга́ться темноты́ (to be frightened of darkness)
избега́ть/избежа́ть кого́? чего́? (to avoid whom? what?)	избега́ть конкуре́нта (to avoid the competitor), избега́ть встре́чи (to avoid the meeting)

7.2.7 The genitive case without a preposition in some greetings and idioms

For the declension of adjectives, ☞ 11.

In some common greetings, the verb **жела́ть** (to wish), which requires the genitive case, is omitted. The phrases with the omitted verb **жела́ть** become idioms:

Счастли́вого пути́!	Have a nice trip!
Споко́йной но́чи!	Good night!
Прия́тного аппети́та!	Bon appetit!
Счастли́вого Но́вого го́да!	Happy New Year!
Мя́гкой поса́дки!	Have a safe landing!
Уда́чи!	Good luck!
Успе́ха/успе́хов!	(I/we etc. wish you) success!

When writing holiday greetings the verb **жела́ть** (to wish) is **not** omitted and takes an object in the genitive case. The person to whom the greetings are addressed is in the dative case: ☞ 8.

Russians usually start their holiday greetings using the verb **поздравля́ть** (to congratulate) followed by the preposition **с** (with) and the noun in the instrumental case: ☞ 9.3. The traditional wishes introduced by the verb **жела́ть** (to wish) complete the greetings. For example:

Дорога́я Мари́я!	Dear Maria,
Поздравля́ю тебя́ с Рождество́м!	I wish you a Merry Christmas!
Жела́ю тебе́ сча́стья, здоро́вья и ра́дости.	I wish you happiness, health and joy.
Верони́ка	Veronica

Examples of card greetings:

И от души́ тебе́ жела́ем	From the bottom of the heart we wish you
Здоро́вья, сча́стья, до́лгих лет ...	Health, happiness, long life.
Жела́ем сча́стья и здоро́вья,	We wish you happiness and health,
Жела́ем бо́дрости и сил ...	We wish you to be in good spirits and have strength.

Note that the adjectives and the pronoun **весь** in the genitive case are also used in the above greetings. For adjectives declension ☞ 11.1. For the declension of **весь** ☞ 14.6.1

Упражне́ния

1. Put the noun in brackets into the correct form:
1. Э́то маши́на (Ната́ша).
2. Э́то велосипе́д (брат).
3. Э́то кле́тка (попуга́й).
4. Э́то ко́шка (подру́га).
5. Э́то бе́рег (мо́ре).

У Мари́и **нет кни́ги**.	Maria does not have/has not got a book.
У Мари́и **не́ было экза́мена**.	Maria did not have/has not had an exam.
У Мари́и **не бу́дет ле́кций**.	Maria will not have lectures.

◕ In Russian, the negative possessive construction is similar to the construction that describes an object's absence: ☞ 7.2.5.

7.3.1.3 Omission of the verb есть (to have, to be) in affirmative possessive constructions and constructions that indicate presence

For constructions that indicate presence ☞ 5.1.1

For affirmative possessive constructions ☞ 7.3.1.1

Level 2, 3

In the present tense, the verb **есть** is usually omitted from possessive affirmative constructions or constructions that indicate presence when they describe:

- **Appearance, personality, mood or health condition:**

У ба́бушки седы́е **во́лосы**.	Grandmother has got grey hair.
У Са́ши **прекра́сный хара́ктер**.	Sasha has a nice personality.
У де́душки **до́брое се́рдце**.	Grandfather is a kind person.
У ма́тери всегда́ **хоро́шее настрое́ние**.	Mother is always in high spirits.
У Ма́ши **грипп**.	Masha has flu.

◕ In Russian, unlike English, questions/comments about **настрое́ние** (mood/spirit) are common:

Как **настрое́ние**?	Are you in good spirits today?
У Мари́и сего́дня **плохо́е настрое́ние**.	Maria feels down/low today.

- **A scheduled event: пра́здники** (holidays), **встре́чи** (meetings), **экза́мены** (examinations):

У студе́нтов **ле́кции по понеде́льникам**.	The students have lectures on Mondays.
У бизнесме́на **встре́ча в час**.	The businessman has a meeting at 1 o'clock.
У ма́мы **день рожде́ния в ма́е**.	Mother has her birthday in May.

- **Weather conditions:**

На у́лице **дождь**.	It is raining outside
Сего́дня си́льный **ве́тер**.	It is very windy today.

◕ In Russian, the verb of motion **идти́** (to go), in a figurative sense, replaces the verb **есть** (to be) when talking about rain or snow: дождь идёт (it is raining), снег идёт (it is snowing). For more information, ☞ 24.7.

- **Descriptions of inseparable parts of an object:** экра́н компью́тера (computer screen), потоло́к, сте́ны, о́кна, пол в ко́мнате (ceiling, walls, windows, the floor in a room):

В ко́мнате **большо́е окно́**.	There is a big window in the room.
У ноутбу́ка **ма́ленький экра́н**.	The laptop has a small screen.

- **When the construction emphasises quality or quantity rather than 'ownership' or 'relationship':**

У Мари́и **прекра́сная** семья́.	Maria has a nice family.
У друзе́й **ра́зные** интере́сы.	The friends have different interests.
У ребёнка **больши́е** спосо́бности.	The child is very able.
У Бори́са **интере́сная** рабо́та.	Boris has an interesting job.
У Еле́ны **три** сестры́ и **два** бра́та.	Helen has three sisters and two brothers.

◕ **Есть** is not omitted from the possessive affirmative construction and construction indicating presence when a speaker needs to emphasise the fact of possession or presence:

У ребёнка **есть спосо́бности к му́зыке**?	Does the child have a gift for music?
Да. У ребёнка **есть спосо́бности**.	Yes, he does.
У Верони́ки **есть аллерги́я** на э́то лека́рство?	Is Veronica allergic to this medicine?

Да, **есть.**	Yes, she is.
Из объявле́ния «Их разы́скивает мили́ция»:	Extract from the description:
Престу́пник – высо́кий по́лный мужчи́на.	'The most wanted': The criminal is a
Осо́бые приме́ты: **есть шрам** на пра́вой щеке́.	tall, big man. Special features: He **has a scar** on his right cheek.

👁 The verb **бу́дет** (to be) in the future tense can also be omitted in the situations described above. The verb **был, -а, -о, -и** (to be) in the past tense cannot be omitted. None of **нет, не́ бы́ло, не бу́дет** (to be) can be omitted in negative possessive constructions or constructions that describe absence.

7.3.2 Using the genitive case with prepositions

The genitive case can be used with many prepositions. The preposition **у** is the most common as it forms an essential part of Russian possessive constructions (☞ 7.3.1). Other prepositions that are most frequently used with the genitive case are listed in the summary table below. The list is not exhaustive, but it does cover the most common prepositions:

Context	Location	Moving from and to	Expression of time	Prepositional constructions
The question that the noun answers	**где?** (where?)	**отку́да?** (from where?), **куда́?** (to where?), **где?** (where?)	**когда́?** (when?)	various, depending on context
Preposition used	**напро́тив** (opposite) **от** (from): **от** is used after adverbs **недалеко́** (not far away) **далеко́** (far way) **вблизи́** (near by) **сле́ва** (on the left) **спра́ва** (on the right) **о́коло/во́зле/у** (near/near by) **у** (at one's place) **вокру́г** (around) **вдоль** (along) **впереди́** (in front of) **позади́/сза́ди** (behind) **среди́/посреди́** (in the middle of) **внутри́** (inside)	**из/с/от** (from) **до** (to) **ми́мо** (past) **из-за** (from behind/ beyond) **из-под** (from under) **вдоль** (along)	**без** (to) **до** (before/until) **по́сле** (after) **во вре́мя** (during/at) **с ... до** (from ... to) **с ... до** (from ... to)	**без** (without) **для** (for whom/for what) **из-за** (because of) **из-под** (purpose of container) **кро́ме** (except/ besides) **про́тив/от** (against) **от** (from/for) **ввиду́** (in view of) **вме́сто** (instead of) **вне** (beyond/ outside of) **ра́ди** (for the sake of)
Examples	☞ 7.3.2.1	☞ 7.3.2.2	☞ 7.3.2.3	☞ 7.3.2.4

Comments on the table

- Nouns in three cases (genitive, instrumental and prepositional) can be used to indicate location. The choice of case depends on the noun's meaning and the preposition that governs the noun.
- Nouns in four cases (accusative, genitive, dative and instrumental) can describe unidirectional movements. The choice of case depends on the noun's meaning and the preposition that governs the noun.
- Nouns in all cases except the nominative can be used in time expressions. The choice of case depends on the noun's meaning and the preposition that governs the noun.

7.3.2.1 Using prepositions with the genitive case in the description of location

Several prepositions are used with the genitive case to indicate precise location. The verb **находи́ться** (to be located/to be situated) and the short-form participle **располо́жен -а, -о, -ы** (to be located/to be situated) are often used in these descriptions. The text below gives the context of when the most common prepositions with the genitive are used.

Сообще́ние господи́на Смирно́ва его́ деловы́м партнёрам об университе́тском городке́, где бу́дет проходи́ть конфере́нция	Mr Smirnoff's e-mail to his business partners about the university campus where the conference will be held:
Конфере́нция бу́дет проходи́ть в Моско́вском госуда́рственном университе́те им. М. В. Ломоно́сова (МГУ). МГУ нахо́дится **о́коло ста́нции** метро́ «Университе́т». **Во́зле ста́нции** метро́ есть кио́ски, где продаю́т кни́ги и газе́ты. **У кио́сков** всегда́ мно́го наро́ду. **Не** о́чень **далеко́ от университе́та** располо́жены Де́тский музыка́льный теа́тр и цирк. К сожале́нию, ва́ша гости́ница нахо́дится **далеко́ от МГУ**. Но для госте́й конфере́нции бу́дет ходи́ть маршру́тное такси́ («маршру́тка»). МГУ – это о́чень большо́й студе́нческий го́род. Гла́вное зда́ние университе́та нахо́дится **посреди́ студе́нческого городка́**. Регистра́ция делега́тов конфере́нции бу́дет проходи́ть **внутри́ гла́вного зда́ния. Напро́тив гла́вного зда́ния** – па́мятник М. В. Ломоно́сову. **Вокру́г па́мятника** – краси́вый сквер. **Вдоль доро́жек** в скве́ре стоя́т скаме́йки, где лю́бят сиде́ть студе́нты. **Позади́ па́мятника** – Ломоно́совский проспе́кт и библиоте́ка. **Сле́ва от па́мятника** нахо́дится физи́ческий факульте́т, **спра́ва от па́мятника** – хими́ческий факульте́т. Там бу́дут проходи́ть семина́ры. В после́дний день конфере́нции вы та́кже смо́жете побыва́ть в гостя́х **у ре́ктора**.	The conference will be held at the Lomonosov Moscow State University (MGU). MGU is located **near** 'University' metro station. **Near** the station there are some kiosks where books and newspapers are sold. By the kiosks there are always a lot of people. **Not very far away from** the university are the Children's Music Theatre and circus. Unfortunately, your hotel is **far away from** MGU. However, for guests of the conference there will be a shuttle bus. MGU is a very big campus. The main building is **in the middle** of the campus. Delegate registration will be held **inside** the main building. The Lomonosov monument is **opposite** the main building. **Around** the monument is a beautiful public garden. **Along** the paths in the garden there are benches where students like to sit. **Behind** the monument are the library and Lomonosov Avenue. The physics department is **on the left of** the monument. The chemistry department is **on the right**. The seminars will be held there. On the last day of the conference, you can visit the Principal (or '*Rector*' in the USA) **at** his private residence.

7.3.2.2 Using the genitive case with verbs of motion and other verbs describing movement

Nouns in all cases, except the nominative case, can describe various movements. The genitive case, with the prepositions listed in the table (☞ 7.3.2), indicates:

- The start point of the movement: **из/с/от** (from), **из-за** (from behind/beyond), **из-под** (from under)
- The end point of the movement: **до** (to)
- The route of the journey: **мимо** (past), **вдоль** (along)

The fourteen *verbs of motion* are mainly used with the genitive case when describing the start and end point of a movement or the route of a journey:

выйти из автобуса	to get off the bus
уйти с работы	to leave a job
уехать от родителей	to leave one's parents
выехать из-за угла	to drive round from behind the corner
вылезти из-под стола	to get out from under the table
доехать до Красной площади	to reach Red Square
дойти до лифта	to reach the lift
пройти мимо магазина	to go past the shop

For the verbs of motion, ☞ 24 and 25.

In Russian, there are many verbs other than fourteen verbs of motion that can describe various movements. Some of them require the genitive case with the prepositions listed at the beginning of this section. The most frequently occurring verbs that describe movement (other than the verbs of motion) are listed below:

добираться/добраться до	to reach (to)
выбрасывать/выбросить из	to throw out from
бросать/бросить мимо	to throw past
возвращаться/вернуться из/от/с	to return from
вставать/встать с	to get up from
вставать/встать из-за	to get up from behind
получать/получить что от кого	to receive something from someone

The following questions are common when asking for directions:

Как добраться до ...?	How can I reach... (general question)?
Как доехать до ...?	How can I reach a place by means of transport?
Как дойти до ...?	How can I reach a place by foot?

The English preposition *from* can be translated into Russian using three different prepositions, **из, с** and **от**, when describing unidirectional movement. Translation of the preposition *from* depends on the indication of the start point of the movement:

		Examples
The preposition *из* is used	if the start point of a movement is a location that can be described by the prepositional case with the preposition **в** (in/at): building, enclosed location or a geographical location etc.	быть **в** доме (to be inside the house) – уйти **из** дома (to leave a house) жить **в** России (to live in Russia) – уехать **из** России (to leave Russia)

		Examples
The preposition c is used	if the start point of the movement is a location that can be described by the prepositional case with the preposition **на** (on/at): being at an event, open space location etc.	быть **на** уро́ке (to be at the lesson) – уйти́ **с** уро́ка (to leave the lesson) отдыха́ть **на** мо́ре (to relax by the seashore) – уе́хать **с** мо́ря (to leave the seashore)
The preposition om is used	if the start point of the movement is a location that can be described by the genitive case with the preposition **y** (near/by). **От** is also used when describing movement from one's place or receiving something from someone.	стоя́ть **y** кио́ска (to stand next to the kiosk) – отойти́ **от** кио́ска (to move away from the kiosk) быть **y** врача́ (to visit the doctor) – уйти́ **от** врача́ (to leave the doctor's office)

On using the prepositions **в** and **на** with the prepositional case, ☞ 10.2.1.

For use of prepositions with the verbs of motion and other verbs describing movement, ☞ 25.7.

Level 2, 3 ### 7.3.2.3 Using the genitive case with prepositions in time expressions

The genitive case is used with prepositions in some time expressions that:

- Indicate time before, after or during an event:

до обе́да	before lunch
по́сле обе́да	after lunch
во вре́мя обе́да	during/at lunch

- Mark the beginning and end of a time period (using the clock, parts of the day, weeks, years or seasons):

с девяти́ до шести́	from 9 to 6 o'clock
с утра́ до ве́чера	from morning to evening
с весны́ до о́сени	from spring to autumn

- Mark the beginning and end of a time period using the words **нача́ло**, **коне́ц** or in expressions of age and some idioms:

от нача́ла до конца́	from beginning to end
от двух до пяти́	from two to five years of age
от зарпла́ты до зарпла́ты	from payday to payday

◈ The preposition **пе́ред** (before) followed by the instrumental case is often used as a synonym of the preposition **до** (before): ☞ 9.3.

- The genitive case is used with the preposition **без** (without) when telling the time in popular speech. This construction is used when indicating '*minutes to the hour*' in the second half of the clock:

без десяти́ пять	ten to five
без двадцати́ пяти́ де́вять	twenty-five to nine
без че́тверти двена́дцать	quarter to twelve

◈ The examples above have the following structure: the preposition governs the cardinal number in the genitive case. The number indicates the minutes. The cardinal number in the nominative concludes the phrase.

For the declension of cardinal numbers and time expressions, ☞ 15.1 and 15.3.

<table>
<tr><td>Level
2, 3</td><td></td></tr>
</table>

7.3.2.4 Using the genitive case in prepositional constructions

👁 The preposition **для** (for whom/what for) followed by an animate noun or personal pronoun in the genitive case is similar to the construction using the dative case without a preposition:

Genitive	Dative	Translation
пода́рок **для ма́мы**	пода́рок **ма́ме**	a present **for/to mother**
э́то **для Вас**	э́то **Вам**	it is **for you**
игру́шка **для сы́на**	игру́шка **сы́ну**	a toy **for/to the son**

Inanimate nouns in this construction are usually used with the preposition **для** followed by the genitive case: для рабо́ты (for the work), для де́ла (for business), для це́ли (for the purpose).

👁 The preposition **из-за** (because of) followed by a noun or personal pronoun in the genitive case can be replaced by a subordinate clause introduced by the conjunction **потому́ что** (because):

Genitive	Subordinate clause introduced by **потому́ что**	Translation
Мы не гуля́ем **из-за дождя́**.	Мы не гуля́ем **потому́**, **что** идёт дождь.	We are not walking **because of the rain/because it is raining.**
Из-за ссо́ры с дру́гом я не пошёл на вечери́нку.	Я не пошёл на вечери́нку **потому́, что** я поссо́рился с дру́гом.	I did not go to the party **because of a quarrel/because I had a quarrel with my friend.**

The preposition **без** (without) followed by the genitive case is often used in opposition to the preposition **с** (with) followed by the instrumental case:

В кафе́:	In the café
Официа́нт: Вы бу́дете чай **с молоко́м и са́харом**?	Waiter: Will you take **milk and sugar** with your tea?
Клие́нт: Чай **без молока́** и **без са́хара**, но **с лимо́ном**, пожа́луйста.	Client: Tea without **milk** and **sugar** but with **lemon**.

The prepositions **из-под** (purpose of a container), **кро́ме** (except, besides), **вме́сто** (instead of) and **про́тив/от** (against) are common in popular speech:

буты́лка **из-под молока́**	milk bottle
ба́нка **из-под мёда**	honey jar
все, **кро́ме Ви́ктора**	everybody except Victor
всё, **кро́ме то́рта**	everything except the cake
вме́сто профе́ссора	instead of the professor
вме́сто уро́ка	instead of the lesson
вакци́на **про́тив гри́ппа**	flu vaccine
лека́рство **от просту́ды**	medicine for a cold
дви́гаться **про́тив тече́ния**	to move against the current
ключ **от кварти́ры**	key to the flat

The prepositions **ввиду́** (in view of), **вне** (beyond/outside of) and **ра́ди** (for the sake of) are common in writing:

ввиду́ измене́ний в расписа́нии	owing to changes to the schedule
ра́ди сла́вы и де́нег	for the sake of glory and money
... э́та ночь для меня́ **вне зако́на**.	... this night for me is outside the law.
Я пишу́ – по ноча́м бо́льше тем.	I write more at night.

Two prepositions **от ... до** (from ... to) convey the idea of distance between two places:

| от Москвы́ до Петербу́рга | from Moscow to St Petersburg |
| от Земли́ до Луны́ | from the Earth to the Moon |

Level
2, 3

7.3.3 Verbs that require the genitive case with a preposition

Several verbs require the genitive case with a preposition. The preposition **от** is the most frequently occurring preposition that governs a noun in the genitive case after the verb.

👁 As Russian sentences have flexible word order, a noun or pronoun in the genitive case does not always appear immediately after the verb that requires that case. Furthermore, the same verb can take several different cases. Also, note that the use of prepositions may differ in Russian and English. A (non-exhaustive) list of the most frequently occurring verbs that take the genitive case is given below, and should be memorised. In the list, both verbal aspects are provided, if both aspects are used in this context; the imperfective aspect appears first, and then the perfective. Note that all words derived or formed from the listed verbs (nouns, participles, gerunds) normally require the same preposition and case. For example: **защища́ть от враго́в** (to defend from enemies), **защи́та от ве́тра** (protection from wind), and **защити́в от клеветы́** (having protected from slander).

Verbs	Examples
защища́ть/защи́тить кого́? что? от кого́? от чего́? (to defend/to protect whom? what? from whom? from what?)	защища́ть плане́ту от загрязне́ния (to protect the planet from pollution)
заслоня́ть/заслони́ть кого́? что? от кого́? от чего́? (to shield/to cover whom? what? from whom? from what?)	заслони́ть ребёнка от ве́тра (to shield the child from the wind)
отка́зываться/отказа́ться от чего́? (to refuse, to decline what?)	отказа́ться от по́мощи (to refuse help)
освобожда́ть/освободи́ть кого́? что? от кого́? от чего́? (to free whom? what? from whom? from what?)	освобожда́ть зало́жников от террори́стов (to free hostages from terrorists)
освобожда́ться /освободи́ться от кого́? от чего́? (to free oneself from whom? from what?)	освободи́ться от опе́ки/от зави́симости (to free oneself from guardianship/from addiction)
пря́тать/спря́тать что? кого́? от чего́? от кого́? (to hide what? whom? from what? from whom?)	пря́тать еду́ от хи́щников в норе́ (to hide food from predators in a burrow)
пря́таться/спря́таться от кого́? от чего́? (to hide from whom? from what?)	пря́таться от дождя́ под наве́сом (to shelter from the rain under the awning)
лечи́ть/вы́лечить кого́? (что?) от чего́? (to treat medically whom? what? from what?)	лечи́ть пацие́нта от инсу́льта (to treat a patient for stroke)
лечи́ться/вы́лечиться/излечи́ться от чего́? (to receive medical treatment impf. for what? to recover pf. from what?)	вы́лечиться от СПИ́Да (to recover from AIDS)

The preposition **y** is frequently used to govern, usually, an animate noun in the genitive case, when the noun describes the source of information or any material things. The preposition **y** appears after the following verbs: **спра́шивать/спроси́ть** (to ask (a question)), **проси́ть/попроси́ть** (to request/to ask for), **занима́ть/заня́ть**, **брать/взять**, **ода́лживать/одолжи́ть** (to borrow): **спроси́ть у Ни́ны** (to ask Nina).

Упражне́ния

Level 1, 2

1. Replace the affirmative constructions with negative ones:
Моде́ль: У Петра́ есть де́ньги – У Петра́ нет де́нег.

1. У Мари́и сейча́с кани́кулы.
2. У Ви́ктора есть рабо́та.
3. У друзе́й есть вре́мя.
4. У ба́бушки есть до́мик в дере́вне.
5. У бизнесме́на есть при́быль.
6. У Никола́я есть вну́ки.

Level 2, 3

2. Give a negative answer:

1. Сего́дня бу́дет матч?
2. В стране́ бы́ли вы́боры президе́нта?
3. У профсою́зов (trade unions) есть подде́ржка в Росси́и?
4. У писа́теля есть сюже́т для но́вого рома́на?
5. У заво́да бу́дут зака́зы на това́ры?

Level 2, 3

3. Insert the verb «есть» if appropriate:

1. У моде́ли всегда́ .... краси́вая причёска.
2. У студе́нта .... слова́рь?
3. На у́лице .... си́льный ве́тер.
4. У Петра́ .... тру́дный хара́ктер.
5. У мое́й сестры́ .... грипп.
6. У ма́мы сего́дня .... плохо́е настрое́ние.

Level 2, 3

4. Use the correct preposition:

1. Мы спря́тались ... ве́тра.
2. Пассажи́ры отказа́лись ... по́мощи.
3. Больно́й вы́лечился ... СПИ́Да.
4. Пожа́рные спасли́ люде́й ... ги́бели.
5. Мо́йте ру́ки ... и ... обе́да.
6. Библиоте́ка откры́та ... девяти́ ... четырёх.
7. Мы плывём ... тече́ния.
8. Ви́ктор прочи́тал кни́гу ... нача́ла ... конца́.
9. Он отказа́лся ... приглаше́ния ... ссо́ры с дру́гом.

Level 2, 3

Обобща́ющее упражне́ние

5. Put the words in brackets into the genitive case. Add prepositions, if appropriate.

1. Подру́га (господи́н Смирно́в) пло́хо себя́ чу́вствует. 2. Господи́н Смирно́в сего́дня опозда́л на рабо́ту (боле́знь) свое́й (подру́га Ири́на). 3. Ве́чером (Ири́на) подняла́сь температу́ра. 4. У́тром (Ири́на) появи́лся ка́шель и на́сморк. 5. Пото́м (Ири́на) заболе́ло го́рло. 6. Снача́ла господи́н Смирно́в купи́л лека́рство (ка́шель и на́сморк). 7. Пото́м он пригото́вил (Ири́на) за́втрак. 8. Она́ вы́пила (чай) (са́хар и молоко́) и съе́ла два (я́блоко). 9. Пото́м им пришло́сь вы́звать врача́. 10. Они́ жда́ли врача́ (обе́д). 11. Врач пришёл, сде́лал Ири́не уко́л (температу́ра) и сказа́л, что (Ири́на) грипп. 12. Ей придётся лежа́ть (коне́ц) (неде́ля).

8 Nouns: dative case

For the concept of the six-case system and the principles of noun declension, ☞ 4.

The dative case is one of the six Russian cases. In a sentence or phrase, the dative case has several roles. It can be used with or without a preposition. This chapter provides a summary of noun endings in the dative case and explains its grammatical roles.

Level 1, 2

8.1 Summary table of noun endings in the instrumental case

Singular masculine and neuter nouns	Hard stem and stem ending with г, к, х, ж, ш, щ, ц	-у
	Soft stem	-ю
Singular feminine nouns	All nouns except those ending in -ия and -ь	-е
	Nouns ending in -ия and -ь	-и
Plural nouns	Hard stem and stem ending with г, к, х, ж, ш, щ, ц	-ам
	Soft stem	-ям

- Some nouns have so-called '*fleeting*' vowels -о/-е/-ё in the final syllable in any case other than nominative singular: пирожо́к – пирожку́ (pie), оте́ц – отцу́ (father) etc. The nouns мать (mother) and дочь (daughter) have the suffix -ер inserted in all cases but the accusative: ма́тери, до́чери. The change ё to ь occurs in the noun лёд/льду (ice): по льду (on ice). For the fleeting vowels, ☞ 4.5
- For hard and soft endings and the spelling rules, ☞ 1.3 and 1.4.

8.2 Using the dative case without a preposition

Level 1, 2

8.2.1 The main role of the dative case without a preposition

In a sentence, a noun or pronoun in the dative case indicates an indirect object, 'an addressee' or 'a recipient', to whom an action is directed. 'An addressee' or 'a recipient' can be animate or inanimate. A noun or pronoun in the dative case answers the question кому́? (to whom?/ for whom?) or чему́? (to/for what?). In a sentence, a noun/pronoun in the dative case frequently accompanies a noun in the accusative case that indicates a direct object. The common structure of a sentence that contains the subject and both direct and indirect object is as follows:

Кто – де́лает – что – кому́ **ИЛИ** Кто – де́лает – кому́ – что	Who (subject) – does (verb) – what (direct object) – to whom (indirect object, addressee) **OR** Who (subject) – does (verb) – to whom (indirect object, addressee) – what (direct object)
Мари́я пи́шет **письмо́** (accusative, direct object) **Петру́** (dative, addressee).	Maria writes **a letter to Peter**.
Мари́я пи́шет **Петру́** (dative, addressee) **письмо́** (accusative, direct object).	Maria writes **Peter a letter**.
Дочь покупа́ет **пода́рок** (accusative, direct object) **ма́тери** (dative, addressee).	The daughter buys a **present for her mother**.
Дочь покупа́ет **ма́тери** (dative, addressee) **пода́рок** (accusative, direct object).	The daughter buys **her mother a present**.

◈ In Russian, there is no equivalent of the English preposition *to* to indicate the addressee of an action.

The dative case is used to indicate an addressee in the following expressions:

- **In correspondence.** For example, the name, title and position of the person to whom a letter or e-mail is addressed are in the dative case: господи́ну президе́нту (to Mr President), господи́ну Смирно́ву (to Mr Smirnoff), профе́ссору Фёдорову (to Professor Fyodorov), Джéймсу Бо́нду (to James Bond).
- **When describing monuments** erected in someone's honour. Names, titles and professions of the honoured persons are in the dative case: па́мятник космона́вту Ю́рию Гага́рину (the monument to the cosmonaut Yuri Gagarin), па́мятник Пу́шкину (Pushkin's monument).
  ◈ Note the genitive case is used when describing the person or the event in whose honour a place or an establishment was named (☞ 7.2.1).
- **With nouns derived from verbs that require the dative case** (☞ 8.2.4): отве́т дру́гу (answer to a friend), посы́лка студе́нту (parcel to a student), сообще́ние дире́ктору (e-mail to a director), по́мощь ветера́нам (help to veterans), сове́т де́вушке (advice to a girl).

<table>
<tr><td>Level
1, 2</td></tr>
</table>

8.2.2 Other meanings of the dative case without a preposition: stating age

The dative case without a preposition is used to convey age. An age expression has the following structure:

- A noun indicating a person/inanimate object, whose age is stated, is in the dative case.

If a cardinal numeral is followed by the noun **год** (year), the form of the noun **год** depends on the last figure in the numeral. For example:

Ско́лько лет **ма́льчику, де́вочке, близнеца́м**?	How old is/are the boy/girl/twins?
Ма́льчику (dative) пять лет (genitive plural).	The boy is 5 years old.
Де́вочке (dative) два го́да (genitive singular).	The girl is two years old.
Близнеца́м (dative) год (nominative).	The twins are one year old.

For the use of cases after numbers, ☞ 15.3.

Level
2, 3 ### 8.2.3 Using the dative case without a preposition in impersonal constructions

For the concept, types and use of impersonal sentences, ☞ 30. ☞ 30.3 for information on the use of:

- the verb **нра́виться/понра́виться** (to like)
- short-form adjectives **ну́жен, нужна́, нужны́** (need)
- modal words **на́до** (need), **мо́жно** (permitted), **нельзя́** (forbidden) etc., with the dative case

Russian *impersonal* sentences do not have a subject. They have only one core element, a predicate, and describe a state or action that occurs as if without external forces: **Хо́лодно.** (It is cold.) **Интере́сно.** (It is interesting.)

However, if the context of an impersonal sentence requires explaining who experiences a certain condition, this information is usually conveyed by a noun or personal pronoun in the dative case:

- **Мари́и** хо́лодно. (**Maria** is cold (literally: it is cold for Maria).)
- **Ви́ктору** интере́сно. (**Victor** is interested (literally: it is interesting for Victor).)

A noun or personal pronoun in the dative case functions as 'the addressee' to whom the action is directed. The noun/pronoun in the dative case answers the question **кому́**? (to whom?).

Level
2, 3 ### 8.2.4 Verbs that require a noun in the dative case without a preposition

In Russian, several verbs require a noun in the dative case as their indirect object.

👁 As Russian sentences have flexible word order, a noun or pronoun in the dative case does not always appear immediately after the verb that requires that case. Furthermore, the same verb can take several different cases. A (non-exhaustive) list of the most frequently occurring verbs that take the dative case is given below, and should be memorised. In the list, both verbal aspects are provided, if both aspects are used in this context; the imperfective aspect appears first, and then the perfective. Note that all words derived or formed from the listed verbs (nouns, participles, gerunds) normally require the same case. For example:

сообщи́ть дру́гу	to inform a friend
сообще́ние дру́гу	a message to a friend
сообщи́в дру́гу	having spoken to a friend

Verbs indicating communication	Examples
говори́ть/сказа́ть кому́? о чём? (to say to whom? about what?)	**сказа́ть дру́гу** о приглаше́нии (to tell a friend about an invitation)
расска́зывать/рассказа́ть кому́? о чём? (to tell whom? about what?)	**рассказа́ть полице́йскому** о происше́ствии (to tell a policeman about the incident)
сообща́ть/сообщи́ть кому́? о чём? (to inform whom? about what?)	**сообщи́ть студе́нтам** об экза́мене (to inform students about an examination)
объявля́ть/объяви́ть кому́? о чём? (to announce to whom? about what?)	**объяви́ть депута́там** о заседа́нии (to announce a meeting to MPs)
напомина́ть/напо́мнить кому́? о чём? (to remind whom? about what?)	**напо́мнить шко́льникам** о сочине́нии (to remind the pupils about an essay)
писа́ть/написа́ть кому́? о чём? (to write to whom? about what?)	**писа́ть ба́бушке** о вну́ке (to write to a grandmother about her grandchild)

читáть/прочитáть комý? о чём?/что? (to read to whom? what?/about what?)	**читáть дéтям** скáзку (to read children a fairy tale)
отвечáть/отвéтить комý? на что? (to answer whom? what?)	**отвéтить дрýгу** на письмó (to answer a friend's letter)
объяснять/объяснить комý? что? (to explain to whom? what?)	**объяснить сотрýдникам** прáвила (to explain the rules to staff)
совéтовать/посовéтовать комý? что дéлать? (to advise whom? to do what?)	**совéтовать знакóмым** посмотрéть гóрод (to advise acquaintances to see a city)
звонить/позвонить комý? (to call, to ring whom?)	**позвонить секретарю** (to call the secretary)
мешáть/помешáть комý? (to disturb whom?/ to prevent someone doing something)	**мешáть брáту** слýшать мýзыку (to prevent one's brother from listening to music)

Verbs indicating emotions, beliefs, likes and dislikes	Examples
вéрить/повéрить комý? чемý? (to believe whom? what?)	**повéрить сплéтням** (to believe rumours)
рáдоваться/обрáдоваться комý? чемý? (to be happy for whom? about what?)	**рáдоваться новостя́м** (to be happy to hear the news)
удивля́ться/удиви́ться комý? чемý? (to be surprised by whom? by what?)	**удиви́ться звонкý** (to be surprised by the phone call)
нрáвиться/понрáвиться (to like whom? what? = who? what? to please someone/ something)'	**бизнесмéну нрáвится** договóр (the businessman likes the agreement/the agreement pleases the businessman)
сочýвствовать/посочýвствовать комý? чемý? (to sympathise with whom? with what?)	**сочýвствовать** Вáшей **утрáте** (to sympathise with your loss)
доверя́ть/довéрить комý? чемý? (to trust whom? what?)	**доверя́ть дрýгу** (to trust a friend)
зави́довать/позави́довать комý? чемý? (to envy whom? what?)	**зави́довать сопéрнику** (to envy a competitor)
льсти́ть/польсти́ть комý? (to flatter whom?)	**льсти́ть начáльнику** (to flatter a boss)
угрожáть комý? чемý? (to threaten whom?)	**угрожáть** офицéру (to threaten an officer)

Verbs describing selling, passing on to, giving etc.	Examples
гото́вить/пригото́вить что? кому? (to prepare, to cook what? for whom?)	**гото́вить** у́жин **гостя́м** (to cook dinner for the guests)
дава́ть/дать что? кому? (to give what? to whom?)	**дать** кни́гу **библиоте́карю** (to give a book to the librarian)
дари́ть/подари́ть что? кому? (to give as a present what? to whom?)	**подари́ть** компью́тер **сы́ну** (to give a computer (as a present) to a son)
сдава́ть/сдать что? кому? (to be examined by whom? or to submit what? to whom?)	**сдава́ть** экза́мен **коми́ссии** (to be examined by a committee), **сдава́ть** сочине́ние **преподава́телю** (to submit an essay to a tutor/instructor)
продава́ть/прода́ть что? кому? (to sell what? to whom?)	**продава́ть** цветы́ **покупа́телям** (to sell flowers to the customers)
посыла́ть/посла́ть что? кому? (to send what? to whom?)	**посла́ть** посы́лку **роди́телям** (to send a parcel to one's parents)
отдава́ть/отда́ть что? кому? (to return what? to whom?)	**отда́ть** долг **ба́нку** (to pay off the loan to the bank)
передава́ть/переда́ть что? кому? (to pass what? to whom?)	**переда́йте Мари́и** привет (pass my regards to Maria)
покупа́ть/купи́ть что? кому? (to buy what? for whom?)	**купи́ть** пода́рки **ро́дственникам** (to buy presents for relatives)
предлага́ть/предложи́ть что? кому? (to offer/to propose what? to whom?)	**предлага́ть** това́р **клие́нтам** (to offer the goods to the clients)
пока́зывать/показа́ть что? кому? (to show what? to whom?)	**показа́ть** сувени́ры **тури́стам** (to show the souvenirs to the tourists)

Verbs describing assistance, rules, learning	Examples
помога́ть/помо́чь кому? (to help whom?)	**помога́ть сосе́ду** (to help a neighbour)
соде́йствовать/соде́йствовать кому? чему? (to co-operate with whom? with what?)	**соде́йствовать установле́нию** ми́ра (to co-operate with the peace process)
принадлежа́ть кому? (to belong to whom?)	**принадлежа́ть госуда́рству** (to belong to the state)
препя́тствовать/**воспрепя́тствовать** кому? чему? (to hinder what? whom?)	**препя́тствовать проведе́нию** рефо́рм (to hinder the reforms)
запреща́ть/запрети́ть кому? что де́лать? (to forbid whom? to do what?)	**запрети́ть де́тям** купа́ться в о́зере (to forbid children to swim in a lake)

Verbs describing assistance, rules, learning	Examples
позволя́ть/позво́лить кому́? что де́лать? (to allow whom? to do what?)	**позво́лить сотру́днику** рабо́тать до́ма (to allow a member of staff to work from home)
разреша́ть/разреши́ть кому́? что де́лать? (to allow whom? to do what?)	**разреши́ть мужчи́не** кури́ть сига́ру (to allow the man to smoke a cigar)
сле́довать/после́довать чему́? (to follow what?)	**сле́довать сове́ту** (to follow advice)
обуча́ть/обучи́ть кого́? чему́? (to teach whom? what?)	**обуча́ть** студе́нта **пла́ванию** (to teach a student swimming)
учи́ть/научи́ть кого́? чему́? (to teach whom? what?/to do what?)	**научи́ть** прия́теля **заба́вным слова́м** (to teach a friend amusing words)

8.2.5 Using adjectives that require a noun in the dative case without a preposition

A few short- and long-form adjectives require a noun in the dative case as their indirect object. They must be memorised:

благода́рен (благода́рна, благода́рны)/ благода́рный (-ая,-ое,-ые) кому́? чему́? за что? (to be grateful to whom? to what? what for?)	Мы **благода́рны друзья́м** за по́мощь. We are grateful to our friends for their help.
ве́рен (верна́, верны́)/ве́рный (-ая, -ое, ые) кому́? чему́? (to be faithful to whom? to what?)	Они́ **верны́ при́нципам** и **тради́циям**. They are faithful to their principles and traditions.
рад (ра́да, ра́ды) кому́? чему́? (to be glad/happy about what? about whom?)	Де́ти **ра́ды пода́ркам**. Children are happy to receive presents.
знако́м (знако́ма, знако́мы)/знако́мый (-ая, -ое, -ые) что? кто? кому́? (what? who? to be familiar to whom? to what?)	**Студе́нтам знако́мы** пра́вила. The rules are familiar to the students.
изве́стен (изве́стна, изве́стны)/изве́стный (-ая, -ое, ые) что? кто? кому́? (what? who? to be known to whom? to what?)	**Жи́телям изве́стны** ме́стные тради́ции. Local traditions are known to people.
подо́бен (подо́бна, подо́бны)/подо́бный (-ая, -ое, -ые) кому́? чему́? (as/like/similar to whom? to what?): mainly used in poetry and literature	Ме́жду ту́чами и мо́рем го́рдо ре́ет Буреве́стник, **чёрной мо́лнии подо́бный** (Го́рький). Between the clouds and the sea proudly soars the stormy petrel, like a streak of black lightning.

Comment on the table

- The short and long forms of the adjective **знако́мый** can be used with the preposition **с** and the instrumental case as well: Студе́нты (nominative) **знако́мы с пра́вилами** (instrumental). (The students are familiar with the rules.)

Упражнéния

1. Put the nouns in brackets into the correct form.

1. Сергéй обещáл (Натáша) бóльше не курúть.
2. Профéссор посовéтовал (студéнты) прочитáть статью.
3. Úра купúла (брат) билéты на матч.
4. Мáша послáла сообщéние (друзья).
5. Это пáмятник (Юрий Гагáрин).
6. Скóлько лет (преподавáтель)?
7. (Ребёнок) 3 гóда.

2. Put the nouns in brackets into the correct form.

1. Мы сочýвствуем (гóре) друзéй.
2. Судья напóмнил (свидéтели) об отвéтственности.
3. Передáйте (рóдственники) мой сердéчный привéт.
4. Актёр раздавáл (поклóнники) свои автóграфы.
5. Бездóмные рáды вáшей (пóмощь).
6. Эта теóрия знакóма (исслéдователи).

8.3 Using the dative case with a preposition

The dative case can be used with several prepositions. The table summarises the prepositions that can appear in the dative case and indicates the context in which they are used:

Context	The question that the noun answers	Preposition used	Examples
In time expressions	когдá? (when?)	**по** (on) + dative plural; **к** (by/ towards)	по суббóтам (on Saturdays), по вечерáм (in the evenings), к средé (by Wednesday), к утрý (by/towards morning)
To indicate movement towards a place	кудá? (where to?)	**к** (towards); **навстрéчу** (towards)	подъéхать к стáнции (to approach the station), подойти к дóму (to approach home), идти навстрéчу вéтру (to go towards the wind)
To indicate a person who is visited	к комý? (to whom?)	**к** (to a person or his/her place)	идти к врачý (to go to see a doctor), éхать к друзьям (to visit friends)
To describe movement along a surface or to emphasise the multidirectional nature of a movement	где? (where?)	**по** (along/ around)	бежáть по ýлице (to run along a street), плыть по волнáм (to swim through the waves), ходúть по кóмнате (walk around the room), возúть когó-либо по гóроду (to drive someone around a city)
In idioms and phrases (for the most frequently occurring phrases ☞ 8.3.1)	various	**благодаря** (thanks to); **вопреки** (despite); **по** (by/in/on/due to); **соглáсно** (in accordance with)	благодаря усúлиям (thanks to effort), вопреки прогнóзам (despite the prognoses), говорúть по телефóну (to talk on phone), передавáть по рáдио (to transmit on radio), соглáсно соглашéнию (in accordance with an agreement)

Comments on the table

- Nouns in all cases, except the nominative, can be used in time expressions. The choice of the case depends on the noun's meaning and the preposition that governs the noun.
- Nouns in three cases (accusative, genitive and dative) can describe the end point of a journey. The choice of case depends on the verb of motion's meaning and the preposition that governs the noun.
- For verbs of motion, ☞ 24–25; for a summary of prepositions used with verbs of motion, ☞ 25.7.
- Nouns in the dative and genitive cases can describe movement along a surface or emphasise the multidirectional nature of a movement. The choice of case depends on the verb of motion's meaning and the preposition that governs the noun.

Level
2, 3

8.3.1 Using the dative case with a preposition in idioms and phrases

Nouns in the dative case appear in several idioms/phrases. The use of prepositions differs in Russian and English. The (non-exhaustive) lists given below cover the most frequently occurring verbs, and should be memorised.

The dative case with the preposition *по* (on, in, by, over, according to) is used in phrases to indicate:

- **Means of communication:** сообщать/сообщить (to inform), передавать/передать (to transmit), выступать/выступить (to perform) **по радио** (on radio)/**по телевизору** (on TV), слушать/послушать **по радио** (to listen to the radio), смотреть /посмотреть **по телевизору** (to watch TV), находить/найти (to find) **по интернету** (on the Internet), говорить (to speak), разговаривать (to speak), звонить/позвонить (to call) **по телефону** (on phone), посылать/послать, отправлять/отправить (to send) **по почте** (by post), **по электронной почте** (by e-mail).
- **Course of action**: заходить/зайти (to call on), звонить/позвонить (to call) **по делу/по делам** (on business):

Вы просто так зашли или **по делу**?	Have you called on me without any reason or on business?
Пропустить урок **по болезни**.	To miss a lesson due to illness.

- **Subject of learning:** лекция (lecture), урок (lesson), курс (course), экзамен (examination), тест (test), учебник (textbook) **по предмету** (on the subject): урок **по истории** (lesson on history), учебник **по русскому языку** (Russian textbook).
- **Expertise:** специалист **по лингвистике** (expert in linguistics), **по профессии** они строители (they are builders by profession).
- **Some rules:** ехать **по расписанию** (to go according to schedule), работать **по правилам** (to work according to the rules).
- **Distribution of objects to a number of people:** Всем сестрам **по серьгам** (пословица). (A pair of earrings to each sister: proverb, meaning a fair distribution.) For the use of numerals with cases, ☞ 15.3.

The dative case with the preposition *к* (for) is used:

- **To indicate feelings:** страсть **к поэзии** (passion for poetry), любовь **к семье** (love for family), доверие **к друзьям** (trust in friends), презрение **к врагам** (contempt for enemies), слабость **к красоте** (weakness for beauty), интерес **к русскому языку** (interest in Russian).
- **In idioms:** к счастью (fortunately), к сожалению (unfortunately), к моему стыду (to my shame), к моему удивлению (to my surprise).

Упражне́ния

1. Put the nouns in brackets into the dative case. Add prepositions as appropriate.

1. Специали́ст (лингви́стика) прочита́л ле́кцию.
2. Интере́с (языки́) растёт среди́ молодёжи.
3. Мне на́до зае́хать (прия́тель) по доро́ге домо́й.
4. (Сча́стье) я сдала́ экза́мен!
5. (Сожале́ние) спаса́телям не удало́сь спасти́ люде́й.
6. Они́ занима́ются на тренажёрах (пя́тница).
7. Аспира́нт позвони́л профе́ссору (де́ло).
8. (У́тро) пенсионе́ры бе́гают (пляж).

Обобща́ющее упражне́ние

1. Put the words in brackets into the correct form. Add a preposition, if appropriate.

Господи́н Смирно́в покупа́ет пода́рки

1. Дни рожде́ния всех ро́дственников в семье́ господи́на Смирно́ва в декабре́, поэ́тому он до́лжен гото́виться (пра́здники), а он так не лю́бит бе́гать (магази́ны). 2. (Господи́н Смирно́в) на́до купи́ть пода́рки (роди́тели, дя́ди, тёти, племя́нники-близнецы́, племя́нницы), двою́родным (сёстры), их (мужья́), (бра́тья) и их (жёны). 3. Он ду́мает, что купи́ть свое́й большо́й (семья́). 4. Его́ (племя́нницы и племя́нники) то́лько два го́да. 5. Они́ бу́дут ра́ды (игру́шки). 6. (Сча́стье) господи́н Смирно́в услы́шал рекла́му (ра́дио) о распрода́же книг (исто́рия) и альбо́мов (иску́сство). 7. Э́ти пода́рки понра́вятся его́ (бра́тья и сёстры). 8. Но что подари́ть други́м (ро́дственники)? 9. (Господи́н Смирно́в) нужна́ по́мощь его́ подру́ги Ири́ны. 10. Он обяза́тельно после́дует её (сове́т).

9 Nouns: instrumental case

For the concept of the six-case system and the principles of noun declension, ☞ 4.

The instrumental case is one of the six Russian cases. In a sentence or a phrase, the instrumental case has several roles. It can be used with or without a preposition.

This chapter provides a summary of noun endings in the instrumental case and explains its grammatical roles.

Level 1, 2

9.1 Summary table of noun endings in the instrumental case

Singular masculine and neuter nouns	hard stem	-ом
	soft stem	-ем (unstressed)
		-ём (stressed)
	stem ending with ж, ш, ч, щ, ц	-ом (stressed)
	stem ending with ж, ш, ч, щ, ц	-ем (unstressed)
Singular feminine nouns	hard stem	-ой
	soft stem	-ей (unstressed)
		-ёй (stressed)
	special ending for nouns ending with -ь	-ью
Plural nouns	hard stem	-ами
	soft stem	-ями

- Some nouns have so-called '*fleeting*' vowels **о/е/ё** in the final syllable in any case other than nominative singular: **день – днём** (day), **отéц – отцóм** (father) etc. The nouns **мать** (mother) and **дочь** (daughter) have the suffix **-ер-** inserted in all cases but the accusative: **мáтерью**, **дóчерью**. Changes **ё/ь** occurs in the noun **лёд/льдом** (ice): **чай со льдóм** (iced tea) etc. For the fleeting vowels, ☞ 4.5.
- For hard and soft endings and the spelling rules, ☞ 1.3 and 1.4.

Level 2

9.1.1 Irregular noun endings

The plural instrumental case has one additional soft ending, **-ьми**:

- The following feminine nouns with a dictionary form ending in **-ь** have alternative endings **-ями/-ьми**: **лошадя́ми/лошадьми́** (horses), **дверя́ми/дверьми́** (doors), **костя́ми/костьми́** (bones), **плетя́ми/плетьми́** (whips). The ending **-ьми** is common in popular speech.
- The nouns **дочь** (daughter), **лю́ди** (people) and **де́ти** (children) have the ending **-ьми** instead of **-ями**: **дочерьми́**, **людьми́**, **детьми́**.

9.2 Using the instrumental case without a preposition

Level 1, 2

9.2.1 The main role of the instrumental case

The main role of the instrumental case without a preposition is to indicate *the means of an action* or *the manner of an action*. Nouns in the instrumental case, in this context, answer the question **чем?** (with what?) or **как?** (how?). For example:

- Писа́ть ру́чк**ой** (to write with a pen), есть ло́жк**ой** (to eat with a spoon), лечи́ть гипно́з**ом** (to treat by hypnosis), разре́зать ла́зер**ом** (to cut with a laser).
- Говори́ть шёпот**ом** (to whisper), продава́ть деся́тк**ами** (to sell by tens), счита́ть со́т**нями** (to count by hundreds).
- Тро́йка мчи́тся стрел**о́й** (The troika is racing like an arrow). Often the noun in the instrumental case can be replaced by a phrase containing the word **сло́вно/как** (like) and a noun in the nominative case: Тро́йка мчи́тся **как/сло́вно стрела́** (The troika is racing like an arrow).
- Е́хать авто́бус**ом** (to go by bus), лете́ть самолёт**ом** (to go by plane). The prepositional case with the preposition **на** (by) is used more often than the instrumental case to convey the same idea: е́хать **на авто́бусе** (to go by bus), лете́ть **на самолёте** (to go by plane) (☞ 10.3.2).

👁 In Russian, there is no equivalent of the English prepositions *by/with* in a phrase/sentence that describes the means or manner of an action.

Level 1, 2

9.2.2 Other meanings of the instrumental case without a preposition

The instrumental case without a preposition is used to denote parts of the day and seasons. The noun in the instrumental case answers the question **когда́** (when?):

Nominative	Instrumental
зима́ (winter)	зимо́й (in the winter)
весна́ (spring)	весно́й (in the spring)
ле́то (summer)	ле́том (in the summer)
о́сень (autumn)	о́сенью (in the autumn)
у́тро (morning)	у́тром (in the morning)
день (day/afternoon)	днём (in the afternoon)
ве́чер (evening)	ве́чером (in the evening)
ночь (night)	но́чью (in the night)

In the plural, the dative case with the preposition **по** (by) can replace the instrumental case without a preposition to convey the same idea (☞ 8.3). For example:

- не спать **ноча́ми** (instrumental) or не спать **по ноча́м** (dative) – not to sleep for nights (on end)
- рабо́тать **вечера́ми** (instrumental) or рабо́тать **по вечера́м** (dative) – to work in the evenings

Level 2, 3

The instrumental case without a preposition is also used to denote:

- **The route of a journey:** пройти́ по́лем (to go across the field), прое́хать двора́ми (to go through the yards). The dative case with the preposition **по** (by/along) and the accusative case with the preposition **че́рез** (across) can replace the instrumental case without a preposition to convey the same idea (☞ 8.3 and 6.3.1, respectively). For example:

пройти **по полю** (dative, to go across the field)/пройти **через поле** (accusative, to go across the field)

проехать **по дворам** (dative, to go through the yards)/проехать **через дворы** (accusative, to go through the yards).

- **Comparison:** часом раньше (an hour earlier), днём позже (a day later). The accusative case with the preposition **на** can replace the instrumental case without a preposition to convey the same idea (☞ 6.3.2). For example: **на час** раньше (an hour early), **на день** позже (a day later).

- **Measurements:** высотой (in height, inanimate nouns), ростом (in height, people or animals), длиной (in length), шириной (in width/breadth), толщиной (in thickness/depth), глубиной (in depth, of lake, of pool etc): высотой 5 метров (5 metres in height), глубиной 1 километр (1 kilometre in depth).

9.2.3 Using the instrumental case without a preposition in passive or impersonal constructions

For the passive voice, ☞ 21.3; for impersonal sentences, ☞ 30.

The instrumental case without a preposition indicates a person or a natural phenomenon that is responsible for the action in passive and impersonal constructions. Nouns in the instrumental case, in this context, answer the question **кем?** (by whom?) or **чем?** (with/by what?). For example:

Роман был написан **модным писателем.**	The novel was written **by a fashionable writer.**
Все дома разрушены **ураганом.**	All the houses were destroyed **by the hurricane.**
Луга залило **водой.**	The meadows are flooded **with water.**

9.2.4 Using the instrumental case without a preposition as a predicate

A noun in the instrumental case without a preposition can serve as a core element of a compound predicate (a verbal phrase) when describing quality, status, type or class:

Они **будут космонавтами.**	They **will be astronauts.**
Ельцин **был первым президентом** Российской Федерации.	Yeltsin **was the first President** of the Russian Federation

In the examples above, the noun in the instrumental case is part of the predicate and qualifies the subject of the sentences. **быть** (to be) is the verb-link and connects the noun in the instrumental case and the subject of the sentence. **Быть** can only be used in the past or future tenses. The noun in the instrumental case, in this context, emphasises *the temporary nature* of the described quality, status, type or class:

Гагарин **был первым космонавтом.**	Gagarin was the first astronaut.
Они **будут музыкантами.**	They are going to be musicians.

👁 In this context, a noun in the instrumental case can be replaced with a noun in the nominative case. Conversely, the noun in the nominative case emphasises *the permanent nature* of the described quality, status, type or class:

Она **была настоящая красавица.**	She was a real beauty.
Толстой **был великий писатель.**	Tolstoy was a great writer.

In the present tense, the verb-link **быть** (to be) is omitted and the noun which qualifies the subject of the sentence is used in the nominative case:

Она **настоящая красавица.**	She is a real beauty.
Толстой – **великий писатель.**	Tolstoy is a great writer.

For the use of the nominative case in this context, ☞ 5.2; information on **быть** (to be), ☞ 16.2.

Besides **быть**, several verbs can serve as a verb-link between the subject of the sentence and the core element of a predicate in the instrumental case without a preposition. They are:

- являться (to be, used in formal writing)
  Москва́ **явля́ется** крупне́йшим **мегапо́лисом** Росси́и

  Moscow is the biggest megalopolis (metropolis) of Russia.

- станови́ться /стать (to become)
  Они́ **ста́ли** прекра́сными **специали́стами**.

  They became excellent specialists.

- счита́ться (to be considered)
  Он **счита́ется** хоро́шим **хиру́ргом**.

  He is considered to be a good surgeon.

- называться/назва́ться (to be called)
  Напи́ток из хле́ба **называ́ется ква́сом**.

  The drink made from bread is called *kvas*.

- остава́ться/оста́ться (to remain as)
  Она́ **оста́лась краса́вицей** и в ста́рости.

  She remained a beauty in her old age.

- ока́зываться/оказа́ться (to turn out to be)
  Он **оказа́лся** настоя́щим **дру́гом**.

  He turned out to be a real friend.

- каза́ться/показа́ться (to seem/appear)
  Тень **показа́лась** нам **чудо́вищем**.

  The shadow seemed to us a monster.

Level 2, 3

9.2.5 Short-form adjectives that require a noun in the instrumental case without a preposition

There are several short-form adjectives that require a noun in the instrumental case without a preposition. The list of the most frequently occurring adjectives that take the instrumental case must be memorised:

бо́лен, больна́, больны́ чем? (to be ill with what?)	Она́ **больна́ анги́ной**. She is ill with tonsilitis.
за́нят, зня́та, за́няты чем? (to be busy with what?)	Они́ **за́няты де́лом**. They are busy with their business.
дово́лен, дово́льна, дово́льны кем? чем? (to be happy with what? with whom?)	Профе́ссор **дово́лен докла́дом**. The professor is happy with his paper.
изве́стен, изве́стна, изве́стны чем?(to be known by what? by whom?)	Крым **изве́стен ви́нами**. Crimea is famous for its wines.
бога́т, бога́та, бога́ты чем? (to be rich in what?)	Сиби́рь **бога́та не́фтью**. Siberia is rich in oil.
бе́ден, бедна́, бедны́ чем? (to be poor in what?)	Ту́ндра **бедна́ расти́тельностью**. The tundra has poor vegetation.

Level 2, 3

9.2.6 Verbs that require a noun in the instrumental case without a preposition

There are several verbs that require a noun in the instrumental case without a preposition.

👁 As Russian sentences have flexible word order, a noun or pronoun in the instrumental case does not always appear immediately after the verb that requires that case. Furthermore, the same verb can take several different cases. A (non-exhaustive) list of the most frequently occurring verbs that take the instrumental case is given below, and should be memorised. In the list, both verbal aspects are provided, if both aspects are used in this context; the imperfective aspect appears first, and then the perfective. Note that all words derived or formed from the listed verbs (nouns, participles, gerunds) normally require the same case: for example

увлека́ться спо́ртом	to be keen on sport
увлече́ние спо́ртом	passion for sport
увлечённый спо́ртом	keen on sport
увлека́ясь спо́ртом	being keen on sport

Verbs indicating profession, position or rank	Examples
рабо́тать кем? где? (to work as what? where?)	Она́ **рабо́тает учи́телем** в шко́ле. She works as a teacher at a school.
служи́ть кем? где? (to serve as what? age?)	Он **слу́жит генера́лом** в Министе́рстве. He serves as a general in the Ministry.
выбира́ть/вы́брать, избира́ть/избра́ть кого́? кем? куда́? (to elect whom? as what? to where?)	Их **избра́ли депута́тами** в Ду́му. They were elected as MPs to the Duma.
назнача́ть/назна́чить кого́? кем? (to appoint whom? as what?)	Его́ **назна́чили дире́ктором**. He was appointed as a director.

Verbs indicating interests or occupation	Examples
интересова́ться/заинтересова́ться чем? кем? (to be interested in what? in whom?)	Они́ **интересу́ются поли́тикой**. They are interested in politics.
увлека́ться/увле́чься чем? кем? (to be keen on what? on whom?)	Мы **увлека́емся исто́рией**. We are keen on history.
занима́ться/заня́ться/позанима́ться чем? (to be engaged in/to be occupied with what?)	Они́ **занима́ются спо́ртом**. They do sport.

Verbs describing physical or emotional state	Examples
восхища́ться/восхити́ться кем? чем? (to be enchanted by whom? by what?)	Тури́сты **восхища́ются Байка́лом**. Tourists are enchanted by Baikal.
восторга́ться кем? чем? (to be delighted by whom? by what?)	Они́ **восторга́ются но́вым фи́льмом**. They are delighted by the new film.
любова́ться/полюбова́ться/залюбова́ться кем? чем? (to admire whom? what?)	Они́ **любу́ются прекра́сным ви́дом**. They admire the beautiful view.
наслажда́ться/наслади́ться чем? (to enjoy/to take pleasure in what?)	Мы **наслажда́емся изы́сканным вку́сом**. We enjoy the delicate taste.
горди́ться/возгорди́ться кем? чем? (to be proud of whom? of what?)	Мать **горди́тся успе́хами** дете́й. Mother is proud of the success of her children.
возмуща́ться/возмути́ться кем? чем? (to be indignant at whom? with what?)	Учи́тель **возмуща́ется плохи́м поведе́нием** шко́льника. The teacher is indignant with the pupil's poor behaviour.
боле́ть/заболе́ть чем? (to be ill with what?)	Они́ **боле́ют гри́ппом**. They are ill with flu.

Verbs describing physical or emotional state	Examples
жéртвовать/пожéртвовать кем? чем? (to sacrifice whom? what?)	Герóй **пожéртвовал жúзнью**. The hero has sacrificed his life.
рисковáть/рискнýть чем? (to take a risk with what?)	Пожáрные **рискýют жúзнью**. Firefighters risk their lives.

Verbs indicating command or possession	Examples
управлáть чем? (to operate/drive/manage what?)	Онú **управлáют машúной**. They operate a machine.
руководúть чем? (to manage what?)	Дирéктор **руководúт завóдом**. The director manages a factory.
комáндовать чем? (to be in command of what?)	Он **комáндует флóтом**. He is in command of the navy.
владéть чем? (to own/to possess what?/to have skills/knowledge in what?)	Миллионéр **владéет бáнками**. The millionaire owns banks. Переводчик **владéет мнóгими языкáми**. An interpreter knows many languages.
обладáть чем? (to have, most common with words describing skills/knowledge)	Онú **обладáют** большúми **спосóбностями**. They are very gifted people.
пóльзоваться чем? (to use what?)	Все **пóльзуются компьютером**. Everybody uses a computer.

Упражнéния

Level 1, 2

1. Put the words in brackets into the correct form:

1. Мы рéжем хлеб (нож).
2. Китáйские блюда едáт (пáлочки).
3. Úра рисýет (карандáш).
4. Онá вернýлась домóй (пóезд).
5. Лóшадь мчúтся (стрелá).
6. Медсестрá мáзала рýку (крем).
7. Турúсты катáются на лыжах (зимá).
8. Снег тáет (веснá).
9. Рабóчие встают рáно (ýтро).

Level 2, 3

2. Provide a description of a bookcase, in Russian, using the instrumental case as appropriate:

a. height 1.80 m
b. width 1.50 m
c. depth 35 cm

3. Insert the phrase in the correct form:

1. Терешкóва былá пéрвой (жéнщина-космонáвт).
2. Оттáва являéтся (столúца) Канáды.
3. Хозáйство развивáется быстрыми (тéмпы).
4. Адмирáл комáндует (флот).
5. Турúсты восхищáются (музéи, мосты и дворцы) гóрода.
6. Выпускникú остáлись (приáтели) на всю жизнь.

7. Солда́ты ежедне́вно риску́ют (жизнь).

8. Ви́ктор увлека́ется (поп-му́зыка, пла́вание, гольф).

9.3 Using the instrumental case with a preposition

The instrumental case can be used with several prepositions. The table summarises the prepositions that can appear in the instrumental case and indicates the context in which they are used:

Context	The question that the noun answers	Preposition used	Examples
In time expressions	когда́? (when?)	**пе́ред** (before), **за** (during/at)	пе́ред обе́дом (before lunch); за у́жином (at dinner)
To indicate a location (real and in a figurative sense, such as dishes' names)	где? (where?)	**под** (under), **над** (above), **за** (at), **пе́ред** (in front of), **ме́жду** (between), **ря́дом с** (next to)	под столо́м (under the table), над крова́тью (above the bed), ме́жду кре́слом и дива́ном (between armchair and sofa), ры́ба запечённая под со́усом (baked fish with sauce)
To indicate a joint action and mixed substances	с кем?/с чем? (with whom?/ with what?)	**с** (with), **вме́сте с** (together with)	мы с дру́гом (my friend and I), кот с соба́кой (a cat with a dog), ка́ша с молоко́м (kasha (porridge) with milk)
To describe features of the appearance of a person or inanimate object	с чем? (with what?)	**с** (with)	де́вушка с дли́нными волоса́ми (a girl with long hair), мужчи́на с бородо́й (a man with a beard), дом с мезони́ном (a house with a mezzanine)
To indicate manner of action	как? (how?)	**с** (with)	есть с аппети́том (to eat with an appetite), говори́ть с акце́нтом (to speak with an accent), писа́ть с оши́бками (to write with mistakes)
To indicate the purpose of an action	за чем? (what for?)	**за** (for/in order to)	идти́ за хле́бом (to go to buy some bread)

Comments on the table

- Nouns in all cases, except the nominative, can be used in time expressions. The choice of the case depends on the noun's meaning and the preposition that governs the noun.
- Nouns in three cases (genitive, instrumental and prepositional) can be used to indicate location. The choice of the case depends on the noun's meaning and the preposition that governs the noun.
- Many Russian verbs that indicate a joint or reciprocal action require a noun in the instrumental case with the preposition **с** (with): ☞ 9.3.1.
- If a speaker is talking about a group of people that includes themself, they say '*we with someone else*': **Мы с дру́гом** идём в бар. (My friend and I go to a bar.) **Мы с роди́телями** е́дем на да́чу. (My parents and I go to the dacha.)

- An added substance is described by using the preposition **с** (with) and a noun in the instrumental case: кока-ко́ла **со льдо́м** (coke with ice), ви́ски **с со́довой** (whisky with soda), джин **с то́ником** (gin and tonic), чай **с молоко́м** (tea with milk), чай **с лимо́ном** (tea with lemon), ко́фе **со сли́вками** (coffee with cream).

С чем Вы пьёте чай? – Я пью чай **с са́харом** и **с молоко́м**.	How do you take your tea? – I take my tea **with sugar and milk**.

- In Russian, the preposition **с** (with) and a noun in the instrumental case is used when describing the fillings of pies, sandwiches, multiple-layer dishes, side dishes, type of soups etc:

пиро́г **с ры́бой**	fish pie
бутербро́д **с сы́ром** и **помидо́рами**	cheese and tomato sandwich
суп **с гриба́ми**	mushroom soup
ры́ба с **карто́фелем** фри	fish and chips

- The following expressions, indicating the manner of an action, are frequently used:

с удово́льствием	with pleasure
с го́рдостью	with pride
с трудо́м	with difficulty
с удивле́нием	with surprise
с интере́сом	with interest
с восто́ргом	with delight
с презре́нием	with contempt

- In popular speech, the expression that indicates the purpose of the action **за чем**? (what for) often replaces the more formal construction introduced by the conjunction **что́бы** (in order to): Он пошёл на по́чту, **что́бы получи́ть посы́лку**. Он пошёл на по́чту **за посы́лкой**. (He went to the post office to get the parcel.) For sentences with **что́бы**, ☞ 29.2.5.

Level 2, 3

9.3.1 Verbs that take a noun in the instrumental case with a preposition

Several verbs require a noun in the instrumental case with a preposition.

👁 As Russian sentences have flexible word order, a noun or pronoun in the instrumental case does not always appear immediately after the verb that requires that case. Furthermore, the same verb can take several different cases. Also, note that the use of prepositions may differ in Russian and English. A (non-exhaustive) list of the most frequently occurring verbs that take the instrumental case is given below, and should be memorised. In the list, both verbal aspects are provided, if both aspects are used in this context; the imperfective aspect appears first, and then the perfective. Note that all words derived or formed from the listed verbs (nouns, participles, gerunds) normally require the same preposition and case: for example

встреча́ться с друзья́ми	to meet friends
встре́ча с друзья́ми	a/the meeting with friends
встреча́ясь с друзья́ми	meeting friends

The majority of reflexive verbs that indicate joint or reciprocal meaning take a noun in the instrumental case with the preposition *с* (with).

For more about reflexive verbs with reciprocal meaning, ☞ 23.2.

Verbs	Examples
встреча́ться/встре́титься с кем? с чем? (to meet whom?/what?)	встреча́ться **с друзья́ми** (to meet friends)
ви́деться/уви́деться с кем? (to see whom?)	уви́деться **с роди́телями** (to see one's parents)

Verbs	Examples
догова́риваться/договори́ться с кем? о чём?(to agree with whom? about what?)	договори́ться о встре́че **с партнёром** (to agree about a meeting with a partner)
знако́миться/познако́миться с кем? с чем? (to introduce/to meet whom? what?)	познако́миться **с но́вым сотру́дником** (to meet a new member of staff)
здоро́ваться/поздоро́ваться с кем?(to say hello to whom?)	поздоро́ваться **с прия́телем** (to say hello to an acquaintance)
проща́ться/попроща́ться с кем? (to say goodbye to whom?)	попроща́ться **со знако́мым** (to say goodbye to an acquaintance)
разводи́ться/развести́сь с кем? (to divorce whom?)	развести́сь **с жено́й** (to divorce one's wife)
расстава́ться/расста́ться с кем? (to separate from whom?)	расста́ться **с дру́гом** (to separate from a friend)
сове́товаться/посове́товаться с кем? (to get advice from whom?)	сове́товаться **со специали́стом** (to get advice from an expert)
ссо́риться/поссо́риться с кем? (to quarrel with whom?)	ссо́риться **с сосе́дом** (to quarrel with a neighbour)
мири́ться/помири́ться с кем? (to make peace with whom?)	мири́ться **с дру́гом** (to make peace with a friend)
смиря́ться/смири́ться с чем? (to accept what?)	смири́ться **с утра́той** (to accept a loss)
воева́ть с кем? (to fight whom?)	воева́ть **с враго́м** (to fight the enemy)
игра́ть/сыгра́ть что?/во что? с кем? (to play what? with whom?)	игра́ть в футбо́л **с бра́том** (to play football with a brother)

Holiday greetings

The verb **поздравля́ть/поздра́вить** followed by the preposition **с** (with) and a noun in the instrumental case functions as the equivalent of English holiday greetings. The verb is often omitted in these greetings:

Поздравля́ем с Но́вым го́дом!/С Но́вым го́дом!	Happy New Year!
Поздравля́ем с Рождество́м!/С Рождество́м!	Merry Christmas!
Поздравля́ем с Днём рожде́ния!/С Днём рожде́ния!	Happy birthday!
Поздравля́ем с пра́здником!/С пра́здником!	Happy holidays!

Some verbs take a noun in the instrumental case with the preposition над (over/at/on):

Verbs	Examples
смея́ться/посмея́ться над кем? над чем? (to laugh at whom? at what?)	смея́ться **над шу́ткой** (to laugh at the joke)
ду́мать/поду́мать над чем? (to think over what?)	ду́мать **над предложе́нием** (to think over the proposal)
рабо́тать/порабо́тать над чем? (to work on what?)	рабо́тать **над прое́ктом** (to work on the project)

Level 2, 3

Упражнéния

1. Put the nouns in brackets into the instrumental case. Add the appropriate preposition to match the sense of the sentence:

1. (Лóндон) и (Москвá) имéется ежеднéвное воздýшное сообщéние.
2. Нúна пошлá на рынок (óвощи).
3. Принимáйте лекáрство (едá).
4. (Гóрдость) родúтели дýмают о сыне.
5. (Университéт) стоúт пáмятник егó основáтелю.
6. Мы поздрáвили друзéй (прáздникаи).
7. Концéрт организовáли (открытое нéбо).
8. Учёные рабóтали (статья́) о клúмате.
9. Мы (коллéги) пошлú в бар пóсле рабóты.
10. Кока-кóлу (лёд) и джúн (тóник), пожáлуйста.

Level 2, 3

2. Match words from the two columns to make a phrase. Add the appropriate preposition:

Модéль: мирúться, друг, с – мирúться с дрýгом

1. познакóмиться	1. ýгол
2. кóфе	2. шýтки
3. пирóг	3. женá
4. смея́ться	4. сосéд
5. развестúсь	5. слúвки
6. спря́таться	6. грибы́

Level 2, 3

Обобщáющее упражнéние

3. Put the words in brackets into the instrumental case. Add a preposition, if appropriate.

Рýсская бáня

1. Сегóдня вéчером господúн Смирнóв встречáется (коллéги) из Áнглии. 2. Онú пéрвый раз в Россúи и (удовóльствие) знакóмятся (традúции и обычаи) страны́. 3. Онú óчень довóльны (гостеприúмство) своúх рýсских коллéг и восхищáются (красотá) Москвы́. 4. Сегóдня онú идýт (господúн Смирнóв) в бáню. 5. Коллéги господúна Смирнóва (любопытство) слýшали егó расскáз о рýсской традúции пáриться (вéник) в бáне. 6. Пéред (вход) в парнýю господúн Смирнóв совéтует накрыть гóлову (полотéнце) и покáзывает, как пóльзоваться (вéник). 7. Сначáла нáдо побúть (вéник) рýки и нóги, а потóм – спúну. 8. Éсли у вас есть проблéмы (здорóвье), бáня вылечит все болéзни (пар). 9. Пóсле бáни рýсские пьют чай (лимóн, мёд, варéнье). 10. К чáю подаю́т пирогú (грибы́, рыба, мя́со, я́блоки, я́годы). Как говоря́т в Россúи: «С лёгким пáром!».

Словáрь:
пáриться – to sweat (as in steam bath)
вéник – besom
парнáя – steam room
С лёгким пáром! – idiom: Enjoy your steam bath!

10 Nouns: prepositional case

For the concept of the six-case system and the principles of noun declension, ☞ 4.

The prepositional case is one of the six Russian cases. This chapter provides a summary of noun endings in the prepositional case and explains its grammatical role.

Level 1, 2

10.1 Summary table of regular noun endings in the prepositional case

Singular nouns	All nouns, except those ending with **-ий/-ия/-ие** and feminine nouns ending with **ь**	**-е-у** (☞ 10.1.1)
	Nouns ending with **-ий/-ия/-ие** and feminine nouns ending with **ь**	**-и**
Plural nouns	Hard stem and stem ending with **г, к, х, ж,, ш, щ, -ч** and **ц**	**-ах**
	Soft stem	**-ях**

Comments on the table

- Some nouns have so-called '*fleeting*' vowels **o/e/ё** in the final syllable in any case other than nominative singular: день – дне (day), отéц – отцé (father), ýгол – углý (corner). The nouns **мать** (mother) and **дочь** (daughter) have the suffix -ер- inserted in all cases except the accusative: мáтери, дóчери. Changes **ё/ь** occurs in the noun лёд/льду (ice): хоккéй на льду (ice hockey). For the fleeting vowels, ☞ 4.5.
- For hard and soft endings and the spelling rules, ☞ 1.3 and 1.4.

Level 1, 2

10.1.1 Irregular noun endings

Several masculine nouns in the singular have, in the prepositional case, an irregular ending -у/-ю after the prepositions **в** (in/at) and **на** (on/at). The same nouns used with any other prepositions in the prepositional case take the regular endings as described above. The most common nouns with irregular endings are given below. Compare:

Where are you?	What are you thinking (about?)
на полý (on the floor)	**о пóле** (about the floor)
на/в углý (on/in the corner)	**об углé** (about the corner)
на/в шкафý (on/in the cupboard)	**о шкáфе** (about the cupboard)
в садý (in the garden)	**о сáде** (about the garden)
в лесý (in the forest)	**о лéсе** (about the forest)
на снегý (in the snow)	**о снéге** (about the snow)

на берегу́ (on the shore)	**о бе́реге** (about the shore)
на мосту́ (on the bridge)	**о мосте́** (about the bridge)
в порту́ (at/in the port)	**о по́рте** (about the port)
в аэропорту́ at/in the airport)	**об аэропо́рте** (about the airport)
в бою́ (in the fight/battle)	**о бо́е** (about the fight/battle)
в краю́ (on the edge/in the region)	**о кра́е** (about the edge/the region)
в носу́ (in the nose)	**о но́се** (about the nose)
в глазу́ (in the eye)	**о гла́зе** (about the eye)
в году́ (in a/the year)	**о го́де** (about a/the year)

Level
1, 2
10.2 The grammatical roles of the prepositional case

The prepositional case can only be used with prepositions. The main role of the prepositional case, in a sentence or phrase, is to indicate location. The noun in the prepositional case answers the question **где?** (where?) and is used with the prepositions **в** (in) or **на** (on/at). The prepositional case is one of three cases that can indicate location. Nouns in the other two cases, instrumental and genitive, take prepositions other than **в** (in) and **на** (on/at).

Level
1, 2
10.2.1 Using the prepositions в (in/at) and на (on/at)

The Russian equivalents of the English prepositions *in*, *at* and *on* do not fully coincide. The vowel **o** is sometimes added to the preposition **в** to ease pronunciation if the preposition is attached to a noun starting with two or more consonants.

The preposition **в** (in/at) is used to indicate:	The preposition **на** (on/at) is used to indicate:
Being inside: в су́мке (in a bag), в ли́фте (in a lift)	Being on the surface: на столе́ (on the table), на земле́ (on land)
Designated space: в зда́нии (in a building), в лесу́ (in the woods), в па́рке (in a park), в саду́ (in the garden), во дворе́ (in the yard)	Outdoors location such as street, square, avenue, junction, field, road, path, motorway etc.: на у́лице (on the street), на шоссе́ (on the motorway)
Geographical locations: в Аме́рике (in America – a continent/country), в Ло́ндоне (in London – a city/town), в дере́вне Леснико́во (in Lesnikovo village – a village/settlement), в Моско́вском райо́не (in Moscow district)	Location on the shore/on the bank of a river, lake, sea, ocean: на берегу́ (on the shore), на Байка́ле (on Lake Baikal) **на** ку́бе (on islands)
Being a part of a group: в па́ртии (in the party), в университе́те (at university), в шко́ле (at school), в кла́ссе (in class)	The points of the compass: на се́вере (in the north), на ю́ге (in the south), на восто́ке (in the east), на за́паде (in the west)
Also: в гора́х (in the mountains), в мо́ре (in the sea)	Attending an event: на о́пере (at the opera), на вы́ставке (at an exhibition), на уро́ке (at a lesson)

The preposition **в** (in/at) is used to indicate:	The preposition **на** (on/at) is used to indicate:
Exceptions (location at the following places): на вокза́ле (at/in the railway station), **на** ста́нции (in the station), **на** по́чте (at/in the post office), **на** фа́брике/**на** заво́де (at/in factory) **на** стадио́не (at/in the stadium), **на** ры́нке (at/in the market), **на** да́че (at/in the country house), **на/в** ку́хне (in the kitchen), **на** этаже́ (on a floor), **на** фло́те (in the navy), **на** Ура́ле (in the Urals), **на** Кавка́зе (in the Caucasus), **на** Ро́дине (in the Motherland)	

 Use of the prepositions **в** and **на** follows the same principles in the accusative and prepositional cases: ☞ 6.3.1.1.

10.3 Other roles of the prepositional case

10.3.1 Use of the prepositional case in time expressions

The prepositional case can be used to indicate time. A noun in the prepositional case, in this context, can answer the questions **когда́** (when?), **в како́м году́** (what year?) **в како́м ме́сяце** (what month?), **на како́й неде́ле** (what week?):

- Year (with the preposition **в**): **в** про́шлом году́ (last year), **в** э́том году́ (this year), **в** сле́дующем году́ (next year), **в** 2011 году́
- Month (with the preposition **в**): **в** январе́ (in January), **в** сентябре́ (in September).
- Week (with the preposition **на**): **на** про́шлой неде́ле (last week), **на** э́той неде́ле (this week), **на** сле́дующей неде́ле (next week).
- The political regime of the times (with the preposition **при**): **при** сове́тской вла́сти (in Soviet times), **при** Петре́ Вели́ком (in Peter the Great's times).

10.3.2 Use of the prepositional case in prepositional constructions

The prepositional case can:

- Indicate the noun taking the preposition **о/об** (about): Он **мечта́ет о свида́нии**. (He **is thinking about a date**.) Фильм **об инопланетя́нах**. (The film **is about aliens**.) The consonant **б** is sometimes added to the preposition **о** to ease pronunciation if the preposition is followed by a noun starting with a vowel. The noun in the prepositional case, in this context, answers the questions **о чём?** (what about?), **о ком?** (whom about?). The preposition **про** (about) has the same meaning as the preposition **о**. The preposition **про** governs the noun in the accusative case and is common in popular speech: ☞ 6 and 6.3.3
- Indicate means of transport (with the preposition **на**): éхать **на** по́езде (to go by train), лете́ть **на** самолёте (to go by plane). The noun in the prepositional case, in this context, answers the question **на чём?** (by what?): ☞ 9.2.1.

10.4 Verbs that require the prepositional case

Several verbs require the prepositional case.

 As Russian sentences have flexible word order, a noun or pronoun in the prepositional case does not always appear immediately after the verb that requires that case. Furthermore, the same verb can take several different cases. Also, note that the use of prepositions may differ in

Russian and English. A (non-exhaustive) list of the most frequently occurring verbs that take the prepositional case is given below, and should be memorised. In the list, both verbal aspects are provided, if both aspects are used in this context; the imperfective aspect appears first, and then the perfective. Note that all words derived or formed from the listed verbs (nouns, participles, gerunds) normally require the same preposition and case: for example

говори́ть о пробле́ме	to speak about the problem
разгово́р о пробле́ме	conversation about the problem
говоря́ о пробле́ме	speaking about the problem.

Verbs that are followed by the preposition *o* and a noun or personal pronoun in the prepositional case:

Verbs	Examples
говори́ть/сказа́ть о чём? о ком? кому́? (to say/to tell/to speak about what? about whom? to whom?)	сказа́ть о пробле́ме полице́йскому (to tell a policeman about the problem)
расска́зывать/рассказа́ть о чём? о ком? кому́? (to tell about what? about whom? to whom?)	рассказа́ть о кло́унах ребёнку (to tell a child about clowns)
спра́шивать/спроси́ть о чём? о ком? кого́? (to ask whom? about what? about whom?)	спроси́ть ба́бушку о её здоро́вье (to ask grandmother about her health)
узнава́ть/узна́ть о чём? о ком? у кого́? от кого́? (to learn about what? about whom? from whom?)	узна́ть о собра́нии от секретаря́/у секретаря́ (to learn about a meeting from the secretary)
слы́шать/услы́шать о чём? о ком? от кого́? отку́да? (to hear about what? about whom? from whom? from where?)	услы́шать о происше́ствии из газе́т (to hear about the incident from the newspapers)
сообща́ть/сообщи́ть о чём? о ком? кому́? (to inform about what? about whom? to whom?)	сообщи́ть о конце́рте друзья́м (to inform friends about the concert)
объявля́ть/объяви́ть о чём? о ком? кому́? (to announce about what? about whom? to whom?)	объяви́ть об экску́рсии тури́стам (to announce an excursion to the tourists)
ду́мать/поду́мать о чём? о ком? (to think about what? about whom?)	ду́мать об о́тпуске (to think about a holiday)
беспоко́иться о чём? о ком? (to be worried/anxious about what? about whom?)	беспоко́иться о здоро́вье (to be worried about one's health)
писа́ть/написа́ть что? о чём? о ком? кому́? (to write what? about what? about whom? to whom?)	написа́ть о прое́кте нача́льнику (to write about the project to the boss)
чита́ть/прочита́ть что? о чём? о ком? кому́? (to read what? about what? about whom? to whom?)	прочита́ть кни́гу о приро́де (to read a book about nature)
по́мнить/вспомина́ть/вспо́мнить что? кого́? о чём? о ком? (to remember what? whom? about what? about whom?)	по́мнить о дру́ге (to remember about a friend), вспо́мнить о встре́че (to remember about the meeting)
забыва́ть/забы́ть что? о чём? о ком? (to forget what? about what? about whom?)	забы́ть о собра́нии (to forget about a meeting)

Verbs	Examples
напоминáть/напóмнить о чём? о ком? кому́? (to remind about what? about whom? to whom?)	напóмнить об экзáмене студéнтам (to remind students about the examination)
мечтáть о чём? о ком? (to dream about what? about whom?)	мечтáть о поéздке (to dream about a trip)
петь/спеть о чём? о ком? кому́? (to sing about what? about whom? to whom?)	петь о любви́ подру́ге (to sing about love to a girlfriend)

Verbs that are followed by the preposition *в* and a noun or personal pronoun in the prepositional case:

Verbs	Examples
сомневáться в чём? в ком? (to doubt what? whom?)	сомневáться в результáте (to doubt the result)
нуждáться в чём? в ком? (to be in need of what? whom?)	нуждáться в поддéржке (to be in need of support)
убеждáть/убеди́ть когó? в чём? (to convince whom? of what?)	убеди́ть дру́га в егó оши́бке (to convince a friend of his mistake)
обвиня́ть/обвини́ть когó? в чём? (to accuse whom? of what?)	обвини́ть диктáтора в преступлéниях (to accuse a dictator of crimes)
подозревáть когó? в чём? (to suspect whom? of what?)	подозревáть престу́пника во лжи́ (to suspect a criminal of lying)
откáзывать/отказáть в чём? кому́? (to refuse/to deny what? to whom?)	отказáть в пóмощи незнакóмцу (to refuse to help a stranger)
учáствовать в чём? (to participate in what?)	учáствовать в конферéнции (to participate in a conference)

The verb *to get married* in Russian:

 There are two expressions that mean *to get married*, one for a man and the other for a woman. The expression **жени́ться на ком?** (followed by the prepositional case) indicates that it is a man who gets married. The expression **выходи́ть/вы́йти зáмуж за когó?** (followed by the accusative case) indicates that it is a woman who gets married.

Упражнéния

1. Answer the questions, using the words in brackets in the correct form with the appropriate preposition:

1. Где пальтó? .... (шкаф).
2. Где бизнесмéн? .... (óфис).
3. Где студéнт? .... (лéкция).
4. Где тури́ст? .... (сад).
5. Где Архáнгельск? .... (сéвер).
6. Где Нью-Йóрк? .... (Амéрика).

Level 1, 2 **2.** Answer the the questions, using the words in brackets in the correct form with the appropriate preposition:

A. О чём

1. .... мечта́ет ро́бот? (ко́смос).
2. .... спра́шивает Э́лла? (общежи́тие).

B. О ком

1. .... ду́мает дочь? (мать).
2. .... пи́шет исто́рик? (царь).

C. На чём

1. Тури́сты летя́т в Крым? (самолёт)
2. Ди́ма е́дет в университе́т? (велосипе́д)

Level 2, 3 **3.** Put the nouns in brackets into the prepositional case. Add the appropriate preposition.

1. ... (Горбачёв) начала́сь перестро́йка.
2. ... 1945-ом (год) зако́нчилась втора́я мирова́я война́.
3. У Верони́ки день рожде́ния ... (октя́брь).
4. Прави́тельство объяви́ло ... (ме́ры) про́тив террори́зма.
5. Банк отказа́л Мари́и ... (креди́т).
6. Больно́й нужда́ется (подде́ржка) ... семьи́.
7. Трубаду́ры (minstrels) пе́ли серена́ды ... (любо́вь).
8. Депута́т забы́л ... (заседа́ние).

Level 2, 3 **Обобща́ющее упражне́ние**

4. Put the words in brackets into the prepositional case.

Сего́дня на (у́лицы) Москвы́ прово́дят социологи́ческий опро́с «О (что) мечта́ет молодёжь?». Господи́н Смирно́в согласи́лся запо́лнить анке́ту:

Вопро́сы анке́ты	
1. Вы ча́сто ду́маете о (семья́, дом, де́ти, роди́тели, ро́дственники)?	6. Вы беспоко́итесь о своём (здоро́вье)?
2. Вы расска́зываете о свои́х (проблéмы, стра́хи, фо́бии) бли́зким?	7. Вы лю́бите чита́ть о (путеше́ствия, приро́да)?
3. Вы мечта́ете о (бога́тство, сла́ва, почёт, уваже́ние, поку́пка) но́вой иномáрки?	8. Вы слу́шаете програ́ммы о (поли́тика и поли́тики)?
4. Вы ду́маете о (повыше́ние) по слу́жбе?	9. Вы разгова́риваете с друзья́ми о (пого́да)?
5. Вы лю́бите смотре́ть фи́льмы об (инопланетя́не)?	10. Вы ча́сто забыва́ете о ва́жных (встре́чи)?

11 Adjectives

Adjectives are words that describe a noun. This is called *attributive* use. In a sentence or phrase, an adjective usually precedes the noun it qualifies: **ру́сская** грамма́тика (**Russian** grammar), **здоро́вый и счастли́вый** челове́к (**healthy and happy** person). However, in a sentence, the adjective can also follow the noun it qualifies: Э́тот костю́м, **тако́й дорого́й и краси́вый**, я реши́л не надева́ть. (I have decided not to wear this suit **that is so expensive and smart**.)

Adjectives can also be used as a core-part of a predicate. If an adjective is used as a predicate it describes the subject of the sentence. The subject and adjective are connected by the verb **быть** (to be) or by any other verb with a meaning similar to **быть** (☞ 16.2). This is called *predicative* use: Они́ **бы́ли здоро́выми и счастли́выми.** (They **were healthy and happy**.)

Adjectives can be divided into three groups – *qualitative*, *possessive* and *relational*. The largest group of adjectives (*qualitative*) describes categories such as colour, size, taste, temperature, abstract qualities: **кра́сный** (red), **ма́ленький** (small), **горя́чий** (hot). Qualitative adjectives can have *long* and *short* forms as well as *comparative* and *superlative* forms. Many *adverbs* are derived from these adjectives (☞ 13).

The smaller *possessive* and *relational* groups of adjective can have only a long form, and they do not form *comparatives* or *superlatives*. *Adverbs* are not derived from these groups.

Relational adjectives describe the material that an object is made of, content or ingredients, time, nationality or origins: **металли́ческий** (metallic), **зи́мний** спорт (winter sport), **Моско́вский** городско́й сове́т (Moscow City Council).

Possessive adjectives indicate: the user of the object: **де́тский** сад (children's nursery); ownership: **ма́мина** шу́ба (mother's fur coat).

Long adjectives must show *agreement* with the *noun* they qualify, in *gender, number* and *case*. For example:

Я чита́ю англи́йскую газе́ту и ру́сский журна́л.	I read an English language newspaper and a Russian magazine

The adjective англи́йскую (English) is in the *feminine, singular, accusative case*, because it describes a *feminine singular noun in the accusative case* – **газе́ту**. The adjective ру́сский (Russian) is in the *masculine, singular, accusative case*, because it describes a *masculine singular noun in the accusative case* – **журна́л**.

Short adjectives are used only as predicates. They agree with the subject of the sentence in number, gender and case.

11.1 Declension

Only long-form adjectives decline. The *masculine* and *neuter* adjectives follow the same pattern; *feminine* adjectives follow a different pattern. The *plural* form includes all genders. The declension of adjectives is shown in the summary tables below. They are arranged according to *hard* or *soft endings* and the influence of the spelling rules: ☞ 1.3–1.4.

11.1.1 Adjectives with hard endings

Adjectives with hard endings that are stressed have a dictionary form ending with **-ой.**
Adjectives with hard endings that are not stressed have a dictionary form ending with **-ый**; for
example: интере́сный (interesting), зубно́й (dental).

For the declension of animate and inanimate nouns, 4.2.1.1 and 4.3.

Summary Table 11.I

Case	Singular adjectives			Plural adjectives (all genders)
	Masculine	Neuter	Feminine	
N	-ый интере́сный	-ое интере́сное	-ая интере́сная	-ые интере́сные
A	as genitive, if describing an animate noun; as nominative, if describing an inanimate noun	as nominative	-ую	as genitive, if describing an animate noun; as nominative, if describing an inanimate noun
	интере́сного (animate) интере́сный (inanimate)	интере́сное	интере́сную	интере́сных (animate) интере́сные (inanimate)
G	-ого интере́сного	-ого интере́сного	-ой интере́сной	-ых интере́сных
D	-ому интере́сному	-ому интере́сному	-ой интере́сной	-ым интере́сным
I	-ым интере́сным	-ым интере́сным	-ой интере́сной	-ыми интере́сными
P	-ом интере́сном	-ом интере́сном	-ой интере́сной	-ых интере́сных

For example:

> Мы ви́дели интере́сных люде́й
> (animate, plural, accusative).

We saw interesting people.

> Мы ходи́ли к зубно́му врачу́
> (dative, singular, masculine).

We went to the dentist.

11.1.2 Adjectives with soft endings

Adjectives with the soft endings have a dictionary form that ends with **-ий.** For example:
ле́тний (summer).

Summary Table 11.II

Case	Singular adjectives			Plural adjectives (all genders)
	Masculine	**Neuter**	**Feminine**	
N	**-ий** ле́тн**ий**	**-ее** ле́тн**ее**	**-яя** ле́тн**яя**	**-ие** ле́тн**ие**
A	as genitive, if describing an animate noun; as nominative, if describing an inanimate noun	as nominative	**-юю**	as genitive, if describing an animate noun; as nominative, if describing an inanimate noun
	ле́тн**его** (animate) ле́тн**ий** (inanimate)	ле́тн**ее**	ле́тн**юю**	ле́тн**их** (animate) ле́тн**ие** (inanimate)
G	**-его** ле́тн**его**	**-его** ле́тн**его**	**-ей** ле́тн**ей**	**-их** ле́тн**их**
D	**-ему** ле́тн**ему**	**-ему** ле́тн**ему**	**-ей** ле́тн**ей**	**-им** ле́тн**им**
I	**-им** ле́тн**им**	**-им** ле́тн**им**	**-ей** ле́тн**ей**	**-ими** ле́тн**ими**
P	**-ем** ле́тн**ем**	**-ем** ле́тн**ем**	**-ей** ле́тн**ей**	**-их** ле́тн**их**

For example:

Студе́нты мечта́ют о ле́тн**их** кани́кул**ах** (plural, prepositional).

The students are dreaming of their summer holidays.

11.1.3 Adjectives that are affected by spelling rules

For the spelling rules, ☞ 1.3

11.1.3.1 Adjectives that have stems ending in **к, г, х, ш, щ, ж** and **ч** are affected by the spelling rules (☞ 1.3.1–1.3.2). The rules explain which letters cannot appear after these consonants. In general, the adjectives that are affected by the spelling rules (those with a dictionary form ending with **-ий** or **-ой**, for example: **глубо́кий** (deep), **большо́й** (big)) follow the modified pattern of adjectives with hard endings. This pattern is called the 'mixed' declension.

Summary Table 11.III

Case	Singular adjectives			Plural adjectives (all genders)
	Masculine	**Neuter**	**Feminine**	
N	**-ий** глубо́к**ий**	**-ое** глубо́к**ое**	**-ая** глубо́к**ая**	**-ие** глубо́к**ие**
A	as genitive, if describing an animate noun; as nominative, if describing an inanimate noun	as nominative	**-ую**	as genitive, if describing an animate noun; as nominative, if describing an inanimate noun

	глубо́кого (animate) глубо́кий (inanimate)	глубо́кое	глубо́кую	глубо́ких (animate) глубо́кие (inanimate)
G	-ого глубо́кого	-ого глубо́кого	-ой глубо́кой	-их глубо́ких
D	-ому глубо́кому	-ому глубо́кому	-ой глубо́кой	-им глубо́ким
I	-им глубо́ким	-им глубо́ким	-ой глубо́кой	-ими глубо́кими
P	-ом глубо́ком	-ом глубо́ком	-ой глубо́кой	-их глубо́ких

For example:

> Мы чита́ем краси́вые афи́ши (plural accusative)
> Большо́го теа́тра (singular, masculine, genitive).

We are reading beautiful posters of the Bolshoi theatre.

11.1.3.2 Adjectives with stems ending in **ж, ч, ш** and **щ** are affected by spelling rule 3 (☞ 1.3.3). The rule explains the choice between stressed letter **-о** and unstressed letter **-е** after these consonants.

Summary Table 11.IV

Case	Singular adjectives			Plural adjectives (all genders)
	Masculine	**Neuter**	**Feminine**	
N	**-ий/-ой** хоро́ший/большо́й	**-ее** (if unstressed) хоро́шее **-ое** (if stressed) большо́е	**-ая** хоро́шая/ больша́я	**-ие** хоро́шие/больши́е
A	as genitive, if describing an animate noun; as nominative, if describing an inanimate noun	as nominative	**-ую**	as genitive, if describing an animate noun; as nominative, if describing an inanimate noun
	хоро́шего/большо́го (animate) хоро́ший/большо́й (inanimate)	**-ее** (if unstressed) хоро́шее **-ое** (if stressed) большо́е	хоро́шую	хоро́ших/больши́х (animate) хоро́шие/больши́е (inanimate)
G	**-его** (if unstressed) хоро́шего **-ого** (if stressed) большо́го	**-его** (if unstressed) хоро́шего **-ого** (if stressed) большо́го	**-ей** (if unstressed) хоро́шей **-ой** (if stressed) большо́й	**-их** хоро́ших/больши́х

D	**-ему** (if unstressed) хорóш**ему**	**-ему** (if unstressed) хорóш**ему**	**-ей** (if unstressed) хорóш**ей**	**-им** хорóш**им**/больш**и́м**
	-ому (if stressed) больш**óму**	**-ому** (if stressed) больш**óму**	**-ой** (if stressed) больш**óй**	
I	**-им** хорóш**им**/больш**и́м**	**-им** хорóш**им**/ больш**и́м**	**-ей** (if unstressed) хорóш**ей**	**-ими** хорóш**ими**/ больш**и́ми**
			-ой (if stressed) больш**óй**	
P	**-ем** (if unstressed) хорóш**ем**	**-ем** (if unstressed) хорóш**ем**	**-ей** (if unstressed) хорóш**ей**	**-их** хорóш**их**/больш**и́х**
	-ом (if stressed) больш**óм**	**-ом** (if stressed) больш**óм**	**-ой** (if stressed) больш**óй**	

For example:

> Мы подари́ли хорóш**ему** дру́г**у** (masculine, singular, dative) айпóд с больш**óй** пáмять**ю** (feminine, singular, instrumental).

> We gave our good friend an iPod with a large memory.

Level 3

11.1.4 Declension of possessive adjectives

Possessive adjectives (☞ introduction to this chapter) are formed from nouns by adding the suffixes -**ин**-, -**ов**- or -**ий**-. Possessive adjectives follow the pronominal declension of a word like наш *our* (☞ 14.4.1). The endings look like those of both nouns and adjectives. Summary Tables 11.V and 11.VI give examples of this pattern:

Summary Table 11.V

Case	Singular adjectives			Plural adjectives (all genders)
	Masculine	**Neuter**	**Feminine**	
N	no ending мáмин/отцóв	**-о** мáмин**о**/отцóв**о**	**-а** мáмин**а**/ отцóв**а**	**-ы** мáмин**ы**/отцóв**ы**
A	as genitive, if describing an animate noun; as nominative, if describing an inanimate noun	as nominative	**-у**	as genitive, if describing an animate noun; as nominative, if describing an inanimate noun
	мáмин**ого**/отцóв**а** (animate) мáмин/отцóв (inanimate)	мáмин**о**/отцóв**о**	мáмин**у**/ отцóв**у**	мáмин**ых** /отцóв**ых** (animate) мáмин**ы**/отцóв**ы** (inanimate)
G	**-ого** мáмин**ого**/отцóв**а**	**-ого** мáмин**ого**/отцóв**а**	**-ой** мáмин**ой**/ отцóв**ой**	**-ых** мáмин**ых**/отцóв**ых**

D	-ому ма́мин**ому**/отцо́в**у**	-ому ма́мин**ому**/ отцо́в**у**	-ой ма́мин**ой**/ отцо́в**ой**	-ым ма́мин**ым**/отцо́в**ым**
I	-ым ма́мин**ым**/отцо́в**ым**	-ым ма́мин**ым**/ отцо́в**ым**	-ой ма́мин**ой**/ отцо́в**ой**	-ыми ма́мин**ыми**/отцо́в**ыми**
P	-ом ма́мин**ом**/отцо́в**ом**	-ом ма́мин**ом**/ отцо́в**ом**	-ой ма́мин**ой**/ отцо́в**ой**	-ых ма́мин**ых**/отцо́в**ых**

Summary Table 11.VI

Case	Singular adjectives			Plural adjectives (all genders)
	Masculine	**Neuter**	**Feminine**	
N	no ending соба́ч**ий**	-е соба́чь**е**	-а соба́чь**я**	-и соба́чь**и**
A	as genitive, if describing an animate noun; as nominative, if describing an inanimate noun	as nominative	-ю	as genitive, if describing an animate noun; as nominative, if describing an inanimate noun
	соба́чь**его** (animate) соба́ч**ий** (inanimate)	соба́чь**е**	соба́чь**ю**	соба́чь**их** (animate) соба́чь**и** (inanimate)
G	-его соба́чь**его**	-его соба́чь**его**	-ей соба́чь**ей**	-их соба́чь**их**
D	-ему соба́чь**ему**	-ему соба́чь**ему**	-ей соба́чь**ей**	-им соба́чь**им**
I	-им соба́чь**им**	-им соба́чь**им**	-ей соба́чь**ей**	-ими соба́чь**ими**
P	-ем соба́чь**ем**	-ем соба́чь**ем**	-ей соба́чь**ей**	-их соба́чь**их**

For example:

На столе́ мно́го Та́нин**ых** кни́г (genitive plural).

There are many of Tanya's books on the table.

На семина́ре мы говори́ли о «Соба́чь**ем** се́рдце» (neuter, singular, prepositional) Булга́кова.

At the seminar we discussed 'Heart of a Dog' by Bulgakov.

Level 1, 2

11.2 Adjectives used as nouns

Several nouns are derived from adjectival phrases, for example, **сла́дкое блю́до** (sweet dessert), **ва́нная ко́мната** (bathroom). In a sentence these adjectives function as independent nouns. However, they still decline as adjectives. The noun that was originally a core-part of the adjectival phrase is left unsaid. For example:

Они́ пришли́ в го́сти с моро́жен**ым** (neuter, singular, instrumental).	They brought ice-cream with them.
Зайди́ в бу́лочн**ую** (feminine, singular, accusative), пожа́луйста.	Could you please pop into the bakery.

The most common adjectives that are used as nouns are listed below:

сла́дкое	sweet dessert	пивна́я	pub/bar
пе́рвое	starter	пра́чечная	laundry
второ́е	main course	набережная	embankment
тре́тье	dessert	заку́сочная	snack-bar
моро́женое	ice-cream	го́рничная	maid
гости́ная	sitting room	сбо́рная	sports team
ва́нная	bathroom	столо́вая	dining room/canteen
бу́лочная	bakery	бли́нная	pancake place

Упражне́ния

Level 1

1. Complete the sentences with adjectives, from the list below, in the correct form. The letters in brackets indicate the case:

ва́жные, но́вые, ру́сские наро́дные, спорти́вный, серьёзные, зубно́й, кита́йский.

1. Я не зна́ю .... сосе́дей. (A)
2. Адвока́т встре́тился с .... клие́нтами. (I)
3. В э́том магази́не продаю́т .... оде́жду. (A)
4. Нам на́до идти́ к .... врачу́. (D)
5. Вы слы́шали о .... рестора́не в це́нтре го́рода? (P)
6. В ми́ре мно́го .... пробле́м. (G)
7. Тури́стам нра́вятся .... пе́сни. (N)

Level 2, 3

2. Complete the sentences by putting the phrases in brackets into the correct form.

1. Шко́льники занима́ются (худо́жественная гимна́стика) в (де́тская спорти́вная шко́ла).
2. Он роди́лся в (ма́ленькая дере́вня) недалеко́ от (стари́нный ру́сский го́род).
3. У Ни́ны (огро́мная кварти́ра) с (больши́е о́кна) в (многоэта́жное зда́ние).
4. Он лю́бит (совреме́нная оде́жда).
5. (Бли́зкие ро́дственники) подари́ли Ми́ше (мо́дный дорого́й айпо́д (iPod)).
6. На (вече́рний конце́рт) (популя́рная рок-гру́ппа) не́ было (свобо́дные места́).

Level 2, 3

Обобща́ющее упражне́ние

3. Complete the story by putting the phrases in brackets into the appropriate form.

Да́ча семьи́ Смирно́вых

1. У семьи́ Смирно́вых, как и у большинства́ (ру́сские се́мьи), есть да́ча в (ма́ленькая дере́вня) недалеко́ от Москвы́. 2. Смирно́вы называ́ют э́тот (ста́рый дереве́нский дом) (родово́е гнездо́). 3. Все поколе́ния Смирно́вых лю́бят собира́ться в (небольшо́й ую́тный двухэта́жный дом) с (резно́е деревя́нное крыльцо́), (огро́мный све́тлый черда́к) и (тёмный холо́дный по́греб). 4. Этот дом постро́ил де́душка господи́на Смирно́ва в нача́ле (про́шлый век). 5. Дом окружён куста́ми (бе́лая сире́нь), (чёрная сморо́да) и (садо́вая мали́на). 6. Подня́вшись по (скрипу́чие ступе́ньки) крыльца́, вы попадёте в (дли́нный

у́зкий) коридо́р. 7. Коридо́р приведёт вас в (просто́рная ко́мната) с (настоя́щая ру́сская печь) в углу́. 8. Ра́ньше в таки́х печа́х не то́лько гото́вили (вку́сные обе́ды) и пекли́ (румя́ные пироги́), но и мы́лись. 9. А наверху́ (ру́сская печь) спа́ли. 10. У (ру́сская печь) стои́т (большо́й деревя́нный стол), накры́тый (бе́лая льняна́я ска́терть). 11. На столе́ всегда́ шуми́т (ста́рый ме́дный самова́р). 12. Смирно́вы лю́бят собира́ться за (большо́й стол) (тёплые ле́тние, и холо́дные зи́мние вечера́) за ча́ем с (горя́чие вку́сные пироги́).

12 Adjectives: comparative, superlative and short- and long-form adjectives

Level 1, 2

12.1 Comparative and superlative forms of adjectives

Only *qualitative* adjectives (☞ 11) can form *comparative* and *superlative* forms. For example:

Москва́-река́ – **дли́нная**, река́ Во́лга – **длинне́е**, река́ Енисе́й – **са́мая дли́нная**.	The river Moskva is *long*, but the river Volga is *longer* (*comparative*), the river Yenisey is the *longest* (*superlative*).

12.2 Formation of the comparative forms of adjectives

There are two ways to form the comparative:

- The simple (one-word) comparative with an added suffix (☞ 12.2.1)
- The compound comparative (☞ 12.2.2)

Both forms of comparatives are common in informal and formal speech and are used in a similar way. Simple comparatives are non-declinable. The compound comparative consists of a non-declinable word and a declinable word (☞ 12.2.2).

12.2.1 Formation of the simple comparative

Simple comparatives are formed by adding one of the suffixes -**е** or -**ее** to the adjective's stem. The suffix -**е** is added to stems ending in **г, к, х, д, т, ст, з** and, to stems of some irregular adjectives. Comparatives that do not fit this pattern are formed by adding the suffix -**ее**.

The stress of the comparatives has a distinctive pattern:

- The stress never falls on the suffix -**е**: **ши́ре** (wider).
- The stress in comparatives ending with -**ее** (except for polysyllabic comparatives) falls on the first letter of the suffix -**ее**: **добре́е** (kinder).
- The stress in polysyllabic comparatives of three or more syllables ending with -**ее** always falls on the stem: **интере́снее** (more interesting).

To form the simple comparative:

- Drop the ending of the adjective (last two letters): **у́мн**ый (clever), **молод**о́й (young).
- Add the suffix -**ее** or -**е** to the stem of the adjective: **умне́е** (cleverer), **моло́же** (younger).

When adding the suffix -**е** the following consonant changes occur in the stem ending:

Г-->Ж	З-->Ж	СТ-->Щ	К-->Ч
Д-->Ж	Х-->Ш		Т-->Ч

The list below includes the most frequently used comparatives formed with the suffix -**е,** including some irregular comparatives:

Dictionary form of the adjective	Comparative
большо́й (big)	бо́льше
ма́ленький (small)	ме́ньше
молодо́й (young)	моло́же
ста́рый (old)	ста́рше
высо́кий tall)	вы́ше
ни́зкий (low)	ни́же
плохо́й (bad)	ху́же
хоро́ший (good)	лу́чше
широ́кий (wide)	ши́ре
у́зкий (narrow)	у́же
далёкий (far)	да́льше
ти́хий (quiet, silent)	ти́ше
лёгкий (light)	ле́гче
коро́ткий (short)	коро́че
гро́мкий (loud)	гро́мче
просто́й (simple)	про́ще
стро́гий (strict)	стро́же
бли́зкий (near)	бли́же
бога́тый (rich)	бога́че
дорого́й (dear/expensive)	доро́же
дешёвый (cheap)	деше́вле
то́лстый (fat)	то́лще
то́нкий (thin)	то́ньше

12.2.2 Formation of the compound comparative

The compound comparative is formed by adding the non-declinable words **бо́лее** (more) or **ме́нее** (less) to the dictionary form of the adjective:

Ле́кция сего́дня **бо́лее интере́сная**.	Today's lecture is more interesting.
Э́то **бо́лее ую́тный** дом.	This is a more cosy/cosier house.
Э́то **ме́нее ую́тный** дом.	This is a less cosy house.

Although the words **бо́лее** (more) and **ме́нее** (less) do not decline, the adjective that forms the second part of the compound comparative agrees in gender, number and case with the noun it qualifies:

В э́тот раз мы останови́лись в **бо́лее** (non-declinable) деше́в**ой** гости́ни**це** (feminine, singular, prepositional).	This time we stayed in a cheaper hotel.

12.3 Using the comparatives

The comparative construction is introduced by the conjunction **чем** (than). The noun introduced by **чем** is always used in the nominative case (☞ 5.3):

Я **моло́же, чем** Ви́ктор и Мари́я (nominative).	I am younger than Victor and Maria.

If **чем** (than) is omitted, the noun(s) in the comparative construction is (are) used in the genitive case (☞ 7.2.4):

Я **моло́же** Ви́ктора и Мари́и (genitive). I am younger than Victor and Maria.

Level 3

To make the comparison precise, some additional information can be added to the comparative phrase, with:

- Expressions of quantity with numerals:

Я моло́же его **на пять** (accusative) **лет** (genitive). I am 5 years younger than him.

Сестра́ **двумя́ года́ми** (instrumental) ста́рше меня́. My sister is 2 years older than me.

Она́ **в три** (accusative) **ра́за** (genitive) ста́рше меня́. She is three times as old as me.

- The words **гора́здо**, **намно́го** (much) followed by the comparative:

О́зеро Байка́л **намно́го** глу́бже о́зера Lake Baikal is much deeper than
Лох-Несс. Loch Ness.

Level 1, 2

12.4 The superlative form of the adjective

12.4.1 Formation of the superlative form of the adjective

There are two ways to form the superlative by using:

- The compound superlative (☞ 12.4.1.1–3)
- The simple (one-word) superlative with an added suffix or prefix (☞ 12.4.2)

Level 1, 2

12.4.1.1 The compound superlative with pronoun са́мый (the most)

The compound superlative is the most common form of superlative. It is used in formal and informal speech. It is formed by adding the pronoun **са́мый** (the most) to the dictionary form of the adjective. For example:

Са́мый тала́нтливый the most talented

Са́мый глубо́кий the deepest

Both parts of the compound superlative, the pronoun **са́мый** and the adjective, agree in gender, number and case with the noun they qualify. For example:

В э́той кни́ге расска́зывается о са́м**ых** дре́вних In this book are described the
город**а́х** (plural prepositional) ми́ра. most ancient cities in the world.

Мы познако́мились с са́м**ым** мо́дн**ым** We met the most fashionable
писа́тел**ем** (masculine, singular, instrumental). writer.

In informal speech, the pronoun **са́мый** can be omitted if it is followed by the declining adjectives **лу́чший** (the best) and **ху́дший** (the worst) (☞ 12.4.2):

Э́то на́ша (са́мая) лу́чшая студе́нтка. This is our best student.

Э́то (са́мый) ху́дший бар в го́роде. This is the worst bar in town.

12.4.1.2 The compound superlative with наибо́лее (the most) and наиме́нее (the least)

In writing **са́мый** is often replaced by the non-declinable words **наибо́лее** (the most) and **наиме́нее** (the least):

Наиме́нее тала́нтливый the least talented

Наибо́лее глубо́кий the deepest

👁 Although the word **наибо́лее** does not decline, the adjective in this superlative construction agrees in gender, number and case with the noun it qualifies:

Прошла́ встре́ча с **наибо́лее** тала́нтливыми спортсме́нами (plural instrumental).	A meeting was held with the most talented sportsmen.

12.4.1.3 The compound superlative with the pronoun все (all)

Level 2, 3

The compound superlative can also be formed by using the comparative form of the adjective and the pronoun **все** (all) in the genitive case **всех** (of all):

тала́нтливее **всех**	most talented singer
глу́бже **всех**	the deepest

This superlative does not decline.

12.4.2 Formation of the simple superlative

Level 3

Simple superlatives are common in writing. They can be formed:

- By adding the suffix **-ейш-** or **-айш-** to the stem of the adjective. The suffix **-айш-** is added to a stem that ends with **г, к, х**. The suffix **-ейш-** is used for the rest of the adjectives: ближа́йший (the nearest), нове́йший (the newest). When adding the suffix **-айш-** the last consonant of the stem is modified: **г-->ж, к-->ч, х-->ш**.
- By adding the prefix **наи-** to the simple superlative with suffixes **-ейш-** or **-айш-**: **наи**красиве́йший (the most beautiful)

Recently, a new way of forming superlatives has been adopted in spoken Russian. This is by adding the Anglicism **су́пер** (super) to the adjective:

У супермужчи́ны до́лжен быть **супер**чи́стый автобомоби́ль.	Superman must have a super-clean car.

👁 There is one further way of forming the superlative adjective. The following declinable adjectives are used as superlatives:

лу́чший	the best	**ху́дший**	the worst
наиме́ньший	the smallest	**наибо́льший**	the biggest

All simple superlative forms decline and agree in gender, number and case with the noun they qualify:

На конфере́нции говори́ли **о нове́йших, суперсло́жных техноло́гиях** (plural, prepositional).	At the conference they discussed the newest super-complicated technologies.

12.5 Long and short forms of adjectives

Level 2, 3

For long-form adjectives, 🕮 11.

Only *qualitative* adjectives (🕮 11) can have a *short* form. Short-form adjectives do not decline. They have only number and gender categories.

12.5.1 Formation of short-form adjectives

To form the short-form adjective from the long-form adjective:

- Drop the ending of the long-form of adjective (last two letters): молодо́й (young), ну́жный (necessary/need).
- Add nothing for the masculine form, add **-a** for the feminine form, add **-o** for the neuter form, add **-ы** for the plural:

мо́лод (m), молода́ (f), мо́лодо (n), мо́лоды (pl)
ну́жен (m), нужна́ (f), ну́жно (n), нужны́ (pl)

- If the stem has two consonants at the end, then, in the masculine form, a 'fleeting' vowel is inserted between the consonants (☞ 4.5): ну́жен (m).

👁 Stress in the feminine and plural short-form adjectives often moves from stem to ending.

12.6 Using short-form adjectives

Level 1, 2

Short-form adjectives are used as a core-element of a predicate and they do not decline. They describe the subject of the sentence and agree in gender and number with the subject. They are most common in writing. A few short-from adjectives, such as ну́жен/нужна́/ну́жно/нужны́ (need), бо́лен/больна́/больны́ (sick/ill), are also common in everyday speech.

The subject and the adjective are connected by the verb **быть** (to be) or by any other verbs that have a similar meaning to **быть** (☞ 16.2). **Быть** is omitted in the present tense, but is present in the past and future tenses. In the past and present tenses **быть** agrees in gender and number with both the short-form adjective and the subject of the sentence. For example:

Past tense:

Они́ (pl) **бы́ли больны́** (pl)	They were ill.
Де́душка (masc sing) **был бо́лен** (masc sing).	Grandfather was ill.
Ба́бушка (fem sing) **была́ больна́** (fem sing).	Grandmother was ill.

Future tense:

Врачи́ (3rd person pl) **бу́дут внима́тельны** (3rd person pl) к пацие́нтам.	The doctors will pay attention to the patients.

Упражне́ния

Level 1

1. Put the adjectives in brackets into the simple comparative form.
1. Сего́дня уро́к .... (тру́дный), чем вчера́.
2. Велосипе́д .... (дешёвый), чем маши́на.
3. Икра́ .... (дорого́й), чем ры́ба.
4. Во́дка .... (кре́пкий), чем вино́.

Level 1

2. Put the adjectives in brackets into the compound superlative form with the word **са́мый:**
Вы зна́ете ...
1. Како́е о́зеро .... (глубо́кий)?
2. Кака́я река́ .... (дли́нный)?
3. Каки́е го́ры .... (высо́кий)?
4. Како́й язы́к .... (тру́дный)?

Level 2

3. Complete the sentences using the simple (one-word) comparative adjective:
1. Кри́зис оказа́лся гора́здо .... (тяжёлый), чем ожида́ли.
2. Наш де́душка ..... (молодо́й) на́шей ба́бушки.
3. Но́вый прое́кт оказа́лся ..... (плохо́й) ста́рого.
4. Фру́кты в суперма́ркете .... (дорого́й), чем на ры́нке.
5. Брат .... (мла́дший) сестры́ на 2 го́да.

Level 2, 3

4. Put the adjectives in brackets into all possible superlative forms:
На на́шей плане́те:
1. Кантьо́н Ко́лка в Колу́мбии .... (глубо́кий) каньо́н.
2. Сеу́л .... (густонаселённый) го́род.
3. Река́ Ро в США .... (коро́ткая) река́.
4. Морска́я змея́ .... (ядови́тый и опа́сный) морско́е живо́тное.

13 Adverbs

Adverbs are indeclinable. They respond to the questions: **когда́?** (when?), **где?** (where?), **куда́?** (where to?), **отку́да?** (where from?), **как?** (how?), **в како́й сте́пени?/наско́лько?** (to what degree?/how?), **почему́?** (why?), **заче́м/с како́й це́лью?** (what for?).

Adverbs mainly qualify verbs:

Как бежи́т спортсме́н? – Спортсме́н бежи́т **бы́стро**.	**How does** the sportsman **run**? – The sportsman **runs fast**.
Где он **живёт?** – Он живёт **там, сле́ва от** суперма́ркета.	Where does he live? – He lives **there, to the left of** the supermarket.

Additionally, adverbs can qualify:

- Adjectives: **О́чень интере́сная** пробле́ма. (A **very interesting** problem.)
- Other adverbs: Фильм продолжа́лся **сли́шком до́лго**. (The film lasted **too long**.)

Level 2, 3

13.1 Adverb formation

Adverbs derive from various parts of speech: adjectives, nouns, pronouns, verbs, gerunds, participles. Adverbs are formed by adding suffixes (☞ 13.1.1), prefixes (☞ 13.1.2) or both (☞ 13.1.3) to the stem of the word that will form the adverb. The list of suffixes and prefixes in these sections is not exhaustive, but it covers the most common adverb formations.

Additionally, some nouns or gerunds can function as adverbs when they qualify a verb.These adverbs look identical to the words from which they are derived. For example:

- Adverbs **у́тром** (in the morning), **ле́том** (in summer), **шёпотом** (in a whisper) are derived from the nouns in the instrumental case **у́тром, ле́том, шёпотом** (☞ 9.2.2).
- Adverbs **мо́лча** (in silence), **лёжа** (in lying position), **припева́ючи** (great, literally 'singing') are derived from the gerunds **мо́лча, лёжа, припева́ючи** (☞ 27).

13.1.1 The largest number of adverbs is formed by adding the suffixes **-o** or **-e** to adjectives that describe quality (☞ 11) or to participles (☞ 26).

To form the adverb:

- Drop the adjective or participle ending (last two letters):
  смешно́й (funny) – смешн-
  и́скренн**ий** (sincere) – искренн-
  угрожа́ющ**ий** (threatening) – угрожающ-
- Add the suffix **-e-** to adjectival or participle stems ending with **-ж, -ш, -ч, -щ**: угрожа́юще.
- Add the suffix **-e-** to the stem if the adjective ends with **-ний** in the dictionary form: и́скренне.
- Add the suffix **-o-** to any stem other than those described above: смешно́.

Indefinite adverbs are formed in the same way as indefinite pronouns (☞ 14.9) by adding the suffixes **-нибудь**, **-то** or **-либо** to the indeclinable question words **где?** (where?), **куда?** (where to?), **откуда?** (from where?), **когда?** (when?) and **как?** (how?): как-нибудь (somehow/some time), где-то (somewhere).

13.1.2 Some adverbs are formed by adding the prefix **по-** to the dative case of possessive pronouns: **по-мо́ему** (in my opinion), **по-тво́ему** (in your opinion) etc. (☞ 14.4.1).

Other adverbs are formed by adding the prefix **в-/во-** to the genitive plural of ordinal numbers: **во**-пе́рвых, **во**-вторы́х, **в**-тре́тьих etc. (☞ 15.2).

For negative pronouns, ☞ 14.10.

13.1.3 Several adverbs are formed by adding the prefix **по-** and suffix **-и** to the stem of adjectives ending in **-ский**, **-цкий** or **-ический**. The prefix **по-** and the suffix **-ьи** are added to stems of possessive adjectives ending in **-ий** (☞ 11).

To form the adverb:

- Drop the adjective or participle ending (last two letters):
  ру́сский (Russian) – русск-
  неме́цкий (German) – немец-
  челове́чий (human) – человеч-
- Add the prefix **по-** and the suffix **-и** or **-ьи** as explained above:
  по-ру́сски
  по-неме́цки
  по-челове́чьи

Some adverbs derived from adjectives ending in **-ский**, **-цкий** or **-ический** do not have the prefix **по-**: ирони́чески (ironic), факти́чески (actually).

Other common prefixes are used to form adverbs from adjectives with the suffix **-о-**:

на: **на́**сухо (very dry) **на**ве́чно (for good), **на**до́лго (for long time).

за: **за́**живо (alive), **за́**мертво (dead), **за́**ново (new).

в: **в**ле́во (to the left), **в**пра́во (to the right).

с (and the suffix **-а**): **с**ле́ва (on the left), **с**пра́ва (on the right).

13.2 Adverb types

Level 2, 3

Adverbs can be divided into several groups depending on their meaning.

13.2.1 Adverbs of manner form the largest group and describe how an action is carried out. They respond to the question **как?** (how?). For example:

Хорошо́/пло́хо (well/badly)	Ви́ктор у́чится **хорошо́**. Victor studies well.
Ти́хо/гро́мко (quietly/loudly)	Му́зька игра́ет **гро́мко.** The music is loud.
По-но́вому/по-ста́рому (new/old style)	Всё **по-ста́рому.** All is as it was before.
Шёпотом (whispering)	Они́ разгова́ривают **шёпотом**. They speak in a whisper.

13.2.2 Adverbs of location include adverbs that describe the location, start or end point of a movement. They include responses to the questions **где?** (where?), **куда?** (where to?), **откуда?** (where from?):

Где? (where?)	Куда? (to where?)	Откуда? (from where?)	Translation
здесь/тут	сюда́	отсю́да	here
там	туда́	отту́да	there
наверху́	наве́рх	све́рху	above/upstairs
внизу́	вниз	сни́зу	below/downstairs
сле́ва	нале́во	сле́ва	left
спра́ва	напра́во	спра́ва	right
впереди́	вперёд	спе́реди	in front of
позади́	наза́д	сза́ди	behind
снару́жи	нару́жу	снару́жи	outside
внутри́	внутрь	изнутри́	inside
везде́/всю́ду	–	отовсю́ду	everywhere
далеко́/вдали́	далеко́/вдаль	издалека́/и́здали	far away
до́ма	домо́й	*See comments*	at home/home

Comments: To respond to the question 'from where?' the noun **дом** (house) in the genitive case is used: из до́ма/из до́му (from home).

Adverbs responding to the questions **куда?** and **откуда?** are common with verbs of motion (☞ 24–25). Adverbs responding the question **где?** describe location/position of the object.

13.2.3 Adverbs of time respond to the question **когда?** and include:

вчера́	yesterday	у́тром	in the morning
сего́дня	today	ве́чером	in the evening
за́втра	tomorrow	днём	afternoon
послеза́втра	the day after tomorrow	но́чью	at night
позавчера́	the day before yesterday	зимо́й	in winter
иногда́	sometimes	весно́й	in spring
ра́ньше	earlier	ле́том	in summer
сейча́с	now	о́сенью	in winter
давно́	a long time ago	одна́жды	once

13.2.4 Adverbs of degree respond to the question **в како́й сте́пени?/наско́лько?** (to what degree?/how?) and include: **о́чень** (very), **сли́шком** ('too'), **значи́тельно/чрезвыча́йно** (considerably), **чуть/чуть-чу́ть** (little), **еле-е́ле** (very slowly). For example:

Мы **о́чень** уста́ли.	We are very tired.
Мы **сли́шком** по́здно прие́хали.	We arrived too late.
В про́бке маши́ны дви́гались **еле-е́ле**.	In the traffic jam the cars were moving really slowly.

13.2.5 **Adverbs of reason** respond to the question **почему́?** (why?): сде́лать что́-нибудь сгоряча́, сослепу, по-глу́пости (to do something without thinking, without seeing it, out of stupidity).

13.2.6 **Adverbs of purpose** respond to the questions **заче́м/с ка́кой це́лью?** (for what?):

назло́ (out of spite)
наро́чно (on purpose)

13.2.7 **Indefinite adverbs** refer to unknown or uncertified:

- location: где́-то, где́-нибудь, где́-либо (somewhere)
- destination: куда́-то, куда́-нибудь, куда́-либо (to somewhere); отку́да-то, отку́да-нибудь, отку́да-либо (from somewhere)
- time: когда́-то, когда́-нибудь, когда́-либо (some time/once upon a time).

For the formation of indefinite adverbs, ☞ 13.1.1.

Use of the indefinite adverbs and the choice between the suffixes **-то, -нибудь** and **-либо** is determined by the same rule as the use of indefinite pronouns: ☞ 14.9.1. For example:

Когда́-нибудь они́ побыва́ют в Росси́и.	Some time they will go to Russia.
Где́-то далеко́, **где́**-то далеко́	Somewhere far away (twice)
Иду́т грибны́е дожди́.	It is raining during sunshine.
(Рожде́ственский)	

Another group of indefinite adverbs is formed by adding the prefix **кое**: кое-где́, кое-куда́, кое-отку́да, кое-ка́к. They have the same connotation and use as indefinite pronouns with added prefix **кое-** (☞ 14.9.1.3).

13.2.8 Negative adverbs

Russian has two types of negative adverb:

- One type is formed by adding the negative particle **ни-** to the question words **где?** (where?), **куда?** (where to?), **отку́да?** (where from?), **когда?** (when?): нигде́ (nowhere), никуда́ (to nowhere), ниотку́да (from nowhere), никогда́ (never).
- The other type is formed by adding the negative particle **не-** to the same question words: не́где, не́откуда, не́куда (indicates lack of space), не́когда (indicates lack of time).

The use of negative adverbs is determined by the same rule as the use of negative pronouns: ☞ 14.10.1 and 14.10.2.

Like negative pronouns with **ни-**, adverbs with **ни-** are used in negative personal constructions that usually have a subject and verb. Negative adverbs intensify the negativity that negative form of the verb expresses:

Мы посмотре́ли фильм «**Никогда́** не говори́ **никогда́**».	We watched the film 'Never Say Never Again'
Мы ещё **нигде́** не успе́ли побыва́ть.	We did not have time to visit any places.

Like negative pronouns with **не-**, adverbs with **не-** are used only in impersonal sentences that do not have a subject (☞ 30.3). Verbs in these sentences are always used in the affirmative form of the infinitive with the person in the dative case. Negative adverbs explain why the action cannot be carried out:

Lack of time	Са́ше **не́когда** отдыха́ть.	Sasha does not have time to relax.
Lack of place	Бездо́мному **не́где** жить.	The homeless man does not have a place to live.

(Explain what happens with a preposition. Не́ от кyge is answer to ex 3 no. 5, but has not been covered)

13.3 Comparative and superlative forms of adverbs

Adverbs have a limited number of comparatives and superlatives.

13.3.1 Comparative forms of adverbs

Only those adverbs that meet the following criteria can form comparative and superlative forms:

- They must end in **-o/-e**
- They must be derived from adjectives that describe quality (☞ 11)

Comparative forms of adverbs are formed in the same way and are identical to the comparative forms of adjectives. All adverbs that meet the criteria mentioned above can have a simple comparative form (☞ 12.2.1). It is mainly adverbs with more than two syllables that have compound comparative forms (☞ 12.2.2). For example:

Adjective	Simple comparative form of adjective	Adverb	Simple comparative form of adverb
быстрый (fast)	быстрее (faster)	быстро (fast)	быстрее (faster)
хороший (good)	лучше (better)	хорошо (good)	лучше (better)

Adjective	Compound comparative form of adjective	Adverb	Compound comparative form of adverb
красивый (beautiful)	более красивый (more beautiful)	красиво (beautiful/ly)	более красиво (more beautiful)
	менее красивый (less beautiful)		менее красиво (less beautiful)

13.3.2 Superlative forms of adverbs

Adverbs do not have all the superlative forms that adjectives have (☞ 12.4):

- Simple one-word superlatives of adverbs are rarely used: нижайше/покорнейше (most humble)
- The most common form of adverb superlative is the compound superlative that has the comparative form of the adverb and the genitive case of the pronoun **весь/все** (all) (☞ 12.4.1.3)
- **Всех** (genitive plural) is used when comparing something or someone with other objects or people: Он знает эти правила лучше **всех**. (He knows these rules **better then anyone else**.)
- **Всего** (genitive singular) is used when comparing different options for the speaker himself/herself: Лучше **всего** он запоминает правила, если записывает их. (He **best [of all] remembers** the rules when he writes them down.)

Superlative adverbs formed by using **наиболее** (most), **наименее** (least) followed by the adverb's dictionary form are common in writing: наиболее интересно (the most interesting).

13.3.3 Using superlative and comparative forms of adjectives and adverbs

Although comparative and superlative forms of adjectives and adverbs look identical and are formed in the same way, they have different roles in a sentence:

- Adverbs qualify verbs: Гепа́рд **бе́гает быстре́е** ти́гра./Гепа́рд **бе́гает быстре́е**, чем тигр. (A cheetah **runs faster** than a tiger.) Гепа́рд **бе́гает быстре́е всех**. (A cheetah **runs faster than everyone** (all other animals).)
- Adjectives qualify nouns or pronouns: Гепа́рд **быстре́е ти́гра**./Гепа́рд **быстре́е**, чем тигр (☞ 12.3). (**A cheetah is faster** than a tiger.) Гепа́рд – **са́мое бы́строе живо́тное**. (The cheetah is **the fastest animal**.)

Упражне́ния

1. Form adverbs from the following adjectives:

1. англи́йский; 2. интере́сный; 3. ме́дленный; 4. соба́чий; 5. и́скренний; 6. дру́жеский

2. Insert the appropriate adverb from the list provided:

туда́, ду́шно, за́втра, ску́чно, неда́вно, отовсю́ду, домо́й.

1. Здесь о́чень ....
2. На ле́кции о́чень ....
3. По́сле рабо́ты она́ е́дет ....
4. Они́ бы́ли в Финля́ндии ....
5. .... доноси́лись кри́ки.
6. Я пое́ду ....

3. Insert the appropriate negative adverb. Form the adverb by adding the particle **ни-** or **не-** to the adverb given in brackets:

1. Мы .... (где) не ви́дели официа́нта.
2. Она́ ещё .... (когда́) не была́ в Ве́нгрии.
3. На Но́вый год нам .... (куда́) пойти́.
4. В трамва́е......... (где) сесть. Мест нет.
5. Жа́нне .... (куда́) получа́ть сообще́ния.
6. Э́тот карто́фель .... (отку́да) не привози́ли. Его́ выра́щивают здесь.

Обобща́ющее упражне́ние

4. Complete the text by inserting the following adverbs in comparative or superlative forms as appropriate:

ча́сто, мно́го, ре́дко, хорошо́, интере́сно, бли́зко, я́рко, увлека́тельно, бы́стро, си́льно, гро́мко, оживлённо, прово́рно

Господи́н Смирно́в идёт на футбо́льный матч

1. Господи́н Смирно́в, как и мно́гие коренны́е москвичи́, боле́ет за моско́вское «Дина́мо». Сего́дня он со свое́й подру́гой Ири́ной идёт смотре́ть матч «Дина́мо»–«Зени́т». Ири́на не о́чень лю́бит футбо́л. Она́ ду́мает, что следи́ть за те́ннисным ма́тчем намно́го ...., а смотре́ть, наприме́р, фигу́рное ката́ние да́же ещё .... 2. Господи́н Смирно́в с Ири́ной за́няли свои́ места́ на трибу́не, и Ири́на посмотре́ла вокру́г. Ей показа́лось, что боле́льщиков «Дина́мо» пришло́ намно́го ...., чем боле́льщиков «Зени́та». 3. Оде́ты они́ бы́ли .... и крича́ли .... 4. «Кто же сего́дня бу́дет бе́гать .... всех и забьёт .... всех голо́в?, – ду́мала Ири́на. 5. Наконе́ц, футболи́сты вы́шли на по́ле, и игра́ начала́сь. Напада́ющий «Дина́мо» оказа́лся .... всех, и всё .... и .... продвига́лся к воро́там «Зени́та», но вдруг его́ толкну́ли, и он упа́л. 6. Боле́льщики обе́их кома́нд зашуме́ли .... 7. Судья́ до́лжен был реши́ть, кто кого́ толкну́л .... 8. К концу́ пе́рвого та́йма игроки́ ста́ли наруша́ть пра́вила всё ...., и судье́ пришло́сь удали́ть не́сколько игроко́в. 9. Во второ́м та́йме кома́нды игра́ли .... 10. Они́ .... наруша́ли пра́вила, и игра́ станови́лась всё .... и .... 11. «Как жаль, что в .... моме́нт прозвуча́л свисто́к, и игра́ зако́нчилась в ничью́ - поду́мала Ири́на. «В це́лом, бы́ло неплохо́. Сто́ит пойти́ на футбо́л ещё раз!» – реши́ла она́.

14 Pronouns

Level
1, 2,3 Pronouns are words that qualify or replace a noun. They divide into several groups depending
on their function in a sentence. See the indicated sections for information on each group:

- Personal pronouns (☞ 14.1) replace nouns and function as nouns.
- Reflexive pronouns (☞ 14.2) have a specific meaning of '-self' and point to the person who acts in a sentence.
- Possessive (☞ 14.4), demonstrative (☞ 14.5) and determinative (☞ 14.6) pronouns qualify nouns or pronouns in a sentence.
- Interrogative pronouns (☞ 14.7) are question words.
- Relative pronouns (☞ 14.8) are an essential element of a type of subordinate clause called 'relative'. Relative pronouns introduce a relative clause and can function as subject or object of a relative clause.
- Some indefinite (☞ 14.9) and negative (☞ 14.10) pronouns can replace nouns and function as nouns. Others qualify nouns or pronouns.
- Reciprocal pronouns (☞ 14.11) have the specific meaning of two persons acting together ('each other').

Level
1, 2 ## 14.1 Personal pronouns

The Russian personal pronouns include:

Person	Singular	Plural
1st	я (I)	мы (we)
2nd	ты (you, informal)	вы/Вы (you, formal or referring to a group)
3rd	он (he)	они (they)
	она (she)	
	оно (it)	

In a sentence, personal pronouns function as nouns. They decline (☞ 14.1.1) and reflect the case, gender and number of the noun they replace. For example:

Using nouns	Replacing the nouns by the appropriate pronouns
Друзья (nominative, plural) показали Марии (dative, singular, feminine) и Ивану (dative, singular, masculine) сад.	Они (the pronoun они reflects the plural number and the nominative case of the noun друзья) показали ей (the pronoun ей reflects the singular number, feminine gender and the dative case of the noun Марии) и ему (the pronoun ему reflects the singular number, masculine gender and the dative case of the noun Ивану) сад.
The friends showed **Maria** and **Ivan** the garden	**They** showed **her** and **him** the garden.

Russian has two pronouns *you*:

- The pronoun **ты** is informal and used to address children, members of the family or close friends.
- The pronoun **Вы** is used to address a person in formal situations. The pronoun and all its forms are written with the capital letter **В**.
- The same pronoun, **вы**, is used to address a group. In this case, the pronoun and all its forms are written with the small letter **в**.

14.1.1 Declension of personal pronouns

The personal pronouns follow their own pattern:

Case	I	you (*informal*)	he	she	it
N	я	ты	он	она́	оно́
A	меня́	тебя́	его́	её	его́
G	меня́	тебя́	его́	её	его́
D	мне	тебе́	ему́	ей	ему́
I	мной/ мно́ю	тобо́й/ тобо́ю	им	ей/е́ю	им
P	мне/обо мне́	тебе́	нём	ней	нём
	we	**you** (*formal or plural*)	**they**		
N	мы	Вы/вы	они́		
A	нас	Вас/вас	их		
G	нас	Вас/вас	их		
D	нам	Вам/вам	им		
I	на́ми	Ва́ми/ва́ми	и́ми		
P	нас	Вас/вас	них		

Comments on the table

- Forms of the instrumental case **мно́й/мно́ю**, **тобо́й/тобо́ю** and **ей/е́ю** are alternatives. The forms ending with -**ою** and the form **е́ю** are common in writing.
- If a pronoun begins with a vowel, the letter -**н**- is added to the pronoun after prepositions having one letter or syllable: с **ним** (with him), к **ней** (to her).
- No additional letters are added to pronouns beginning with a vowel after polysyllabic prepositions: благодаря́ **им** (thanks to them), навстре́чу **ей** (towards her).
- If the preposition **о** governs the pronoun **мне** in the prepositional case, two letters are added to the preposition (обо). This rule applies only to the pronoun **мне**.

Examples of the use of the personal pronouns in various cases:

For the concept of the six-case system and the meaning of the individual cases, ☞ 4–10.

Со мно́ю (instrumental) вот что происхо́дит, **Ко мне** (dative) мой ста́рый друг не хо́дит. (Евтуше́нко)	What is happening is happening to me, My old friend does not come to me.
Жди **меня́** (accusative), и **я** (nominative) верну́сь. (Си́монов)	Wait for me and I will be back.

Весе́нней но́чью ду́май **обо мне́** (prepositional). (Евтуше́нко)

Think of me during the spring night.

Для меня́ (genitive) нет **тебя́** (genitive) прекра́сней. (Анто́нов)

There is no one better than you for me.

14.2 Reflexive pronoun себя́ (self)

The reflexive pronoun **себя́** (self) can only refer to a noun or personal pronoun. It is equivalent to the English form *self* and can be used to emphasise that one does something oneself. **Себя́** declines like the personal pronoun ты (☞ 14.1.1), but does not have a nominative form: себя́ (accusative), себя́ (genitive), себе́ (dative), собо́й/собо́ю (instrumental, себе́ (prepositional).

Себя́ cannot reflect either the number or gender of the pronoun to which it refers.

Себя́ is common in popular speech and idioms:

Кот смо́трит **на себя́** в зе́ркало.	The cat looks at himself in the mirror.
Как ты **себя́** чу́вствуешь?	How do you feel today?
На дверя́х магази́на напи́сано: «**К себе́**» и́ли «**От себя́**».	On shop doors is written: 'Pull' and 'Push'.

Себя́ is often used with pronoun **сам** (self), which has a similar meaning: ☞ 14.6.1.

14.3 Possessive, demonstrative and determinative pronouns

In a sentence, possessive (☞ 14.4), demonstrative (☞ 14.5) and determinative (☞ 14.6) pronouns qualify a noun. They agree in case, gender and number with the noun they qualify.

14.4 Possessive pronouns

Possessive pronouns express the idea of ownership: Э́то **моя́ кварти́ра.** (This is my flat.) The Russian possessive pronouns include:

мой (m), моя́ (f), моё (n), мой (pl)	my	наш (m), на́ша (f), на́ше (n), на́ши (pl)	our
твой (m), твоя́ (f), твоё (n), твои́ (pl)	your (*informal*)	В/ваш (m), В/ва́ша (f), В/ва́ше (n), В/ва́ши (pl)	your (*formal or referring to a group*)
его́	his/its	их	their
её	her	свой (m), своя́ (f), своё (n), свой (pl)	one's own

Unlike the other possessive pronouns, **его** (his/its), **её** (her) and **их** (their) are indeclinable and therefore cannot agree in gender, number and case with the noun they qualify: Я ду́маю о **его́** сообще́нии и **его́** звонке́. (I am thinking of his e-mail and his call.)

14.4.1 Declension of the possessive pronouns

The pronouns **мой**, **твой** and **свой** have the following pattern:

Case	Singular		
	Masculine	**Feminine**	**Neuter**
N	мой/свой	моя́/своя́	моё/своё
A	as genitive, if describing an animate noun; as nominative, if describing an inanimate noun мо**его́**/сво**его́** (animate) мой/свой (inanimate)	мою́/свою́	моё/своё
G	мо**его́**/сво**его́**	мо**е́й**/сво**е́й**	мо**его́**/сво**его́**
D	мо**ему́**/сво**ему́**	мо**е́й**/сво**е́й**	мо**ему́**/сво**ему́**
I	мо**и́м**/сво**и́м**	мо**е́й**/сво**е́й**	мо**и́м**/сво**и́м**
P	мо**ём**/сво**ём**	мо**е́й**/сво**е́й**	мо**ём**/сво**ём**
	Plural		
N	мо**и́**		
A	as genitive, if describing an animate noun; as nominative, if describing an inanimate noun		
	мо**и́х** (animate) мо**и́** (inanimate)		
G	мо**и́х**		
D	мо**и́м**		
I	мо**и́ми**		
P	мо**и́х**		

The pronouns **наш** and **ваш** have the following pattern:

Case	Singular		
	Masculine	**Feminine**	**Neuter**
N	наш/ваш	на́ш**а**/ва́ш**а**	на́ш**е**/ва́ш**е**
A	as genitive, if describing an animate noun; as nominative, if describing an inanimate noun	на́ш**у**/ва́ш**у**	на́ш**е**/ва́ш**е**
	на́ш**его**/ва́ш**его** (animate) наш/ваш (inanimate)		
G	на́ш**его**/ва́ш**его**	на́ш**ей**/ва́ш**ей**	на́ш**его**/ва́ш**его**
D	на́ш**ему**/ва́ш**ему**	на́ш**ей**/ва́ш**ей**	на́ш**ему**/ва́ш**ему**
I	на́ш**им**/ва́ш**им**	на́ш**ей**/ва́ш**ей**	на́ш**им**/ва́ш**им**
P	на́ш**их**/ва́ш**их**	на́ш**ей**/ва́ш**ей**	на́ш**их**/ва́ш**их**

		Plural
N		на́ши/ва́ши
A		as genitive, if describing an animate noun; as nominative, if describing an inanimate noun
		на́ш**их** /ва́ш**их** (animate) на́ш**и**/ва́ш**и** (inanimate)
G		на́ш**их**/ва́ш**их**
D		на́ш**им**/ва́ш**им**
I		на́ш**ими**/ва́ш**ими**
P		на́ш**их**/ва́ш**их**

Level 2

14.4.2 Possessive pronoun свой (one's own)

The pronoun **свой** emphasises ownership. It does not have any meaning on its own and therefore is used to replace a possessive pronoun in a sentence with some limitations:

- **Свой** does not usually describe the subject of the sentence itself and therefore does not appear in the nominative case, except in some proverbs and idioms: **Своя́ руба́шка** бли́же к те́лу (посло́вица). (Everyone puts their own interest first; literally: One's own shirt is near to one's own body. Proverb.)
- **Свой** usually describes an object of the sentence that is related to the subject and is usually used in cases other than the nominative.
- **Свой** emphasises that the object and subject of the sentence are related.

14.4.2.1 Using свой

If the subject of the sentence is in the 1st person (я, ты), **свой** is used as an alternative to the possessive pronoun **мой** or **наш**. The use of an alternative does not change the meaning of the sentence:

Мы горди́мся **на́шими** успе́хами /Мы горди́мся **свои́ми** успе́хами.	We are proud of our success.

If the subject of the sentence is in the 2nd person (ты, вы), **свой** is the preferred form of possessive pronoun. The use of an alternative does not change the meaning of the sentence:

Ты е́здил в о́тпуск со **свои́ми** ро́дственниками?	Did you go on holiday with your relatives?

If the subject of the sentence is in the 3rd person (он, она́, они́ or any nouns that can be replaced by them), the pronouns **свой**, **его́**, **её**, **их** are used to express a different meaning:

- **Свой** emphasises that the object of the sentence is related to the subject.
- **Его́, её, их** emphasise that the object of the sentence is not related to the subject.

Compare:

Учёные пи́шут о результа́тах **свои́х опытов**. (The scientists write about the results of **their experiments**.)	Учёные пи́шут о результа́тах **их о́пытов**. (The scientists write about the results of **somebody else's experiments**.)
Господи́н Смирно́в влюблён **в свою́ подру́гу**. (Mr Smirnoff is in love with **his girlfriend**.)	Господи́н Смирно́в влюблён в **его́ подру́гу**. (Mr Smirnoff is in love with **somebody else's girlfriend**.)

Additionally, **свой** can function as an independent adjective when conveying the meaning of belonging to a group. For example:

Он – **свой па́рень**.	He is one of our lads.
Мы посмотре́ли фильм «**Свой** среди́ чужи́х, чужо́й среди́ **свои́х**».	We watched the film 'At Home among Strangers, a Stranger at Home'.
Всему́ **своё вре́мя**.	There is a right time for everything.

evel 2

14.5 Demonstrative pronouns

Demonstrative pronouns point out an object or person: **Э́тот** ноутбу́к мой, а **тот** –Ви́ктора. (This laptop is mine, but that one is Victor's.)

The Russian demonstrative pronouns include:

э́тот (m), э́та (f), э́то (n), э́ти (pl)	this	тот (m), та (f), то (n), те (pl)	that
э́то	this/that/it		
тако́й (m), така́я (f), тако́е (n), таки́е (pl)	such	тако́в (m), takoвá (f), таково́ (n), таковы́ (pl) (mainly used in idioms and in writing)	such

14.5.1 Pronouns э́то (this/that/it) and э́тот (this)

Russian has two pronouns **э́то** and **э́тот** that are translated into English with the same word '*this*'. However **Э́то** and **Э́тот** have different functions in a sentence and different grammatical categories.

The indeclinable pronoun **Э́то** is used as the subject of a sentence when indicating a person or object:

Э́то профе́ссор.	**This** is a professor.
Э́то о́зеро.	**This** is a lake.
Что э́то?	What's this/that?
Кто э́то?	Who is this/that?

Э́то can also appear as the subject of the whole phrase and can be translated into English as 'it'/'this'/'that':

Э́то про́сто замеча́тельно!	It/that is really great!

The declinable pronoun **э́тот** has gender, number and case and qualifies a subject or object of a sentence:

Э́тот фильм был снят в про́шлом году́.	This film was shot last year.	**Э́тот** qualifies the subject of the sentence **фильм**.
Бизнесме́н прочита́л **э́то** интере́сное сообще́ние.	The businessman read this interesting e-mail.	**Э́то** qualifies the object of the sentence **сообще́ние**.

🔊 The declinable neuter form of **э́тот** ('**э́то**') looks identical to the indeclinable pronoun **э́то**. The declinable '**э́то**' is often used as a noun; it functions as an object in a sentence and is usually translated as 'that':

Ты действи́тельно э́того хо́чешь?	Are you sure you want that?

14.5.2 Declension of the demonstrative pronouns

The pronouns **э́тот** and **тот** follow the following pattern:

Case	Singular		
	Masculine	Feminine	Neuter
N	э́тот/тот	э́та/та	э́то/то
A	as genitive, if describing an animate noun; as nominative, if describing an inanimate noun	э́ту/ту	э́то
	э́того/того́ (animate) э́тот/тот (inanimate)		
G	э́того/того́	э́той/той	э́того/того́
D	э́тому/тому́	э́той/той	э́тому/тому́
I	э́тим/тем	э́той/той	э́тим/тем
P	э́том/том	э́той/той	э́том/том
	Plural		
N	э́ти/те		
A	as genitive, if describing an animate noun; as nominative, if describing an inanimate noun		
	э́тих/тех (animate) э́ти/те (inanimate)		
G	э́тих/тех		
D	э́тим/тем		
I	э́тими/те́ми		
P	э́тих/тех		

The pronouns **тако́й** and **тако́в** decline as follows:

	Singular		
Case	Masculine	Feminine	Neuter
N	тако́й/тако́в	така́я/takова́	тако́е/таково́
A	as genitive, if describing an animate noun; as nominative, if describing an inanimate noun	таку́ю/takову́	тако́е/таково́
	тако́го/таково́го (animate) тако́й/таково́й (inanimate)		
G	тако́го/таково́го	тако́й/takову́	тако́го/таково́го
D	тако́му/таково́му	тако́й/таково́й	тако́му/таково́му
I	таки́м/таковы́м	тако́й/таково́й	таки́м/таковы́м

P	таком/таковом		такой/таковой	таком/таковом
	Plural			
N	такие/таковы́			
A	as genitive, if describing an animate noun; as nominative, if describing an inanimate noun			
	таки́х/таковы́х (animate) такие/таковы́ (inanimate)			
G	таки́х/таковы́х			
D	таки́м/таковы́м			
I	таки́ми/таковы́ми			
P	таки́х/таковы́х			

Examples using demonstrative pronouns with different cases:

Зри́тели не ожида́ли **тако́й развя́зки** (genitive) сюже́та.	The audience did not expect such an end to the plot.
Э́тот мир (singular, masculine, nominative) приду́ман не на́ми. (Дербенёв)	This world was not invented by us.
Археологи рабо́тали **на э́тих раско́пках** (plural prepositional) пе́рвый раз.	The archaeologists worked at this dig for the first time.
Тури́сты поста́вили пала́тки **на то́м берегу́** (singular, masculine, prepositional) реки́.	The tourists pitched their tents on the other side of the river.

14.6 Determinative pronouns

The determinative pronouns include:

- Emphatic pronouns: **сам, -а, -о, -и** (-self) and **са́мый, -ая, -ое, -ые** (the very)
- Pronouns that indicate the total number of objects: **весь, вся, всё, все** (all), **ка́ждый, -ая, -ое, -ые** (every), **вся́кий, -ая, -ое, -ие** (any), **любо́й, -ая, -ое, -ые** (any).

Determinative pronouns qualify a noun or pronoun. They decline, and agree in gender, number and case with the noun they qualify.

14.6.1 Declension of determinative pronouns

Са́мый, ка́ждый and **любо́й** decline like adjectives with a hard ending (☞ 11.1.1). **Вся́кий** declines like an adjective whose declension is affected by a spelling rule (☞ 11.1.3).

Сам declines as follows:

Case	Singular			
	Masculine		**Feminine**	**Neuter**
N	сам		сама́	само́
A	as genitive, if describing an animate noun; as nominative, if describing an inanimate noun		саму́ (самоё –old form)	само́
	самого́ (animate) сам (inanimate)			

G	самого́		само́й	самого́
D	самому́		само́й	самому́
I	сами́м		само́й	сами́м
P	само́м		само́й	само́м
	Plural			
N	са́ми			
A	as genitive, if describing an animate noun; as nominative, if describing an inanimate noun			
	сами́х (animate) са́ми (inanimate)			
G	сами́х			
D	сами́м			
I	сами́ми			
P	сами́х			

Весь declines as follows:

	Singular			
Case	**Masculine**		**Feminine**	**Neuter**
N	весь		вся	всё
A	as genitive, if describing an animate noun; as nominative, if describing an inanimate noun		всю	всё
	всего́ (animate) весь (inanimate)			
G	всего́		всей	всего́
D	всему́		всей	всему́
I	всем		всей	всем
P	всём		всей	всём
	Plural			
N	все			
A	as genitive, if describing an animate noun; as nominative, if describing an inanimate noun			
	всех (animate) все (inanimate)			
G	всех			
D	всем			
I	все́ми			
P	всех			

Comments on the table

- If the preposition **o** governs the pronoun **всём/всей/всех** in the prepositional case, two letters are added to the preposition (**обо**): обо всéх/обо всём.
- If a preposition consists of a single consonant or ends with a consonant, **-o** is added to the preposition before **весь** in all cases except the nominative: ко всéм, безо всéх.

Examples using determinative pronouns with different cases:

Кáждый охóтник (singular, masculine, nominative) желáет знать, где сидúт фазáн. (Дéтская считáлка)	Every hunter wishes to know where the pheasant is. (Nursery rhyme)
Передáча «Вы́жить **любóй ценóй** (singular, feminine, instrumental)» пóльзуется популя́рностью у телезрúтелей.	The programme 'Ultimate Survival' is popular among audiences.
Всегó дóброго/**Всег**ó хорóшего (masculine, singular, genitive)!	All the best!
Все лю́ди (nominative plural) стремя́тся к мúру **во всём** мúре.	All people strive to achieve peace in the whole world.

14.6.2 Using Сам and Сáмый

Сам is frequently used with the reflexive pronoun **себя́** to intensify reflexive meaning. Both pronouns agree in:

Пожилáя одинóкая жéнщина писáла пúсьма **самá себé** (dative).	The lonely old lady wrote letters to herself.
Нéкоторые лю́ди разговáривают **сáми с собóй** во снé (instrumental).	Some people talk to themselves in their sleep.
Сегóдня покáзывают прогрáмму «**Сам себé** режиссёр» (dative).	Today the programme 'You've been framed' is on.

Сáмый means *the very*:

Кремль нахóдится **в сáмом цéнтре** Москвы́.	The Kremlin is in the very centre of Moscow.

Additionally, **сáмый** is used to form:

- Compound superlatives of adjectives (☞ 12.4.1.1).
- The word *the same*

14.6.2.1 The Russian equivalent of *the same* has three parts, two declinable pronouns **тот** and **сáмый** and one indeclinable particle **же**: **тóт же сáмый** (the same).

	Singular		
Case	Masculine	Feminine	Neuter
N	тóт же сáмый	тá же сáмая	тó же сáмое
A	as genitive, if describing an animate noun; as nominative, if describing an inanimate noun	тý же сáмую	тó же сáмое
	тогó же сáмого (animate) тóт же сáмый (inanimate)		
G	тогó же сáмого	тóй же сáмой	тогó же сáмого

Case	Singular			
	Masculine		**Feminine**	**Neuter**
D	тому́ же са́мому		то́й же са́мой	тому́ же са́мому
I	тем же са́мым		то́й же са́мой	тем же са́мым
P	то́м же са́мом		то́й же са́мой	то́м же са́мом
	Plural			
N	те́ же са́мые			
A	as genitive, if describing an animate noun; as nominative, if describing an inanimate noun			
	тех же са́мых (animate) те́ же са́мые (inanimate)			
G	тех же са́мых			
D	тому́ же са́мому			
I	те́ми же са́мыми			
P	тех же са́мых			

Level 1, 2

14.7 Interrogative pronouns

The interrogative pronouns include these *declinable* question words:

кто (who)	како́й, -ая, -ое, -ие (what/what kind of)	ско́лько (how many/how much)
что (what)	кото́рый, -ая, -ое, -ие (which)	
	чей, чья, чьё, чьи (whose)	

- **Како́й, кото́рый** and **чей** have case, gender and number; **кто**, **что** and **ско́лько** have case only.
- **Кто** and **что** are question words about a noun. Their case corresponds to the case of the noun to which the question refers: **Кого́** (accusative) вы зна́ете? (Whom do you know?) **О чём** (prepositional) вы говори́те? (What are you talking about?) On agreement between кто, что and the predicate of the sentence ☞ 14.8.2.
- **Како́й, кото́рый** and **чей** agree in gender, number and case with the noun they qualify: **Како́го челове́ка** (singular, masculine, accusative) вы встре́тили? (Which person have you met?) **Чьих веще́й** (genitive plural) здесь нет? (Whose things are not here?)
- **Кото́рый** declines like an adjective with a hard ending (☞ 11.1.1).
- **Како́й** declines like an adjective affected by spelling rules (☞ 11.1.3).
- **Ско́лько** is used to ask about quantity and is always followed by a noun in the genitive plural: Ско́лько **звёзд** (genitive plural) на не́бе? (How many stars are there in the sky?) Ско́лько **студе́нтов** (genitive plural) в гру́ппе? (How many students are there in the group?) On using nouns with numbers, ☞ 15.3.1.

14.7.1 Declension of interrogative pronouns кто, что, ско́лько and чей

Кто, **что** and **ско́лько** decline as follows:

Case	кто	что	ско́лько
N	кто	что	ско́лько
A	кого́	что	as genitive, if describing an animate noun; as nominative, if describing an inanimate noun
			ско́льких (animate) ско́лько (inanimate)
G	кого́	чего́	ско́льких
D	кому́	чему́	ско́льким
I	кем	чем	ско́лькими
P	ком	чём	ско́льких

Чей declines as follows:

Case	Singular Masculine	Neuter	Feminine
N	чей	чьё	чья
A	as genitive, if describing an animate noun; as nominative, if describing an inanimate noun	чьё	чью
	чьего́ (animate) чей (inanimate)		
G	чьего́	чьего́	чьей
D	чьему́	чьему́	чьей
I	чьим	чьим	чей/чьёю
P	чьём	чьём	чьей
Plural			
N	чьи		
A	as genitive, if describing an animate noun; as nominative, if describing an inanimate noun		
	чьих (animate) чьи (inanimate)		
G	чьих		
D	чьим		
I	чьи́ми		
P	чьих		

Level
1, 2

Упражне́ния

1. Complete the sentences by putting the pronouns in brackets into the required form:

1. Да́йте .... (я), пожа́луйста, ча́шку ко́фе.
2. Мо́жно .... (Вы) помо́чь?
3. Приходи́те к .... (мы) в го́сти.
4. Де́ти разгова́ривают о .... (он).
5. Ко́ля рабо́тает с .... (ты)?
6. (Они́) .... сего́дня нет на уро́ке.

Level
1, 2

2. Put the phrases in brackets into the correct form:

1. Друг подари́л .... (моя́ сестра́) конфе́ты.
2. К .... (наш сосе́д) приходи́ли го́сти.
3. Переда́йте, пожа́луйста, ... (Ваш брат) серде́чный приве́т.
4. На .... (их у́лица) мно́го зе́лени.
5. Не меша́йте .... (э́тот челове́к).
6. Да́йте мне .... (э́та откры́тка) и .... (тот слова́рь).
7. Писа́тель опи́сывает сюже́т .... (таки́е ве́рные слова́).

Level
2

3. Choose the appropriate possessive pronoun and make sure it and the noun it qualifies are in the appropriate form:

1. Челове́к крича́л не .... (его́/свой го́лос).
2. Им на́до зако́нчить .... (их/своя́ рабо́та).
3. В .... (моя́/своя́ ко́мната) о́чень ую́тно.
4. В .... (его́/свой стихи́) поэ́т опи́сывает приро́ду.
5. Ви́ктор сказа́л, что .... (его́/своя́ жена́) о́чень лю́бит .... (её/своя́ рабо́та).

Level
2, 3

14.8 Relative pronouns

The interrogative pronouns (☞ 14.7) **кто** (who), **что** (what), **кото́рый** (which), **како́й** (what/ what kind of) and **чей** (whose) can function as relative pronouns in a complex sentence. Complex sentences usually have one main clause and one or more subordinate clauses. The main clause contains the complete idea. Subordinate clauses clarify or expand on information provided in the main clause and cannot exist independently. Relative pronouns are an essential element of one particular type of subordinate clause, the relative clause.

14.8.1 Using the relative pronoun кото́рый

Кото́рый is used in relative clauses and can clarify **any noun** in the main clause. Like an adjective, a relative clause responds to the questions **како́й** (what? what kind of?). For example:

Како́й фильм ты бу́дешь смотре́ть?	**What** film you are going to watch?
Я бу́ду смотре́ть фильм, **кото́рый вы́играл «О́скара» в э́том году́.**	I will watch a film **which won the Oscar this year.**

English relative clauses can be introduced by the relative pronouns **which, that** or **who/whom**. The Russian equivalent of these three English pronouns is the relative pronoun **кото́рый**. Unlike in English, **кото́рый** cannot be omitted from the sentence. For example:

Я зна́ю студе́нта, **кото́рый** у́чится в Москве́.	I know a student **who** is studying at Moscow.
Я жду́ с нетерпе́нием встре́чи с дру́гом, **кото́рого** я не ви́дел мно́го лет.	I am looking forward to seeing a friend **whom** I have not seen for many years.
Мы купи́ли кни́гу, **о кото́рой** все говоря́т.	We bought the book about **which** everybody is talking.
Счета́, **кото́рые** откры́л клие́нт, бу́дут заморо́жены.	The accounts that a client has opened will be frozen.

| Моро́женое, **кото́рое** я купи́л на вокза́ле, оказа́лось невку́сным. | The ice-cream I bought at the station did not taste good. |

👁 The gender and number of **кото́рый** corresponds to the gender and number of the noun that **кото́рый** clarifies in the main clause. However, the case of **кото́рый** reflects its grammatical role in the relative clause. **Кото́рый** can be:

- The subject of the relative clause in the nominative case
- A direct object in the accusative case
- An indirect object with various prepositions in the dative, instrumental or genitive cases.

Therefore, the case of **кото́рый** often differs from the case of the noun that it clarifies. For example:

| Студе́нты встре́тились с молоды́м худо́жником, **кото́рый** получи́л гла́вный приз на ко́нкурсе. | The students met the artist **who** had received first prize in the competition. |

In this example **кото́рый** clarifies the masculine singular noun **с худо́жником**. Therefore, **кото́рый** is used in the masculine singular. In the relative clause, **кото́рый** is the subject of the sentence. Therefore **кото́рый** is used in the nominative case.

| Мы подняли́сь на колоко́льню, **о кото́рой** прочита́ли в путеводи́теле. | We went up the bell-tower about which we had read in the guide-book. |

In this example, о кото́рой clarifies the feminine singular noun **на колоко́льню**. Therefore, it is used in the feminine singular. In the relative clause **о кото́рой** is the indirect object of the sentence governed by the preposition *about* that takes the prepositional case. Therefore, **кото́рый** is used in the prepositional case.

14.8.2 Using the pronouns кто (who) and что (that/which)

Кто and **что** are used in relative clauses to clarify **any pronoun** in the main clause. Most frequently **кто** and **что** refer to the determinative pronouns **весь, ка́ждый, любо́й** and the demonstrative pronoun **тот** (👁 14.5–14.6).

Кто is equivalent to the English **who. Что** is equivalent to the English **that** or **which.** Unlike in English, **кто** and **что** cannot be omitted from the sentence. For example:

| И **тот, кто** с пе́сней по жи́зни шага́ет, Тот никогда́ и нигде́ не пропадёт. (Ле́бедев-Кума́ч) На тра́урном ми́тинге вспомина́ли **всех тех, кто** поги́б во вре́мя тера́кта. Бы́ло на́звано и́мя **ка́ждого, кто** потеря́л свою́ жизнь. | And he who marches through life with song, He will never ever lose. At the remembrance meeting, they remembered those who died in the terrorist attack. The names of every one of those who lost their lives were read out. |
| Попроси́те **любо́го, кто** войдёт в ко́мнату, закры́ть окно́. **Всё** хорошо́, **что** хорошо́ конча́ется. | Ask anyone who enters the room to close the window. All's well that ends well. |

👁 **Кто** and **что** decline, but do not have gender or number. The case of **кто** and **что** reflects their grammatical role in the subordinate clause. For example:

Он забы́л всё, **о чём** ему́ рассказа́ли.	He has forgotten everything he was told.
Произошло́ то, **к чему́** все давно́ гото́вились.	Something that everybody has been preparing for has happened.
Все удиви́лись тому́, **что** он сказа́л.	Everybody was surprised at what he said.

Я не знал всех, **кто** пришёл на вечери́нку.   I didn't know everyone who came to the party.

In the first example, **о чём** is the indirect object of the relative clause and is governed by the preposition *about* that takes the prepositional case.

In the second example, **к чему́** is the indirect object of the relative clause and is used with a verb that requires the dative case (**гото́виться к**).

In the third example, **что** is the direct object of the relative clause and is used in the accusative case with no preposition.

In the last example, **кто** is the subject of the relative clause and is used in the nominative case.

👁 If **кто** or **что** are the subject of the main or relative clause, they require the verb in a certain form:

- **кто** usually agrees with the verb in the 3rd person singular in the present and future tenses and in the masculine singular in the past tense. However, **кто** can agree with a verb in the plural. This can occur if **кто** is the subject of a verbal phrase that consists of a verbal link and the noun in the plural form:

  Те, кто де́сять лет наза́д **бы́ли студе́нтами** (predicate   Those who were students
  consisting of verbal link 'to be' and noun in the   at our university ten years ago
  plural) на́шего университе́та, сейча́с занима́ют   now hold important posts
  высо́кие посты́ в прави́тельстве.   in the government.

- **что** always requires the verb in the 3rd person singular in the present and future tenses and in the neuter singular in the past tense:

  Никто́ не ожида́л того́, **что случи́лось**.   No one expected what happened.

14.8.3 Using Чей (whose) and Како́й (what kind of)

Чей clarifies a noun in a sentence. **Чей** (whose) can be replaced by the appropriate form of **кото́рый**.

Я ли́чно зна́ю худо́жника, **чьи рабо́ты/**   I personally know the artist whose
рабо́ты кото́рого продаю́тся на аукцио́не.   works are being sold at the auction.

Како́й is mainly used with the demonstrative pronoun **тако́й**:

А я **тако́й, како́й** я есть,   I am who I am,
Как ди́кий куст колю́чий. (Марко́вцев)   I am like a wild thorn bush.
Тури́сты посети́ли вы́ставку   The tourists visited an exhibition entitled
«Крым **тако́й, како́й** он есть».   'Crimea as it is now'.

14.9 Indefinite pronouns

Level 2, 3

Indefinite pronouns are used when speaking about unknown or unspecified persons, objects, places, time etc. Russian indefinite pronouns are equivalent to the English pronouns with the prefixes *some-* or *any-*:

Кто́-то игра́ет на гита́ре.   **Someone** is playing the guitar.
Я ду́маю, что с ним **что́-то** случи́лось.   I think **something** has happened to him.
Заходи́ **ка́к-нибудь**!   Come and see me **some time**!

Indefinite pronouns are formed by adding the indeclinable particles -**то**, -**нибудь**, -**либо** or **кое**- (some/any) to the declinable interrogative pronouns **кто**, **что**, **како́й** and **чей** (☞ 14.7). The indefinite pronouns therefore have a declinable root that follows the pattern of the interrogative pronouns, and an indeclinable suffix. On the declension of **кто, что** and **чей**, ☞ 14.7.1. **Како́й** declines like an adjective affected by spelling rule 2 (☞ 1.3.2, 11.1.3.1).

The indefinite pronouns include:

кто́-то, кто́-нибудь, кто́-либо (someone/ anyone)	како́й-то, како́й-нибудь, како́й-либо (some sort of)	кое-кто́ (some), кое-что́ (a few), кое-како́й (some/one or two)
что́-то, что́-нибудь, что́-либо (something/ anything)	чей-то, чей-нибудь, чей-либо (someone's)	

Pronouns formed with the particles **-то** and **-нибудь** are common in written and spoken language. The pronouns formed with the particle **-либо** have the same meaning as those with the particle **-нибудь**; they are mainly used in writing. The pronouns formed with the particles **кое-** are the least common.

For the indefinite adverbs (somehow, somewhere etc.), ☞ 13.2.7.

👁 14.9.1 Using indefinite pronouns

14.9.1.1 The particle **-то** indicates that the speaker is referring to persons, objects, places, time unknown to them, whilst the speaker's audience could have more information on the matter. Indefinite pronouns with **-то** appear most frequently in affirmative statements with the past tense and present tense verbs indicating an action in progress:

Кто́-то оста́вил на столе́ паке́т.	**Somebody** has left a package on the table.
Кто́-то звони́т в дверь. Откро́й!	**Somebody** is ringing the doorbell. Open the door!
В ко́мнате **что́-то** упа́ло.	**Something** in the room has fallen down.

14.9.1.2 The particles **-нибудь** or **-либо** indicate that the speaker and their audience are unfamiliar with the persons, objects, places, time to which the speaker is referring. Indefinite pronouns with the particles **-нибудь** or **-либо** appear most frequently in questions, imperative sentences, sentences with future tense verbs or present tense verbs indicating habitual action. For example:

Кто́-нибудь зна́ет, где живёт Та́ня?	Does anyone know where Tanya lives?
Ты пригото́вил **что́-нибудь** на у́жин?	Have you made anything for dinner?
Кто́-нибу́дь, помоги́те, челове́ку пло́хо.	Someone, please help. The person is unwell.
Я куплю́ **како́й-нибудь** сок на за́втрак.	I will buy some sort of juice for breakfast.
Мы пода́рим ребёнку **каку́ю-нибудь** игру́шку.	We will give the child some sort of toy.
Там всегда́ **кто́-нибудь** поёт.	There is always someone singing there.
Бу́дут ли проводи́ться **каки́е-либо** экспериме́нты в лаборато́рии?	Will some experiments be carried out in the laboratory?
Пацие́нт бу́дет осмо́трен **кем-либо** из хиру́ргов.	The patient will be examined by one of the surgeons.

14.9.1.3 The particle **кое-** indicates that the speaker knows the persons, objects, places, time about which they are talking. However, they prefer not to reveal this information to their audience:

| Мне на́до **кое-что́** тебе́ сказа́ть. | I need to tell you something. |
| У нас всегда́ остана́вливается **кое-кто́** из ро́дственников. | We always have some relatives staying with us. |

Pronouns with the particle **кое-** may have negative connotations, depending on the context:

Кое-кто́ кое-где́ не хо́чет жить че́стно.	There are some people, somewhere, who do not want to live by honest means.

14.9.2 Declension of indefinite pronouns

Indefinite pronouns consist of one declinable and one indeclinable element:

- The declinable elements **кто**, **что**, **како́й**, **чей** decline like interrogative pronouns (☞ 14.7): кого́-то, кому́-то, чём-нибудь, чего́-нибудь.
- **Како́й** and **чей** also have gender and number: како́го-нибудь, каку́ю-нибудь, каки́х-либо, чью́-то, чьи́х-то.
- The particles -**то**, -**нибудь**, -**либо** and **кое-** form the indeclinable element of the pronoun.
- Prepositions that govern pronouns with particles -**то**, -**нибудь** and -**либо** precede the pronoun: с ке́м-нибудь, о чём-то, без чего́-то, у како́го-либо.
- Prepositions that govern pronouns with the particle **кое-** are placed between particle and pronoun: кое у кого́, кое о чём, кое с каки́м.

14.9.3 Other indefinite pronouns

Additionally, the following small number of indefinite pronouns is mainly used in writing: не́кто (certain), не́что (something), не́кий, -ая, -ое, -ие (certain), не́который, -ая, -ое, -ие (some) and не́сколько (several).

- **Не́кто** (certain) and **не́что** (something) exist only in the nominative and accusative cases:

Позвони́л не́кто господи́н Смит.	A certain Mr Smith called.
Они́ уви́дели не́что ужа́сное.	They saw something horrible.

- **Не́кий**, -ая, -ое, -ие (certain) and **не́который**, -ая, -ое, -ие (some) decline, have gender and number and function like adjectives:

Не́которые лю́ди предпочита́ют де́лать поку́пки в интерне́т-магази́не.	Some people prefer to do their shopping through the Internet.

- **Не́сколько** (several) is used as a number that indicates indefinite quantity: ☞ 15.10.

<table><tr><td>Level 2, 3</td></tr></table>

◉ 14.10 Negative pronouns

Russian has two types of negative pronouns:

- One type is formed by adding the negative particle **ни-** to the interrogative (☞ 14.10.1)
- The other type is formed by adding the negative particle **не-** to the interrogative (☞ 14.10.2).

All negative pronouns decline and follow the pattern of the interrogative pronouns (☞ 14.7). Pronouns that are based on **како́й** and **чей** also have gender and number. Prepositions that govern negative pronouns are placed between particle and pronoun: ни у кого́, ни о чём, ни с ке́м, не́ о ком, не́ у кого, не́ с чем.

◉ The two types of negative pronoun convey different meanings and are used in different types of sentences. Note that Russian sentences can have an unlimited number of negatives.

14.10.1 Negative pronouns with the particle ни-

The negative pronouns **никто́**, **ничто́**, **никако́й**, **ниче́й** are used in negative constructions that usually have a subject and verb. The negative form of the verb conveys the idea of absence of action itself or a negative result of the action. Negative pronouns intensify the negativity that negative form of the verb expresses. The verb is used with the negative particle **не-** and negative pronouns with negative particle **ни-**:

Сосе́ди **ничего́ не** слы́шали.	The neighbours heard nothing/did not hear anything.

Свиде́тели **ничего́** не сказа́ли.   The witnesses said nothing/did not say anything.

Он **ни с ке́м не обща́лся**.   He did not communicate with anyone./He communicated with no one.

The negative pronouns have the following patterns

The accusative case coincides with the genitive case. Note that a preposition is placed between two elements of the pronoun.

N	никто́	ничто́
A	as genitive никого́/ни на кого́	as genitive ничего́/ни на что́
G	никого́/ни у кого́	ничего́/ни у чего́
D	никому́/ни к кому́	ничему́/ни к чему́
I	нике́м/ни с ке́м	ниче́м/ни с че́м
P	ни о ко́м	ни о чём

Case	Singular		
	Masculine	**Feminine**	**Neuter**
N	никако́й/ниче́й	никака́я/ничья́	никако́е/ничьё
A	as genitive никако́го/ничьего́	as genitive никако́й/ничье́й	as genitive никако́го/ничьего́
G	никако́го/ничьего́	никако́й/ничье́й	никако́го/ничьего́
D	никако́му/ничьему́	никако́й/ничье́й	никако́му/ничьему́
I	никаки́м/ничьи́м	никако́й/ничье́й	никаки́м/ничьи́м
P	ни о како́м/ни о чьём	ни о како́й/ни о чье́й	ни о како́м/ни о чьём
	Plural		
N	никаки́е/ничьи́		
A	as genitive никаки́х/ничьи́х		
G	никаки́х/ничьи́х		
D	никаки́м/ничьи́м		
I	никаки́ми/ничьи́ми		
P	ни о каки́х/ни о чьи́х		

14.10.2 Negative pronouns with the particle не́

The negative pronouns **не́кого**, **не́чего** are used only in impersonal sentences that do not have a subject (☞ 30.3). The verb in sentences with **не́кого**, **не́чего** is always used in the affirmative form of the infinitive with the person in the dative case. The negative pronouns **не́кого**, **не́чего** explain why the intended action cannot be carried out:

Reason why an action cannot be carried out	Russian sentence	English equivalent
Lack of object of the action	О́ле **не́** с кем обща́ться.	Olia **has no one** to talk to.
	Нам **не́**чего вспо́мнить.	They **have nothing** to remember.
	Пенсионе́ру **не́**чего де́лать.	A retired person **has nothing** to do.

For declension of negative pronouns with the particle **не**, ☞ 30.3.2; for using negative pronouns with the particles **не** and **ни**, ☞ 30.3.3.

14.11 Reciprocal pronoun друг дру́га (each other)

The first part of the pronoun **друг дру́га** is indeclinable. The second declines like a noun **друг** (friend). Any prepositions added to **друг дру́га** are placed between the two parts of the pronoun:

N	друг дру́га
A	as genitive друг дру́га
G	друг (у) дру́га
D	друг (к) дру́гу
I	друг (с) дру́гом
P	друг (о) дру́ге

Level 2, 3

Упражне́ния

1. Fill the gaps with the relative pronoun **кото́рый** in the correct form (the first eight lines are part of a poem):

1. Вот дом, (a) .... постро́ил Джек.
А э́то пшени́ца, (b) .... в тёмном чула́не храни́тся
В до́ме, (c) .... постро́ил Джек.
Вот пёс без хвоста́, (d) .... за ши́ворот тре́плет кота́,
(e) .... пуга́ет и ло́вит сини́цу,
(f) .... ча́сто вору́ет пшени́цу,
(g) .... в тёмном чула́не храни́тся
В до́ме, (h) .... постро́ил Джек.
(Марша́к)

2. Мы ходи́ли в клуб о .... писа́ли газе́ты.
3. Они́ смея́лись над шу́ткой, ... рассказа́л Ви́ктор.

4. Я уви́дел челове́ка, лицо́ .... показа́лось мне знако́мым.

5. Студе́нты слу́шали ле́кцию учёного, у .... бы́ло мно́го публика́ций.

Level 2, 3

Обобща́ющее упражне́ние

2. Complete the text by putting the pronouns in brackets into the required form:

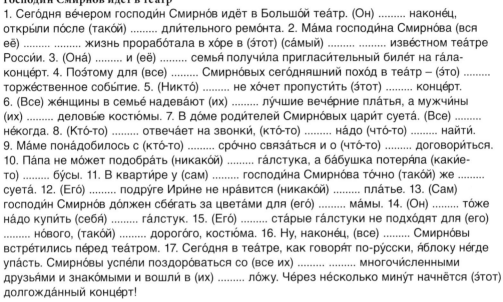

Господи́н Смирно́в идёт в теа́тр

1. Сего́дня ве́чером господи́н Смирно́в идёт в Большо́й теа́тр. (Он) .... наконе́ц, откры́ли по́сле (тако́й) .... дли́тельного ремо́нта. 2. Ма́ма господи́на Смирно́ва (вся её) .... жизнь прорабо́тала в хо́ре в (э́тот) (са́мый) .... изве́стном теа́тре Росси́и. 3. (Она́) .... и (её) .... семья́ получи́ла пригласи́тельный биле́т на га́ла-конце́рт. 4. Поэ́тому для (все) .... Смирно́вых сего́дняшний похо́д в теа́тр – (э́то) .... торже́ственное собы́тие. 5. (Никто́) .... не хо́чет пропусти́ть (э́тот) .... конце́рт. 6. (Все) же́нщины в семье́ надева́ют (их) .... лу́чшие вече́рние пла́тья, а мужчи́ны (их) .... деловы́е костю́мы. 7. В до́ме роди́телей Смирно́вых цари́т суета́. (Все) .... не́когда. 8. (Кто́-то) .... отвеча́ет на звонки́, (кто́-то) .... на́до (что́-то) .... найти́. 9. Ма́ме понадо́билось с (кто́-то) .... сро́чно связа́ться и о (что́-то) .... договори́ться. 10. Па́па не мо́жет подобра́ть (никако́й) .... га́лстука, а ба́бушка потеря́ла (каки́е-то) .... бу́сы. 11. В кварти́ре у (сам) .... господи́на Смирно́ва то́чно (тако́й) же .... суета́. 12. (Его́) .... подру́ге Ири́не не нра́вится (никако́й) .... пла́тье. 13. (Сам) господи́н Смирно́в до́лжен сбе́гать за цвета́ми для (его́) .... ма́мы. 14. (Он) .... то́же на́до купи́ть (себя́) .... га́лстук. 15. (Его́) .... ста́рые га́лстуки не подхо́дят для (его́) .... но́вого, (тако́й) .... дорого́го, костю́ма. 16. Ну, наконе́ц, (все) .... Смирно́вы встре́тились пе́ред теа́тром. 17. Сего́дня в теа́тре, как говоря́т по-ру́сски, я́блоку не́где упа́сть. Смирно́вы успе́ли поздоро́ваться со (все их) .... многочи́сленными друзья́ми и знако́мыми и вошли́ в (их) .... ло́жу. Че́рез не́сколько мину́т начнётся (э́тот) долгожда́нный конце́рт!

15 Numbers

Level
1, 2, 3
Numbers are divided into three groups:

- Cardinal numbers indicate quantity (☞ 15.1): оди́н (one), де́сять (ten).
- Ordinal numbers indicate the order of objects in a set (☞15.2): пе́рвый (first), второ́й (second).
- Collective numbers indicate the number of objects in a group (☞15.9): дво́е (group of two), тро́е (group of three).

There are several words that describe indefinite quantity (☞ 15.10): мно́го книг (many books), ма́ло журна́лов (few magazines). Additionally some nouns and adverbs are often used to express quantity (☞ 15.12).

Level
1, 2
15.1 Cardinal numbers

Cardinal numbers in figures and words:

0 ноль (нуль)	20 два́дцать
1 оди́н (m), одна́ (f), одно́ (n)	30 три́дцать
2 два (m, n), две (f)	40 со́рок
3 три	50 пятьдеся́т
4 четы́ре	60 шестьдеся́т
5 пять	70 се́мьдесят
6 шесть	80 во́семьдесят
7 семь	90 девяно́сто
8 во́семь	100 сто
9 де́вять	200 две́сти
10 де́сять	300 три́ста
11 оди́ннадцать	400 четы́реста
12 двена́дцать	500 пятьсо́т
13 трина́дцать	600 шестьсо́т
14 четы́рнадцать	700 семьсо́т
15 пятна́дцать	800 восемьсо́т

16 шестна́дцать	900 девятьсо́т
17 семна́дцать	1 000 ты́сяча
18 восемна́дцать	1 000 000 миллио́н
19 девятна́дцать	1 000 000 000 миллиа́рд
	1 000 000 000 000 триллио́н

15.1.1 Cardinal number structure

- Numbers between оди́н (1) and де́сять (10), со́рок (40) and сто (100) consist of one root or element.
- The numbers ты́сяча (1 000), миллио́н (1 000 000), миллиа́рд (1 000 000 000), триллио́н (1 000 000 000 000) are nouns that are used as cardinal numbers.
- All numbers other than 1–10, 40, 100, 1 000, 1 000 000 and 1 000 000 000 are formed by using two roots (elements). For example, оди́ннадцать has roots **оди́н-** and **-надцать**; пятьсо́т has roots **пять-** and **сот**.
- Compound numbers are formed from the appropriate one-word numbers. For example, восемьсо́т со́рок семь (847), ты́сяча пятна́дцать (1 015).
- If a compound number includes one of the nouns **ты́сяча** (1 000), **миллио́н** (1 000 000), **миллиа́рд** (1 000 000 000) and is higher than ты́сяча девятьсо́т девяно́сто де́вять (1 999), it follows the rule described in section 15.3.1.1.

15.1.2 Main characteristics of cardinal numbers

Level 1, 2

Cardinal numbers have the following characteristics:

- All cardinal numbers decline (☞ 15.1.3).
- Number 'one' has three genders: **оди́н** (masculine), **одна́** (feminine), **одно́** (neuter) and agrees in gender with the noun it qualifies:
  оди́н рубль (one rouble) – masculine
  одна́ кни́га (one book) – feminine
  одно́ упражне́ние (one exercise) – neuter
- Also, 'one' has singular and plural forms. The plural form **одни́** is used to count nouns that have plural form only (☞ 3.5):
  одни́ вы́боры one election/s одни́ джи́нсы one pair of jeans
- Additionally, the plural **одни́** and singular **оди́н/одна́** can have the special meaning 'alone, on their own'. The plural **одни́** can also function as the equivalent of the English word *some*:
  Мы сиде́ли **одни́**. We were sitting **alone**.
  Он пришёл **оди́н**. He came **on his own**.
  Одни́ говоря́т, что ... Some say that ...
- Number 'two' has three genders that are expressed by two forms: **два** indicates masculine and neuter, **две** indicates feminine:
  два стола́/окна́ two tables/windows **две** ко́мнаты two rooms
- Numbers other than 'one' and 'two' do not have gender or number

For the forms of nouns that follow cardinal numbers, ☞ 15.3.

15.1.3 Declension of cardinal numbers

Level 2, 3

The declension of cardinal numbers is shown in Summary Tables 15.I–15.VII.

Summary Table 15.I: declension of number 'one'

Number 'one' declines like the pronoun э́тот/э́та/э́то/э́ти (this, that) (☞ 14.5.2):

Case	Singular		
	Masculine	**Neuter**	**Feminine**
N	no ending оди́н	**-о** одно́	**-а** одна́
A	as genitive, if describing an animate noun; as nominative, if describing an inanimate noun	as nominative	**-у**
	одного́ (animate) оди́н (inanimate)	одно́	одну́
G	**-ого** одного́	**-ого** одного́	**-ой** одно́й
D	**-ому** одному́	**-ому** одному́	**-ой** одно́й
I	**-им** одни́м	**-им** одни́м	**-ой** одно́й
P	**-ом** одно́м	**-ом** одно́м	**-ой** одно́й
	Plural (all genders)		
N	**-и** одни́		
A	as genitive, if describing an animate noun; as nominative, if describing an inanimate noun		
	одни́х (animate) одни́ (inanimate)		
G	**-их** одни́х		
D	**-им** одни́м		
I	**-ими** одни́ми		
P	**-их** одни́х		

Summary Table 15.II: declension of numbers 'two', 'three' and 'four'

Case	Numbers 2, 3 and 4			
	два (masculine and neuter)	две (feminine)	три	четы́ре
N	два	две	три	четы́ре
A	as genitive, if describing an animate noun; as nominative, if describing an inanimate noun			
	двух (animate) два (inanimate)		трёх (animate) три (inanimate)	четырёх (animate) четы́ре (inanimate)
G	двух	двух	трёх	четырёх
D	двум	двум	трём	четырём
I	двумя́	двумя́	тремя́	четырьмя́
P	двух	двух	трёх	четырёх

Summary Table 15.III: declension of numbers 5–20 and 30

The numbers 5–20 and 30 follow a pattern similar to feminine singular nouns ending with -ь (☞ 4.2.3):

Case	Numbers 5–20 and 30		
N	пять	оди́ннадцать	три́дцать
A	пять	оди́ннадцать	три́дцать
G	пяти́	оди́ннадцати	тридцати́
D	пяти́	оди́ннадцати	тридцати́
I	пятью́	оди́ннадцатью	тридцатью́
P	пяти́	оди́ннадцати	тридцати́

Summary Table 15.IV: declension of numbers 40, 90 and 100

Case	Numbers 40, 90 and 100		
N	со́рок	девяно́сто	сто
A	со́рок	девяно́сто	сто
G	сорока́	девяно́ста	ста
D	сорока́	девяно́ста	ста
I	сорока́	девяно́ста	ста
P	сорока́	девяно́ста	ста

Summary Tables 15.V and 15.VI: declension of numbers 50–80 and 200–900

Numbers 50–80 and 200–900 consist of two roots (elements) like other cardinal numbers (☞ introduction to this chapter). However, in these numbers **both roots** decline.

- Start roots with a number between 5 and 8 follow the pattern described in Summary Table 15.III.
- Start roots with a number between 2 and 4 follow the pattern described in Summary Table 15.II.
- End roots with the number 100 follow the modified pattern described in Summary Table 15.IV. An end root with number 10 declines like a feminine noun ending in -ь (☞ 4.2.3).

Summary Table 15.V: declension of numbers 50–80

Case	Numbers 50–80	
N	пятьдеся́т	во́семьдесят
A	пятьдеся́т	во́семьдесят
G	пяти́десяти	восьми́десяти
D	пяти́десяти	восьми́десяти
I	пятью́десятью	восемью́десятью or восьмью́десятью
P	пяти́десяти	восьми́десяти

Summary Table 15.VI: declension of numbers 200–900

Case	Numbers 200–900			
N	две́сти	три́ста	четы́реста	семьсо́т
A	две́сти	три́ста	четы́реста	семьсо́т
G	двухсо́т	трёхсо́т	четырёхсо́т	семисо́т
D	двумста́м	трёмста́м	четырёмста́м	семиста́м
I	двумяста́ми	тремяста́ми	четырьмяста́ми	семьюста́ми
P	двухста́х	трёхста́х	четырёхста́х	семиста́х

Summary Table 15.VII: declension of numbers тысяча (1 000), миллион (1 000 000), миллиард (1 000 000 000), триллион (1 000 000 000 000)

The words **тысяча, миллион** and **миллиард** are nouns and follow regular noun patterns.
тысяча follows the pattern of feminine nouns with hard endings affected by a spelling rule
(☞ 4.2.2).
Миллион, миллиард, триллион follow the pattern of masculine nouns with hard endings
(☞ 4.2.1):

Case	Numbers 1 000, 1 000 000 and 1 000 000 000			
	Singular		**Plural**	
N	тысяча	миллион	тысячи	миллионы
A	тысячу	миллион	тысячи	миллионы
G	тысячи	миллиона	тысяч	миллионов
D	тысяче	миллиону	тысячам	миллионам
I	тысячей	миллионом	тысячами	миллионами
P	тысяче	миллионе	тысячах	миллионах

15.2 Ordinal numbers

Level 2, 3

Ordinal numbers describe the position of an object in a set. In a sentence, they function in the same way as long-form adjectives. They decline in the same way as adjectives and have gender and number (☞ 11). They agree with the noun they qualify, in gender, number and case.

15.2.1 List of ordinal numbers in figures and words

1st первый/первая/первое	11th одиннадцатый/-ая/-ое
2nd второй/вторая/второе	12th двенадцатый/-ая/-ое
3rd третий/третья/третье	13th тринадцатый/-ая/-ое
4th четвёртый/четвёртая/четвёртое	14th четырнадцатый/-ая/-ое
5th пятый/пятая/пятое	15th пятнадцатый/-ая/-ое
6th шестой/шестая/шестое	16th шестнадцатый/-ая/-ое
7th седьмой/седьмая/седьмое	17th семнадцатый/-ая/-ое
8th восьмой/восьмая/восьмое	18th восемнадцатый/-ая/-ое
9th девятый/девятая/девятое	19th девятнадцатый/-ая/-ое
10th десятый/десятая/десятое	20th двадцатый/-ая/-ое

Compound numbers

21st двадцать первый	50th пятидесятый
22nd двадцать второй	60th шестидесятый
...	70th семидесятый
30th тридцатый	80th восьмидесятый
31st тридцать первый	90th девяностый
...	100th сотый
40th сороковой	200th двухсотый
42nd сорок второй	300th трёхсотый
43rd сорок третий	400th четырёхсотый
...	500th пятисотый
	600th шестисотый

	700th семисо́тый 800th восьмисо́тый 900th девятисо́тый 1000th ты́сячный 2000th двухты́сячный 3000th трёхты́сячный 10 000th десятиты́сячный 100 000th стоты́сячный 1 000 000th миллио́нный 1 000 000 000th миллиа́рдный

15.2.2 Declension of ordinal numbers

All ordinal numbers, except **тре́тий** (3rd), decline like adjectives with hard endings that are not affected by spelling rules (☞ 11.1.1). **тре́тий** (3rd) declines like an adjective with a soft ending that is not affected by spelling rules (☞ 11.1.2).

Summary Table 15.VIII: declension of ordinal numbers with hard endings

Case	Singular Masculine	Neuter	Feminine
N	пе́рв**ый**	пе́рв**ое**	пе́рв**ая**
A	as genitive, if describing an animate noun; as nominative, if describing an inanimate noun пе́рв**ого** (animate) пе́рв**ый** (inanimate)	пе́рв**ое**	пе́рв**ую**
G	пе́рв**ого**	пе́рв**ого**	пе́рв**ой**
D	пе́рв**ому**	пе́рв**ому**	пе́рв**ой**
I	пе́рв**ым**	пе́рв**ым**	пе́рв**ой**
P	пе́рв**ом**	пе́рв**ом**	пе́рв**ой**
	Plural (all genders)		
N	пе́рв**ые**		
A	as genitive, if describing an animate noun; as nominative, if describing an inanimate noun		
	пе́рв**ых** (animate) пе́рв**ые** (inanimate)		
G	пе́рв**ых**		
D	пе́рв**ым**		
I	пе́рв**ыми**		
P	пе́рв**ых**		

Summary Table 15.IX: declension of the ordinal number *третий*

Тре́тий declines like a possessive adjective ending with **-ий** (☞ 11.1.4, Summary Table 11.VI).

Case	Singular		Neuter	Feminine
	Masculine		**Neuter**	**Feminine**
N	тре́т**ий**		тре́т**ье**	тре́т**ья**
A	as genitive, if describing an animate noun; as nominative, if describing an inanimate noun		тре́т**ье**	тре́т**ью**
	тре́т**ьего** (animate) тре́т**ий** (inanimate)			
G	тре́т**ьего**		тре́т**ьего**	тре́т**ьей**
D	тре́т**ьему**		тре́т**ьему**	тре́т**ьей**
I	тре́т**ьим**		тре́т**ьим**	тре́т**ьей**
P	тре́т**ьем**		тре́т**ьем**	тре́т**ьей**
Plural (all genders)				
N	тре́т**ьи**			
A	as genitive, if describing an animate noun; as nominative, if describing an inanimate noun			
	тре́т**ьих** (animate) тре́т**ьи** (inanimate)			
G	тре́т**ьих**			
D	тре́т**ьим**			
I	тре́т**ьими**			
P	тре́т**ьих**			

15.3 Using cardinal and ordinal numbers

15.3.1 Using cardinal numbers with nouns

A cardinal number's agreement with the noun it qualifies can follow one of the two rules described in sections 15.3.1.1 and 15.3.1.2.

15.3.1.1 This rule applies to a phrase that contains either:

- a cardinal number in the nominative case followed by any noun: Сейча́с **два** (nominative) часа́ (a noun). (It is 2 o'clock.) Здесь **три́дцать оди́н** (nominative) студе́нт (a noun). (Here there are thirty-one students.) На столе́ **пять** (nominative) бана́нов. (On the table there are 5 bananas.)

or

- a cardinal number, except 'one' or a compound number ending in 'one', in the accusative case followed by an inanimate noun: Он съел **две** (accusative) гру́ши (inanimate noun) и **три** (accusative) я́блока (inanimate noun). (He ate two pears and three apples.)

The rule reads:

- A noun in the **nominative case** is used after 'one' or numbers that end with 'one'. 'One' also agrees with the gender and number of the noun it qualifies:

  На столе́ лежа́т оди́н рубль (masculine singular nominative), тридцать одна́ копе́йка (feminine singular nominative), одно́ письмо́ (neuter singular nominative) и одни́ очки́ (plural nominative).

  On the table are one rouble, thirty-one kopeks, one letter and one pair of glasses.

  If there is **an adjective** in the phrase, it **agrees** in gender, number and case with the noun it qualifies:

  Вот оди́н зелё**ный** огуре́ц (masculine singular nominative) и одно́ кра́с**ное** я́блоко (neuter singular nominative).

  Here are one green cucumber and one red apple

- A noun in the **genitive singular** is used after 'two', 'three' and 'four' or compound numbers that end with 'two', 'three' and 'four'.
- The number 'two' also agrees in gender with the noun it qualifies:

  В ва́зе два бана́**на** (masculine, genitive, singular), две сли́**вы** (feminine, genitive, singular), и два я́блок**а** (neuter, genitive, singular).

  In the bowl are two bananas, two plums and two apples.

  If there is **an adjective** in the phrase, **it does not fully agree** with the noun it qualifies. The form of the adjective in this context depends on the gender of the noun that it qualifies.

  If the adjective qualifies a masculine or neuter noun, it is used in the genitive plural, although the noun is in the genitive singular:

  Вот два **сла́дких** (genitive plural) апельси́на (genitive singular) и три **ки́слых** (genitive plural) лимо́на (genitive singular).

  Here are two sweet oranges and three bitter lemons.

  If the adjective qualifies a feminine noun, it is used in the nominative plural, although the noun is in the genitive singular:

  Здесь откры́ли три **но́вые** (nominative plural) дискоте́ки (genitive singular).

  Here three new discos were opened.

  In contemporary Russian, there is an alternative form of the adjective that qualifies the feminine noun, which is common in popular speech and poetry. The adjective can appear in the plural genitive case:

  Две **ве́чных** (genitive plural) подру́ги (genitive singular)– любо́вь и разлу́ка – не хо́дят одна́ без друго́й. (Окуджа́ва)

  The two eternal friends – love and separation– do not go the one without the other.

- The genitive plural is used after any number except 'one', 'two', 'three' and 'four' or compound numbers that end with 'one', 'two', 'three' or 'four'. There is no gender to the number:

  В ва́зе пять бана́**нов** (genitive plural), шесть слив (genitive plural) и два́дцать я́блок (genitive plural).

  In the bowl are five bananas, six plums and twenty apples.

  If there is **an adjective** in the phrase, it **agrees** in gender, number and case with the noun it qualifies:

  Они́ купи́ли семь **краси́вых** откры́ток (genitive plural).

  They bought seven nice postcards.

- Ты́сяча (1 000), миллио́н (1 000 000), миллиа́рд (1 000 000 000) and higher numbers follow the pattern described above.

The nouns **ты́сяча, миллио́н, миллиа́рд** are in the nominative singular after the number 'one' or numbers that end with 'one'. 'One' agrees with the following noun in gender: одна́ ты́сяча (1 000) – feminine, nominative, singular.

The nouns **тысяча, миллио́н, миллиа́рд** are in the genitive singular after the numbers 'two', 'three' and 'four' or numbers that end with 'two', 'three' and 'four'. 'Two' agrees with the following noun in gender: дв**е** ты́сяч**и** (2 000) – feminine, genitive, singular. On gender and number, ☞ 15.1.2.

The nouns **тысяча, миллио́н, миллиа́рд** are in the genitive plural after any number except 'one', 'two', 'three' and 'four' or numbers that end with 'one', 'two', 'three' or 'four'. There is no gender to the number: пять ты́сяч (5 000) – genitive plural.

15.3.1.2 This rule applies to a phrase that contains either:

- a cardinal number in the genitive, dative, instrumental or prepositional case followed by any noun.

or

- a cardinal number in the accusative case followed by an animate noun.

The rule reads:

- All cardinal numbers agree with the case of the noun they qualify (for the declension of cardinal numbers, ☞ 15.1.3): В кафе́ я встре́тился с шест**ью** (instrumental) това́рищ**ами** (plural instrumental). (In a café I met (with) six friends.)

Additionally:

- The number 'one', or any compound number ending in 'one', agrees in gender and number with the noun it qualifies: Мы купи́ли одн**у́** гру́шу (feminine accusative), оди́н лимо́н (masculine accusative) и одн**о́** моро́жено**е** (neuter accusative). (We bought a pear, a lemon and an ice-cream.) ☞ See section 15.1.2.

If there is **an adjective** in the phrase, it **agrees** in gender, number and case with the noun it qualifies: Я познако́мился с одно́й молодо́й де́вушкой (feminine, singular, instrumental) и тремя́ молоды́ми людьми́ (plural instrumental). (We met (with) one young girl and three young men.)

15.3.1.3 Using the nouns год (year) and челове́к (person) after cardinal numbers

The nouns **год** (year) and **челове́к** (person) have the following plural forms in the nominative case: год – го́д**ы** and челове́к – **лю́ди**. The plural forms in all cases except the genitive are derived from these plural nominative forms. The plural genitive forms of these nouns differ when they appear after cardinal numbers except 'one', 'two', 'three' and 'four' or numbers that end with 'one', 'two', 'three' or 'four':

- **лет** is the genitive plural of **год**
- **челове́к** is the genitive plural of **челове́к**

For example:

Мы про́жили здесь пять **лет**.	We have been living / we have lived here for 5 years.
Два́дцать **челове́к** пришли́ на встре́чу.	Twenty people attended the meeting.

The genitive form **люде́й** is used after numbers indicating indefinite quantity: ☞ 7.2.2.1.

15.3.1.4 The issue of agreement

In a sentence, if a phrase consisting of a number (a cardinal number other than 'one', a collective or an indefinite number – ☞ 15.9, 15.10) and a noun is the subject of the sentence, it can relate to the predicate in two different ways. The predicate can have alternative forms of the 3rd person plural or 3rd person singular in the present tense and future tenses, and 3rd person plural or neuter singular in the past tense:

- The predicate is frequently used in the plural when it follows the subject of the sentence and the subject is animate:

Три бизнесме́на **е́дут/пое́дут** в Москву́.   Three businessmen are going to Moscow.

Че́тверо тури́стов **посмотре́ли** Эрмита́ж.   Four tourists visited the Hermitage.

- The perfective verb that *precedes* the subject is frequently used in the neuter singular:

  На вечери́нку **пришло́** пять челове́к.   Five people attended the party.

- The short-form passive participle usually appears in the singular form if it relates to a phrase with a number:

  Бы́ло постро́ено два до́ма.   Two houses were built.

15.4 Telling the time

Both 24-hour and 12-hour clocks are used to respond to the questions **Кото́рый час?** and **Ско́лько вре́мени?** (What is the time?)

For precise official times, such as in timetables, event schedules, TV and radio programmes, the 24-hour clock is usually used. In everyday use, the 12-hour clock is preferred. Both cardinal and ordinal numbers are used to express clock times.

15.4.1 The 12-hour clock

To express the exact time on the hour, the cardinal numbers are used. The number is followed by the appropriate form (☞ 15.3) of the noun **час** (hour). For example:

Сейча́с час.   It's now one o'clock. (The number is omitted only in this expression).

Сейча́с два часа́.   It's 2 o'clock.

Сейча́с пять часо́в.   It's 5 o'clock.

To indicate '*minutes past the hour*' in the first half of the clock, the following construction is used:

- A cardinal number in the nominative case starts the phrase.
- The number is followed by the noun **мину́та** (minute). The form of **мину́та** depends on the number it follows (☞ 15.3).
- An ordinal number in the genitive singular masculine ends the phrase. This qualifies the noun **час** (hour) (which is in fact omitted) and agrees with it in gender, number and case. This ordinal number refers to the forthcoming hour. For example:

2.10 – де́сять мину́т тре́тьего

12.20 – два́дцать мину́т пе́рвого

On using the genitive case in this construction, ☞ 7.2.3.2.

To indicate '*minutes to the hour*' in the second half of the clock, a cardinal number in the genitive case with the preposition **без** (without) is used. A cardinal number in the nominative, referring to the forthcoming hour, ends the phrase. For example:

6.55 – без пяти́ семь

8.35 – без двадцати́ пяти́ де́вять

6.45 – без пятна́дцати семь or без че́тверти (a quarter) семь

On using the genitive case in this construction, ☞ 7.3.2.3; on the cardinal numbers' declension, ☞ 15.1.3.

The nouns **у́тро** (morning) and **ве́чер** (evening) are used in the singular genitive case as equivalents to the English **am** and **pm** respectively. However, they are only used after the exact hour and are often omitted:

во́семь часо́в ве́чера (8 pm)

шесть часо́в утра́ (6 am)

15.4.2 The 24-hour clock

In the 24-hour clock, the exact numbers are expressed; both **час** (hour) and **минýта** (minute) are omitted:

24.00 двáдцать четы́ре ноль-ноль
21.10 двáдцать оди́н де́сять

15.5 Responding to questions regarding time

To respond to the questions **Когдá?** (When?) and **В котóром часý?** (At what time?) the following constructions are used.

Level 2, 3

The 12-hour clock:

- The preposition **в** (at) is added to a time expression that indicates the exact hour:
в час (at one o'clock)
в пять часóв (at five o'clock)
- The preposition **в** (at) is not used in a time expression starting with the preposition **без**:
без пяти́ де́вять (five to nine)
- The preposition **в** (at) is often omitted from a time expression that indicates the first half of the clock:
пять минýт девя́того (8.05)
че́тверть вторóго (1.15)
- The preposition **в** (at) is added to a time expression indicating half an hour. The noun полови́на (half) is used in the prepositional case in this expression:
в полови́не вторóго (1.30).
The 24-hour clock:
- The preposition **в** (at) is added to the time expression: в 20.05 (20.05).

Level 2, 3

15.5.1 Other time expressions

The following time expressions are common in everyday speech:

- **óколо** (about): óколо двух часóв (about 2 o'clock)
- **часá в четы́ре** (about 4 o'clock): the change of word order in this phrase indicates the idea of 'proximity'
- **к** (by): к двум часáм (by 2 o'clock)
- **с ... до: с** двух **до** пяти́ (from 2 until 5 o'clock)
- **пóлдень** (midday)
- **пóлночь** (midnight)
- **полторá часá** (one and a half hours)
- **полчасá** (half an hour)
- **че́тверть чáса** (quarter of an hour)

Level 1, 2

15.6 Talking about age

Cardinal numbers are used when talking about age. An age expression has the following structure:

- The noun indicating the person/inanimate object whose age is stated is in the dative case.
- The cardinal number is followed by the nouns **год** (year), **месяц** (month), **день** (day), **неделя** (week), or **тысячелéтие** (millennium). The form of the noun depends on the last figure in the number. For example:

Де́вочке два **гóда**.	The girl is two years old.
Мáльчику шесть **лет.**	The boy is six years old.
Ребёнку оди́н **мéсяц**.	The baby is one month old.

On using nouns after a cardinal number, ☞ 15.3.1; on using nouns in the dative case, ☞ 8.2.2; on using the noun **год** in the genitive plural, ☞ 15.3.1.3.

In the present tense, **быть** (to be) is omitted from an expression of age. In the past and future tenses, **быть** and **исполня́ться/испо́лниться** (to turn) are used:

Актёру бы́ло со́рок лет.	The actor was 40.
Ба́бушке бу́дет 65 лет.	Grandmother is going to be 65.
Ей исполня́ется 100 лет.	She is turning 100.

The following idioms expressing age are common in popular speech:

- **за** (over): Ей **за** пятьдеся́т. (She is over 50.)
- **на** (in): Ему́ **на** шесто́й **деся́ток**. (He is in his fifties (his 6th decade)).

<table>
<tr><td>Level
2</td></tr>
</table>

15.7 Using numbers to express date, months, years and days of the week

15.7.1 The prepositional case is used to respond to the question **когда́** (when?) when indicating millennium, century, year, month or week (☞ 10.3.1). For example: в но́вом тысячеле́тии (in the new millennium), в январе́ (in January), на про́шлой неде́ле (last week).

The preposition **в** (in) governs the nouns **тысячеле́тие** (millennium), **век** (century), **год** (year) and **ме́сяц** (month). The preposition **на** (on) governs the noun **неде́ля** (week).

Numbers indicating years start with cardinal numbers and end with ordinal numbers. The ordinal number appears in the masculine singular form because it qualifies the masculine noun **год** (year):

1962 – ты́сяча девятьсо́т шестьдеся́т (cardinal numbers) **второ́й** (ordinal number) **год**
2011 – две ты́сячи (cardinal numbers) **оди́ннадцатый** (ordinal number) **год**
When responding to the question когда́ (when?) only the last ordinal number declines and appears in the prepositional case. In the prepositional case, the noun год has the irregular ending -y (☞10.1.1):

In 1962 – в ты́сяча девятьсо́т шестьдеся́т (cardinal numbers) второ́**м** (ordinal number) **году́**

In 2011 – в две ты́сячи (cardinal numbers) оди́ннадцато**м** (ordinal number) **году́**

15.7.2 The accusative case with the preposition **в** (on) is used to respond to the question **когда́** (when?) when indicating days of the week (☞ 6.3.2):

в понеде́льник	on Monday
в суббо́ту	on Saturday

15.7.3 The genitive case is used to respond to the question **когда́** (when?), when indicating the date:

Ю́рий Гага́рин полете́л в ко́смос двена́дцат**ого** апре́л**я** ты́сяча девятьсо́т шестьдеся́т пе́рв**ого** го́д**а**.	Yuri Gagarin flew into space on the 12th of April 1961.

For this date expression, ☞ 7.2.3.1. Note, there is no preposition in this expression. All components of the date, including month and year, are in the genitive case. Only the last ordinal number of the year declines; it appears in the genitive case.

☞ Other time expressions are covered in sections 6.3.2, 7.2.3.1, 7.2.3.2, 8.2.2, 9.2.2 and 10.3.1.

Level 3

15.8 Ordinal numbers expressing fractions and decimals

The following words express fractions:

- половина (half)
- четверть (quarter)
- треть (one third)

On using **половина** (half) and its shortened form, **пол-**, ☞ 7.2.2.2.

To express decimal numbers the following the phrases are used:

- Целая (доля) – the whole ('share')
- Десятая (доля) – (0,1), сотая доля (0,01), тысячная доля (0,001) etc.
- The feminine noun **доля** is omitted, but assumed. The adjective **целый** and any ordinal number **десятый**, **сотый** etc. agree in gender with the noun **доля**.
- After 'one', **целый**, **десятый**, **сотый** etc. are in the nominative singular. After any other numbers, they are in the genitive plural.
- A comma is used as a separator in decimal numbers.

For example:

0,1 – ноль целых, одна десятая   1,2 – одна целая и две десятых

Level 2, 3

15.9 Collective numbers

Collective numbers indicate the number of objects in a group. These belong to this group:

- The pronoun **óба** (masculine and neuter), **óбе** (feminine) – 'both'
- The noun **пáра** (pair/couple)
- Special forms of numbers between two and ten: двóе (2), трóе (3), чéтверо (4), пятеро (5), шéстеро (6), сéмеро (7), вóсьмеро (8), дéвятеро (9), дéсятеро (10).

Collective numbers decline, but do not have gender or number, with one exception: the pronoun **óба** (both). **Óба** expresses masculine and neuter gender and **óбе** expresses feminine gender: óба пáрня (both chaps), óбе дéвушки (both girls).

15.9.1 Declension of collective numbers

The declension of collective numbers is similar to that of plural adjectives (☞ 11.1). **Óба/óбе**, **двóе** and **трóе** follow the pattern of adjectives with soft endings. The other collective numbers follow the pattern of adjectives with hard endings.

Case	Collective numbers			
N	óба (masculine and neuter)	óбе (feminine)	двóе	чéтверо
A	as genitive, if describing an animate noun; as nominative, if describing an inanimate noun			
	обóих (animate) óба (inanimate)	обéих (animate) óбе (inanimate)	двоих (animate) двóе (inanimate)	четверых (animate) чéтверо (inanimate)
G	обóих	обéих	двоих	четверых
D	обóим	обéим	двоим	четверым
I	обóими	обéими	двоими	четверыми
P	обóих	обéих	двоих	четверых

Level
2, 3

15.9.2 Using collective numbers

Collective numbers have limited use:

- Numbers between **двóе** (two) and **дéсятеро** (ten) are only used to indicate animate nouns of masculine and common gender (☞ 2.3.1 and 2.3.6). They are common in popular speech when describing groups of children, young animals or people with the same occupation: трóе детéй (three children), чéтверо котя́т (three kittens), двóе коллéг (two colleagues).
- In a sentence, collective numbers can act as an independent word: Нас бы́ло дéсятеро. (There were ten of us.)
- **Óба/óбе** can be used with animate and inanimate nouns of all genders: óба глáза (both eyes), óбе сестры́ (both sisters).
- **Пáра** (pair/couple) is often used with many nouns that have only plural forms (☞ 3.5) or to indicate a couple of people or animals: пáра очкóв (pair of glasses), две супру́жеские пáры (two married couples), пáра гнеды́х (two bay horses).

When a collective number is followed by a noun, the following rule applies to the form of the noun:

- If **óба** is in the nominative case, it is followed by a noun in the genitive singular. **Óба** also agrees in gender with the noun it qualifies: óбе звезды́ экрáна (both movie stars), óба президéнта (both presidents).
- If **óба** is in the accusative case and is followed by an inanimate noun, the noun appears in the genitive singular. **Óба** also agrees in gender with the noun it qualifies: Миллионéр купи́л óба зáмка. The millionaire bought both castles.
- If there is **an adjective** in a phrase as described above, it **does not fully agree** with the noun it qualifies. The form of the adjective in this context depends on the gender of the noun that the adjective qualifies:
  - If the adjective qualifies a masculine or neuter noun, it is used in the genitive plural, although the noun is in the genitive singular: На столé óба **нóвых** (genitive plural) **журнáла** (genitive singular). (Both new magazines are on the table.)
  - If the adjective qualifies a feminine noun, it is used in the nominative plural, although the noun is in the genitive singular: Они́ купи́ли óбе **интерéсные** (nominative plural) **кни́ги** (genitive singular). (They bought both interesting books.)
  - If óба/óбе appears other than as described above, it agrees in gender, number and case with the noun it qualifies: Я люблю́ обóих брáтьев и обéих сестёр. (I love both my brothers and both my sisters.)
- A noun in the plural is used after all collective numbers, except **óба/óбе**. If there is **an adjective** in a phrase, it **agrees** in case and number with the noun it qualifies: Мы посмотрéли фильм о семеры́х смéлых друзья́х. (We watched a film about seven brave friends.)

15.9.2.1 Using collective numbers with nouns that have only a plural form

Nouns that have only a plural form (☞ 3.5) use collective numbers to describe quantities between two and four: дво́е сане́й (two sledges), тро́е брюк (three pairs of trousers).

To describe a higher quantity, two alternative constructions are used with these nouns. For example:

пя́теро су́ток	пять су́ток
ше́стеро часо́в	шесть часо́в (6 clocks)
во́сьмеро воро́т	во́семь воро́т

After 'one', nouns that have only a plural form are used in the nominative. The number 'one' is in the plural form (☞ 15.1.2): одни́ по́хороны (one funeral).

Level 2

15.10 Expressions of indefinite quantity

There are a number of words that can describe quantity, including:

мно́го (a lot)	немно́го (a little)
ско́лько (how much/how many)	сто́лько (so much/so many)
ма́ло (a little)	нема́ло (a few)
не́сколько (a few/several)	мно́гие (many)
немно́гие (not many)	

The question words **ско́лько?** (how much?/how many?), the pronouns **не́сколько** (several/a few), **сто́лько** (so much/so many) and the adjectives **мно́гие** (many), **немно́гие** (not many) decline and follow the pattern of plural adjectives with soft endings (☞ 11.1). For example:

Case	Indefinite expression
N	не́сколько
A	as genitive, if describing an animate noun; as nominative, if describing an inanimate noun
	не́скольких (animate) не́сколько (inanimate)
G	не́скольких
D	не́скольким
I	не́сколькими
P	не́скольких

The adverbs **мно́го, ма́ло, немно́го** do not decline.

After words of indefinite quantity, the noun is always used in the genitive plural:

| В библиоте́ке мно́го **уче́бников** (genitive plural). | In the library there are many textbooks. |

Any adjective to a phrase agrees in case and number with the noun it qualifies:

| В газе́тах написа́ли о не́скольких но́вых музе́ях (prepositional plural). | The newspapers wrote about several new museums. |

15.11 Using nouns as numbers

In Russian, there are several nouns that are used as cardinal numbers: thousand, million, billion. They have all a noun's characteristics: gender, number and case. Other nouns that express the idea of quantity include:

- Banknotes: со́тня (100 roubles), деся́тка (10 roubles).
- Grades and marks in Russian primary, secondary and higher education: **едини́ца/кол** (fail below any standard), **дво́йка** (fail), **тро́йка** (satisfactory/pass), **четвёрка** (good), **пятёрка** (excellent).

These numbers, едини́ца (1), дво́йка (2), тро́йка (3), четвёрка (4), пятёрка (5), шестёрка (6), семёрка (7) восьмёрка (8), девя́тка (9), деся́тка (10), can indicate:

- The number of a tram, trolleybus or bus:

| Извини́те, здесь **тро́йка** хо́дит? | Excuse me, does the number three (tram) come past here? |

- The names of cards in card games:

| **семёрка** бубён | seven of diamonds |
| козырна́я **шестёрка** | six of trumps |

- Number of babies born: дво́йня (twins), тро́йня (triplets)

| Она́ родила́ **дво́йню**. | She gave birth to twins. |

- Additionally, the noun **тро́йка** (3) can indicate a three-piece suit, a three-man commission or three horses:

Он купи́л дорогу́ю **тро́йку**.	He bought an expensive three-piece suit.
Во времена́ ста́линских репре́ссий **тро́йки** вы́несли пригово́ры бо́лее 400-ам ты́сячам челове́к.	During Stalin's repressions, three-man commissions passed sentence on more than 400,000 people.
Вот мчи́тся **тро́йка** удала́я вдоль по столбово́й (ру́сская наро́дная пе́сня).	The daring troika (three horses) races along the road marked by poles. (Russian folk song).

The nouns **деся́ток** (10) and **пято́к** (5) are used to count the number of eggs or buttons:

| Мы купи́ли пято́к яи́ц и два деся́тка пу́говиц. | We bought five eggs and twenty buttons. |

15.12 Other expression of quantity

Common expressions of quantity include:

- Expressions of multiplying: вдво́е (twice), втро́е (three times), вче́тверо (four times) etc.; два́жды (twice), три́жды (three times). After 'ten', the expression в ... раз (... times) is used: в оди́ннадцать раз (eleven times), в два́дцать раз (twenty times).
- Expressions of community: вдвоём (group of two), втроём (group of three), вчетверо́м (group of four), впятеро́м (group of five): Мы пошли́ в кино́ втроём. (The three of us went to the cinema.)
- Expressions of repetition and sequence (common in writing): во-пе́рвых (firstly), во-вторы́х (secondly), в-тре́тьих (thirdly).

- To express the idea of distributing something, the following construction is used:
  - The preposition **по** followed by a cardinal number in the accusative case.
  - The number is followed by a noun in the nominative or genitive case depending on the number the noun follows (☞ 15.3.1):

Alternatively, the idea of distributing something can be expressed by the preposition по followed by a noun in the dative case:

Дети получили по два яблока и три конфеты.	The children got two apples and three sweets each.
Всем сёстрам **по серьгам** (пословица).	A pair of earrings to each sister (proverb: meaning a fair distribution).

Упражнения

1. Complete the sentences by putting the phrases in brackets into the correct form:

1. Наташе подарили 23 (красные розы).
2. Миллионер купил 31 (новые машины).
3. Мальчик съел 1 (жёлтая дыня) и 2 (сладкое яблоко).
4. В спектакле заняты 5 (молодые актёры).
5. У Марины сегодня 6 (интересные встречи).

2. Replace the English phrases by their Russian equivalents in the correct form:

1. Гости должны прийти (by 7 o'clock).
2. Бассейн открыт (from 11 am to 10 pm).
3. Я начинаю работать (at 8.45) и заканчиваю (at 5.30)
4. Магазины закрыты на обед (between 1 pm and 2 pm).
5. Мы встречаемся (at 1 o'clock).

Обобщающее упражнение

3. Answer the quiz questions using the answers provided. Write the numbers in words:

Господин Смирнов отвечает на вопросы викторины (quiz)

Сегодня в любимом кафе господина Смирнова «Ёлки-Палки» проводится викторина для всех любителей кроссвордов. Пожалуйста, помогите господину Смирнову ответить на вопросы:

Вопросы	Ответы
1. Когда началась вторая мировая война?	01.IX.1939
2. Когда умер Лев Толстой?	20.XI.1910
3. Когда Колумб открыл Америку?	1492 г.
4. Когда родился и умер Шекспир?	1564 – 1616
5. В каком веке на Руси приняли христианство?	10 век
6. Какой день – самый длинный в году?	21.VI

16 Verbs

Verbs define an action (to do something etc.) or a state (to exist, to know etc).

The basic dictionary form of a verb is *the infinitive*, for example, **де́лать** (to do), **быть** (to be). For the infinitive, ☞ 16.1 and 20.6.

Level 1, 2
Russian verbs have the following grammatical categories:

- **Tense.** Russian verbs have three tenses that give us the time during which the action takes place, in *the present, past* or *future*. For each of the three tenses, ☞ 17, 18 and 19 respectively.
- ◉ **Aspect.** Most Russian verbs have two verbal aspects called *imperfective* and *perfective*. An aspect does not change the verb meaning, but defines the nature of an action. It determines whether the action is complete or incomplete, single or multiple, defined or undefined. For the verbal aspects, ☞ 20.

Level 2, 3
- **Transitivity.** Transitivity is a grammatical category that clarifies the relationship between a verb and object in a sentence. It helps us to establish whether the verb must take a direct object to convey the message correctly (transitive verbs) or whether it cannot have an object (intransitive verbs). For transitive and intransitive verbs, ☞ 21.1, 21.2
- **Voice.** Voice is a grammatical category that clarifies the relationship between a verb and subject in a sentence. The verb describes what the subject does itself (active voice), or what is done to the subject by someone or something else (passive voice). For the passive and active voices, ☞ 21.3.
- **Mood.** A verb can be in one of four moods: *indicative, imperative, conditional* or *subjunctive*. The verbal mood defines the speaker's attitude towards the action and establishes whether the speaker describes a real, desirable or hypothetical action. For the four moods, ☞ 22.

Level 2, 3
Additionally, note:

- Two verbal forms derive from the verb: the *participle* (*verbal adjective*) and the *gerund* (*verbal adverb*). Both participles and gerunds are common in writing. For participles and gerunds, ☞ 26 and 27 respectively.
- There are many verbs called reflexive verbs. They are formed by adding the particle **-ся/-сь** to a verb ending. **-ся/-сь** can modify a verb's meaning in different ways. For reflexive verbs, ☞ 23.
- There are several verbs called *impersonal*. They have a limited number of forms and can be used only in a special type of sentence that has no subject. These sentences also are called *impersonal*. For impersonal sentences in general and impersonal verbs in particular, ☞ 30 and 30.4.

Function in a sentence

The verb serves as the predicate to the subject of the sentence. This means the verb explains the action or state of the subject. All verbs change their endings to agree with the subject. The exception to this rule is a few impersonal verbs (☞ 30.4).

In the present and future tenses, the verb agrees with the subject in person and number (☞ 17 and 19 respectively). In the past tense, the verb agrees with the subject in gender and number (☞ 18).

evel
, 2

16.1 The infinitive

The infinitive is the dictionary form of a verb. The English equivalent of Russian infinitives is the verbal form introduced by *to* – (**to do, to** be etc.). The Russian infinitive can end with **-ть, -ти** or **-чь.**

- **-ть** is the most common infinitive ending and is added to the stem of the verb after a vowel: быть (to be), де́лать (to do).
- **-ти** is the less common infinitive ending and is added to the stem of the verb after a consonant: идти́ (to go), найти́ (to find).
- Only a small number of verbs have their infinitive ending with **-чь**: мочь (to be able/can), печь (to bake). Unlike the infinitive endings **-ть** and **-ти**, **-чь** is part of the verbal stem. When past tense verbs, present tense verbs, future perfective verbs are formed from the verbs in **-чь**, the letter **ч** changes: **ч-г** (бере́чь, берегу́, etc.), **ч-г-ж** (мочь, могу́, мо́жешь etc.) or **ч-к** (печь, пеку́, печёшь, etc.).

The infinitives of reflexive verbs have the particle **–ся** added to **-ть** and **–чь** (after the soft sign): улыба́ться (to smile), увле́чься (to be keen on/to be carried away). The particle **-сь** is added to **-ти** (after a vowel): спасти́сь (to save oneself), найти́сь (to be found/to turn up).

In Russian, most verbs have two infinitives – imperfective and perfective. Both infinitives are clearly marked in a dictionary – де́лать (to do) – imperfective (impf), сде́лать (to do) – perfective (pf).

For verbal aspect in general, ☞ 20; for use of the verbal aspects of the infinitive, ☞ 20.6.

16.1.1 Using the infinitive

The imperfective and perfective infinitives can be used in two ways:

- to form the present, past or future tenses of a verb
- as an essential unchangeable part of compound verbal forms (☞ 16.1.2).

👁 When choosing between imperfective and perfective infinitives, bear in mind the general concept of verbal aspect, and what verbal form you intend to form by using the infinitive. The following verbal forms are formed from the imperfective and perfective infinitives:

Imperfective infinitive	Perfective infinitive
Present tense (☞ 17).	**No present tense**
Past tense of imperfective verbs (☞ 18).	**Past tense** of perfective verbs (☞ 18).
Compound future tense of imperfective verbs (☞ 16.1.2).	Simple future tense **of perfective verbs** (☞ 19).

Comments on the table

👁 Some verbal stems are modified when forming the present tense of imperfective verbs (☞ 17.1) or the future tense of perfective verbs.

evel
, 2

16.1.2 Using the infinitive as an essential part of compound verbal forms

In Russian, the infinitive can be used as an essential part of the following compound verbal forms:

- With **быть** (to be) to form the future tense of imperfective verbs: Я бу́ду де́лать (I will do), они́ бу́дут де́лать (they will do) etc. Only imperfective infinitives can be used in this tense. For the compound future tense, ☞ 19.1.2.

- With many personal verbs:

Мари́я о́чень **лю́бит пла́вать и игра́ть** в волейбо́л.	Maria **loves swimming and playing** volleyball.
Он **на́чал рабо́тать** в Москве́ в про́шлом году́.	He **started working** in Moscow last year.

- A Russian infinitive that follows a verb is often translated into English by using the *gerund*. For example,

Я люблю́ **пла́вать.**	I love **swimming.**
Переста́ньте **болта́ть.**	Stop **talking**.

- With short-form adjectives such as **рад, -а, -ы** (to be pleased); **сча́стлив, -а, ы** (to be happy); **до́лжен, -а, -ы** (must); **наме́рен, -а, -ы** (to intend); **гото́в -а, -ы** (to be ready):

Дире́ктор **до́лжен рассмотре́ть** но́вое предложе́ние.	The director **must consider** a new proposal.

For short-form adjectives, ☞ 12.5.

👁 Some additional rules on how to choose between imperfective and perfective infinitives may apply when an infinitive appears after certain verbs (☞ 20.6.1.1).

Level 2, 3 The infinitive is frequently used in *impersonal sentences* as an essential part of a compound verbal form (for impersonal sentences, ☞ 30):

- With a modal word such as **на́до, ну́жно, необходи́мо** (necessary), **не на́до, не ну́жно** (not necessary), **возмо́жно** (possible), **не́возмо́жно** (impossible), **мо́жно** (to be permitted), **нельзя́** (not permitted/not allowed):

Нельзя́ кури́ть.	**No smoking.**
Мо́жно войти́?	**May** I **come in?**
Извини́те, мне **на́до идти́.**	Excuse me, **I need to go.**

- With an adverb:

Как **хорошо́ гуля́ть** по ле́су ра́нним у́тром.	**It is great walking** in a forest early in the morning.

- With negative pronouns or adverbs with the prefix **не-**:

Мне **не́куда идти́.**	I **have no place to go.**

👁 Some additional rules on how to choose between imperfective and perfective infinitives may apply when an infinitive appears after some modal words (☞ 20.6.1.2).

The infinitive can also appear in a sentence as its subject:

Кури́ть – здоро́вью вреди́ть.	**Smoking** damages your health.
Быть и́ли **не быть.** Вот в чём вопро́с. (Шекспи́р)	**To be**, or not **to be**, that is the question. (Shakespeare)
У меня́ появи́лась **возмо́жность порабо́тать** за грани́цей.	I have **the opportunity to work** abroad.

Level 1, 2

16.2 The verb быть (to be)

The verb **быть** (to be) has only aspect, the imperfective. It can be used:

- As an independent verb (☞ 18.2, 19.1.1):

Мы там **бы́ли.**	We **were** there.

- As a verbal link in a compound verbal form (☞ 12.6, 26.2.2):

Ры́нок **был закры́т.**	The market **was closed.**

- To form the compound imperfective future tense (☞ 19.1.1):

Он **бу́дет рабо́тать** за́втра.	He **will work** tomorrow.

16.2.1 Omission of быть (to be) in the present tense

Unlike in English, **быть** (to be) is not used in the Russian present tense. Therefore, in the present tense there is no verb in the basic Russian sentence that:

- Names or classifies an object: Кто э́то? (Who **is** this?) Э́то профе́ссор. (This **is** a professor.) Что э́то? (What **is** this?) Э́то суперма́ркет. (This **is** a supermarket.) A dash is usually used between two nouns in the nominative case instead of the verb **быть** (to be):

   Господи́н Смирно́в – представи́тель   Mr Smirnoff **is** a company representative.
   компа́нии.

- Indicates location:

   Кремль на Кра́сной пло́щади.   The Kremlin **is** on Red Square.
   Сотру́дники в о́фисе.   The staff **are** in the office.

- Points something out: **Вот**, пожа́луйста. (**Here** it **is**.) **Вот** моя́ дере́вня, **вот** мой дом родно́й (Су́риков). (**Here is** my village, **here is** my house.) The word **вот** serves as the English equivalent to *here is*.

- **Быть** (to be) is omitted as a verbal link to the subject of the sentence with adjectives, short-form participles, adverbs or modal words:

   Я **сча́стлив**.   I **am happy**.
   Мы **ра́ды** с Ва́ми **познако́миться**.   We **are pleased to meet** you.
   Его́ сад **ме́ньше** моего́.   His garden **is smaller** than mine.

For more information, ☞ 12.5.

level 3

16.2.2 Equivalents of быть (to be)

Several verbs have a meaning close to **быть** (to be). They are frequently used to replace **быть** in writing:

- **Явля́ться**, impf. (to be/to appear to be) takes a noun in the instrumental case (☞ 9):

   Господи́н Смирно́в **явля́ется**   Mr Smirnoff **is** a company representative
   представи́телем компа́нии   at a trade-fair.
   на я́рмарке.
   Кита́й **явля́ется** са́мым кру́пным   China **is** the biggest exporter in the world.
   экспортёром в ми́ре.

- **Яви́ться**, pf. (to be/to attend/to present) answers the questions **куда́?** (where to), **когда́?** (when):

   Вы **обя́заны яви́ться в суд**   You are **obliged to be present in**
   в ука́занное вре́мя.   **court** at the time indicated.

- **Счита́ться**, impf. (to consider/to regard as) takes a noun in the instrumental case (☞ 9):

   О́зеро Байка́л **счита́ется** са́мым   Lake Baikal **is considered to be** the
   глубо́ким и чи́стым **о́зером** плане́ты.   deepest and cleanest lake on our planet.

- **Числи́ться**, **состоя́ть**, impf. (to be/to be on paper) takes a noun in the instrumental case (☞ 9):

   – Говоря́т, Вы бы́ли режиссёром?   – They say you were a producer?
   – Был. Верне́е, **числи́лся**.   – Yes, I was. It is better to say,
   (Довла́тов).   I **held the post** of a producer, but I did
        nothing.

- **Исполня́ться**, impf. – **испо́лниться**, pf. (to be/to turn).

   Одно́й из са́мых ста́рых жи́тельниц   One of the oldest female citizens
   плане́ты в э́том году́ **испо́лнилось**   in the world **turned** 114 this year.
   114 лет.

- **Находи́ться**, impf. (to be located/to be situated). **Находи́ться** is common in writing and popular speech:

   Извини́те, где **нахо́дится** городска́я   Excuse me, where **are** the local council
   администра́ция?   offices (situated)?

- **Есть** (is/are) is an old form of **быть** in the present tense. It is used, in scientific style, poetry or idioms:

Это **есть** наш после́дний и реши́тельный бой. (Интернациона́л)	This **is** the final struggle. (Internationale)
Нау́ка есть оди́н из наибо́лее эффекти́вных спо́собов добыва́ния но́вого зна́ния о ми́ре (Интерне́т).	Science **is** one of the most effective ways of gaining new knowledge about the world.

However, the verb **есть** is an essential part of the constructions *one has something* and *there is / there are*:

У меня́ есть друг.	**I have** a friend.
В до́ме есть лифт.	**There is** a lift in the house.

For **есть**, ☞ 5.1.1, 7.3.1.

Other equivalents of быть are:

- **Быва́ть**, impf. – **побыва́ть**, pf. (to be/to exist or to visit) is especially common in popular speech in all tenses. Because it can have both aspects, it is used to emphasise a repeated or a single action:

До́брых дел никогда́ **не быва́ет** (impf., repeated action) мно́го.	Charity **is** never too much.
Он ча́сто **быва́ет** (impf., repeated action) в отдалённых райо́нах, встреча́ется с избира́телями.	He often **visits** remote districts and meets his constituents.
Духово́й орке́стр **побыва́л** (pf., single action) на ежего́дном фестива́ле. Вы когда́-нибудь **быва́ли** (impf., repeated action) на приёме в Кремле́?	The brass band **visited** the annual festival. **Have** you ever **been** to an official reception in the Kremlin?

- **Наступа́ть**, impf. – **наступи́ть**, pf. (to be) is used when describing time, seasons or sound:

Наступи́ла весна́.	Spring **has arrived**/It **is** spring.
Наступа́ет тишина́.	It **is getting** quiet.

- **Станови́ться**, impf. – **стать**, pf. (to become/it is getting) is used in impersonal sentences when describing physical and emotional conditions or natural phenomena:

Стано́вится светло́.	It **is getting** light.
Ста́ло светло́.	It **became** light.
Ему́ **ста́ло** тру́дно дыша́ть.	He **started having** breathing difficulties.

Level 1, 2

16.2.3 Using быть (to be) in the past and future tenses

The verb **быть** (to be) does have past and present tenses and is not omitted from sentences. For how to form the past tense of **быть**, ☞ 18.2; for how to form the future tense of **быть**, ☞ 19.1.1.

In the past tense, **быть** must agree with the subject of the sentence in gender and number and, in the future tense, in person and number. In a sentence, **быть** can appear:

16.2.3.1 As a predicate (a verb) to the subject of the sentence:

Где вы **бы́ли**?	Where **were** you?
Мы **бы́ли** в кино́.	We **were** in the cinema.
Ты **бу́дешь** за́втра на рабо́те?	**Will** you **be** at work tomorrow?
Да, обяза́тельно **бу́ду**.	For sure, I **will be**.

Level 2, 3

16.2.3.2 As a verbal link and as a part of a compound predicate (a compound verbal form).
Быть connects the subject of the sentence with short-form and comparative adjectives, short-form participles, adverbs or modal words (for more information on each form ☞ the appropriate section given in brackets). For examples see page 153.

A short-form adjective (☞ 12.5):	
Мы **бы́ли ра́ды** Вас ви́деть.	We were **pleased** to see you.
Мы **бу́дем** о́чень **ра́ды** Вас ви́деть.	We **will be very pleased** to see you.
A comparative adjective (☞ 12.1):	
Це́ны на ры́нке **бы́ли ни́же**, чем в суперма́ркете.	The prices in the market **were lower** than the supermarket.
Це́ны на ры́нке **бу́дут ни́же**, чем в суперма́ркете.	The prices in the market **will be lower** than the supermarket.
A short-form participle (☞ 26.2):	
Фестива́ль **был откры́т**.	The festival **was opened**.
Фестива́ль **бу́дет откры́т**.	The festival **will be opened**.
An adverb (☞ 13):	
В гора́х **бы́ло хо́лодно**.	It **was cold** in the mountains.
В гора́х **бу́дет хо́лодно**.	It **will be** cold in the mountains.
A modal word (☞ 30.1):	
Секрета́рю **на́до бы́ло** подгото́вить отчёт.	The secretary **needed to** prepare a report.
Секрета́рю **на́до бу́дет** подгото́вить отчёт.	The secretary **will need** to prepare a report.
A noun or a long-form adjective in the instrumental or nominative case (☞ 9.2.4):	
Ве́ра **была́** /**бу́дет** прекра́сным **врачо́м**.	Vera **was/will be a** great **doctor**.
Спекта́кль **был** /**бу́дет интере́сным**.	The show **was/will be interesting**.
Пу́шкин **был поэ́т от** Бо́га.	Pushkin **was** blessed as **a poet**.

Упражне́ния

evel
, 2

1. Complete the sentences using **быть** in the appropriate form:

1. Вчера́ Ни́на .... в кита́йском рестора́не.
2. За́втра Са́ша .... на рабо́те.
3. Мы с подру́гой .... отдыха́ть на пля́же.
4. В воскресе́нье я уже́ .... в пути́.
5. На про́шлой неде́ле мы .... на дискоте́ке.

evel
, 3

2. Complete the sentences using the verbs **быва́ть, станови́ться, наступа́ть, явля́ться, находи́ться** or **счита́ться** in the appropriate form:

1. Пари́ж .... столи́цей Фра́нции.
2. В сле́дующем году́ И́ра ча́сто .... в гостя́х у ба́бушки.
3. Всегда́, когда́ .... ле́то, ... тепло́.
4. Ра́ньше Пётр .... поря́дочным челове́ком.
5. Эрмита́ж .... в Са́нкт-Петербу́рге.

17 Verbs: present tense

Level 1, 2
The Russian verb has only one present tense, which is imperfective. For verbal aspect, ☞ 20.

Russian and English tenses do not fully correspond. Therefore, understanding the context helps to translate verbs correctly from/to English. For example:

Ка́ждый день я **чита́ю.**	I **read every day**.
Сейча́с я **чита́ю.**	I **am reading now**.

In a sentence, the present tense verb must agree with the subject in person and number. This means the verb changes its ending or *conjugates* in accordance with the form of the subject. The subject of the sentence appears in the sentence in the nominative case. For the nominative case, ☞ 5.

Below is the complete set of eight personal pronouns that represent the 1st, 2nd and 3rd persons in the singular and plural:

Person	Russian personal pronoun corresponding to the person	English personal pronoun corresponding to the person
1st singular	я	I
2nd singular	ты	you (*informal, familiar form singular*)
3rd singular	он/она́/оно́	he/she/it
1st plural	мы	we
2nd plural	Вы	you (*formal, when addressing one person*)
	вы	you (*plural*)
3rd plural	они́	they

17.1 Present tense formation

Russian verbs can be divided into two conjugations (types) as follows.

- **The first conjugation**
  The most common endings of the first-conjugation infinitives are **-ать/-ять/-еть/-оть/ -уть/-ти/-чь.**
  Monosyllabic verbs ending in **-ить** (for example, **жить** (to leave), **пить** (to drink) etc.) are also first-conjugation verbs.
- **The second conjugation**
  The most common ending of the second-conjugation infinitives is **-ить.**
  Some verbs ending in **-ать** and **-еть** are second-conjugation verbs. For example:
  –Some verbs ending in **-еть: терпе́ть** (to endure/tolerate), **верте́ть** (to spit), **оби́деть** (to offend), **зави́сеть** (to depend on), **ненави́деть** (to hate), **ви́деть** (to see), **смотре́ть** (to look/watch).
  –Some verbs ending in **-ать: гнать** (to chase/drive), **держа́ть** (hold), **слы́шать** (to hear), **дыша́ть** (to breathe).
  –Some verbs ending in **-чать: крича́ть** (to shout), **молча́ть** (to be silent).

However, there are several exceptions to this pattern that must be memorised. Therefore it is necessary to check in a dictionary which provides irregular verb endings to see to which *conjugation* (type) a verb belongs.

Level
1, 2

17.1.1 Formation of conjugation I verbs

To form the present tense of conjugation I verbs:

- Remove **the last two letters** of the infinitive, for example, рабо́тать (to work) – рабо́та-, идти́ (to go) – ид-.
- Add the following personal ending to the stem:

Person	Ending
1st singular	-ю/-у
2nd singular	-ешь/-ёшь
3rd singular	-ет/-ёт
1st plural	-ем/-ём
2nd plural	-ете/-ёте
3rd plural	-ют/-ут

Note some variations in the pattern:

A рабо́тать (to work) рабо́та-	B писа́ть (to write) пиш-	C идти́ (to go) ид-	D рисова́ть (to draw) рису-	E воева́ть (to fight) вою-	F дава́ть (to give) да-	G печь (to bake) пек-
Я рабо́таю	пишу́	иду́	рису́ю	вою́ю	даю́	пеку́
Ты рабо́таешь	пи́шешь	идёшь	рису́ешь	вою́ешь	даёшь	печёшь
Он/она́/оно́ рабо́тает	пи́шет	идёт	рису́ет	вою́ет	даёт	печёт
Мы рабо́таем	пи́шем	идём	рису́ем	вою́ем	даём	печём
Вы рабо́таете	пи́шете	идёте	рису́ете	вою́ете	даёте	печёте
Они́ рабо́тают	пи́шут	иду́т	рису́ют	вою́ют	даю́т	пеку́т

Comments on some variations in the pattern of conjugation I verbs shown above:

- **All examples:** In the 1st person singular and 3rd person plural forms **-ю** appears after a vowel and **-у** after a consonant.
- **Examples C and G:** If the stem of the verb ends in a consonant and the stress falls on the ending, **-e** in the ending is replaced by **-ё.**
- **Examples D and E:** If the infinitive has suffixes **-ева-/-ова-**, drop **-ва** and

  –replace **-e** or **-o** with **-у** after a hard consonant: танцева́ть – танцу́ю; рисова́ть – рису́ю.
  –replace **-e** with **-ю** after a soft consonant: воева́ть – вою́ю.

  Then add the appropriate ending.
  For the hard and soft consonants, ☞ 1.4.

- **Example F:** If the infinitive has the suffix -**ава,** drop -**ва.** Then add the appropriate ending. If the stress falls on the ending, -**e** in the ending is replaced by -**ё.**
  Note the infinitive form with suffix -**ыва** is not affected. It follows pattern A; for example, опа́здывать (to be late): опа́здываю, опа́здываешь etc.
- 👁 **Examples B and G:** Many verbs are affected by consonant alternation (change) to the stem. In particular, the 1st singular (я) and the 3rd plural (они́) forms are affected. For a list of the most common consonant changes in the stem, ☞ 17.1.2.

17.1.2 Consonant alternation (changes) in conjugation I verbs

👁 In the present tense, the most frequent consonant alternations (changes) occur in the stem of conjugation I verbs that end in -**ать.** Note the consonant change and loss of the letter -**a** in these examples:

с—ш	писа́ть (to write): пишу́, пи́шешь, пи́шет, пи́шем, пи́шете, пи́шут
х—ш	паха́ть (to plough): пашу́, па́шешь, па́шет, па́шем, па́шете, па́шут
з—ж	ре́зать (to cut/to slice): ре́жу, ре́жешь, ре́жет, ре́жем, ре́жете, ре́жут
г-ж	дви́гать (to move/to be motivated): дви́жу, дви́жешь, дви́жет, дви́жем, дви́жете, дви́жут
д-ж	глода́ть (to gnaw): гложу́, гло́жешь, гло́жет, гло́жем, гло́жете, гло́жут
ск—щ	иска́ть (to look for): ищу́, и́щешь, и́щет, и́щем, и́щете, и́щут
т—щ	ропта́ть (to grumble): ропщу́, ро́пщешь, ро́пщет, ро́пщем, ро́пщете, ро́пщут
т—ч	пря́тать (to hide): пря́чу, пря́чешь, пря́чет, пря́чем, пря́чете, пря́чут
к—ч	пла́кать (to weep): пла́чу, пла́чешь, пла́чет, пла́чем, пла́чете, пла́чут
б-бл	колеба́ть (to shake): коле́блю, коле́блешь, коле́блет, коле́блем, коле́блете, коле́блют
м-пл	дрема́ть (to doze): дремлю́, дре́млешь, дре́млет, дре́млем, дре́млете, дре́млют
п-л	сы́пать (to sprinkle) : сы́плю, сы́плешь, сы́плет, сы́плем, сы́плете, сы́плют

- The verb **дви́гать** and its reflexive pair **дви́гаться** have two meanings and follow two different patterns. The verb follows the pattern, described in the table above, when used in figurative sense or in technical terms: Престу́пниками дви́жет жа́дность (The criminals are motivated by greed). Турби́на дви́жется (The turbine is moving). The verbs follow a different pattern with no consonant change (дви́гаю, дви́гаешь, дви́гают) when used with the literal meaning "to move": Они́ дви́гают дива́н (They are moving a sofa).
- Some verbs that follow the pattern described in the above table have alternative endings without consonant changes: **маха́ть** (to wave) – маха́ю, маха́ешь, маха́ют etc.; **ка́пать** (to drip) – ка́паю, ка́паешь, ка́пают.

- The consonant change **сл-шл** occurs in the future tense (☞ 19.1.3) of the perfective verb **послáть** (to send) and other verbs formed from the same root: пошлю́, пошлёшь, пошлёт, пошлём, пошлёте, пошлю́т.
- Many first-conjugation verbs affected by consonant change have distinctive stress patterns. If their infinitives have the stress on the ending, the 1st person singular keeps the stress on the ending. The rest of the conjugation has the stress moved to the stem. If their infinitives have the stress on the stem, the stress remains in its original position.

Verbs ending with **-чь** have the following changes in the stem:

ч–к	печь (to bake) : пеку́, печёшь, печёт, печём, печёте, пеку́т
ч–г–ж	мочь (to be able/can) : могу́, мо́жешь, мо́жет, мо́жем, мо́жете, мо́гут

Some verbs are irregular. Among them:

éхать (to go in or on a vehicle) : éду, éдешь, éдет, éдем, éдете, éдут

👁 Many monosyllabic verbs belong to conjugation I and have present tense stems that are different from their infinitive stems:

жить (to live)	пить (to drink)	ждать (to wait)	звать (to call)	брать (to take)
жив-	пь-	жд-	зов-	бер-
я живу́	пью	жду	зову́	беру́
ты живёшь	пьёшь	ждёшь	зовёшь	берёшь
он/онá/онó живёт	пьёт	ждёт	зовёт	берёт
мы живём	пьём	ждём	зовём	берём
вы живёте	пьёте	ждёте	зовёте	берёте
они́ живу́т	пьют	ждут	зову́т	беру́т

17.1.3 Formation of conjugation II verbs

To form the present tense of conjugation II verbs:

- Remove **the last three letters** of the infinitive form, for example, говори́ть (to speak) – говор-, молчáть (to keep silent) – молч-.
- Add the following personal endings to the stem:

Person	Ending
1st singular	-ю/-у
2nd singular	-ишь
3rd singular	-ит
1st plural	-им

Person	Ending
2nd plural	-ите
3rd plural	-ят/-ат

Note some variations in the pattern:

A говори́ть (to speak) говори-	B молча́ть (to be silent) молч-	C люби́ть (to love) люб-
я говорю́	молчу́	люблю́
ты говори́шь	молчи́шь	лю́бишь
он/она́/оно́ говори́т	молчи́т	лю́бит
мы говори́м	молчи́м	лю́бим
вы говори́те	молчи́те	лю́бите
они говоря́т	молча́т	лю́бят

Comments on some variations in the pattern of conjugation II verbs:

- All conjugation II present tense stems end in a consonant. If a consonant is affected by spelling rule 1 (г, к, х, ж, ш, ч, щ, ц), -**у** appears in the 1st person singular and -**a** appears in the 3rd person plural. For the spelling rules, ☞ 1.3.1.
- After any other consonants -**ю** and -**я** are used respectively in the 1st person singular and the 3rd person plural.
- Many verbs are affected by consonant alternation (change) to the stem. Often these changes affect only the 1st person singular. The verb **люби́ть** (pattern C) is an example. For a list of the most common consonant changes in the stem, ☞ 17.1.4.
- Many second-conjugation verbs have distinctive stress patterns (with some exceptions). If their infinitives have the stress on the ending, the first person singular keeps the stress on the ending. The rest of the conjugation has the stress moved to the stem. If their infinitives have the stress on the stem, the stress remains in its original position.

<table>
<tr><td>Level
2, 3</td><td></td></tr>
</table>

17.1.4 Consonant alternation (changes) in conjugation II verbs

👁 The following alternation (changes) frequently occur in the stem of conjugation II verbs. It affects only the 1st person singular. The rest of the endings follow the standard pattern:

б–бл	люби́ть (to love) – люблю́, ... лю́бят
п–пл	спать (to sleep) – сплю, ... спят
в–вл	гото́вить (to cook/to prepare) – гото́влю, ... гото́вят
м–мл	корми́ть (to feed) – кормлю́, ... ко́рмят
ф–фл	графи́ть (to rule paper) – графлю́, ... графя́т
т–ч	плати́ть (to pay) – плачу́, ... пла́тят
ст–щ	чи́стить (to clean) – чи́щу, ...чи́стят
д–ж	ходи́ть (to go) – хожу́, ... хо́дят

з—ж	возить (to transport) – вожу, ... водят
с—ш	носить (to carry) – ношу, ... носят

17.1.5 Mixed-conjugation verbs

Some verbs follow their own pattern and contain endings of both conjugations. For example:

есть (to eat)	хотеть (to want/wish)	бежать (to run)
я **ем** (special form)	хочу (I/II)	бегу (I/II)
ты **ешь** (special form)	хочешь (I)	бежишь (II)
он, она, оно **ест** (special form)	хочет (I)	бежит (II)
мы едим (II)	хотим (II)	бежим (II)
вы едите (II)	хотите (II)	бежите (II)
они едят (II)	хотят (II)	бегут (I)

17.2 Reflexive verbs in the present tense

For the use of reflexive verbs, ☞ 23.

To form the present tense of a reflexive verb:

- Identify the verb conjugation (☞ see section 17.1): заниматься (to be occupied) – conjugation I, учиться (to study) – conjugation II.
- Drop the four last letters of the conjugation I infinitive: **занима-.**
- Drop the five last letters of the conjugation II infinitive: **уч-.**
- Follow the patterns for the conjugation I or II verbs (☞ see section 17.1).
- Add **-ся** after a consonant or the letter **-ь**, or **-сь** after a vowel. For example:

Conjugation I	Conjugation II
я занима**юсь**	уч**усь**
ты занима**ешься**	учишься
он (она, оно) занима**ется**	учится
мы занима**емся**	учимся
вы занима**етесь**	учитесь
они занима**ются**	учатся

Упражне́ния

1. Fill in the gaps using the verb given in brackets in the appropriate form of the present tense:

1. Гру́ппа тури́стов .... (отдыха́ть) в лесу́. Пенсионе́ры .... (собира́ть) грибы́, ...
(игра́ть) в домино́, ... (разгова́ривать) и .... (обсужда́ть) после́дние но́вости.
2. Верони́ка ве́село .... (танцева́ть) на дискоте́ке.
3. Худо́жник .... (рисова́ть) карти́ну, писа́тель .... (писа́ть) но́вый рома́н, пе́карь ....
(печь) хлеб, а продаве́ц .... (продава́ть) сувени́ры.

2. Use the verbs in brackets in the appropriate form of the present tense:

1. Как Вас .... (звать)?
2. Кто .... (иска́ть), тот всегда́ найдёт.
3. Студе́нты .... (брать) кни́ги в библиоте́ке.
4. На за́втрак я .... (пить) ко́фе и .... (есть) ка́шу.
5. Шко́льники .... (ждать) результа́тов экза́мена.
6. Это непра́вда. Вы .... (лгать).
7. Вы .... (мочь) мне помо́чь?
8. О́ля гро́мко .... (пла́кать).

3. Complete the Russian proverbs using the appropriate verbs, in the present tense, from the list provided:
разруша́ть, провожа́ть, начина́ть, боле́ть, конча́ть, погиба́ть:

1. По оде́жке встреча́ют, а по уму́ ....
2. Дека́брь год ...., а зи́му ....
3. Мир стро́ит, а война́ ....
4. Сме́лый побежда́ет, а трус ....
5. Челове́к от лени ...., а от труда́ здорове́ет.

Обобща́ющее упражне́ние

4. Use the infinitive verbs below in the 3rd person singular present tense to describe Mr Smirnoff's typical summer holiday on a beach.

Встава́ть ра́но у́тром, принима́ть душ, бри́ться, одева́ться, занима́ться в тренажёрном за́ле, купа́ться в мо́ре, лежа́ть на пля́же, загора́ть, ката́ться на во́дных лы́жах/на велосипе́де, игра́ть в те́ннис/в гольф, расслабля́ться, танцева́ть на дискоте́ке, петь пе́сни, пить пи́во в ба́ре, е́здить на экску́рсию, есть шашлыки́, устава́ть, спать до́лго, ви́деть сны.

18 Verbs: past tense

vel 2
There is only one past tense in Russian. However, both imperfective and perfective verbs can be used in the past tense. For verbal aspect, ☞ 20. Imperfective verbs in the past tense describe an ongoing action, a general statement/fact or an action in progress. Perfective verbs in the past tense describe a completed single action or the result of an action that occurred in the past.

Russian and English tenses do not fully correspond. Therefore, translation to/from English depends on understanding the context and meaning of the Russian verbal aspects. For example:

Мы це́лый день **пекли́** (impf. past) пироги́.	We **were making** pies for the whole day/ we spent the whole day making pies.
Мы **испекли́** (pf. past) пять пирого́в.	We **made/have made** five pies.

Past tense verbs do not *conjugate* (agree with a subject in person and number). Instead, all Russian past tense verbs function as short-form adjectives and agree with the subject of the sentence in gender and number. For example:

Он де́лал (m, singular).	He did.
Она́ де́лала (f, singular).	She did.
Они́ де́лали (pl).	They did.

For the short adjectives, ☞ 12.5.

evel 2

18.1 Past-tense formation

Both the imperfective and the perfective verbs are formed in the same way in the past tense. However, two different infinitives, imperfective and perfective, are used to form, respectively, imperfective and perfective past tense verbs. Both infinitives are clearly marked in dictionaries; for example, де́лать, impf. (to do), сде́лать, pf. (to do).

To form the past tense:

- Remove the last two letters of the infinitive form (dictionary form) **-ть/-ти/-чь**, for example де́лать, impf. (to do), сде́лать, pf. (to do).
- Add the suffix **-л** to the stem: де́лал, impf. (did, was doing), сде́лал, pf. (did/has done).
- Then, for the masculine singular form, add nothing after **-л**: де́лал, сде́лал.
- For the feminine singular form, add **-а** after **-л**: де́лала, сде́лала.
- For the neuter singular form, add **-о** after **-л**: де́лало, сде́лало.
- For all plural forms, add **-и** after **-л**: де́лали, сде́лали.
- To form the past tense of reflexive verbs, follow the standard pattern described above, then add **-ся** after a consonant or the letter **-ь** or **-сь** after a vowel; for example, интересова́ться (to be interested) – интересова́лся (m), интересова́лась (f), интересова́лось (n), интересова́лись (pl).

When speaking about yourself in the past tense, it is necessary to remember your own gender. The gender of the past-tense verb must correspond to the gender of the speaker. When using the polite form **Вы** (you) in the past tense, the verb requires the plural form of the verb. For example:

– Что Вы **де́лали** (pl) вчера́, Ири́на?	'What did you do/were you doing yesterday, Irina?'
– Я **отдыха́ла** (f).	'I relaxed/was relaxing.'

– Что Вы **де́лали** (pl) вчера́, Джон?   'What did you do/were you doing
                                          yesterday, John?'
– Я **отдыха́л** (m).   'I relaxed/was relaxing.'

Level 1, 2

18.2 The verb быть (to be) in the past tense

For more information on **быть** (to be), ☞ 16.2.

To form the past tense of **быть**, follow the standard pattern described above: ☞ 18.1. **Быть** has the following past tense forms: был (m), была́ (f), бы́ло (n), бы́ли (pl).

Level 2, 3

18.3 Irregular past tense verbs

Several verbs follow a special pattern in the past tense. They are listed below.

- The verb **идти́** and its derived forms are formed by using a different stem: **шёл, шла, шло, шли** etc. If an added prefix ends with a consonant the vowel **о** is added to the prefix: **вошёл, вошла́, обошёл** etc.
- Verbs that have infinitives ending with -**ти** (except идти́), -**чь** and -**ереть**, the verb **лезть** and their derived forms. Note the absence of the suffix -**л**- in the masculine form after the consonants **з, с, г, к** and **р**, and the appearance of the letter **ё** under stress. Some verbs ending in -**сти** are exceptions to this rule (see comments below).

везти́ (to transport)	вёз, везла́, везло́, везли́
нести́ (to carry)	нёс, несла́, несло́, несли́
расти́ (to grow)	рос, росла́, росло́, росли́
мочь (can, to be able to)	мог, могла́, могло́, могли́
помо́чь (to help)	помо́г, помогла́, помогло́, помогли́
печь (to bake)	пёк, пекла́, пекло́, пекли́
лечь (to lay down)	лёг, легла́, легло́, легли́
течь (to leak/to flow)	тёк, текла́, текло́, текли́
умере́ть (to die)	у́мер, умерла́, умерло́, умерли́
протере́ть (to rub through/to grate)	протёр, протерла́, протерло́, протерли́
лезть (to climb)	*лез, лезла́, лезло́, лезли́*

- Verbs that have infinitives ending with -**сти** and their derived forms keep the suffix -**л**- in all forms, if their present and future tense stems end with -**д** or -**т**. For example:

вести́: веду́, веду́т (to lead)	вёл, вела́, вело́, вели́
цвести́: цвету́, цвету́т (to blossom)	**цвёл**, цвела́, цвело́, цвели́

- Verbs that have infinitives ending with -**сть** and their derived forms drop the three last letters of the infinitive to form the past tense:

есть (to eat)	*ел, е́ла, е́ло, е́ли*
сесть (to sit down)	*сел, се́ла, се́ло, се́ли*

- Most imperfective and perfective verbs ending with -**нуть** drop the suffix -**ну**- in the past tense. They lose the suffix -**л**- in the masculine form, if the stem ends with a consonant, and keep -**л**-, if the stem ends with a vowel:

мёрзнуть/замёрзнуть (to freeze)	(за)мёрз, (за)мёрзла, (за)мёрзло, (за)мёрзли
мо́кнуть/промо́кнуть (to get wet)	(про)мо́к, (про)мо́кла, (про)мо́кло, (про)мо́кли
вя́нуть/завя́нуть (to fade)	(за)вя́л, (за)вя́ла, (за)вя́ло, (за)вя́ли

- Perfective verbs ending in -**нуть** keep the suffixes -**ну**- and -**л**- in all forms, if they describe a single instantaneous action action. For example:

кри́кнуть (to shout)	кри́кнул, кри́кнула, кри́кнуло, кри́кнули
пры́гнуть (to jump)	пры́гнул, пры́гнула, пры́гнуло, пры́гнули

- Some verbs, if they have only *perfective* forms ending with **-нуть**, drop the suffix **-ну-** in the past tense and also the suffix -л- in the masculine form:

Привы́кнуть (to get used to)	привы́к, привы́кла, привы́кло, привы́кли
Дости́гнуть (to reach)	дости́г, дости́гла, дости́гло, дости́гли
Исче́знуть (to disappear)	исче́з, исче́зла, исче́зло, исче́зли

Упражне́ния

1. Rewrite the sentences in the past tense:

1. Ве́ра хо́дит в шко́лу.
2. Ма́льчик чита́ет кни́гу.
3. Столо́вая не рабо́тает.
4. Студе́нт интересу́ется те́ннисом.
5. Они́ спят до́лго.

2. Rewrite the sentences in the past tense:

1. По́вар трёт сыр.
2. Ба́бушка печёт пиро́г с гриба́ми.
3. Официа́нт несёт блю́до на подно́се.
4. Он выра́щивает петру́шку в саду́.
5. «Ско́рая по́мощь» везёт пацие́нта в больни́цу.
6. Го́сти едя́т блины́ с икро́й.
7. Кот пры́гает на стол.
8. Они́ привы́кнут к жаре́.
9. Ребёнок хорошо́ танцу́ет и рису́ет.
10. Река́ течёт по равни́не.
11. Когда́ де́ти иду́т в шко́лу, они́ разгова́ривают и смею́тся.

Обобща́ющее упражне́ние

3. Use the infinitive verbs below in the past tense to describe Mr Smirnoff's typical winter holiday.

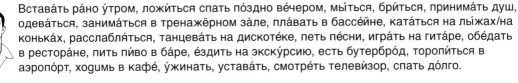

Встава́ть ра́но у́тром, ложи́ться спать по́здно ве́чером, мы́ться, бри́ться, принима́ть душ, одева́ться, занима́ться в тренажёрном за́ле, пла́вать в бассе́йне, ката́ться на лы́жах/на конька́х, расслабля́ться, танцева́ть на дискоте́ке, петь пе́сни, игра́ть на гита́ре, обе́дать в рестора́не, пить пи́во в ба́ре, е́здить на экску́рсию, есть бутербро́д, торопи́ться в аэропо́рт, ходи́мь в кафе́, у́жинать, устава́ть, смотре́ть телеви́зор, спать до́лго.

19 Verbs: future tense

Level 1, 2 In Russian, imperfective and perfective verbs form their future tenses in two different ways. Imperfective verbs have the compound form of the future tense and perfective verbs have the simple form: ☞ 19.1.2 and 19.1.3. Imperfective verbs in the future tense describe an action in progress/repeated action or an intention of doing something in the future. Perfective verbs in the future tense describe a complete single action that will occur. For verbal aspect, ☞ 20.

Russian and English tenses do not fully correspond. Therefore, translation to/from English depends on understanding the context and meaning of the Russian verbal aspects. For example:

За́втра на обе́д мы **бу́дем гото́вить** (impf) борщ.	Tomorrow we **intend to make/ will be making** borshch for lunch.
За́втра на обе́д мы **пригото́вим** (pf) борщ.	Tomorrow we **will make** borshch for lunch.

19.1 Future tense formation

Level 1, 2 ### 19.1.1 The verb быть (to be) in the future tense

The verb **быть** (to be) has only one aspect (the imperfective) and forms the future tense in its own way. For more on **быть**, ☞ 16.2.

To form the future tense of **быть**:

- Use the stem **буд-**. Note the stem differs from the infinitive stem of the verb **бы-**.
- Follow the pattern of a regular conjugation I verb in the present tense: ☞ 17.1.1.

1st person singular	я бу́д**у**
2nd person singular	ты бу́д**ешь**
3rd person singular	он, она́, оно́ бу́д**ет**
1st person plural	мы бу́д**ем**
2nd person plural	вы бу́д**ете**
3rd person plural	они́ бу́д**ут**

The verb **быть** in the future tense can appear in a sentence as a self-contained verb and as a predicate to the subject of the sentence. **Быть** must agree with the subject of the sentence in person and number. For example:

Мы бу́дем на вы́ставке в сре́ду.	**We will be** at the exhibition on Wednesday.
Я там **бу́ду.**	**I will be** there.

Level 1, 2 ### 19.1.2 Formation of the imperfective (compound) future tense

Russian imperfective verbs have a compound form of the future tense. The tense contains the verb **быть** in the appropriate form of the future tense (☞ 19.1.1) and the imperfective infinitive of the verb that carries the meaning. Note that only an imperfective infinitive can be used to form the compound future tense.

In a sentence, **быть** (to be) must agree with the subject in person and number. The imperfective infinitive does not change. For example:

Я **бу́ду** рабо́тать.   **I will** work.
Мы **бу́дем** отдыха́ть.   **We will** relax.

To form the imperfective (compound) future tense:

- Take the appropriate form of **быть (to be)** in the future tense (☞ 19.1.1): я бу́ду, ты бу́дешь, они́ бу́дут etc.
- Add the imperfective infinitive of the verb that carries the meaning. For example

Я **бу́ду чита́ть**.   **I will read/will be reading**.
Они́ **бу́дут чита́ть**.   They **will read/will be reading**.

19.1.3 Formation of the perfective (simple form) of the future tense

Russian perfective verbs have a future tense called the '*simple*' future tense because it contains only one verb. The simple future tense of perfective verbs is formed in exactly the same way as the present tense of imperfective verbs.

For the formation of the present tense, ☞ 17.1.

Imperfective verbs in the present tense and perfective verbs in the simple future tense follow exactly the same rules and patterns. Both imperfective present-tense verbs and perfective future-tense verbs belong to either conjugation I or conjugation II, or are mixed-conjugation verbs, and follow the pattern described above (☞ 17.1). However, imperfective present tense verbs and perfective future tense verbs are formed from two different infinitives, imperfective and perfective respectively. The verbal aspect is clearly marked in dictionaries. This prevents confusing them when using the present and the future tenses.

Compare:

Present tense	Perfective future
де́лать – to do (imperfective infinitive)	**с**де́лать – to do (perfective infinitive)
я де́ла**ю**	я **с**де́ла**ю**
ты де́ла**ешь**	ты **с**де́ла**ешь**
он/она́/оно́ де́ла**ет**	он/она́/оно́ **с**де́ла**ет**
мы де́ла**ем**	мы **с**де́ла**ем**
вы де́ла**ете**	вы **с**де́ла**ете**
они́ де́ла**ют**	они́ **с**де́ла**ют**

Упражне́ния

1. Put the imperfective verbs in brackets into the future tense:
1. Мы .... (изуча́ть) ру́сский язы́к.
2. Профе́ссор .... (рабо́тать) с на́ми.
3. Я .... (есть) блины́.
4. Ле́том они́ .... (пла́вать) в реке́.
5. Вы .... (обе́дать)?

Обобща́ющее упражне́ние

2. Use the perfective verbs given below in the infinitive to describe, in the 1st person singular future tense, Mr Smirnoff's trip to lake Baikal.

Встать ра́но у́тром, вы́звать такси́, поза́втракать на́спех, вы́пить ча́ю, прие́хать на вокза́л, вскочи́ть в по́езд, расположи́ться в ую́тном купе́, познако́миться с сосе́дями по купе́, пообе́дать в ваго́не-рестора́не, прие́хать в Ирку́тск, переночева́ть в гости́нице, отпра́виться на о́зеро, пойма́ть мно́го ры́бы, искупа́ться в о́зере, верну́ться домо́й, рассказа́ть друзья́м о пое́здке.

20 Verbs: verbal aspect

Level
1, 2

In Russian, verbal aspect is one of the core grammatical concepts, together with the three tenses – past, present and future (for information on the tenses, ☞ 17, 18 and 19 respectively). Russian tenses give us the time during which the action takes place – in *the present*, *past* or *future*. However, verbal aspect is the essence of the description of an action. Verbal aspect describes an action in the following ways:

Imperfective aspect	Perfective aspect
• Describes an incomplete action that is/was/will be in progress.	• Describes a complete action and focuses on the result achieved by the action ('Done!').
• Describes a repeated action that occurs/occurred/will occur more than once.	• Describes a single action that occurred/will occur only once.
• Confirms that the action took place, is taking place or will take place without indicating whether the action was completed and the result was achieved.	

Most Russian verbs have two verbal aspects, called *imperfective* and *perfective*. Only a few verbs have just one aspect. In dictionaries, the aspect of the verb is indicated by the abbreviations *impf* (imperfective) and *pf* (perfective); aspect pairs are cross-referenced.

👁 Russian verbal aspect may present some difficulties for the following reasons:

- Use of the verbal aspect depends on three factors: the context, the nature of the action described and what information about this action the speaker wants to give. Use of the verbal aspect requires keeping in mind all these factors.
- Sometimes the context may be unclear or ambiguous and therefore use of the verbal aspect depends on the speaker's personal interpretation of the context.
- English and Russian language users have different ways of expressing concepts of time and action, which do not always correspond. Translation from/to English depends on context and on what information is important for the speaker in this context.

👁 20.1 Formation of verbal aspect

In Russian there is no single unified pattern on the formation of perfective and imperfective verbs. Most aspectual pairs are formed by various verbal stem modifications (adding prefixes, adding or changing suffixes). Although some prefixes and suffixes used in the verbal aspect formation might have similar meaning, all aspectual pairs need to be checked in a dictionary.

For the formation and meaning of verbal aspects of verbs of motion, ☞ 25.5.

The most common ways to form the perfective are as follows (☞ sections given in brackets):

- By adding a prefix to the imperfective stem (☞ 20.1.1).
- By making some internal changes to the imperfective stem (☞ 20.1.5).
- By using a different verb (☞ 20.1.6).

Level
1, 2

Perfective verbs formed from the imperfective have the following characteristics:

- The meaning of the verb is not always changed.
- The majority of perfective verbs focus on an end to the action ('Done!') and emphasise that the described action is single and complete. For example, **де́лать** (to do, impf) – **сде́лать** (to finish doing, pf); **чита́ть** (to read, impf) – **прочита́ть** (to finish reading, pf).

Level
2, 3

- Some perfective verbs focus either on the beginning of an action or on its duration rather than on the end of the action. However, they still convey the idea that the described action is single and complete (☞ 20.1.2).

20.1.1 Formation of the perfective aspect by adding a prefix

The perfective aspect of the verb can be formed by adding a prefix to the imperfective stem. Some examples of prefixes frequently used to form the perfective form are listed below. In all the examples given, the perfective verbs with the added prefix have the same meaning as their imperfective pair, but emphasise that a single and complete action is over:

Prefix	Examples	
	Imperfective	**Perfective**
про-	чита́ть (to read)	прочита́ть
на-	писа́ть (to write) печа́тать (to print) рисова́ть (to draw)	написа́ть напеча́тать нарисова́ть
вы-	пить (to drink) учи́ть (to learn/to study)	вы́пить вы́учить
с-	есть (to eat) петь (to sing) де́лать (to do) игра́ть (to play) мочь (can /to be able to)	съесть* спеть сде́лать сыгра́ть* смочь
при-	гото́вить (to prepare /to cook)	пригото́вить
по-	смотре́ть (to watch /to look at) звони́ть (to ring/to make a call) за́втракать (to have breakfast) обе́дать (to have lunch) у́жинать (to have dinner) стро́ить (to build)	посмотре́ть позвони́ть поза́втракать пообе́дать поу́жинать постро́ить
за-	плати́ть (to pay)	заплати́ть
* съесть: note the addition of the **ъ** after the prefix; сыгра́ть: note the vowel change **и/ы** in the root.		

Curiously, there is only one verb, *to buy*, whose perfective form has no prefix, but whose imperfective form does: **покупа́ть** (impf) – **купи́ть** (pf).

<table>
<tr><td>Level
2, 3</td><td>

20.1.2 Prefixes за-, по- and про-

</td></tr>
</table>

The meaning of the prefixes **за-**, **по-** and **про-** may differ from verb to verb. Some perfective verbs with added **за-**, **по-** and **про-** focus on the end of a single and complete action (☞ the table in 20.1.1). However, other perfective verbs with added prefixes **за-**, **по-** and **про-** focus on the beginning or duration of a single and complete action rather than on the end. All three prefixes have specific meanings when added to verbs of motion (☞ 25.1.3).

- **За-** may emphasise the beginning of the action when added to some imperfective verbs. Many of these verbs describe a sound: хло́пать – захло́пать (to applaud); крича́ть – закрича́ть (to shout/to scream); петь – запе́ть (to sing); игра́ть – заигра́ть (to play music); молча́ть – замолча́ть (to be silent); ла́ять – зала́ять (to bark); пла́кать – запла́кать (to cry) etc.
- **По-** may emphasise the short duration of the action when added to some verbs: рабо́тать – порабо́тать (to work); спать – поспа́ть (to sleep); говори́ть – поговори́ть (to talk); есть – пое́сть (to eat).
- **Про-** may emphasise an action of long duration: рабо́тать – прорабо́тать (to work); жить – прожи́ть (to live); учи́ться – проучи́ться (to study); занима́ться – прозанима́ться (to be occupied).

<table>
<tr><td>Level
2, 3</td><td>

20.1.3 Perfective forms of the verbs ви́деть, знать and слы́шать

</td></tr>
</table>

The prefix **у-** added to the imperfective verbs **ви́деть**, **знать** and **слы́шать** form their perfective pair with a slight modification to the verb meaning:

Meaning of the imperfective form	Meaning of the perfective form
ви́деть (to see/to have visual ability/ to meet someone)	уви́деть (to catch sight of) – the perfective form loses the verb meanings 'to meet someone' and 'to have visual ability'
слы́шать (to hear/to have a sense of hearing)	услы́шать (to hear) – the perfective form loses the verb meaning 'to have a sense of hearing'
знать (to know)	узна́ть (to find out/to learn) – the perfective form has the modified meaning of 'to learn' and 'to find out'

<table>
<tr><td>Level
3</td><td>

20.1.4 Prefixes that change the verb meaning

</td></tr>
</table>

Some prefixes added to some basic imperfective verbs change the meaning of the verb and make the verb perfective. For example:

писа́ть (to write)	**вы́**писать (to prescribe/to subscribe)
писа́ть (to write)	**с**писа́ть (to copy)
писа́ть (to write)	**за**писа́ть (to write down)
писа́ть (to write)	**о**писа́ть (to describe)
писа́ть (to write)	**под**писа́ть (to sign)
писа́ть (to write)	**пере**писа́ть (to rewrite/to copy).

If the prefix changes the meaning of the verb, a new imperfective verb with modified meaning is formed by adding the suffix **-ыва/-ива** or **-ва** to the stem of the perfective verb with prefix. So the aspect pairs in this case are considered as follows:

Imperfective aspect (describes an on-going action)	Perfective aspect (describes a single complete action)
выпи́сывать (to prescribe/to subscribe/to write out)	вы́писать (to prescribe/to subscribe/to write out)
спи́сывать (to copy)	списа́ть (to copy)
запи́сывать (to write down)	записа́ть (to write down)
опи́сывать (to describe)	описа́ть (to describe)
подпи́сывать (to sign)	подписа́ть (to sign)
перепи́сывать (to rewrite/to copy)	переписа́ть (to rewrite/to copy)

It is possible to see some similarities in use and meaning of some prefixes. However, there is no single unified pattern for how the added prefixes change the verb meaning. Some prefixes may have multiple meanings, depending on the verb. Therefore, the meaning of all verbs with added prefixes needs to be checked in a dictionary. The examples below show how some frequently occurring prefixes added to a verb change the verb meaning. (For verbs of motion with prefixes, ☞ 25.)

Prefix	Meaning	Example
в-	to join/to insert	вступа́ть/вступи́ть (to join a group) вставля́ть/вста́вить (insert)
вы-	to take away	выбра́сывать/вы́бросить (to throw)
до-	to do something to a certain point	дочи́тывать/дочита́ть до середи́ны (to read half the book) дожива́ть/дожи́ть до рассве́та (to survive to dawn) допи́сывать/дописа́ть до конца́ страни́цы (to write to the end of the page)
за-	to get/to gain/to close	загота́вливать/загото́вить (to store) захва́тывать/захвати́ть (to seize) заклéивать/заклéить (to seal) завя́зывать/завяза́ть (to fasten)
на-	to add/to press	наклéивать/наклéить; налепля́ть/налепи́ть (to stick something on something) нажима́ть/нажа́ть; нада́вливать/надави́ть (to press)
недо-	to underdo	недоеда́ть/недоéсть (to not finish your meal) недоса́ливать/недосоли́ть (to not add enough salt) недова́ривать/недовари́ть (to undercook)
о-/об-	to complete	осма́тривать/осмотрéть (to examine/to look thoroughly) обду́мывать/обду́мать (to think through)
пере-	to re-do	перестра́ивать/перестро́ить (to rebuild) перечи́тывать/перечита́ть (to reread) передéлывать/передéлать (to re-do)
	to change	переса́живаться/пересéсть (to change transport) переду́мывать/переду́мать (to change one's mind) переключа́ть/переключи́ть (to change a TV programme etc.) переводи́ть/перевести́ (to translate)

Prefix	Meaning	Example
	to overdo	переса́ливать/пересо́лить (to add too much salt) перееда́ть/перее́сть (to overeat) перева́ривать/перева́рить (to overcook)
при-	to do a little	приоткрыва́ть/приоткры́ть (to open a bit) приса́живаться/присе́сть (to sit on the edge) приостана́вливать/приостанови́ть (to suspend)
	to invent/to gain	приду́мывать/приду́мать (to make up) приобрета́ть/приобрести́ (to gain)
раз-/рас-	to open	развя́зывать/развяза́ть (to untie) раскрыва́ть/раскры́ть (to open)

Level 1, 2 ## 20.1.5 Formation of the aspectual pairs by making some internal changes to the verbal stem

Internal changes to the verbal stem can be made in the following ways:

- By changing a suffix. There are two frequently followed patterns.
  - Often the suffixes **-а/-я** indicate an imperfective verb and are changed for the suffix **-и** to make the verb perfective: реша́ть (impf) – реши́ть (pf), конча́ть (impf) – ко́нчить (pf).
  - The suffixes **-ыва/-ива/-ава** indicate an imperfective verb and are changed for the suffixes **-а/-я** to make the verb perfective: прода**ва́**ть (impf) – прода́ть (pf), опа́з**дыва́**ть (impf) – опозда́ть (pf). Often the change of suffix can be complicated by consonant changes in the stem. Usually, the same consonant change occurs when forming the perfective verbs and conjugating the verb in the present tense: с–ш, т–ч, б–бл etc. (For a list of the most frequent consonant changes, ☞ 17.1.2–17.1.4.)

- By changing or omitting a vowel in the stem. Often the vowels **а, ё, и** and **ы**, in the stem of imperfective verbs, are changed to make the verb perfective: а-о (ка**с**а́ться, to touch, impf., – ко**с**ну́ться, pf.), ё-е (расчё**с**ывать, to comb, impf. – рас**ч**еса́ть, pf.), и-е (ум**и**ра́ть, to die, impf. – ум**е**ре́ть, pf.), ы-о (взд**ы**ха́ть, to sign, impf. – взд**о**хну́ть, pf.). The presence of the 'fleeting' vowels, **ы** and **и**, in the stem often indicates the imperfective aspect. Their omission often indicates the perfective aspect: посыла́ть (to send, impf) – посла́ть (pf), собира́ть (to gather/to collect, impf.) – собра́ть (pf.), вспомина́ть (to remember, impf) – вспо́мнить (pf).

- In a small number of verbs, internal changes of the stem (vowels and consonant change or omission) are complicated by the reflexive particle –ся (for reflexive verbs, ☞ 23). Several reflexive verbs form their perfective pairs with non-reflexive verbs formed from the same stem. They are: сади́ться (to sit down, impf.) – сесть (pf.), ложи́ться (to lie down/to go to bed, impf.) – лечь (pf.), станови́ться (to become, impf.) – стать (pf.).

Some examples of internal changes made to imperfective stems to form perfective verbs are listed below. In all the examples, the perfective verb does not change the meaning of the imperfective one, but emphasises that a single action is completed.

Examples	
Imperfective	**Perfective**
реша́ть (to decide/to solve)	реши́ть

Examples	
конча́ть (to finish)	ко́нчить
продолжа́ть (to continue)	продо́лжить
изуча́ть (to study)	изучи́ть
объясня́ть (to explain)	объясни́ть
отвеча́ть (to answer)	отве́тить
встреча́ть (to meet)	встре́тить
приглаша́ть (to invite)	пригласи́ть
дава́ть (to give)	дать
продава́ть (to sell)	прода́ть
встава́ть (to get up/to stand up)	встать
опа́здывать (to be late)	опозда́ть
расчёсывать (to comb)	расчеса́ть
вспомина́ть (to remember)	вспо́мнить
понима́ть (to understand)	поня́ть
поднима́ть (to lift)	подня́ть
посыла́ть (to send)	посла́ть
собира́ть (to gather/to collect)	собра́ть
созыва́ть (to call for a meeting)	созва́ть
сади́ться (to sit down)	сесть
ложи́ться (to lie down)	лечь
станови́ться (to become)	стать

Level 1, 2

20.1.6 Formation of the perfective aspect by using a verb with a different stem

Some perfective aspects can be formed by using a verb with a different stem. Examples of some frequently occurring aspect pairs are listed below. In all examples, the perfective verb has the same meaning as the imperfective, but emphasises that a single action is completed:

Imperfective	Perfective
говори́ть (to say)	сказа́ть
брать (to take/to borrow)	взять
класть (to put down)	положи́ть
лови́ть (to catch)	пойма́ть

20.2 The context for use of verbal aspect

There are several words frequently used to establish the context for the appropriate use of verbal aspect.

20.2.1 Marker words frequently used with the imperfective aspect

To emphasise the meaning of the imperfective aspect, such as a repeated/habitual action or an action in progress, several words can be used to make the context clear.

● The vocabulary that conveys the idea of repetition is:

Ка́ждый день/ежедне́вно, ка́ждый ве́чер, ка́ждый год/ежего́дно и т. д.	Every day, every evening, every year etc.
По вечера́м/вечера́ми, по ноча́м/ноча́ми, по понеде́льникам и т. д.	In the evenings, in the night, on Mondays etc.
Два ра́за в неде́лю, три ра́за в ме́сяц, раз в две неде́ли/ка́ждую втору́ю неде́лю и т. д.	Twice a week, three times a month, every fortnight etc.
Обы́чно, всегда́, иногда́, никогда́, как пра́вило, постоя́нно, периоди́чески и т. д.	Usually, always, sometimes, never, as a rule, permanently, from time to time etc.
Ча́сто, ре́дко/и́зредка/нечáсто, неоднокра́тно и т. д.	Often, seldom, many times etc.
Как ча́сто?	How often?

For example:

Ири́на **смо́трит** свой люби́мый телесериа́л **ка́ждый день.**	Irina **watches** her favourite television series **every day.**
На про́шлой неде́ле Ири́на **смотре́ла** свой люби́мый телесериа́л **ка́ждый день.**	Last week Irina **watched** her favourite television series **every day.**
На сле́дующей неде́ле Ири́на **бу́дет смотре́ть** свой люби́мый телесериа́л **ка́ждый день.**	Next week Irina **is going to watch /will watch** her favourite television series **every day.**

● The vocabulary that conveys the idea of an action in progress is:

Как до́лго / Ско́лько вре́мени? С двух до трёх утра́, с пяти́ до семи́ ве́чера и т. д.	How long (for)? From 2 am to 3 am, from 5 pm to 7 pm etc.
Как до́лго / Ско́лько вре́мени? Два часа́, три часа́ и т. д	How long for? For two, three hours etc..
До́лго, недо́лго и т. д.	For a long time, for a short while etc.
Це́лый день, ве́чер и т. д.	For a whole day, evening etc.
Весь день, ме́сяц, год и т. д.	For a whole day, month, year etc.
Сейча́с	Now (right now, currently) etc.

For example:

Сейча́с Ми́ша **пи́шет** сочине́ние.	**Right now** Misha **is writing** an essay.
С двух до трёх Ми́ша **писа́л** сочине́ние, а **с пяти́ до шести́ отдыха́л.**	**From 2 to 3 pm** Misha **was writing** an essay and from **5 to 6 pm** he **was relaxing.**

Це́лый день Ми́ша **бу́дет отдыха́ть.** Misha **will be relaxing for the whole day.**

- There are no special marker words that support the use of the imperfective in sentences that give common knowledge or describe skills/ability. For example:
  - Ты **зна́ешь**, кто тако́й Гага́рин? '**Do** you **know** who Gagarin is?'
  - Коне́чно, **зна́ю.** 'Of course I **do.**'
  Мари́я прекра́сно **гото́вит.** Maria **cooks** well.

20.2.2 Marker words frequently used with the perfective aspect

To emphasise both meanings of the perfective aspect, the completeness of an action and that it is a single action, the following words are often used to make the context clear:

То́лько что, уже́ и т. д.	Just (only just), already etc.
Обяза́тельно и т. д.	Surely (without fail) etc.
К двум, к трём часа́м; к суббо́те и т. д.	By 2, 3 o'clock, by Saturday etc.
За два часа́, за неде́лю и т. д.	Within two hours, within a week etc.
Вдруг (внеза́пно), неожи́данно и т. д.	Suddenly, unexpectedly etc.

For example:

Господи́н Смирно́в **то́лько что прие́хал.** Mr Smirnoff **has just arrived.**
Ми́ша **обяза́тельно уберёт** свою́ **For sure,** Misha **will tidy up** his flat
кварти́ру **к семи́ часа́м ве́чера.** **by 7 pm.**

20.2.3 Words frequently used with both the imperfective and perfective aspects

Some words can convey only the idea of the past, present or future and cannot support the idea of a repeated action (impf) or single action (pf), an action in progress (impf) or a completed action (pf). Therefore, they are used with both verbal aspects. The speaker's personal interpretation of context and the information that they wish to give determine the use of the verbal aspect in these situations:

Вчера́, позавчера́, за́втра, послеза́втра и т. д.	Yesterday, the day before yesterday, tomorrow, the day after tomorrow etc.
В суббо́ту, в понеде́льник (дни неде́ли) и т. д.	On Saturday, on Monday (days of the week) etc.
У́тром, ве́чером, днём, но́чью (вре́мя су́ток) и т. д.	In the morning/evening/afternoon/ night (parts of the day) etc.
В сентябре́ (ме́сяцы) и т. д.; в про́шлом/бу́дущем году́, ле́том, зимо́й (времена́ го́да) и т. д.	In September (months) etc; last year/ next year, in the summer, in the winter (seasons) etc.
Давно́, неда́вно и т. д.	Long time ago, recently etc.
В 5 часо́в, в 7 часо́в ве́чера и т. д.	At 5 o'clock, at 7 pm etc.
Число́ – 5-ого декабря́ 1999 го́да; в 2000-ом году́ и т. д.	Date: 5th December 1999; in 2000 etc.
На ско́лько вре́мени? На 5 дней и т. д.	How long for? For 5 days etc.

For example:

Вчера Миша **читал** (impf) новый роман.	Yesterday Misha read/was reading a new novel (the result is unknown or is not relevant).
Вчера Миша **прочитал** (pf) новый роман.	Yesterday Misha finished reading/read/ did read a new novel (he achieved a goal).
Завтра Ирина **будет готовить** (impf) ужин для своих друзей.	**Tomorrow** Irina **will be making** dinner for her friends (Irina intends to do it, but there is no certainty that the result will be achieved).
Завтра в 7 часов Ирина **приготовит** (pf) ужин для своих друзей.	**Tomorrow at 7 pm,** Irina **will make** dinner for her friends (the dinner certainly will be made).

20.3 Use of verbal aspect in the present tense

For verbal aspect, ☞ the introduction to this chapter; for the present tense, ☞ 17.

In the present tense, only the imperfective aspect is used. In Russian, there is only one form of the present tense. Therefore, translation into English depends on the context and its interpretation by a speaker. For example, 'Они работают' can be translated as 'They are working' or 'They work'.

In the text below, you will see the various possible contexts in which the imperfective aspect can be used in the present tense.

Типичный день господина Смирнова. Господин Смирнов **живёт** в Москве и **работает** в Кремле. Он очень **любит** (a true fact) свою работу. Обычно много **работает** (repeated action) и мало **отдыхает** (repeated action). Каждый день он **обедает** (repeated action) в кафе «Ёлки-палки». Смотрите, вот он сейчас **сидит** у окна (action in progress), **ест** (action in progress) блины и **решает** (action in progress) кроссворды.	**A typical day for Mr Smirnoff.** Mr Smirnoff **lives** (true fact/state of being/repeated action) in Moscow and **works** (true fact/state of being/repeated action) in the Kremlin. He **loves** (true fact) his job very much. Usually, he **works** (repeated action) a lot and **relaxes** (repeated action) very little. Every day, he **has** his lunch (repeated action) in the 'Iolki-palki' café. Look, here he **is** now **sitting** (action in progress) next to a window, **eating** (action in progress) pancakes and **solving** (action in progress) a crossword.

20.4 Use of verbal aspect in the past tense

In the Russian past tense both aspects can be used.

For the past tense, ☞ 18. For the use of verbal aspect with verbs of motion in the past tense, ☞ 25.5.

20.4.1 Functions of verbal aspects

The verbal aspects in the past tense follow the general rule outlined in the introduction to this chapter. Additionally, the verbal aspects can be used to emphasise some specific meanings (☞ 20.4.2, 20.4.3, 20.4.4).

In the past tense, imperfective verbs are used:

- To confirm that an action occurred in the past without any indication of whether or not the action was completed and the result achieved. However, the use of the imperfective verb implies that the described action lasted for a while.

Влади́мир Набо́ков **писа́л** свои́ рома́ны на англи́йском языке́, а пото́м **переводи́л** их на ру́сский язы́к.	Vladimir Nabokov **wrote** his novels in English first, and then **translated** them into Russian.
В про́шлом ве́ке **не по́льзовались** компью́тером.	In the 19th century, they **did not use** computers.
В выходны́е мы **гуля́ли** по ле́су и **собира́ли** грибы́.	Last weekend we **walked/were walking** in the wood and **picked/were picking** mushrooms.

- To describe a habitual/repeated action in the past or skills/abilities. Often the use of the verb in this context implies that an action used to occur in the past, but does not occur any more.

| Ра́ньше Ви́ктор **чита́л** газе́ты ка́ждый день. | In the past Victor **used to read** the newspapers every day. |
| Ра́ньше Мари́я вку́сно **гото́вила**. | In the past, Maria **used to cook** well. |

- To describe an action that was in progress. Often the duration is indicated or implied in this context.

| **С двух до трёх** студе́нты **писа́ли** тест. | **From 2 pm to 3 pm**, the students **were taking/took** a test. |

In the past tense, perfective verbs are used

- To describe a single completed action. In any context, the speaker focuses on the achieved result of the action, either affirmative (Done!) or negative (Did not achieve the goal):

| Ви́ктор **прочита́л** кни́гу. | Victor **read/has read** a book (and **finished reading**). |
| Ви́ктор **не прочита́л** кни́гу (кни́ги). | Victor **did not read a book/did not finish reading/has not read** a book. |

- The use of a perfective verb often implies that an action has been in progress for a while and, finally, the goal was achieved as expected:

| Це́лый день Ви́ктор **чита́л** (impf. describes a process) кни́гу и, наконе́ц, **прочита́л** (pf, it is done!) её. | For the whole day, Victor **has been reading** a book and, finally, **has finished reading it.** |

As you can see from the examples above, translation of verbal aspect in the past tense from/to English can vary and depends on context and its interpretation by the speaker.

In the text below, you will see the various possible contexts in which the Russian imperfective and perfective verbs can be used in the past tense.

Господи́н Смирно́в на пе́нсии

До своего́ вы́хода на пе́нсию три́дцать пять лет господи́н Смирно́в **жил** (impf, action was in progress) в Москве́ и **рабо́тал** (impf, action was in progress) в Кремле́. Он о́чень **люби́л** (impf, confirmation that the action occurred) свою́ рабо́ту. Тогда́ он мно́го **рабо́тал** (impf, confirmation that the action occurred) и ма́ло **отдыха́л**

Mr Smirnoff in his retirement

For the thirty-five years before he retired Mr Smirnoff **had been living** (impf, action was in progress) in Moscow and **working** (impf, action was progress) in the Kremlin. He **loved** (impf, confirmation that the action occurred) his job very much. At that time he **worked** (impf, confirmation that the action occurred) a lot and **relaxed** (impf,

(impf, confirmation that the action occurred). Ка́ждый день он **обе́дал** (impf, repeated action) в кафе́ «Ёлки-па́лки». Он ча́сто **вспомина́ет** (impf. present tense) э́то вре́мя, когда́ ка́ждый день он **сиде́л** у окна́ (impf, action was in progress) в свой обе́денный переры́в, **ел** (impf, action was in progress in the past) вку́сные блины́ и **реша́л** (impf, action was in progress) кроссво́рды. Он та́кже лю́бит вспомина́ть (impf. present tense) оди́н моро́зный зи́мний день. В тот день он бы́стро **реши́л** (pf, single completed action) кроссво́рд, **съел** (pf, single completed action) свой ты́сячный блин и **получи́л** (pf, single completed action) замеча́тельный приз от кафе́ – фотоаппара́т.

confirmation that the action occurred) very little. Every day, he **had** his lunch (impf, repeated action) in the 'Iolki-palki' café. He often **remembers** (impf. present tense) the time when he **would sit** (impf, action was in progress) next to a window during his lunch break, **eating** (impf, action was in progress) pancakes and **solving** (impf, action was in progress) a crossword. In addition, he **loves to remember** (impf. present tense) one particular frosty winter's day. On this day he quickly **solved** the crossword (pf, single completed action), **ate** (pf, single completed action) his thousandth pancake and **received** (pf, single completed action) a great prize from the café for this – a camera.

Level 2, 3 ## 20.4.2 Use of imperfective and perfective verbs with an indication of time in the past tense

If a speaker knows the precise duration of an action in the past, the following constructions are used:

- The imperfective verb, followed by an expression of time without a preposition, is used to explain that the action occurred, and lasted for the indicated period, but the goal was not achieved. Alternatively, the result of the action is unknown or not relevant.

Ско́лько вре́мени студе́нт **писа́л** сочине́ние?	**For how long did** the student **write** the essay/**For how long was** the student **writing** the essay?
Студе́нт **писа́л** сочине́ние **час**.	The student **wrote/was writing** the essay **for an hour.**

It is not known if he completed the essay.

- The perfective verb, followed by the expression of time with the preposition **за** (within), is used to emphasise that the goal of the action was achieved within the indicated period.

За ско́лько вре́мени студе́нт **написа́л** сочине́ние?	**How long** did it take the student **to write (to complete)** the essay?
Студе́нт **написа́л** сочине́ние **за час**.	The student **wrote/has written** the essay **within an hour.**

- The imperfective verb, followed by an expression of time with the preposition **за** (for), is used to describe ability/skills to achieve a goal in the indicated period. This construction is less frequent.

За ско́лько вре́мени студе́нт обы́чно **писа́л** сочине́ния?	**How long** did it usually take the student **to write/to complete** the essays?
Студе́нт **обы́чно писа́л** сочине́ния **за час**.	The student **usually managed/was able to write/to complete** the essays within an hour.

20.4.3 Use of the verbal aspect to describe completed and reversed actions in the past tense

Several verbs can describe an action in which the result can be reversed.

- All verbs of motion with prefixes (☞ 25): приходи́ть/прийти́ (to arrive), выноси́ть/вы́нести (to get off), уезжа́ть/уе́хать (to depart) etc.
- The verbs открыва́ть/откры́ть (to open); закрыва́ть/закры́ть (to close); брать/взять (to take/to borrow); занима́ть/заня́ть (to borrow); встава́ть/встать (to get up); ложи́ться/лечь (to lie down); сади́ться/сесть (to sit down); класть/положи́ть (to put); включа́ть/включи́ть (to turn on); выключа́ть/вы́ключить (to turn off) and similar verbs.

If an imperfective verb from the above list is used in the past tense, it implies that the action did take place in the past, but was reversed back to its original point:

Дире́ктор **приходи́л**.	The director **was here** (but he **is gone now**).
Он **приезжа́л в** Москву́.	He **was** in Moscow/visited Moscow (but **is gone now**).
Мы **открыва́ли** окно́.	We **opened** the window (but **closed it again**).
Они́ **бра́ли креди́т** в ба́нке.	They **took a loan** from the bank (but **paid it back**).

If the perfective verb from the above list is used in the past tense, it implies that the goal of the action was achieved in the past, but its result is still relevant to the present:

Дире́ктор **пришёл**.	The director **has arrived** (and he is still here).
Он **прие́хал** в Москву́.	He **has arrived** in Moscow (and is still there).
Мы **откры́ли** окно́.	We **have opened** the window (and it is still open).
Они́ **взя́ли креди́т** в ба́нке.	They **have taken a loan** from the bank (and still owe money to the bank).

If a speaker knows the precise duration of an action in the examples above, the following constructions are used:

- The imperfective verb, followed by an expression of time with the preposition **на** (for), is used to explain that the action occurred in the past, lasted for the indicated period, but its result was reversed back to its original point.

На ско́лько (вре́мени) он **приезжа́л** (impf) в Москву́?	**How long** did he **stay** in Moscow?
Он **приезжа́л** (impf) **на два дня**.	He **stayed (came)** for two days (but is gone now).
На ско́лько (вре́мени) они́ **бра́ли** (impf) креди́т в ба́нке?	**For how long** did they **take** the loan from the bank?
Они́ **бра́ли** (impf) креди́т в ба́нке **на де́сять лет**.	They **took the loan** from the bank **for ten years** (they owed money to the bank for ten years, but paid it back).

- The perfective verb, followed by an expression of time with the preposition **на** (for), is used to emphasise that the goal of the action was achieved within the indicated period and its result is still relevant to the present.

На ско́лько (вре́мени) он **прие́хал** (pf) в Москву́?	How long does he **intend to stay** in Moscow?
Он **прие́хал** (pf) **на два дня**.	He **has come to stay for two days** (he is still in Moscow).
На ско́лько (вре́мени) они́ **взя́ли** креди́т в ба́нке?	**For how long** have they **taken** the loan from the bank?

Они́ **взя́ли** креди́т в ба́нке **на де́сять лет**.	They **have taken the loan** from the bank **for ten years** (they still owe money to the bank).

20.4.4 Other additional meanings of verbal aspect in the past tense

Verbal aspect can carry some additional meanings in sentences with an animate subject.

- If a question is asked by using the imperfective aspect, it can imply that the person who carried out the action did something wrong.

Кто **ста́вил** (impf) кни́ги на по́лки? Я не могу́ ничего́ найти́!	Who **put** the books on the shelves? I cannot find anything!
Из ска́зки «Три медве́дя»: ... По́здно ве́чером вошли́ в дом три медве́дя ... смо́трят и ничего́ не понима́ют:	Extract from the Russian fairy tale 'The three bears': ... Late that night, the three bears got home ... They look around and do not understand what has happened:
– Кто **сиде́л** (impf) на моём сту́ле?! – зарыча́л Миха́йло Ива́нович.–	'Who's been sitting in my chair?!' Mikhailo Ivanovich asked angrily.
А кто **сиде́л** (impf) на моём сту́ле?! – спроси́ла Ма́рья Ива́новна.	'And who's been sitting in my chair?!' Maria Ivanovna asked.

- If a question is asked using the perfective aspect, it can focus on the quality of the single and complete action.

Кто **испёк** (pf) э́тот **вку́сный торт?**	Who **made** this **great cake?**
Кто **так ужа́сно вы́мыл** (pf) посу́ду?	Who **did the washing up so poorly?**

In negative sentences, both aspects are used to convey additional information:

- In negative sentences imperfective verbs emphasise that the action did not occur.

– Ви́ктор, ты **посла́л** сообще́ние?	'Victor, **have you sent/did you send** a message?'
– Нет, я **не посыла́л** (impf).	'No, I **have not/did not**.'

- The use of the perfective in the same context emphasises that an attempt was made to achieve the goal, but it was not a success

– Извини́, я **не смог посла́ть/не посла́л** (pf) сообще́ние.	Sorry, but I **did not manage to send** a message (tried, but failed for whatever reason).

20.5 Use of verbal aspect in the future tense

Both the imperfective and perfective aspects can be used in the future tense. For the future tense, ☞ 19. Verbal aspect in the future tense follows the general rule outlined in the introduction to this chapter, except for the verbs of motion (☞ 24.5.3–24.5.5).

In the future tense, the imperfective verb is used:

- To describe the intention to carry out an action without any indication of whether or not the action is intended to be completed. However, the use of the imperfective verb implies that the described action will last for a while.

За́втра мы **бу́дем загора́ть** на пля́же.	Tomorrow we **are going to sunbathe** on the beach.

- To describe a repeated/habitual action.

В но́вом году́ по вечера́м я **бу́ду рабо́тать** в клу́бе.	In the New Year, I **will work** in the evenings in a sports club.

- To describe an action in progress. Usually, in this context the duration of the action would be indicated.

С пяти́ до шести́ ве́чера мы **бу́дем разгова́ривать** с друзья́ми по ска́йпу. — From 5 pm to 6 pm we will be talking to our friends on Skype.

In the future tense, the perfective verb focuses on the expected result in the future rather than on the intended action. It is used to describe a single complete action. For example:

Я **пошлю́** посы́лку послеза́втра. — I **will send** the parcel the day after tomorrow.

Translation from/to English depends on context and its interpretation by the speaker. Russian perfective verbs in the future tense are usually translated by using the English simple future tense: Мы э́то **сде́лаем**. (We **will do** it.) Russian imperfective verbs in the future tense are usually translated by using the English future continuous tense: Мы **бу́дем** э́то **де́лать**. (We **will be doing** it.)

In the text below, you will see the various possible contexts in which the Russian imperfective and perfective verbs can be used in the future tense:

Господи́н Смирно́в мечта́ет о пе́нсии

Когда́ господи́н Смирно́в вы́йдет на пе́нсию, он **бу́дет жить** (impf, action will occur) в Москве́, но **не бу́дет рабо́тать** (impf, action will occur) в Кремле́. Тогда́ он **бу́дет** мно́го **отдыха́ть** (impf, action will occur). Ка́ждый день он **бу́дет обе́дать** (impf, repeated action) в кафе́ «Ёлки-па́лки». Он ча́сто **мечта́ет** (impf. present tense) о том вре́мени, когда́ он ка́ждый день **бу́дет сиде́ть** у окна́ (impf, repeated action), **бу́дет есть** (impf, repeated action) блины́ и **реша́ть** (impf, repeated action) кроссво́рды. Но до э́того ещё далеко́! А пока́ в кафе́ **прохо́дит** (impf. present tense) ко́нкурс «Кто **съест** (pf, single complete action) ты́сячный блин?». Господи́н Смирно́в **наде́ется** (impf. present tense), что и́менно он **съест** (pf, single complete action) ты́сячный блин, обяза́тельно **вы́играет** (pf, single complete action) ко́нкурс и **полу́чит** (pf, single complete action) приз – фотоаппара́т.

Mr Smirnoff is dreaming about his retirement

When Mr Smirnoff has retired, **he will be living / will live** (impf, action will occur) in Moscow, but **will not be working / will not work** (impf, action will occur) in the Kremlin. Then he **will be relaxing/will relax** (impf, action will occur) a lot. Every day, he **will have** his lunch (impf, repeated action) in the 'lolki-palki' café. He often dreams about this time, when he **will sit** (impf, repeated action) next to a window, **eat** (impf, repeated action) pancakes and **solve** (impf, repeated action) crosswords. However, this time is far away. Meanwhile, in the café a competition called 'Who **will eat** (pf, single complete action) the thousandth pancake?' **is taking place** (impf, present tense). Mr Smirnoff **hopes** (impf, present tense) that it is he who **will eat** (pf, single complete action) the thousandth pancake and for sure **will win** (pf, single complete action) the prize – a camera.

evel 3

20.5.1 Use of imperfective and perfective verbs with an indication of time in the future tense

If a speaker knows the precise duration of an action in the future, the following constructions are used:

- The imperfective verb, followed by an expression of time without a preposition, is used to explain that the intended action will last for the indicated period, but the result of the action is unknown.

Ско́лько вре́мени юри́ст **бу́дет гото́вить** докуме́нты? — For how long will the lawyer be preparing the papers?

Юри́ст **бу́дет гото́вить** докуме́нты **три дня.** — The lawyer **will be preparing** the papers **for three days.**

- The perfective verb, followed by an expression of time with the preposition **за** (within), is used to emphasise that the goal of the action will certainly be achieved, as expected, within the indicated period.

За ско́лько вре́мени юри́ст **подгото́вит** докуме́нты?	**How long will** it **take** the lawyer **to prepare** the papers?
Юри́ст **подгото́вит** докуме́нты **за три дня**.	The lawyer **will prepare** the papers **within three days**.

- Perfective verbs are often followed by the preposition **че́рез** (within/in from now).

Юри́ст **подгото́вит** докуме́нты **че́рез три дня**.	The lawyer **will prepare** the papers **within three days from now**.

Level 3

20.5.2 Use of verbal aspect to describe reversed actions in the future tense

For verbs that can describe reversed action, ☞ 20.4.3.

In the future tense, to describe the duration of an action that can be reversed, perfective verbs are normally used. An exception is the imperfective verbs of motion (☞ 24.5.3–24.5.5). The imperfective and perfective verbs are followed by a time expression with the preposition **на**: **На ско́лько** (вре́мени)? (**For how long?**).

In this example, the perfective verb describes the single complete action in the future within the indicated period.

На ско́лько (вре́мени) они́ **возьму́т** (pf.) креди́т в ба́нке?	**For how long will** they **borrow** the money from the bank?
Они́ **возьму́т** (pf.) креди́т (pf) **на два го́да**.	They **will borrow** the money **for two years**.

In this example, the imperfective verb describes the intention to carry out an action in the future within the indicated period.

На ско́лько (вре́мени) они́ **бу́дут брать** (impf) креди́т в ба́нке?	**For how long are** they **borrowing** the money from the bank?
Они́ **бу́дут брать** (impf) **на два го́да**.	They **are borrowing** the money **for two years**.

Level 1

Упражне́ния

1. Choose the perfective or imperfective form of the verb in brackets. Put the verb in the correct form.

1. Мы то́лько что .... (учи́ть/вы́учить) 100 слов.
2. Мы всегда́ .... (узнава́ть/узна́ть) мно́го но́вого на ле́кциях.
3. Он обы́чно .... (обе́дать/пообе́дать) в кафе́.
4. Сего́дня на за́втрак они́ .... (пить/вы́пить) ча́шку ча́я и .... (есть/съесть) бутербро́д.

Level 2,3

2. Choose the appropriate verbal aspect of the verb in brackets. Put the verb in the correct form:

1. Вчера́ студе́нт .... (сдава́ть/сда́ть) экза́мен, но не .... (сдава́ть/сда́ть) его́.
2. Ви́ктор, кто .... (учи́ть/научи́ть) тебя́ так хорошо́ пла́вать? Ты до́лго .... (учи́ться/научи́ться)?
3. Учёные бу́дут це́лые дни .... (проводи́ть/провести́) в лаборато́рии.
4. Ты уже́ .... (звони́ть/позвони́ть) Са́ше?
5. Когда́ Ви́ктор .... (зака́нчивать/зако́нчить) университе́т, он .... (поступа́ть/поступи́ть) в аспиранту́ру.
6. Ты не .... (снима́ть/снять) боти́нки и оста́вил гря́зные следы́.

Level 3

3. Answer the questions using the words in brackets. Add a preposition, if appropriate:

1. За ско́лько вре́мени Вы пригото́вили обе́д? (час)
2. Как до́лго они́ живу́т здесь? (10 лет)
3. На ско́лько Вы прие́хали в Но́вгород? (2 дня)
4. На ско́лько вы возьмёте ипоте́ку? (25 лет)
5. Когда́ ты пригото́вишь обе́д? (полчаса́)

Level 2

20.6 Use of verbal aspect with the infinitive

The infinitive is a basic verb form. It cannot be conjugated and cannot have a tense on its own. However, it can have aspect. The majority of verbs have two infinitives, imperfective and perfective. On using the infinitive in a sentence, ☞ 16.1.1–16.1.2.

The imperfective and perfective infinitives convey exactly the same idea as the imperfective and perfective verbs, in the present, past and future tenses (☞ introduction to this chapter). The imperfective infinitive describes an action in progress, habitual/repeated action, skills/abilities, or denotes that the action is occurring. The perfective infinitive describes a single complete action focusing on its result.

However, the infinitive rarely appears in a sentence on its own (☞ 16.1.1). Usually the infinitive is used as a complementary part of the verb in a personal form, a modal word or an adverb.

Он **лю́бит отдыха́ть** (the verb in personal form + the infinitive).	He **loves to relax**.
Ему́ **на́до отдыха́ть** (a modal word + the infinitive).	He **needs to relax**.
Здесь **хорошо́ отдыха́ть!** (an adverb + the infinitive)	It **is great to relax** here!

Therefore, usually, the choice of aspect for the infinitive depends on the meaning of the verb, modal word or adverb that the infinitive complements. Translation between English and Russian also depends on the speaker's personal interpretation of the context. For example:

Мари́я **хо́чет** (impf) **чита́ть** (impf).	Maria **wants to do some reading** (now or in general).
Мари́я **захоте́ла** (pf) **чита́ть** (impf).	Maria **wants/wanted to do some reading** or Maria **feels/felt like doing some reading**.
Мари́я **хо́чет** (impf) **прочита́ть** (pf) заключи́тельную кни́гу о Га́ри По́тере.	Maria **wants to read** the final Harry Potter book (to the end).
Мари́я **захоте́ла** (pf) **прочита́ть** (pf) заключи́тельную кни́гу о Га́ри По́тере.	Maria **wants/wanted to read** the final Harry Potter book (to the end) or Maria **feels like/felt like reading** the final Harry Potter book (to the end).

20.6.1 Special use of the verbal aspect with the infinitive

20.6.1.1 Use of the infinitive with some verbs

If the infinitive complements the following verbs, only the imperfective infinitive can be used. Here, the principal verb, and not the complementary infinitive, conveys the aspect meaning:

Level 2

Imperfective	Perfective	Translation
начина́ть	нача́ть	to start/to begin
продолжа́ть	продо́лжить	to continue

	Imperfective	Perfective	Translation
Level 1, 2	конча́ть	ко́нчить	to finish/to end
Level 2, 3	зака́нчивать	зако́нчить	to finish/to graduate
	ока́нчивать	око́нчить	to finish/to graduate
	–	стать (coll)	to start/to begin
	перестава́ть	переста́ть (coll)	to stop
	принима́ться	приня́ться (coll)	to start/to begin
	надоеда́ть	надое́сть	to be fed up
	устава́ть	уста́ть	to be tired
	привыка́ть	привы́кнуть	to get used to
	отвыка́ть	отвы́кнуть	to get out of the habit of
	учи́ться	научи́ться	to gain some skills
	приуча́ть	приучи́ть	to train to do something
	отуча́ть	отучи́ть	to train to lose some habits
	–	разлюби́ть	to lose interest
	–	разучи́ться	to lose skills/ability
	–	полюби́ть	to love
	–	понра́виться	to like
	запреща́ться (запрещено́)	–	to forbid
	избега́ть	–	to avoid

After the verbs **нра́виться** (impf, to like), **люби́ть** (impf, to love) and **мочь** (impf, to be able) both perfective and imperfective infinitives can be used.

After the verbs **успе́ть** (pf, to have time to do something/to manage), **суме́ть** (pf, to be able to manage), **уда́ться** (pf, to succeed), **забы́ть** (to forget) only the perfective infinitive is used.

Level 2, 3

20.6.1.2 Use of the infinitive with some modal words

The use of imperfective or perfective infinitive after the following modal words changes the meaning of the phrase:

- The modal words **на́до/ну́жно/необходи́мо** (need/necessary) and **мо́жно** (possible/to be allowed) followed by the imperfective infinitive convey the idea that 'it is time to act'.

Надо **конча́ть**.	**It is time** to end (something).
Мо́жно **накрыва́ть** на стол.	**It is time** to lay the table.

- The modal words **на́до/ну́жно/необходи́мо** (need/necessary) followed by the perfective infinitive convey the idea of 'necessity to act'.

На́до **ко́нчить**.	**It is necessary** to end (something).

- The modal word **мо́жно** (possible/to be allowed) followed by the perfective infinitive conveys the idea that 'it is permitted to act'.

Мо́жно **накры́ть** на стол.	You **may** lay the table.

- If the word **пора́** means 'it is time', it is usually followed by the imperfective infinitive.

    Пора́ **обе́дать**.   It is time **to have lunch**.

- The modal word **нельзя́** (impossible/not permitted) followed by the imperfective infinitive conveys the idea that 'it is not permitted'.

    В аэропорту́ **нельзя́ оставля́ть**   **It is not permitted to leave** your luggage
    бага́ж без присмо́тра.   unattended in an airport.

- However, if the word **нельзя́** is followed by the perfective infinitive, it conveys the idea that 'it is not physically possible'.

    В аэропорту́ **нельзя́ оста́вить** бага́ж.   **It is not possible to leave** the luggage in
    Ка́мера хране́ния закры́та!   the airport. The left luggage office is closed!

evel
3

20.6.1.3 Other special uses of the verbal aspect with the infinitive

- In negative sentences only the imperfective infinitive can be used after:

    не на́до (не ну́жно)/не́зачем   unnecessary
    не сле́дует   should not
    бесполе́зно   it is no use
    не полага́ется/не при́нято   it is not customary
    не разреша́ется/не разрешено́   not permitted
    не хо́чется   do not feel like
    не сове́товать (in personal forms: do not advise
    я не сове́тую, ты не сове́туешь etc.)

    For example:
    В Росси́и **не при́нято здоро́ваться**   In Russia, **it is not customary to shake**
    че́рез поро́г.   **hands** over the threshold.

    Мне **не хо́чется обща́ться** с ним.   I **do not feel like socialising** with him.

- Only the imperfective infinitive is used after words with the meaning 'to have enough' – хва́тит, дово́льно, доста́точно. For example:

    Хва́тит говори́ть об э́том де́ле.   **That's enough talking** about this matter.

evel
2

20.7 The use of verbal aspects in the imperative

The imperative (an instruction/request/invitation) has only two forms: the 2nd person singular and 2nd person plural. However, the imperative is used in both aspects, imperfective and perfective. For the imperative, ☞ 22.2.

The speaker's choice between imperfective and perfective imperatives is based on the general meaning of the verbal aspect (☞ introduction to this chapter).

The imperfective imperative can contain:

- General advice or an instruction/request to carry out an action for a period of time.

    Всегда́ **мо́йте** ру́ки пе́ред едо́й.   Always **wash** your hands before eating.
    Следи́те за чистото́й в до́ме.   **Keep** the house clean.
    Говори́те ме́дленно и я́сно!   **Speak** slowly and clearly!

- An instruction/request to start an action.

    Пиши́те, пожа́луйста!   Please, **write** (start writing)!
    Чита́йте!   **Read**!

The perfective imperative

- Is an instruction/request to carry out a single action and to complete it. If a speaker gives an instruction using the perfective imperative, they expect to see the result of the request.

    Переда́йте, пожа́луйста, соль.   **Pass** the salt, please.
    Скажи́те, пожа́луйста.   **Tell** me, please
    Прочита́йте, пожа́луйста, пе́рвое   Please read the first sentence.
    предложе́ние.

Level
2, 3

20.7.1 Some special uses of the perfective and imperfective imperatives

The aspect of the imperative can have some additional meanings. For example, the imperfective imperative is used to convey the sense of a very polite invitation. Conversely, the perfective imperative sounds more like an instruction/an order than an invitation. However, this rule is followed only in some selected contexts, for example 'paying a visit' (especially when verbs of motion are involved).

Compare the situations:

В гостя́х. Paying a visit.	Разгово́р с провини́вшимся ученико́м. A conversation with a badly behaved pupil.
The imperfective imperative sounds like a very polite invitation:	The perfective imperative sounds like an instruction:
Входи́те (come in), раздева́йтесь (take your coat off), проходи́те (come through), сади́тесь (sit down), пожа́луйста; чу́вствуйте себя́, как до́ма (make yourself at home).	Зайди́ к дире́ктору по́сле уро́ков. (Go and see the headmaster after lessons.)
Бери́те всё, что хоти́те/бери́те/ку́шайте всё, что на столе́ (help yourself).	Войди́ и объясни́, почему́ ты опя́ть опозда́л. (Come in and explain why you are late.)
Бери́те фру́кты, икру́ (help yourself to some fruit and caviar), налива́йте вино́ (help yourself to wine), пе́йте (drink), кури́те (feel free to smoke), пожа́луйста.	Замолчи́! (Be quiet!)
Заходи́те к нам в любо́е вре́мя! (Call on us at any time!).	Прекрати́ верте́ться! (Stand still!)
Приезжа́йте, пожа́луйста, в го́сти. (Do come and visit us)	this is imperfective

Level
1, 2

20.7.2 Use of aspects of the imperative in negative sentences

Usually, negative imperatives are used in the imperfective form:

Не открыва́йте окно́. Здесь хо́лодно.	Don't open the window. It's cold.
Не кури́те!	Don't smoke!

In negative constructions the perfective form of the imperative is used only if a speaker wants to warn against possible undesirable results of an action:

То́лько, пожа́луйста, **не разбе́й** э́ту ва́зу. Она́ така́я дорога́я!	Please don't break this vase. It is very expensive!
Не **забу́дь** закры́ть дверь. Вчера́ ты оста́вил дверь неза́пертой.	Don't forget to lock the door today. Yesterday you left the door unlocked.

Level
2, 3

Упражне́ния

1. Complete the sentences using the appropriate form of the infinitive in brackets:

1. Подро́стки лю́бят .... (слу́шать/послу́шать) рок-му́зыку.
2. Ле́на отвы́кла ра́но .... (встава́ть/встать).
3. Соба́к на́до .... (выгу́ливать/вы́гулять) ка́ждый день.
4. Больно́му нельзя́ .... (пить/вы́пить) спиртно́е.

5. Звени́т буди́льник! Пора́ .... (встава́ть/встать).

6. Здесь нельзя́ .... (кури́ть/закури́ть).

7. Студе́нты ско́ро начну́т .... (занима́ться/заня́ться) в лаборато́рии.

8. Ви́ктор ко́нчил .... (чита́ть/прочита́ть) статью́.

9. Депута́ты Ду́мы продо́лжили .... (обсужда́ть/обсуди́ть) прое́кт зако́на.

2. Form the imperative from the verb in brackets:

1. Мать говори́т сы́ну: «(Вести́) .... себя́ прили́чно! Не (груби́ть) .... ста́ршим, ... (слу́шать) учителе́й.»

2. Всегда́ (есть) .... мно́го овоще́й и фру́ктов. (Пить) .... со́ки.

3. Никому́ не .... (расска́зывать) о на́шем секре́те. И, пожалу́йста, не .... (проговори́ться) Ма́ше.

4. (Говори́ть) .... гро́мко и ме́дленно, пожа́луйста.

5. (Заходи́ть) .... ко мне за́втра. (Принести́) .... фотогра́фии.

6. На у́лице гололёд. Не .... (упа́сть)!

21 Verbs: transitive and intransitive verbs, active and passive voice

The categories of transitivity and voice have strong connections. They explain the relationships between verb, object and subject in sentences.

Level 2, 3

21.1 Transitivity

Transitivity is a grammatical category that helps us to understand the relationship between a verb and object in a sentence, to establish whether the verb can take a direct object and to convey the message correctly. In both Russian and English verbs are either transitive or intransitive (☞ 21.1.1 and 21.2 respectively). English and Russian verbs do not fully correspond on transitivity. Therefore, we cannot assume that if a verb is transitive in English it will also be transitive in Russian.

The most distinctive feature for recognising an intransitive Russian verb is the ending -ться as all Russian reflexive verbs are intransitive (for reflexive verbs, ☞ 23). However, non-reflexive verbs do not have a distinctive feature to indicate transitivity. Reference books and larger dictionaries provide information as to whether the verb is intransitive or transitive or to indicate specific uses of the verb.

21.1.1 Transitive verbs

In a sentence, a transitive verb must be followed by a direct object. The direct object clarifies the transitive verb. If a transitive verb is without a direct object in a sentence, the idea of the sentence sounds incomplete or unclear. For example:

Верóника **мóет (что?) посýду.**	Veronica **is washing (what?) the dishes.**
Алексéй **надевáет (что?) джúнсы.**	Alex **is putting on (what?) jeans.**

In a sentence, a direct object is represented by a noun or pronoun in the accusative case without a preposition. In a Russian negative sentence a direct object can be represented by a noun or pronoun in the genitive case without a preposition. For example:

Кóля купúл **кнúгу** (accusative case).	Nick bought a book.
Кóля не купúл **кнúги** (genitive case).	Nick did not buy a book.
Кóля не купúл **кнúгу** (accusative case).	Nick did not buy the book (a specific book)

21.2 Intransitive verbs

In a sentence, an intransitive verb cannot take a direct object. If an intransitive verb needs any clarification it must be followed by a phrase with a preposition. A prepositional construction can be represented by a noun or personal pronoun with a preposition in various cases. For example:

Футболúст бежúт **за мячóм.**	A footballer runs **after a ball.**
Баскетболúст бежúт **с мячóм.**	A basketball player runs **with a ball.**

Instrumental and dative cases without prepositions can also follow intransitive verbs:

интересова́ться спо́ртом (to be interested in sport)

In Russian, the following groups of verbs are always intransitive:

- **All reflexive verbs.** (For reflexive verbs, ☞ 23.)
- Eight of the fourteen verbs of motion and the verbal forms derived from them. (For a list of the verbs of motion, ☞ 24.1).

21.3 Voice

Voice is one of the core grammatical categories that clarify relations between the verb and the subject of the sentence. In both Russian and English, there are two voices: *active* and *passive*. The active voice confirms that the subject of the sentence acts itself and explains how. The passive voice describes what is done to the subject of the sentence by someone else or something else that is often called the 'agent'. In the Russian passive construction, a known 'agent' is expressed by the instrumental case with no preposition. Only transitive verbs that take a direct object can have passive voice. Note the following changes when an active construction is converted into a passive one:

- The direct object of an active construction becomes the subject of a passive construction.
- The subject of an active construction becomes the object of a passive construction.

For example:

Active construction	Passive construction
О́пытный **юри́ст подгото́вил** все необходи́мые докуме́нты. (**The** experienced **lawyer prepared** all the necessary papers.)	Все необходи́мые **докуме́нты подгото́влены** о́пытным **юри́стом** ('agent' in the instrumental case). (All the necessary **papers are prepared by an** experienced **lawyer**.)
За́втра **Моско́вский городско́й суд бу́дет рассма́тривать** де́ло про́тив ви́це-мэ́ра Москвы́. (Tomorrow **the Moscow City Court will hold** hearings against the deputy mayor of Moscow.)	За́втра в Моско́вском городско́м су́де **бу́дет рассма́триваться** де́ло ('agent' is omitted) про́тив ви́це-мэ́ра Москвы́. (Tomorrow **hearings will be held** against the deputy mayor of Moscow in the Moscow City Court.)

Passive constructions are mainly used in writing. However, passive impersonal sentences (☞ 30.1) and indefinite-personal sentences (☞ 21.5) are common in popular speech. For example:

Здесь **наку́рено.**	Somebody has been smoking here.
Решено́, е́дем!	It is decided, let's go!
Нас **спроси́ли.**	We were asked.
Их **арестова́ли.**	They were arrested.

21.4 How to express the passive voice

The passive voice can be expressed:

- By a short-form passive participle. Such participles are used in the perfective aspect only and describe a complete action.
  - For short-form passive participles, ☞ 26.2.
  - For the verb-link **быть** (to be) used with short-form passive participles, ☞ 26.2.
- By reflexive verbs. Usually imperfective reflexive verbs are used in the passive sense. They describe an ongoing incomplete action. However, when describing natural phenomena, both imperfective and perfective reflexive verbs can be used: ☞ 23.4.

👁 In Russian, passive constructions are often replaced by indefinite-personal sentences: ☞ 21.5.

21.5 Indefinite-personal sentences with omitted subject

This type of sentence has only one core element – the predicate (the verb). The subject of the sentence ('they') is always omitted, but it is implied that it is animate. The verb reflects the form of the omitted subject – the 3rd person plural form of a personal verb. The verb can be used in all three tenses (present, past and future) and in both aspects (perfective and imperfective):

В газе́тах мно́го **писа́ли** об э́том преступле́нии.	**They wrote** a lot about this crime in the newspapers.
Говоря́т, что он прекра́сный челове́к.	**They say** he is a wonderful man.

👁 In Russian, the personal pronoun **они́** (they) is never used in these indefinite-personal sentences as it would imply that we actually know who is acting in the sentences. Note that the same form of the verb, 3rd person plural, is used to describe one unknown person or an unspecified number of people. For example:

Они́ Вас **спра́шивают.**	**They are asking** for you (Implied: we know who is asking.)
Вас **спра́шивают.**	**Someone is asking** for you. (Implied: unknown person/persons are asking.)

Indefinite-personal sentences are common in popular speech. They often replace passive constructions with reflexive verbs or short-form participles. For example:

Мемориа́л **откры́ли** два го́да наза́д (indefinite-personal sentence).	**They opened** the memorial two years ago.
Мемориа́л **откры́лся** (reflexive verb) два го́да наза́д.	The memorial **was opened** two years ago.
Мемориа́л **был откры́т** (short-form participle) два го́да наза́д.	The memorial **was opened** two years ago.

👁 Some common transitive English verbs are intransitive in Russian. Therefore, they cannot appear in passive constructions. However, they are commonly used in indefinite-personal sentences. Among these verbs are:

говори́ть	to speak a language	сле́довать	to follow
ве́рить	to believe	наблюда́ть за	to watch/to observe
помога́ть	to help	присма́тривать за	to look after
смотре́ть на	to look at	ду́мать о	to think about

For example:

На како́м языке́ **говоря́т** в Португа́лии?	What language **is spoken** in Portugal?
За детьми́ прекра́сно **присма́тривают** в э́тих я́слях.	The children **are looked after** well in this nursery.

evel
2, 3

Упражне́ния

1. Translate into Russian. Keep the passive voice where possible:

1. Too much money was spent on the wedding. Many guests were invited, a lot of food was eaten and a lot of wine was drunk.
2. Moscow was not built at once (idiom).
3. This paper must be rewritten.
4. The thief will be caught and sent to prison.
5. New parking is being built next to the offices.
6. Caution! The doors are closing.

evel
3

2. Rewrite the message that Mr Smirnoff's secretary has left him, replacing personal sentences with indefinite-personal sentences with omitted subject:

Уважа́емый Алекса́ндр Дми́триевич!
1. Кака́я-то де́вушка звони́ла Вам два́жды.
2. Кто́-то принёс для Вас паке́т и оста́вил его́ на столе́.
3. Заходи́л како́й-то мужчи́на и спра́шивал, когда́ Вы бу́дете?
4. Я уточни́ла, вы́ставка открыва́ется за́втра.
5. Я прове́рила, газе́ты писа́ли о Ва́шем докла́де.

22 Verbs: mood

Level
1, 2, 3 A verb can appear in a sentence in one of four moods:

1 *indicative*
2 *imperative*
3 *conditional*
4 *subjunctive*

The verbal mood defines the speaker's attitude towards the action.

Level
1, 2 ## 22.1 The indicative mood

The indicative mood describes an action that the speaker considers real. The indicative mood can be presented by using any verbal form in all three tenses. For example:

Идёт дождь.	It **is raining**.
На у́лице дождь?	**Is** it **raining** outside?
Како́й си́льный дождь!	What heavy rain!
Вчера́ **шёл** дождь.	It **rained** yesterday.
За́втра **бу́дет** дождь.	It **will rain** tomorrow.

Level
1, 2 ## 22.2 The imperative

The verb in the imperative mood is used to give a command, an instruction or advice, or to make a request. The imperative is used as a predicate in a sentence with the subject omitted. The imperative has only two personal forms, 2nd person singular **ты** (you) and 2nd person plural **вы** (you). **Ты** is used to address someone informally. **Вы** is used to address one person formally or a group of people. The imperative can be used in both aspects, imperfective and perfective. For use of verb aspect in the imperative, ☞ 20.7.

Examples of the imperative:

Са́ша, **заходи́, не стесня́йся**!	Sasha, **come in, don't be** shy!
Соблюда́йте пра́вила у́личного движе́ния!	**Follow** the traffic regulations!
Бу́дьте добры́! **Переда́йте**, пожа́луйста, Ната́лье Серге́евне, что звони́л её аспира́нт Ма́рченко.	**Would you be so kind as to tell** Natalia Sergeevna that her PhD student Marchenko called?

In Russian, to make a very polite request the phrase **Бу́дьте добры́**!/**Бу́дьте любе́зны**! (Be so kind) is used with the word **пожа́луйста** (please). For example:

В тра́нспорте – **Бу́дьте добры́**!	In public transport – **Would you be so kind** as to pass (the money) for the ticket (**please**).
Переда́йте на биле́т, **пожа́луйста**!	

22.2.1 Formation of the imperative

Both the imperfective and perfective aspects of the imperative are formed in the same way:

- Use the 3rd person plural of the present tense to form the imperfective imperative and the 3rd person plural of the perfective future tense to form the perfective imperative:
  - де́ла**ют** (they do, imperfective)
  - сде́ла**ют** (they will do, perfective)
  - иду́**т** (they go, imperfective)
  - приду́**т** (they will come, perfective)
  - гото́в**ят** (they cook, imperfective)
  - пригото́в**ят** (they will cook, perfective).

  For present tense and future perfective verb formation, ☞ 17 and 19 respectively.
- Drop the ending of that form: де́ла-/сде́ла-; ид-/прид-; гото́в-/пригото́в-
- Add the appropriate suffix:
  - add -**й**, if the stem ends in a vowel: де́лай-; сде́лай-
  - add -**и**, if the stem ends in a consonant: иди-; приди-
  - add -**ь**, if the stem ends in a consonant and the stress falls on the stem throughout the conjugation (in all forms of the present or future perfective tense): гото́в**ь**
- Add nothing after the suffix for the 2nd person singular form; add -**те** for the 2nd person plural form: де́лай, сде́лай, де́лай**те**, сде́лай**те**.
- For reflexive verbs (ending with -ться): at the end add -**сь** after a vowel and -**ся** after a consonant: умыва́й**тесь**, умыва́й**ся** (wash yourself).

22.2.2 Formation of irregular imperatives

There are some irregular imperatives whose formation does not follow the regular pattern using the 3rd person plural present tense stem:

	from
ешь/е́шьте (eat)	есть (они́ **едя́т**)
пей/пе́йте (drink)	пить (они́ **пьют**)
поезжа́й/поезжа́йте (go)	пое́хать (они́ **пое́дут**)
verbs with the suffix -ва-/-ава-	
встава́й/встава́йте (get up)	встава́ть (они **встаю́т**)
дава́й/дава́йте (give)	дава́ть (они **даю́т**)
достава́й/достава́йте (get)	достава́ть (они **достаю́т**)
узнава́й/узнава́йте (find out)	узнава́ть (они **узнаю́т**)
продава́й/продава́йте (to sell)	продава́ть (они **прода́ю́т**)

22.2.3 Additional ways to express the imperative mood

There are additional ways to convey the imperative mood. The following compound forms are often used in popular speech:

- The imperative of the verb **дава́ть** (in this context the verb means 'to let') followed by the imperfective infinitive or by the perfective verb in the perfective future tense, in the 1st person plural form:

Дава́йте говори́ть друг дру́гу комплиме́нты (Окуджа́ва).

Let us pay each other compliments.

Дава́й помя́нем тех, кто с на́ми был ... (гру́ппа «Любэ́»).

Let us remember who was with us ...

- The particle **пусть/пуска́й** ('let') followed by a noun/pronoun in the nominative case and a personal verb that agrees with the noun/pronoun. Usually this construction is employed when talking about giving an instruction to a 3rd person. The subject of the sentence can be omitted:

Пусть он сам **реша́ет**.

Let him decide for himself.

Пусть всегда́ **бу́дет со́лнце**,

Let the sun be for ever,

Пусть всегда́ **бу́дет не́бо**,

Let the sky be for ever,

Пусть всегда́ **бу́дет ма́ма**,

Let my mum be for ever.

Пусть всегда́ **бу́ду я**. (Оша́нин)

Let me be for ever.

- The particle **да** ('let') followed by a personal verb in the 3rd person singular or plural. This construction is frequently used in slogans, toasts and poetry

Да здра́вствуют му́зы, **да здра́вствует** ра́зум! (Пу́шкин)

Hail, muses! Hail, reason!

A very strong command can be given by using the imperfective infinitive: **Сиде́ть!** (Sit down!) **Лежа́ть!** (Lie down!) **Молча́ть!** (Be quiet!) Very rarely, an adverb can be used as a command: **Ти́хо!** (Silence!)

Verbs of motion with the prefix **по-** are frequently used in the past tense to invite someone to start moving (for the verbs of motion with prefixes, ☞ 25.1): **Пошли́!** (Let us go!)

Он сказа́л – **пое́хали**, он взмахну́л руко́й, Сло́вно вдоль по Пи́терской, Пи́терской Пронёсся над Землёй. (Добронра́вов)

He said, 'Let's go', and waved his hand, As if along Piterskaya street He went around the Earth.

Упражне́ния

Level 1, 2

1. Form the imperatives of the following verbs:

1. уходи́ть
2. пригото́вить
3. критикова́ть

4. есть
5. пить
6. сади́ться

Level 2

Обобща́ющее упражне́ние

2. Complete the e-mails sent by Mr Smirnoff:

    A. to his girl-friend

    B. to his secretary

using imperatives formed from the verbs given:

A. Быть до́брым, звони́ть ма́тери, поздравля́ть с днём рожде́ния, купи́ть цветы́, ждать меня́ у вхо́да в рестора́н.

B. Быть до́брым, посыла́ть факс г. Сми́ту, заказа́ть сто́лик на четверы́х в рестора́не.

22.3 Conditional mood

Level 2, 3

The conditional mood describes a possible or hypothetical action that will/would take place in the past, present or future, if certain conditions are met/would be met. This type of sentence is common in both popular speech and in writing. The choice of verbal aspect in the conditional mood depends on the speaker's interpretation of the situation (for verbal aspect, ☞ 20). The conditional mood is usually expressed by a complex sentence in which a subordinate clause determines conditions to enable the action to occur in the main clause ('if-then'). The subordinate clause can precede or follow the main clause:

Éсли не бу́дет дождя́ (condition), я пойду́ гуля́ть (possible action).	If it doesn't rain, I will go out.
Я пойду́ гуля́ть (possible action), éсли не бу́дет дождя́ (condition).	I will go out, if it doesn't rain.

22.3.1 Types and structure of conditional sentences

There are two types of conditional sentences. One type sets hypothetical conditions for a hypothetical action:

Éсли бы я знал, что он не придёт, **я бы не сиде́л** весь ве́чер до́ма.	**If I had known** he was not going to come, **I would not have spent** the evening at home.

Another type sets real conditions for the action that will occur if these conditions are met:

Éсли я узна́ю, что он не придёт, **я не бу́ду сиде́ть** це́лый ве́чер до́ма.	**If I find out** that he is not going to come, **I will not spend** the evening at home.

The sentence structure with hypothetical conditions is as follows:

- The subordinate clause is introduced by the conjunction **éсли** (if) with the particle **бы** – **éсли бы** (if). **Éсли** and **бы** cannot be separated.
- **Бы** must appear in both the main and subordinate clauses before or after a verb.
- All verbs in the main and subordinate clauses are in the past tense.

The sentence structure with real conditions is as follows:

- The subordinate clause is introduced by the conjunction **éсли** (if).
- No **бы** in this type of sentence.
- All verbs in the main and subordinate clauses are used in tenses that reflect the actual time of the action.

22.3.2 Modified structure of conditional sentences

Level 3

In informal style, changes can be made to the structure of the conditional sentence:

- The subordinate clause can be omitted, if conditions are set on behalf of the speaker (*If I were you*). The expression '**на Ва́шем ме́сте**' is equivalent to the English '*If I were you*'. For example:

(На Ва́шем ме́сте) **я бы не храни́л** де́ньги в э́том ба́нке.	(If I were you), **I would not have kept/I wouldn't keep** money in this bank.

- **Éсли** can be replaced with the words **раз, коль, ко́ли** (if).

Раз ты хо́чешь, я сде́лаю.	**If you want**, I will do it.

22.4 Subjunctive mood

Level 2, 3

22.4.1 Subjunctive: meaning and use

A verb in the subjunctive mood describes a wishful thought. In a simple sentence with one subject, the particle **бы** added to a verb conveys the idea that the described action is not real, but a desirable one. The English equivalents of the Russian subjunctive mood are sentences with the modal verbs *should*, *would* or *could*. The particle **бы** can only be used with past-tense verbs or an infinitive. In a sentence, the particle **бы** can be added to:

- A verb in the past tense, if a speaker makes a request. **Бы** can be placed before or after the verb:

Посла́л бы ты Ви́ктору ещё одно́ сообще́ние, что-то он не отвеча́ет **or** Ты **бы посла́л** Ви́ктору ещё одно́ сообще́ние, что-то он не отвеча́ет.	**Could you please send** Victor another e-mail; for some reason he is not answering.

- A negative verb in the past tense, if a speaker makes an inquiry:

Ты посла́л бы Ви́ктору ещё одно́ сообще́ние? **or** Ты **бы не посла́л** Ви́ктору ещё одно́ сообще́ние?	**Could you please send** Victor another e-mail?

Note, the negative verb conveys the same idea as the positive one (see the example above), but may sound more polite.

- An infinitive, if the speaker is just thinking aloud. **Бы** is placed after the infinitive:

Съесть бы сейча́с моро́женое!	I **would love** to have an ice cream now!
Полежа́ть бы на пля́же!	I **would love** to lie on a beach!

The verbs **хоте́ть** (to want) and **мочь** (to be able) are often used in the subjunctive mood to express a polite invitation or request:

Я **хоте́л бы пригласи́ть** Вас в го́сти.	I **would like to invite** you to visit me.
Мы **бы хоте́ли попроси́ть** вас об одно́м одолже́нии.	We **would like to ask** you to do us a favour.
Вы **могли́ бы уба́вить звук** телеви́зора?	**Could you please turn down** the television?

The negative forms of **хоте́ть** and **мочь** are often used in the subjunctive mood to make an inquiry:

Ты **не мог бы зайти́** в магази́н по доро́ге домо́й?	**Could you please pop into** the shop on your way home?

In the examples above, the particle, **бы** is added to **хоте́ть** and **мочь**, which are in the past tense.

22.4.2 Using clauses introduced by что́бы

If a sentence has more than one subject, a subordinate clause introduced by the conjunction **что́бы** is used to make a request or express desire. The English equivalent of this type of construction is '*I want you to do it*'.

In the subordinate clause, all verbs must be used in the past tense regardless of the actual timing of the action described. **Что́бы** cannot be translated into English. For example:

Диспе́тчер **приказа́л пило́ту, что́бы** он неме́дленно **посади́л** самолёт.	A traffic controller **instructed the pilot to land** the plane immediately.
Попроси́те Ма́шу, **что́бы** она мне **позвони́ла**.	**Ask** Masha **to call** me.

In the main clause, the following words are often used to emphasise a request or express desire:

- Verbs говори́ть – сказа́ть (to say), проси́ть – попроси́ть (to ask), тре́бовать – потре́бовать (to demand), передава́ть – переда́ть (to pass on a message), хоте́ть – захоте́ть (to want), жела́ть – пожела́ть (to wish), предупрежда́ть – предупреди́ть (to warn) etc.
- Modal words на́до, ну́жно, необходи́мо (need/necessary).
- Adverbs ва́жно (important), жела́тельно (desirable) etc.

Note that the conjunction **что́бы** can be used in other contexts: ☞ 29.2.5.

Обобщáющее упражнéние

1. Complete scenarios A and B below with phrases 1–4 to produce:
A. conditional sentences that describe hypothetical conditions for a hypothetical action.
B. conditional sentences that describe real conditions for an action that will occur, if these conditions are met.

1. съéздить в кругосвéтное путешéствие
2. купи́ть зáмок в Шотлáндии
3. помóчь нуждáющимся
4. провести́ всеми́рный кóнкурс кроссвóрдов

A. Éсли бы господи́н Смирнóв вы́играл лотерéйный билéт ...
B. Éсли господи́н Смирнóв вы́играет лотерéйный билéт ...

23 Reflexive verbs

Level 2, 3 The origin of Russian reflexive verbs lies in the combined form of a verb and the pronoun **себя** (yourself) in Old Russian. In contemporary Russian, the particle **-ся (-сь)**, added to a verb after the verb ending, replaces the pronoun **себя** (yourself). The particle **-ся** is added after a consonant or **-ь**, and **-сь** is added after a vowel.

The majority of reflexive verbs derive from transitive non-reflexive verbs with the same root, and form pairs with them, for example: **мыть – мыться** (to wash); **начинать – начинаться** (to begin). All reflexive verbs are intransitive: ☞ 21.1.

For the reflexive verbs in the present, past and future tenses, ☞ 17, 18 and 19 respectively.

The particle **-ся** can modify the meaning of a verb as follows:
- It can stress that an action is directed at oneself (☞ 23.1).
- It can describe a reciprocal action (☞ 23.2).
- It can emphasise ability or permanent quality (☞ 23.3).

Additionally, **-ся** can:
- Make an active verb passive (☞ 23.4).
- Make a transitive verb intransitive, but does not add any additional meaning (☞ 23.5).

There are a number of reflexive verbs that do not have non-reflexive pairs (☞ 23.6).

Level 2, 3 ## 23.1 Reflexive verbs with the meaning of an action directed at oneself

Reflexive verbs in this group derive from transitive non-reflexive verbs and form pairs with them. For example:

Она **моет** (a transitive verb that takes a direct object in the accusative case without a preposition) **руки**.	She **washes her hands**.
Она **моется** (an intransitive verb that cannot take a direct object).	She **washes herself**.

The most commonly used verbs of this kind describe routine actions of 'looking after yourself' and form the following pairs:

Non-reflexive transitive verbs that must take a noun/pronoun in the accusative case without a preposition	Reflexive intransitive verbs that cannot take a noun/pronoun in the accusative case without a preposition
одевать (to dress whom)	одеваться (to dress oneself)
мыть (to wash whom/what)	мыться (to wash oneself)
умывать (to wash whom/what)	умываться (to wash oneself)

Non-reflexive transitive verbs that must take a noun/pronoun in the accusative case without a preposition	Reflexive intransitive verbs that cannot take a noun/pronoun in the accusative case without a preposition
раздева́ть (to undress whom)	раздева́ться (to undress oneself)
вытира́ть (to dry what/whom)	вытира́ться (to dry oneself)
убира́ть (to tidy up what)	убира́ться (to tidy up somewhere)
расчёсывать (to comb what/whom)	расчёсываться (to comb oneself)
причёсывать (to comb what/whom)	причёсываться (to comb oneself)
брить (to shave what/whom)	бри́ться (to shave oneself)
купа́ть (to bathe what/whom)	купа́ться (to bathe oneself)
гото́вить (to cook/to prepare what)	гото́виться (to prepare for something)

23.2 Reflexive verbs with reciprocal meaning

Level 3

Reflexive verbs can describe reciprocal actions. Some reflexive verbs in this group derive from transitive non-reflexive verbs and form pairs with them. For example:

Я **встреча́ю** (a transitive verb that takes a direct object in the accusative case without a preposition) **Ви́ктора** в кафе́.

I am **meeting Victor** in a café.

Мы **встреча́емся** (an intransitive verb that cannot take a direct object) с Ви́ктором в кафе́.

Victor and I meet in a café.

Он **обнима́ет** (a transitive verb that takes a direct object in the accusative case without a preposition) **дру́га**.

He **hugs his friend.**

Они́ **обнима́ются** (an intransitive verb that cannot take a direct object).

They **hug each other.**

The most common pairs of this verb group are a transitive verb followed by a noun or a personal pronoun in the accusative case and an intransitive reflexive verb followed by a noun or a personal pronoun in the instrumental case:

Non-reflexive transitive verb	Reflexive intransitive verb	
встреча́ть (кого? что?)	встреча́ться (с кем? с чем?)	to meet
ви́деть (кого? что?)	ви́деться (с кем?)	to see
мири́ть (кого? что?)	мири́ться (с кем? с чем?)	to reconcile
ссо́рить (кого? что?)	ссо́риться (с кем?)	to quarrel
руга́ть (кого? что?)	руга́ться (с кем?)	to argue
обнима́ть (кого? что?)	обнима́ться (с кем? с чем?)	to hug
целова́ть (кого? что?)	целова́ться (с кем? с чем?)	to kiss
знако́мить (кого? что?)	знако́миться (с кем? с чем?)	to make an acquaintance
представля́ть (кого? что?)	представля́ться (кому?)	to introduce

There are several reflexive verbs describing reciprocal action that do not have a non-reflexive transitive pair. Often they are followed by an indirect object in the instrumental case with the preposition **c** (with):

здоро́ваться (с кем?)	to say hello
проща́ться (с кем?)	to say goodbye
соревнова́ться (с кем?)	to compete
боро́ться (с кем?)	to fight (boxing etc.)
дра́ться (с кем?)	to fight (gangs)
перепи́сываться (с кем)/с кем?	to correspond

23.3 Reflexive verbs with the meaning of ability or permanent quality

Reflexive verbs can describe ability or permanent quality. Reflexive verbs in this group derive from transitive non-reflexive verbs and form pairs with them. For example:

Кот **цара́пает** (a transitive verb that takes a direct object in the accusative case without a preposition) **кре́сло.**	A cat **is scratching an armchair.**
Кот **цара́пается** (an intransitive verb that cannot take a direct object).	A cat **is able to scratch.**

Frequently occurring verbs in this group are:

куса́ть (кого? что?)	куса́ться	to bite
коло́ть (кого? что?)	коло́ться	to prick
лома́ть (кого? что?)	лома́ться	to break
гнуть (кого? что?)	гну́ться	to bend
бода́ть (кого? что?)	бода́ться	to butt
ляга́ть (кого? что?)	ляга́ться	to kick

23.4 Reflexive verbs in passive constructions

The particle -**ся** added to a verb can make the verb passive. For passive sentences, ☞ 21.3; for passive participles, ☞ 26.1.2.3–4 and 26.1.3.

In passive sentences, reflexive verbs are mainly used in the imperfective aspect to describe an ongoing incomplete action. Conversely, short passive participles without -**ся** are used only in the perfective aspect to describe a single complete action. For example:

Все расхо́ды **опла́чиваются** (incomplete ongoing action) ме́стным сове́том.	All expenses **are paid** by the local council.
Все расхо́ды **опла́чены** (a single completed action) ме́стным сове́том.	All expenses **have been paid** by the local council.

When describing natural phenomena, a reflexive verb can be used in both perfective and imperfective aspects:

От моро́за стёкла на о́кнах **покры́лись** (pf)/**покрыва́ются** (impf) замыслова́тыми узо́рами.	Because of the frost, the windows were covered/are being covered by a curious pattern.

The majority of all transitive non-reflexive verbs can form a pair with reflexive verbs with a passive meaning. Compare:

Active construction	Passive construction
Молоды́е **иссле́дователи разраба́тывают** но́вые компью́терные програ́ммы. (The young **researchers develop** new computer programs.)	Но́вые **компью́терные програ́ммы разраба́тываются** молоды́ми иссле́дователями. (New **computer programs are developed** by young researchers.)

Passive constructions with reflexive verbs are common in writing, especially in literary texts:

Цель э́та **достига́лась** де́йствиями наро́дной войны́ (Толсто́й)

This purpose has been achieved by a popular war.

23.5 Reflexive verbs without any additional meanings

There are several frequently occurring reflexive verbs in which the added particle -**ся** makes the verb intransitive, but does not modify the verb meaning. Reflexive verbs in this group derive from transitive non-reflexive verbs and form pairs with them. Verbs in this group can describe:

- The beginning, continuation or end of an action. Usually, a reflexive verb is used with an inanimate subject, and its non-reflexive pair with an animate subject: начина́ть – начина́ться (to begin); продолжа́ть – продолжа́ться (to continue); конча́ть – конча́ться (to finish):

  Спекта́кль **начался́** ра́но.

  The performance **started** early.

  Они́ **на́чали** рабо́тать в шесть утра́.

  They **started** working at 6 o'clock in the morning.

- Some changes in an ongoing process or state of the subject of a sentence or its location: останови́ть – останови́ться (to stop); измени́ть – измени́ться (to change); поднима́ть – поднима́ться (to lift, to go up); спуска́ть – спуска́ться (to go down); улучша́ть – улучша́ться (to improve); ухудша́ть – ухудша́ться (to make worse); снижа́ть – снижа́ться (to lower); повыша́ть – повыша́ться (to raise/to improve) etc.:

  Це́ны на нефть **повы́сились** на 20%.

  Oil prices went up by 20%.

  Прави́тельство **повы́сило** це́ны на бензи́н на 20%.

  The government raised petrol prices by 20%.

- Emotions and feelings: беспоко́ить (to worry/to bother) – беспоко́иться (to be worried); волнова́ть (to excite /to worry) – волнова́ться (to be excited /to be worried), etc.:

  Информа́ция о но́вых тера́ктах в Москве́ **беспоко́ит** мно́гих россия́н.

  Information about the new terrorist attacks in Moscow **worries** many Russians.

  Мно́гие россия́не **беспоко́ятся** из-за но́вых тера́ктов в Москве́.

  Many Russian are worried because of the new terrorist attacks in Moscow.

23.6 Reflexive verbs that are used only with the particle -ся

There are a number of reflexive verbs that do not have non-reflexive pairs. For example:

забо́титься (о ком? о чём?)	to take care of
наде́яться (на кого́? на что?)	to rely on
наде́яться	to hope
горди́ться (кем? чем?)	to be proud of
улыба́ться (кому́?)	to smile

смея́ться (над чем?)	to laugh
явля́ться (чем? кем?)	to be/to appear
любова́ться (чем? кем?)	to admire

👁 Some reflexive verbs may seem, at first sight, to share a root with a non-reflexive verb pair. However, the reflexive and similar-looking non-reflexive verbs may have completely different meanings. For example:

учи́ться (to study where?)	Я учу́сь в университе́те, а она́ у́чится в шко́ле. (I **study at** university, but she **studies at** school.)	учи́ть (to learn by heart/to teach)	Студе́нт у́чит но́вые слова́. (The student **learns** new vocabulary.)
занима́ться (to be occupied/to study)	Он занима́ется в тренажёрном за́ле. (He **exercises** in a gym.)	занима́ть (to borrow)	Молодожёны за́няли де́ньги в ба́нке на сва́дебное путеше́ствие. (The newlyweds **borrowed** money from a bank for their honeymoon.)
состоя́ться (to take place/to be held)	Заседа́ние Ду́мы **состои́тся** в сле́дующую сре́ду. (The Parliamentary session **will be held** next Wednesday.)	состоя́ть из (to consist of)	Докла́д **состои́т из пяти́** разде́лов. (The report **consists of** five chapters.)

23.6.1. Reflexive impersonal verbs

Level 2, 3

Some reflexive verbs are impersonal: ☞ 30.4. A number of reflexive impersonal verbs do not have non-reflexive pairs:

- **нездоро́виться** (to feel unwell) – **Вам нездоро́вится? (Are** you **unwell?)**
- **приходи́ться/прийти́сь** (to have to) – **Подозрева́емому придётся** отве́тить на мно́гие вопро́сы. (The suspect will have to answer many questions.)
- **смерка́ться** (to get dark) – **Смерка́лось. (It was getting dark.)**
- 👁 The verb **нра́виться/понра́виться** (кому? что? кто?) – to like – can function as an impersonal verb and appear in impersonal sentences (☞ 30.4.1): Де́вочке нра́вится чита́ть кни́ги. (The girl likes reading books – impersonal.) However, **нра́виться/понра́виться** can also appear in sentences that have a subject in the nominative case: Де́вочке нра́вится э́та кни́га. (The girl likes this book.) ☞ 5.1.2.

Some reflexive impersonal verbs have non-reflexive pairs that have similar meanings, but are used in personal constructions with the subject in the nominative case:

- **хоте́ться/захоте́ться** (to feel like doing something) – хоте́ть/захоте́ть (to want): **Ей захоте́лось** спать. (She felt like sleeping.) **Она́ захоте́ла** спать. (She wanted to sleep.)

Other examples include:

- **рабо́таться** (to be able to work) – рабо́тать/порабо́тать (to work)
- **спа́ться** (to be able to sleep) – спать/поспа́ть (to sleep)
- **сиде́ться** (to be able to sit still) – сиде́ть/посиде́ть (to sit)

Упражне́ния

1. Rewrite the sentences twice, putting the verbs in brackets firstly into the present tense, then in the past tense:

1. Где Вы .... / .... (учи́ться)?
2. Бизнесме́ны .... / .... (расслабля́ться) по́сле рабо́ты в ба́не.
3. Нача́льник .... / .... (занима́ться) сро́чными дела́ми.
4. Тюле́ни .... / .... (купа́ться) в зали́ве.
5. Поли́тик .... / .... (боя́ться) результатов вы́боров.

2. Insert the appropriate verb in the correct form of the present or the future tense:
куса́ться, нача́ться, продава́ться, разбива́ться, спря́таться

1. За́втра спекта́кль .... в 6 часо́в, а не 7.30.
2. Каки́е това́ры .... в но́вом суперма́ркете?
3. Я наде́юсь, э́та соба́ка не ....?
4. Они́ .... от дождя́ под наве́сом.
5. Мы бу́дем смотре́ть пье́су Б. Шо́у «Дом, где .... сердца́».

24 Verbs of motion: introduction; verbs of motion without prefixes

Level
1, 2, 3 In Russian, many verbs describe a variety of physical movements, for example, **идти** (to go); **гуля́ть** (to walk); **пры́гать** (to jump), **дви́гать/дви́гаться** (to move), **класть** (to put) etc. Fourteen of these verbs form a special group called the 'verbs of motion'. The idea of *unidirectional* and *multidirectional* movements is at the heart of the concept of the fourteen Russian verbs of motion and any verbal forms derived from them. The ways in which English and Russian describe a variety of physical movements do not fully coincide. Unlike in Russian, the concept of unidirectional and multidirectional movements does not play a significant role in English grammar.

The fourteen Russian verbs of motion can be used with or without prefixes. The verbs of motion with prefixes have different meanings to those without prefixes and are used in different contexts. The verbs of motion without prefixes are explained in this chapter. For those with prefixes, ☞ 25. A full list of the dictionary forms of all fourteen verbs of motion can be found in section 24.1.

Level
1, 2, 3 ## 24.1 List of verbs of motion without prefixes

The fourteen Russian verbs that form the special group called the 'verbs of motion' are listed below in their dictionary forms. All verbs of motion have two dictionary forms; both of them are *imperfective*. (For verbal aspect, ☞ 20.) Eight verbs of motion are *intransitive* and six are *transitive*. For the concept of transitivity, ☞ 21). The verb conjugation is marked by the numbers I and II. (For verb conjugation, ☞ 17).

Intransitive verbs of motion (cannot have a direct object)		
Unidirectional	**Multidirectional**	**Translation**
идти́ (I)	ходи́ть (II)	to go (by foot)
е́хать (I)	е́здить (II)	to go (by transport)/to ride
бежа́ть (mixed)	бе́гать (I)	to run
лете́ть (II)	лета́ть (I)	to fly/to go by air transport
плыть(I)	пла́вать (I)	to swim/to sail/to go by water transport
лезть (I)	ла́зить (II)	to climb
ползти́ (I)	по́лзать (I)	to crawl
брести́ (I)	броди́ть (II)	to wander/to stroll

Transitive verbs of motion (must have a direct object)		
Unidirectional	**Multidirectional**	**Translation**
везти́ (I)	вози́ть (II)	to transport
вести́ (I)	води́ть (II)	to lead
нести́ (I)	носи́ть (II)	to carry in one's arms
гнать (II)	гоня́ть (I)	to drive (animals)
кати́ть (II)	ката́ть (I)	to roll
тащи́ть (II)	таска́ть (I)	to drag/pull

24.2 The meanings of the verbs of motion without prefixes

evel 2

Each of the fourteen verbs of motion is part of a pair: **идти́–ходи́ть, е́хать–е́здить, бежа́ть–бе́гать, лете́ть–лета́ть** etc. Both forms of each verb of motion are translated into English in the same way: to go – **идти́/ходи́ть**, to run – **бежа́ть /бе́гать** etc. However, in Russian, each part of the pair is used in different contexts.

All verbs listed in the first column of the above table (starting with the verb **идти́**) describe unidirectional movement. Usually unidirectional movement is presented as a movement that is in progress to a known destination in the present, past or future. All verbs listed in the second column of the above table (starting with the verb **ходи́ть**) describe multidirectional movement. This includes a round trip (return), habitual (repeated) movements or movements in unspecified directions (around/zigzag) in the present, past or future. Additionally, the group of multidirectional verbs can indicate one's ability or skills. Only with a clear understanding of the context can a speaker choose between the paired verbs of motion.

Although the concept of Russian verbs of motion is not fully reflected in English, unidirectional Russian verbs are often translated into English using the *continuous* present, past or future tenses (I am going/I was going/I will be going etc.). Multidirectional Russian verbs are translated into English using the *simple* present, past or future tenses (I go/I went/I will go).

24.3 The verb *to go* in Russian

evel 2

The English verb *to go/to go by* can be translated into Russian by using four different pairs of verbs:

- The verbs **идти́–ходи́ть** describe going on foot (walking). Often the adverb **пешко́м** (on foot) is added to the verbs **идти́–ходи́ть** (to go/to walk) to emphasise the way of travelling: Он **идёт пешко́м**. (He is walking (on foot)). Они́ лю́бят **ходи́ть пешко́м**. (They love walking (on foot)). The English verb *to walk* can also be translated into Russian using the verb **гуля́ть**, which is not part of the verbs of motion group. The verb **гуля́ть** is used with the prepositions **по** (around) or **вдоль** (along) and emphasises walking for pleasure.
- The verbs **е́хать–е́здить** describe travelling by any kind of land transport, including riding: Она́ **е́дет на авто́бусе**. (She is **going by bus**.) В Инди́и **е́здят на слона́х**. (In India, they **ride elephants**.)
- The verbs **лете́ть–лета́ть** describe travelling by any means of air transport: Она́ **лети́т на самолёте**, а он **лети́т на возду́шном ша́ре**. (She **is going by plane**, but he **is going by balloon**.)

- The verbs **плыть–пла́вать** describe travelling by any kind of water transport: Мы **плывём на паро́ме**, а они́ **плыву́т на ло́дке**. (We **are going by ferry**, but they **are going by boat**.)
- The preposition **на** (by) with a noun in the prepositional case is used to specify any means of transport, including riding.

<table>
<tr><td>Level
2, 3</td></tr>
</table>

24.4 Reflexive verbs of motion without prefixes

The transitive verbs of motion without prefixes and verbs derived from them can have a reflexive intransitive form (with the addition of the particle -ся): ☞ 23. When a verb of motion becomes reflexive, its meaning changes. The majority of the reflexive verbs of motion are used in a figurative sense: ☞ 24.7.

The most frequently occurring reflexive verb of motion is **ката́ться** (imperfective)–**поката́ться** (perfective), derived from the verb **ката́ть** (to roll). The verb **ката́ться** is part of the following idioms and indicates doing something for pleasure: **ката́ться на лы́жах** (to ski); **ката́ться на конька́х** (to skate); **ката́ться на са́нках** (to sledge); **ката́ться на велосипе́де** (to cycle); **ката́ться на ло́дке** (to sail for pleasure); **ката́ться на ло́шади** (to ride a horse). Conversely, the verbs **е́хать–е́здить/лете́ть–лета́ть/плыть–пла́вать** (to go) describe travelling by various kinds of transport (neutral, not pleasure). For example:

Зимо́й на росси́йских куро́ртах тури́сты **ката́ются на** лы́жах и конька́х. Ле́том тури́сты **ката́ются на** велосипе́де и на ло́дке. Я **е́зжу** в университе́т **на** велосипе́де.	In the winter, in Russian resorts, tourists **ski** and **skate**. In the summer, tourists **cycle** and **sail**. I **go** to the university **by bike**/I **cycle** to the university.

24.5 Using the verbs of motion without prefixes

<table>
<tr><td>Level
1, 2</td></tr>
</table>

24.5.1 The most frequent use of the verbs of motion without prefixes in the present tense

The most common use, in the present tense, of the unidirectional verbs of motion is to describe a single movement to a known destination, which is occurring as we speak. Conversely, the multidirectional verbs of motion are used to stress the habitual nature of the movement. For example:

A dialogue on the train

– Извини́те, Вы **е́дете** (unidirectional movement is occurring as we speak) на фестива́ль в Эдинбу́рг?	Excuse me; **are** you **going** to the Edinburgh festival?
– Да, я **е́ду** (unidirectional movement is occurring as we speak) в Эдинбу́рг на фестива́ль.	Yes, I **am going** to the Edinburgh festival.
– Вы **е́здите** (habitual movement) на фестива́ль в Эдинбу́рг ка́ждый год?	Do you **go** to the Edinburgh festival every year?
– Нет, я обы́чно **е́зжу** (habitual movement) туда́ раз в два го́да.	No, I usually **go** there every other year.

A dialogue in the street

– Привéт, Ирúна! Сто лет тебя́ не вúдел. Куда́ **идёшь** (unidirectional movement is occurring as we speak)?	Hi Irina! I have not seen you for ages. Where **are you going**?
– Привéт, Вúктор! Я **идý** (unidirectional movement is occurring as we speak) в тренажёрный зал.	Hi, Victor! I **am going** to the gym.
– Я **хожý** (habitual movement) в тренажёрный зал по пя́тницам.	I **go** to the gym on Fridays.
– А я не люблю́ тренажёры. Я **пла́ваю** (habitual movement) в бассéйне по суббóтам.	I don't like the machines. I **swim** in the pool on Saturdays.

Level 1, 2

24.5.2 The most frequent use of the verbs of motion without prefixes in the past tense

The multidirectional verbs are the ones that are most frequently used in the past tense. They are used when describing both a single round-trip movement or multiple round-trip (return) movements in the past and answer the following questions:

- Куда́ Вы ходúли/éздили? (Where did you go?)
- Скóлько раз Вы ходúли/éздили туда́? (How many times did you go there?)

For example:

Прóшлым лéтом мы **éздили** (single return movement, to the area and back) в Австра́лию.

Last summer we went to Australia.

Вчера́ вéчером Вúктор **ходúл** (single return movement, to the area and back) в кинó.

Yesterday evening Victor went to the cinema.

В понедéльник Марúя **возúла** (single return movement, to the area and back) отца́ в больнúцу.

On Monday, Maria took her father to the hospital.

Онú **éздили** (multiple return movement, to the area and back) на Чёрное мóре два́жды.

They went to the Black Sea twice.

Level 1, 2

24.5.3 The most frequent use the verbs of motion without prefixes in the future tense

In the present tense, unidirectional verbs of motion are often used in popular speech to describe one's intentions for the future. This structure is equivalent to when an English verb in the present continuous tense is used to describe an action in the future. For example:

За́втра мы **éдем** (our intentions for the future) в Иркýтск.

Tomorrow we **are going** to Irkutsk.

Пóсле рабóты он **идёт** (his intentions for the future) на вечерúнку.

After work, he **is going** to a party.

Онú **летя́т** (their intentions for the future) на мóре в слéдующий четвéрг.

They **are flying** to the seaside next Thursday.

The perfective verbs of motion with the prefix **по-** are frequently used in the future tense to describe one's definite actions in the future. For verbs of motion with the prefix **по-**, ☞ 25.1.4.

24.5.4 Less frequent use of the unidirectional verbs of motion in the present, past and future tenses

In the present and past tenses, the unidirectional verbs of motion are also used to emphasise the one-way-only nature of a movement, if the context requires. Usually, the direction of the described movement is clearly indicated and the destination is known. The one-way movement can be single or repeated. For example:

Обы́чно я **иду́** на рабо́ту пешко́м, а обра́тно **е́ду** на авто́бусе.	Usually I **walk** to work, but **go back** home by bus.
Сего́дня я **е́ду** на рабо́ту на метро́.	Today I **am going** to work by tube/ underground/subway.

Often the emphasis is made on some particular or unusual circumstances surrounding the one-way movement, if it is a one-off event. For example:

Я сего́дня из-за плохо́й пого́ды **е́ду** на рабо́ту на авто́бусе. Соверше́нно невозмо́жно **идти́** пешко́м!	Today I **am going to** work by bus because of the bad weather. It is impossible to walk today!
Вчера́ из-за ава́рии на шоссе́ я **е́хала до** вокза́ла це́лый час. Я чуть не опозда́ла на по́езд.	Yesterday I was travelling for an hour to the railway station because of an accident on the motorway. I almost missed my train.

In the past tense, the unidirectional verbs of motion are also used to describe a background action in support of the principal action. Therefore, the unidirectional verbs usually appear in a complex sentence with subordinate clauses or in a simple sentence with more than one verb. The description of the background action is usually introduced by one of the conjunctions **пока́, в то вре́мя как** (while/meanwhile), **когда́** (when/while) or **и** (and). Sometimes these conjunctions are omitted, but implied. The principal verb can be used in both perfective and imperfective aspects. Note the verbs of motion describing the background action are used in the imperfective aspect only. For example:

Вчера́, когда́ я **шла** (background action) по у́лице, я **встре́тила** (principal action) дру́га.	Yesterday when I **was going** (I was on my way) along the street I **met** my friend.
Я **шла, шла, шла** (background action). Пирожо́к **нашла́** (principal action).	I was **going, going, going**. I **found** a little pie.

The compounded imperfective future tense of unidirectional verbs is very rarely used. It is used only if it is necessary to stress the precise timing of when an action will be occurring in the future. The Russian verb is translated into English using the future continuous tense (I will be going etc.). For example:

Уже́ 5 часо́в. За́втра в э́то вре́мя мы уже́ **бу́дем лете́ть** в Пари́ж.	It is already 5 o'clock. This time tomorrow, we **will** already **be flying** to Paris.
Когда́ ты **бу́дешь идти́ ми́мо** теа́тра, посмотри́ афи́шу.	When you **pass by/go past** (literally: **will be passing**) the theatre look at the poster. (This form is rarely used.)

24.5.5 Less frequent use of the multidirectional verbs of motion in the present, past and future tenses

In all three tenses, the multidirectional verbs of motion are used to stress movement in non-specified directions (around). For example:

Соба́ка **бе́гает по** по́лю.	The dog **runs/is running** around the field.
Ле́тним ве́чером ла́сточки **бу́дут лета́ть над** по́лем.	In summer evenings, swallows **will be flying/will fly** over the field.
Он до́лго **ходи́л по** ле́су.	He **walked/was walking** around the forest for a long time.

In all three tenses, the multidirectional verbs of motion are also used to indicate ability or skills. For example:

Свѝньи **не лета́ют**.	Pigs **cannot fly**.
Как стра́нно! Оле́г так хорошо́ **пла́вал**, а тепе́рь бои́тся воды́.	How bizarre! Oleg **used to swim** so well and now he is scared of water.
Больно́й ребёнок **бу́дет ходи́ть** то́лько по́сле опера́ции.	The sick child **will be able to walk** only after an operation.

In the past tense, the multidirectional verbs are used to emphasise a habitual action that is not carried out any more. For example:

Пенсионе́ры **ра́ньше** всегда́ **ходи́ли** (they used to it, but do not do it any more) в э́тот клуб игра́ть в би́нго, но клуб закры́ли.	Retired people **used to go** to that club to play bingo, but the club was closed down.
Когда́-то давно́ здесь был огро́мный пруд. Я вспомина́ю, как над ним всегда́ **лета́ли** (they used to it, but do not do it any more) ча́йки.	A long time ago, there was a huge pond here. I remember how seagulls **used to fly** over it.

The compounded imperfective future tense of multidirectional verbs is often used to stress the intention to do something on a regular basis. For example:

По утра́м я **бу́ду бе́гать** в па́рке.	I intend to jog in the park every morning.
В ста́рших кла́ссах де́ти **бу́дут ходи́ть** в шко́лу шесть раз в неде́лю.	In the senior classes the schoolchildren will be attending school six times a week.

24.6 Verbs of motion in the present and past tenses: internal stem modification

For the present and past tenses of verbs, ☞ 17 and 18 respectively. The formation of the compounded future of imperfective verbs is not affected by any irregularities. For the simple future of perfective verbs, ☞ 19.1.3.

24.6.1 Present tense stem modification

All verbs of motion without prefixes that are affected by some changes in the present tense stem are listed below. If the verb of motion is not included in the list, its stem is not affected by internal stem modification.

- Changes in the stem concern only the 1st person singular form of the verbs ходи́ть, е́здить, лете́ть, броди́ть, води́ть, носи́ть and кати́ть.
- Changes in the stem of the verbs е́хать, плыть, брести́, вести́ and **гна**ть remain throughout the conjugation.
- Changes occur in the stem of the verb бежа́ть in the 1st person singular and the 3rd person plural forms.

Infinitive	1st person singular	2nd person singular	3rd person plural
хо**ди́**ть	хо**жу́**	хо́**ди**шь	хо́**дя**т
е́**х**ать	е́**ду**	е́**де**шь	е́**ду**т
е́з**ди**ть	е́з**жу**	е́з**ди**шь	е́з**дя**т
бе**жа́**ть	бе**гу́**	бе**жи́**шь	бе**гу́**т
лете́ть	ле**чу́**	лети́шь	летя́т

Infinitive	1st person singular	2nd person singular	3rd person plural
плыть	плыву́	плывёшь	плыву́т
брести́	бреду́	бредёшь	бреду́т
броди́ть	брожу́	бро́дишь	бро́дят
вести́	веду́	ведёшь	веду́т
води́ть	вожу́	во́дишь	во́дят
носи́ть	ношу́	но́сишь	но́сят
гнать	гоню́	го́нишь	го́нят
кати́ть	качу́	ка́тишь	ка́тят

24.6.2 Irregular past tense (☞ 18.3)

There are several verbs of motion without prefixes that follow a special pattern in the past tense. They are listed below.

- The verb **идти́**. The past tense is formed from a different stem: **шёл, шла, шло, шли**.
- Verbs with infinitives that end with **-ти** (except идти́), and the verb **лезть**. Note the absence of suffix **-л-** in the masculine form after consonants **з** and **с** and the appearance of the letter **ё** under the stress. Some verbs in **-ти** are exceptions to this rule (see comments below). For example:

  везти́ (to transport): вёз, везла́, везло́, везли́
  нести́ (to carry): нёс, несла́, несло́, несли́
  ползти́ (to crawl): полз, ползла́, ползло́, ползли́
  лезть (to climb): лез, ле́зла, ле́зло, ле́зли

- Verbs whose infinitives end with **-ти** keep the suffix **-л-** in all forms, if their present-tense stems end with **-д:**

  вести́: веду́, веду́т (to lead): **вёл**, вела́, вело́, вели́
  брести́: бреду́, бреду́т (to wander/to stroll): **брёл**, брела́, брело́, брели́

Note that all the verbs listed above follow the same pattern when a prefix is added to them. For the irregular past tense of verbs of motion with prefixes, ☞ 25.4.

24.7 Figurative use of verbs of motion without prefixes

Verbs of motion without prefixes are frequently used in a figurative sense, especially in popular speech and idioms. If verbs of motion are used in a figurative sense, they may have only a limited number of forms. The following list of verbs of motion used figuratively is not exhaustive, but it contains the most frequently occurring verbs of motion.

The verb **идти́** (to go), in all tenses, appears in several idioms. Note neither the verb **ходи́ть** (to go) nor any forms derived from it are used in these idioms:

- **Идти́** (to go) replaces **to be** when talking about any event/activity in progress, such as уро́к (lesson), фильм (film), спекта́кль (show), экза́мен (examination), футбо́льный матч (football match); for example, Что **идёт** по телеви́зору/в кино́/в теа́тре? (**What's on** TV/at the cinema/at the theatre?) Ти́хо! Иду́т экза́мены. (Silence! Examinations are in progress.)
- **Идти́** (to go) replaces **to be** when talking about some weather conditions (rain or snow); for example, Дождь/снег **идёт**. (It **is** raining/snowing.)

- **Идти** (to go) replaces **to be** when describing the process of communication; for example, Речь/разговор **идёт о** ... (They **are talking** about ... /the conversation about ... **is in progress**.) Спор **идёт о** ... (They are arguing about ...)
- **Идти** can convey the meaning 'to suit someone', when talking about clothes, hairstyle or habits. Тебе так **идёт** новая **причёска**! (Your new **hair-do suits** you so well!) **Курение** совсем **не идёт** тебе и портит твой имидж. (**Smoking does not suit** you and damages your image.)

Both **идти** and **ходить** (to go), in all tenses, are used when:

- Talking about how a watch/clock is working; for example, Часы **идут**. (The watch/clock **is working**.) Часы давно **не ходят**. (The watch/clock **has not been working** properly for a long time.)
- Describing the movements of vehicles, mainly public transport; for example, Трамвай, поезд, троллейбус, автобус **идёт**. (The tram, train, trolleybus, bus **goes**.) Раньше трамвай No. 5 часто **ходил**. (The No. 5 tram used to **come** frequently in the past.) However, the verbs **ехать** and **ездить** are used to describe the movement of a car: Машина/такси/грузовик **едет** по автостраде (A car/taxi/lorry is driving on a motorway).

Other frequently occurring verbs of motion without prefixes and used in all tenses are:

- **Водить/вести** in the idiom водить/вести машину (to drive). The noun **машина** is an obligatory part of the Russian idiom; for example, Он хорошо **водит машину**. (He **drives** well.)
- **Вести** meaning 'to behave'. The pronoun **себя** is an obligatory part of the idiom; for example, Мальчик хорошо **вёл себя** на уроке. (The boy **behaved himself** at the lesson.)
- **Вести** meaning 'to conduct'; for example, **Вести** урок /войну. (**To conduct** a lesson/a war.) **Вести переписку**. (**To correspond** with.) **Вести хозяйство**. (**To keep house**.) **Вести наблюдение(я)**. (**To observe/watch**.)
- **Водить** in the idiom 'to lie'; for example, Он всех нас **водит за нос**. (He **lies** to all of us.)
- **Носить** (to wear); for example, Он **носит** очки и бороду. (He **wears** glasses and **sports** a beard.)

To describe a fast-going process, the idioms of time are used with the verbs **идти** (to go), **бежать** (to run) and **лететь** (to fly) in the present, past and future tenses: Время **идёт/бежит/летит**. (Time **is flying** by.) Годы/дни/часы **идут/бегут/летят**. (The years/days/hours **are flying** by.)

Several reflexive verbs of motion are used figuratively:

- **Нестись/носиться** (to run; to be obsessed with an idea): Дети **носились** по двору до самого вечера. (The children **run** around the yard until the evening.) «Русь, куда **несёшься** ты? Дай ответ» (Гоголь). (Russia! Where are you going to so fast? Answer me.) Она **носилась** с этим предложением месяц. (She **has been obsessed** with this proposal for a month.)
- **Обходиться/обойтись** (с кем-либо) хорошо/плохо (to treat someone well/badly): Со спасёнными животными плохо **обходились** их хозяева. (The rescued animals were **treated** badly by their owners.)
- **Гнаться/гоняться** за кем?/за чем? (to run after someone/something hoping to catch someone/something): «За нами **гонится** эскадра по пятам» (Высоцкий). (The warships came after us.)
- **Тащиться/таскаться** (to drag oneself along): «Бродяга, судьбу проклиная, **тащился** с сумой на плечах» (Народная песня). (The tramp, cursing his luck, was dragging himself along with a bag on his shoulder.)
- **Катиться/кататься на лыжах** (to ski)/**санках** (to skate) etc. – the verb is a part of the idiom: ☞ 24.4.

Упражне́ния

Level 1, 2

1. Replace the English phrases containing the verbs *to go/to ride* by the appropriate Russian equivalent. Put the verbs and nouns into the correct form and add the appropriate preposition:

1. Про́шлым ле́том друзья́ (to ride camels) в Еги́пте.
2. За́втра Та́ня (to go to Moscow) на по́езде?
3. Ма́ша не лю́бит (to go by plane).
4. Обы́чно студе́нты (to go by foot) в университе́т пешко́м.
5. Вы ра́ньше ча́сто (to go by bike)?

Level 1, 2

2. Insert the appropriate unidirectional or multidirectional verb of motion without prefix in the correct form:

A. Ка́ждый день:
1. Ва́ня .... в шко́лу пешко́м.
2. Ко́шка .... на де́рево.
3 Оте́ц .... до́чку в де́тский сад на маши́не.
4. И́ра .... соба́ку в городско́й парк.

B. Сейча́с:
1. Самолёт .... из Ло́ндона в Петербу́рг.
2. Студе́нты .... пешко́м в библиоте́ку и .... кни́ги.
3. Мы .... на по́езде в Эдинбу́рг.
4. Па́па .... дете́й на мотоци́кле.

C. На про́шлой неде́ле:
1. Ники́тины .... к сы́ну в Австра́лию на самолёте.
2. Ба́бушка .... вну́ка на маши́не в больни́цу.
3. Студе́нты .... на вечери́нку к сосе́дям.
4. Тури́сты .... в го́ры на велосипе́де.

D. За́втра:
1. Мари́на .... к роди́телям на да́чу.
2. А́ся .... в го́сти к сосе́дям по до́му.
3. Ми́ша и Ко́ля .... на вертолёте в Мурма́нск.
4. Мари́я .... дете́й к ба́бушке на маши́не.

Level 2, 3

3. Insert the appropriate verb of motion:

1. Обы́чно Мари́на .... на рабо́ту на авто́бусе, но вчера́ она́ опа́здывала и поэ́тому .... на такси́.
2. Вы не бойтесь воды́, вы уме́ете ....?
3. Вчера́ Ви́ктор .... пешко́м по па́рку и нашёл лотере́йный биле́т.
4. В но́вом году́ мы .... в тренажёрный зал ка́ждый день.
5. Ра́ньше бездо́мный це́лыми дня́ми .... по го́роду.
6. Вчера́ па́па .... на кры́шу, что́бы почини́ть анте́ну.
7. Черепа́хи о́чень ме́дленно ....
8. Про́шлой о́сенью пти́цы ста́ями .... над па́рком.

Обобща́ющее упражне́ние

4. Fill the gaps with the appropriate form of the Russian equivalents of the verbs *to go by foot/to go by transport*, *to swim*, *to jog*:

Level 2, 3

Господи́н Смирно́в встреча́ет ста́рого дру́га

1. – Приве́т, Са́ша! Как дела́? Куда́ ....?
2. – Приве́т, Вале́ра! Спаси́бо, всё норма́льно. Я .... на рабо́ту. Ты не забы́л, что я рабо́таю в Кремле́. Там нахо́дится на́ша компа́ния. Я всегда́ .... на рабо́ту пешко́м. А ты? Куда́ ты ....?

3. – Я то́же .... на рабо́ту. То́лько я рабо́таю далеко́ от це́нтра и мне прихо́дится ....
туда́ на метро́. Ну, иногда́ я .... на рабо́ту на авто́бусе. Ты .... в бассе́йн по суббо́там?
4. – Коне́чно, ... Я люблю́ спорт. А ты?
5. Я .... по па́рку по утра́м. Ну ла́дно, извини́, мне на́до ....
6. Пока́. Счастли́во.

25 Verbs of motion: verbs of motion with prefixes

All verbs of motion with prefixes are formed by adding prefixes to the fourteen verbs of motion without prefixes: ☞ 24.1.

The essential characteristics of the verbs of motion with prefixes are:

- Adding a prefix changes the meaning of the verb: **идти́/ходи́ть** (to go); **прийти́/приходи́ть** (to arrive); **уйти́/уходи́ть** (to depart); **зайти́/заходи́ть** (to pop in) etc. For the meanings of the prefixes, ☞ 25.1.
- Any of up to 20 different prefixes can be added to the verbs of motion. The most frequently occurring verbs of motion, such as **идти́/ходи́ть** (to go), **éхать/éздить** (to go), etc. can take all 20 prefixes. For all possible prefix combinations, ☞ 25.2.
- Each prefix affects all verbs of motion in the same way. For example, **при-** means 'to move here' with all verbs that can be used with **при-**: **прийти́/приходи́ть** (to arrive/to come here); **приплыва́ть/приплы́ть** (to sail here); **приноси́ть/принести́** (to bring here) etc.; **y-** means 'to move away' with all verbs that can be used with -**y**: **уходи́ть/уйти́** (to depart/to move away); **уплыва́ть/уплы́ть** (to sail away); **уноси́ть/унести́** (to take away), etc.
- Some changes may occur in the stem of the verb when a prefix is added; for example: ид–й: **идти́ – прийти́**; д–ж: **éздить – уезжа́ть** etc.: ☞ 25.3.
- All verbs of motion with prefixes have one imperfective and one perfective verb with the same prefix. All *perfective* verbs are formed from the *unidirectional* verbs of motion without prefixes. All *imperfective* verbs are formed from the *multidirectional* verbs of motion without prefixes; for example, **приходи́ть** (imperfective, from multidirectional verb **ходи́ть**) – **прийти́** (perfective, from unidirectional verb **идти́**); **уезжа́ть** (imperfective, from multidirectional verb **éздить**) – **уéхать** (perfective, from unidirectional verb **éхать**), etc. For exceptions to this rule, ☞ 25.1.3–25.1.5; for the complete list of unidirectional and multidirectional verbs, ☞ 24.1.

25.1 Meanings of the prefixes used with verbs of motion

25.1.1 The prefixes при-, у-, в-, вы-, под-, от-, вз-, раз- and с-

The prefixes **при-** and **у-**, **в-** and **вы-**, **под-** and **от-**, **вз-** and **с-**, and **раз-** and **с-** form pairs of prefixes with opposite meanings. When added to a verb of motion, the prefixes emphasise the start and end of a movement (see Summary Table 25.I below–all verbs given as examples in the table are perfective.). Note that if a prefix ends in a consonant and is followed by the letters **й**, **ш** or **гн** the vowel **о** is added to the prefix, and if it is followed by the vowel **e** the letter **ъ** is added to the prefix.

Summary Table 25.I

Prefix meaning	Examples	Preposition that the verb takes and case of the noun that follows
при-: move here (arrive)	прийти́/прие́хать (to arrive) принести́/привести́ (to bring) привезти́ (to deliver)	**куда́** (where to): в + accusative на + accusative к + dative
		отку́да (where from): из + genitive с + genitive от + genitive
у- : move from here (depart)	уйти́/уе́хать (to depart/to leave) унести́/увести́ (to take away)	**отку́да** (where from): из/с/из-за/из-под/от + genitive
		куда́ (where to): в + accusative на + accusative к + dative
в(о)- : move in (inside)	войти́/въе́хать (come in/to enter) внести́ (to bring inside); ввезти́ (to import)	**куда́** (where to): в + accusative на + accusative
		отку́да (where from): из + genitive с + genitive
вы-: move out (outside)	вы́йти/вы́ехать (to get out/ to exit) вы́нести (to take away from inside); вы́везти (to export)	**отку́да** (where from): из/с/из-за/из-под + genitive
		куда́ (where to): в + accusative на + accusative
под(о)- : approach/come up to	подойти́/подъе́хать (to approach) поднести́ (to bring to); подвезти́ (to give a lift)	**куда́** (where to): к + dative
от(о)- : move from	отойти́/отъе́хать (to go away from/to step away) отнести́/отвезти́ (to take away from)	**отку́да** (where from): от + genitive в + accusative (в сторону)
		куда́ (where to): в + accusative на + accusative к + dative
вз(о) /воз- : move up (has limited use)	взлете́ть (to take off) влезть (to climb)	**куда́** (where to): в + accusative на + accusative
		отку́да (where from): с + genitive

Prefix meaning	Examples	Preposition that the verb takes and case of the noun that follows
с(о)-: move down (has limited use)	слете́ть (to fly down) слезть (to climb down)	**отку́да** (where from): с + genitive
		куда́ (where to): в + accusative на + accusative
раз(о)-: to deliver in many different points or to disperse something (the prefix is used only with transitive verbs)	разнести́ (to deliver) развести́ (to deliver)	**куда́** (where to): по + dative
с(о): to deliver to one point from many different points (the prefix is used only with transitive verbs)	снести́ (to deliver) свезти́ (to deliver)	**куда́** (where to): в + accusative на + accusative
раз(о)- (ся): disperse from one point; the prefix is used only with reflexive verbs	разъе́хаться/разбежа́ться (to disperse)	**куда́** (where to): в + accusative на + accusative по + dative
с(о)- (ся): gather to one point; the prefix is used only with reflexive verbs	съе́хаться/сбежа́ться (to gather)	**отку́да** (where from): из + genitive с + genitive от + genitive
		куда́ (where to): в + accusative на + accusative к + dative

Level 3

Additional information:

- Verbs with prefixes **вы-** and **от-** have the additional temporal meaning 'to be away for a short while': Дире́ктор **вы́шел**. (The director **is out for a minute**.) Я **отойду́** на мину́ту. (I **will be back** in a minute.)
- The prefix **от-** added to the transitive verbs of motion (**относи́ть–отнести́; отвози́ть–отвезти́; отводи́ть–отвести́**) emphasises the end point of the movement rather than the start point: Он **отнёс** кни́ги в библиоте́ку. (He **returned** the books to the library.) Я **отвезу́** тебя́ в аэропо́рт. I **will give you a lift** to the airport. For a complete list of the verbs of motion without prefixes, ☞ 24.1.
- The prefixes **вз-** and **с-** are used in specific contexts, mainly with the verbs лете́ть/лета́ть (to fly) and лезть/ла́зить (to climb). In Russian, verbs other than the verbs of motion are used to convey the idea *to go upstairs/to go up* – **поднима́ться** (impf)/**подня́ться** (pf) and *to go downstairs/to go down* – **спуска́ться** (impf)/**спусти́ться** (pf). For example: Он с лёгкостью **подня́лся** на тре́тий эта́ж. (He easily **climbed** to the third floor.) Она́ **спусти́лась** в по́греб за вино́м. (She **went down** to the cellar to get some wine.) To describe upwards movement in any means of air transport, the verb of motion is used: **взлета́ть/взлете́ть** (to take off). However, to convey the idea of landing, verbs other than verbs of motion are used: **приземля́ться /приземли́ться** or **сади́ться/сесть** (to land).
- The prefixes **с-, про-** and **за-** have additional temporal meanings (☞ 25.1.5).

25.1.2 Prefixes про-, пере-, за-, до- and обо-

The prefixes **про-**, **пере-**, **за-**, **до-** and **обо-** do not form semantic pairs. When added to a verb of motion, the prefixes **про-**, **пере-**, **за-** and **обо-** clarify the details of a speaker's route (see Summary Table 25.II below–all verbs given as examples in the table are perfective.). Note, the prefixes **про-**, **пере-**, and **за-** have multiple meanings. The prefix **до-** describes the end point of a movement. If the prefix **об-** is followed by the letters **й**, **ш** or **гн** the vowel **о** is added to the prefix, and if it is followed by the vowel **е** the letter **ъ** is added to the prefix.

Summary Table 25.II

Prefix	Meaning	Examples	Preposition that the verb takes and case of the noun that follows
про-	move through/pass by/move under/ move above; the meaning depends on the following preposition	пройти́ ми́мо (to pass by) пролете́ть над (to fly above)	**где?** (where?) че́рез + accusative под + instrumental ми́мо + genitive над + instrumental
	other meanings: to miss something (a stop, a street etc)	прое́хать остано́вку (to miss one's stop)	no preposition + accusative (свою́ остано́вку)
	to move how far? (a distance)/to move how long? (timing)	прое́хать 5 киломе́тров/ 5 часо́в (to travel for 5 km/5 hours)	no preposition + accusative (ско́лько киломе́тров/часо́в)
пере-	across	перейти́ у́лицу (to cross the street)	**что?** (what?) no preposition + accusative (у́лицу)
		перейти́ че́рез мост (to cross over the bridge)	че́рез (что?) + accusative
	other meanings: to move house	перее́хать (to move house)	**отку́да?** (from where?) из + genitive с + genitive
			куда́? (to where?) в + accusative на + accusative
за-	pop in/call on/call for	зайти́ в магази́н (to pop in)	**куда́?** (where to?) в + accusative на + accusative
		зайти́ к дру́гу (call on a person)	**к кому́?** (on whom?) к + dative

Prefix	Meaning	Examples	Preposition that the verb takes and case of the noun that follows
		зайти́ за хле́бом (to call for)	**за кем?/чем?** (for whom/what) за + instrumental
	other meanings: move behind	зайти́ за дом (to go behind a house)	**куда́?** (where to?) за + accusative
до-	reach the point/to go as far as	дойти́ до (to go as far as)	**до ку́да?** (where to?) до + genitive
об(о)-	move around	обойти́ (to go around)	**вокру́г чего́?** (around what?) вокру́г + genitive что? (what?) no preposition + accusative (дом)

Level 2, 3

25.1.3 Prefixes with temporal meaning по-, с-, за- and про-

The prefixes **по-**, **с-**, **за-**, and **про-** added to the verbs of motion can emphasise either the beginning or length of a movement. Note that if the prefix **с-** is followed by a vowel the letter **ъ** is added to the prefix: **съе́здить**.

The verbs of motion with prefixes that have temporal meaning (**по-**, **с-**, **за-**, and **про-**) form their aspect pairs differently to verbs of motion with other prefixes (☞ 25.1.1 and 25.1.2.). In this situation, the verbs without a prefix are imperfectives and the verbs with added prefixes are their perfective pairs. For example:

идти́ (impf) – пойти́ (pf)   ходи́ть (impf)– походи́ть (pf)
е́хать (impf) – пое́хать (pf)   е́здить (impf) – пое́здить (pf)
бежа́ть (impf) – побежа́ть (pf)   бе́гать (impf) – побе́гать (pf)

👁 Note that the prefixes **с-**, **за-** and **про-** can have other meanings and can be used in different ways (☞ 25.1.1 and 25.1.2).

Level 2, 3

25.1.4 Verbs of motion with the prefix по-

The prefix **по-** added to a unidirectional verb of motion makes the verb perfective and changes the verb in the following way:

- In the future tense and the infinitive form, **по-** stresses an intention: За́втра я **пое́ду** в Москву́. (I **will go** to Moscow tomorrow.) A verb of motion, in the infinitive form, with **по-** is frequently used with the verbs **реша́ть–реши́ть** (to decide) and **хоте́ть–захоте́ть** (to wish): Ле́том мы **реши́ли пое́хать** в Испа́нию. (We **decided to go** to Spain in the summer.) Я **хочу́ пойти́** в кино́. (I **would like to go** to the cinema.)

👁 In the past tense **по-** can be used:

- When emphasising the beginning of a movement (*setting off*): Я не заста́ла подру́гу, она́ **пое́хала** в Ло́ндон. (I missed my friend; she **had set off** for London.)
- When describing a sequence of movements: Он **вы́шел** из до́ма **и пошёл** к авто́бусной остано́вке. (He **left** the house **and began walking** towards the bus stop.) Снача́ла мы **е́хали** по шоссе́, пото́м **пое́хали** по у́зкой лесно́й доро́ге. (At first, we **were driving along** the motorway, then we **began driving along** the narrow forest road.) Note, neither the verb **ходи́ть** nor **идти́** can be used in this context. **Ходи́ть** in the past tense describes a single round trip, from and to the start point; **идти́** describes an on-going background action that is never completed.

- When giving an instruction: Давáй **пошлú**!/**Пошлú**! (**Let's go**!) Ну что ж, **поéхали**! (Well, let's **go**!)

The prefix **по-**, added to multidirectional verbs of motion without prefixes, stresses the short length of a movement in all tenses and the infinitive form: Онá **походúла** по кóмнате и леглá спать. (She **walked for a short while** around the room and went to bed.) Он решúл **поплáвать**. (He has decided to **go for a swim**.)

25.1.5 Verbs of motion with the prefixes с-, про- and за-

The prefixes **с-**, **про-** and **за-** are used only with multidirectional verbs of motion, if the timing is being emphasised.

- The prefix **с-** added to a multidirectional verb makes the verb perfective and conveys the idea of a quick return movement/round trip in the past or future. In popular speech, a verb of motion with **с-** is frequently used in the imperative or infinitive forms: Гóсти идýт, а я забы́ла купúть хлéба. **Сбéгай**, пожáлуйста, в бýлочную, купú пáру бухáнок. (The guests are arriving now, but I forgot to buy some bread. Could you please **go** to the bakery **now and get** a couple of loaves.) Зáвтра мне нáдо **съéздить** в библиотéку. (Tomorrow I need **to go** to the library **(and come back quickly).**)
- Conversely, the prefix **про-** added to multidirectional verbs makes them perfective and conveys the idea of a prolonged multidirectional movement in the past and future: Турúсты **весь день проходúли по** музéям. (The tourists **spent all day** in the museums. – **For the whole day**, the tourists **were going around** the museums.)
- The prefix **за-** added to a multidirectional verb makes the verb perfective and emphasises the beginning of the multidirectional movement in the past or future: Онá нéрвно **заходúла** по кóмнате, ожидáя звонкá. (While waiting for a call, she became tense and **started walking around** the room.)

25.2 Combinations of verbs of motion with prefixes

Various verbs of motion can take a different number of prefixes. All common combinations of verbs of motion with prefixes are presented in Summary Table 25.III. All the prefixes listed describe the start and end points of the movement or its route.

Summary Table 25.III

идтú–ходúть	при-/у-, в-/вы-, под-/от-, вз-/с-, раз(о)-(ся)/с(о)-(ся), за-, про-, до-, пере-, об(о)-
éхать–éздить	при-/у-, в-/вы-, под-/от-, вз-/с, разъ-(ся)/съ-(ся), за-, про-, до-, пере-, объ-
летéть–летáть	при-/у-, в-/вы-, под-/от-, вз-/с, раз-(ся)/с-(ся), за-, про-, до-, пере-, об-
бежáть–бéгать	при-/у-, в-/вы-, под-/от-, вз-/с, раз-(ся)/с-(ся), за-, про-, до-, пере-, о-
плыть–плáвать	при-/у-, вы-, под-/от-, вс-, рас-(ся)/с-(ся), за-, про-, до-, пере-
нестú–носúть	при-/у-, в-/вы-, под-/от-, раз-/с-, за-, про-, до-, пере-, об-
везтú–возúть	при-/у-, в-/вы-, под-/от-, раз-/с-, за-, про-, до-, пере-, об-
вестú–водúть	при-/у-, в-/вы-, под-/от-, раз-/с-, за-, про-, до-, пере-, об-
лезть–лáзить	в-/вы-, с-, за-, про-, до-, пере-
ползтú–пóлзать	при-/у-, в-/вы-, под-/от-, рас-(ся)/с-(ся), за-, про-, до-, пере-, с-

гнать–гоня́ть	при-/у-, в-/вы-, под-(о)/от-, разо-/со-, за-, про-, до-, пере-, об-
катить–ката́ть	при-/у-, в-/вы-, под-/от-, рас-(ся)/с-(ся), за-, про-, до-, пере-, с-
тащи́ть–таска́ть	при-/у-, в-/вы-, под-/от-, рас-/с-, за-, про-, до-, пере-, с-
брести́–броди́ть	при-, раз-(ся), за-, про-, до-

 The **two prefixes with temporal meaning** *по-* and *про-* are used with all fourteen verbs of motion. The **prefixes** *с-* and *за-* with temporal meaning have a limited use, mainly with the verbs **ходи́ть**, **е́здить**, **бе́гать** and **лета́ть**. Additionally, in everyday speech the prefix **из-(ис-)** is added to the verbs **ходи́ть**, **е́здить**, **ла́зить** to emphasise that one has exhausted all possible destinations: **исходи́ть** весь го́род (to go everywhere in the city).

Level 2, 3 — 25.3 Verbs of motion with prefixes in the present and the future tenses: internal stem modification

Most verbs of motion with prefixes are affected by some internal stem changes in the present and future tenses. These changes are similar to the changes that occur in the present-tense stems of verbs of motion without prefixes (☞ 24.6.1). Each added prefix affects all stems of verbs of motion in the same way. Summary Tables 25.IV and 25.V explain these changes.

Summary Table 25.IV

Comments	Future tense of perfective verbs – examples			
Changes affect	**Infinitive**	**1st person singular**	**2nd person singular**	**3rd person plural**
All forms	**идти́: й/йд** Infinitive stem has **-й-**: дойти́, зайти́ etc. Future tense stem has **-йд-**: дойду́, зайду́	дойду́, зайду́	дойдёшь, зайдёшь The verb **прийти́** has **-д-** in all future tense forms (see comments below)	дойду́т, зайду́т
All forms	е́хать: **х/д**	дое́ду, зае́ду	дое́дешь, зае́дешь	дое́дут, зае́дут
Only 1st person singular	лете́ть: **т/ч**	долечу́, залечу́	долети́шь, залети́шь	долетя́т, залетя́т
All forms	плыть: **в**	доплыву́, заплыву́	доплывёшь, заплывёшь	доплыву́т, заплыву́т
1st person singular and 3rd person plural	бежа́ть: **ж/г**	добегу́, забегу́	добежи́шь, забежи́шь	добегу́т, забегу́т
All forms	вести́: **с/д**	доведу́, заведу́	доведёшь, заведёшь	доведу́т, заведу́т

Comments	Future tense of perfective verbs – examples			
All forms	брести́: **ст/д**	добреду́, забреду́	добредёшь, забредёшь	добреду́т, забреду́т
All forms	гнать: **гн/гон**	догоню́, загоню́	дого́нишь, заго́нишь	дого́нят, заго́нят
1st person singular	кати́ть: **т/ч**	докачу́, закачу́	дока́тишь, зака́тишь	дока́тят, зака́тят

- An exception to this pattern is the verb **прийти́**:

я приду́	мы придём
ты придёшь	вы придёте
он придёт	они приду́т

Summary Table 25.V

Comments	Present tense of imperfective verbs – examples			
Changes affect	**Infinitive**	**1st person singular**	**2nd person singular**	**3rd person plural**
Only 1st person singular	ходи́ть: **д/ж**	дохожу́, захожу́	дохо́дишь, захо́дишь	дохо́дят, захо́дят
All forms	е́здить: **езди- / езжа-**	доезжа́ю, заезжа́ю	доезжа́ешь, заезжа́ешь	доезжа́ют, заезжа́ют
All forms	пла́вать: **плава/ плыва-**	доплыва́ю, заплыва́ю	доплыва́ешь, заплыва́ешь	доплыва́ют, заплыва́ют
Only 1st person singular	води́ть: **д/ж**	довожу́, завожу́	дово́дишь, заво́дишь	дово́дят, заво́дят
Only 1st person singular	вози́ть: **з/ж**	довожу́, завожу́	дово́зишь, заво́зишь	дово́зят, заво́зят
Only 1st person singular	носи́ть: **с/ш**	доношу́, заношу́	доно́сишь, зано́сишь	доно́сят, зано́сят
All forms	ла́зить: **лази-/ леза-**	долеза́ю, залеза́ю	долеза́ешь, залеза́ешь	долеза́ют, залеза́ют
All forms	ката́ть: **ката-/ катыва-**	дока́тываю, зака́тываю	дока́тываешь, зака́тываешь	дока́тывают, зака́тывают
All forms	таска́ть: **таска-/ таскива-**	дота́скиваю, зата́скиваю	дота́скиваешь, зата́скиваешь	дота́скивают, зата́скивают
All forms	броди́ть: **броди-/ бреда-**	добреда́ю, забреда́ю	добреда́ешь, забреда́ешь	добреда́ют, забреда́ют

The stems of the following verbs are not affected by internal changes in any tense: лета́ть, бе́гать, нести́, везти́, тащи́ть, по́лзать, ползти́, гоня́ть, лезть.

25.4 Irregular verbs of motion with prefixes in the past tense (☞ 18.3)

There are several verbs of motion with prefixes that follow a special pattern in the past tense:

- The verb **идти** and any verbs with prefixes derived from **идти**: **шёл, шла, шло, шли, пришёл, пришла, пришло, пришли, ушёл, ушла, ушло, ушли** etc. If the prefix ends with a consonant the vowel **-о-** is added to the prefix: **вошёл, вошла, обошёл** etc.
- Verbs whose infinitives end with **–ти** (except идти), the verb **лезть** and their derived forms exhibit absence of the suffix **-л-** in the masculine form after the consonants **з** and **с** and the appearance of the letter **ё** under the stress. Some verbs ending in **-ти** are exceptions to this rule (see comments below). For example:

  вез**ти** (to transport): привёз, привезла, привезло, привезли etc.

  нес**ти** (to carry): унёс, унесла, унесло, унесли etc.

  полз**ти** (to crawl): дополз, доползла, доползло, доползли etc.

  ле**зть** (to climb): залез, залезла, залезло, залезли etc.

- Verbs whose infinitives end with **-ти** and their derived forms keep the suffix **-л-** in all forms, if their present and future tense stems end with **-д:**

  вес**ти**: веду, ведут (to lead): привёл, привела, привело, привели etc.

  брес**ти**: бреду, бредут (to wander/to stroll): добрёл, добрела, добрело, добрели etc.

Level 2, 3

Упражнения

1. Complete the sentences using a suitable verb of motion with prefixes **в-/вы-/при-/у-/под-/от-/вз-/с-**. Put the verb into the appropriate form:

1. Россия .... нефть, газ и лес, а .... готовую продукцию.
2. Хозяин .... свою собаку на прогулку в любую погоду.
3. Школьник постучал в дверь кабинета директора и спросил: «Можно ....?». «Да, ...,» – ответил директор.
4. Давай быстрее! Наш поезд .... через 5 минут.
5. .... в гости в пятницу. Сможешь?
6. Каждый день врач .... на работу в 8 утра, а .... домой в 6 вечера.
7. Извините, вы не .... меня до вокзала?
8. Кот заболел. Надо .... его к ветеринару.
9. Бабушка .... к окну.
10. Птица .... с ветки на землю.
11. Стюардесса объявила, что самолёт .... через 5 минут.

Level 2, 3

2. Complete the sentences using a suitable verb of motion with prefixes **про-/пере-/за-/до-/об-**. Put the verb in the required form:

1. Лошади красиво .... через мост.
2. Улицу следует .... на зелёный свет.
3. Мой знакомый .... мимо меня и даже не поздоровался.
4. Проезд был закрыт, и нам пришлось .... вокруг площади.
5. По дороге в аэропорт я .... к другу за посылкой.
6. Птица .... к нам в окно.
7. Ты сможешь .... эту бурную реку?
8. «Извините, мы сможем .... до Невского проспекта на метро?». «Это недалеко. Вы сможете .... туда пешком».

Level 2, 3

3. Complete the sentences using a suitable form of a verb of motion with prefix **по-**:

1. Летом мы решили .... на Байкал на поезде.
2. Виктор вышел из дома и .... к станции метро.
3. Вы .... со мной на дачу?
4. Говорят, что Гагарин сказал перед взлётом: «Ну что, ...!»

5. Сначáла мы дóлго шли по незнакóмой ýлице, потóм перешли́ чéрез дорóгу и .... по пáрку. Затéм мы остановились, провéрили наш маршрýт по кáрте и .... дáльше.

6. К сожалéнию, я не застáла свою подрýгу дóма. Онá ýже .... в аэропóрт.

4. Complete the sentences using a suitable form of a verb of motion with prefixes that have temporal meaning **по-/про-/за-/с-**:

1. Нам так понрáвились карти́ны э́того худóжника, что мы цéлый день .... по вы́ставке.

2. Мáма попроси́ла сы́на .... за хлéбом.

3. Стáрая собáка .... немнóжко по пáрку и устáла.

4. Прочитáв эсэмéску (SMS, text-message), Мари́на взволнóванно .... по кóмнате.

25.5 Using verbal aspect with verbs of motion with prefixes

The meanings of imperfective and perfective verbs of motion with prefixes correspond to the general concept of the verbal aspects: ☞ 20. For example:

По суббóтам наш друг Ви́ктор **приходи́л** (impf, a repeated action) к нам в гóсти и **приноси́л** (impf, a repeated action) вкýсный торт. Но в прóшлую суббóту, пéрвый раз за мнóго лет, он заболéл и не **пришёл** (pf, a single complete action).	Every Saturday Victor **used to come to visit us and bring** a nice cake. Last Saturday for the first time in many years he was ill and **did not come.**
Зáвтра мы **зайдём** (pf, a single complete action) к Ви́ктору и **принесём** (pf, a single complete action) емý егó люби́мый торт.	Tomorrow we **will call on** Victor and **will bring** him his favourite cake.

Additionally, in Russian the verbal aspect of the verbs of motion with prefixes can emphasise some very specific meanings: ☞ 25.5.1–3.

25.5.1 Special meanings of the verbal aspect in the past tense: actions with reversed results

☞ 20.4.3 and 20.5.2.

All verbs of motion with prefixes can describe an action in which the result can be reversed. In the past tense, any imperfective verb of motion with a prefix can convey the idea that the action did take place in the past, but was reversed back to its original point. This meaning is similar to a description of a round trip in the past using a multidirectional verb of motion without a prefix. For example:

Example	Translation	Meaning (literal translation)
Они́ **éздили** в Москвý.	They **went** to Moscow.	They **were** in Moscow, **but are not there now.**
Они́ **приезжáли** в Москвý.	They **came** to Moscow.	
Мáма **води́ла** ребёнка в шкóлу.	The mother **took the** child to school.	The child **was brought** to school **but is not there now.**
Мáма **приводи́ла** ребёнка в шкóлу.	The mother **brought** the child to school.	

A perfective verb of motion with a prefix can emphasise that the goal of the action was achieved in the past once, its result was not modified in any way and it is still relevant to the present.

Compare:

Imperfective	Perfective
Ваш друг **заходи́л**. (Your friend **called on you, was here,** but he **is gone now.**)	Ваш друг **пришёл**. (Your friend **has arrived and is still here.**)
Я зна́ю челове́ка, кото́рый **входи́л** в ко́мнату. (I know the person, who **came into the room and left again.**)	Я зна́ю челове́ка, кото́рый **вошёл** в ко́мнату. (I know the person who **came into the room and is still here.**)
Како́й за́пах! Кто-нибу́дь приноси́л све́жий ко́фе? (Such a nice smell! **Did** someone **bring** some fresh coffee? – **There is no coffee here any more, but one can still smell it.**)	Како́й за́пах! Кто-нибу́дь **принёс** све́жий ко́фе? (Such a nice smell! **Did** someone **bring** some fresh coffee?)

Level 2, 3 ## 25.5.2 Use of the imperfective and perfective verbs of motion with an indication of time in the past tense

If, in the examples above, a speaker knows the precise duration of an action, time expressions are used thus:

- With the preposition **на** (for): **На ско́лько вре́мени заходи́л** (impf) Ваш друг? (**How long** was your friend here (but he is not here any more)?) Мой друг **заходи́л на па́ру мину́т** (impf). (My friend **called on me, was here for a couple of minutes,** but he **is gone now.**) **На ско́лько вре́мени зашёл** (impf) Ваш друг? (**How long** has your friend come here for (and will be staying)?) Мой друг **зашёл на па́ру мину́т.** (My friend **has arrived and will stay here for couple of minutes.**)
  Note that in the examples above the imperfective verbs of motion describe an action in the past that lasted for the indicated period, but is over now. The perfective verbs of motion describe an action which has occurred in the past, but whose consequences would be felt in the future for the indicated period.
- The perfective verb followed by a time expression with the preposition **за** (within) is used to emphasise that the goal of the action was achieved within the indicated period: **За ско́лько вре́мени** они́ **дое́хали** до Москвы́? (**How long** did it take for them to reach Moscow?) Они́ **дое́хали** до Москвы́ **за во́семь часо́в.** (They **reached** Moscow **within eight hours.**)
- In the past tense, the imperfective verb followed by a time expression with the preposition **за** (for) is used to describe ability/skills to achieve a goal within the indicated period. This construction is less frequent: **За ско́лько вре́мени** они́ **обы́чно доезжа́ли** до Москвы́? (**How long** did it take for them to reach Moscow (usually)?) Они́ **доезжа́ли до** Москвы́ **за во́семь часо́в.** (They usually **reached** Moscow **within eight hours.**)

25.5.3 Special meanings of the verbal aspect in the past tense: negative sentences

In negative sentences both aspects are used to convey some additional information:

- In negative sentences, imperfective verbs emphasise that the action has not occurred: Ви́ктор не приходи́л (impf)? (**Has** Victor come?) Нет, **не приходи́л** (impf). (No, he **has not.**) Почтальо́н **приноси́л** (impf) посы́лку? (Has the postman **brought** the parcel?) Нет, **не приноси́л.** (No, he **has not.**)
- The use of the perfective in the same context emphasises that an attempt was made to achieve the goal, but it was not a success: Извини́, я **не пришёл** (pf). (I am sorry, I **could not make it.**) Почтальо́н **не принёс** (pf) посы́лку. (The postman **could not (was not able to) deliver** the parcel.)

25.5.4 Using the verbs of motion with prefixes in the future tense

Both imperfective verbs of motion with prefixes and unidirectional verbs of motion without prefixes are often used in popular speech to describe one's intentions for the future. This structure is equivalent to when an English verb in the present continuous tense is used to describe an action in the future (☞ also 24.5.5). For example:

Compare:

Они **уезжа́ют** за́втра домо́й.	Они **е́дут** за́втра.
They **are leaving** for home tomorrow.	They **are going** home tomorrow.

If, in the examples above, a speaker knows the precise duration of an action, time expressions are used thus:

- With the preposition **на** (for). Both imperfective and perfective verbs are used to convey the idea of the start point of the journey/movement/stay in the future: **На ско́лько вре́мени** приезжа́ют/прие́дут Ва́ши роди́тели? (**How long** will your parents be staying?)
- The perfective verb followed by a time expression with the preposition **за** (within) is used to emphasise that the goal of the action will be achieved within the indicated period: **За ско́лько вре́мени** они́ **долетя́т** до Ирку́тска? (**How long** will it take for them to reach Irkutsk?) Они́ **долетя́т до** Ирку́тска **за ше́сть часо́в**. (They will have **reached** Irkutsk **within six hours**.)

25.6 Figurative meaning of verbs of motion with prefixes

evel 3

Verbs of motion with prefixes form an essential part of many Russian idioms. Some examples are given below. All verbs in these examples can be used in both the imperfective and perfective verbal aspects and in all tenses.

Verbs of motion with the prefix **вы-**:

- **Выходи́ть/вы́йти за́муж** за + a noun/pronoun in the accusative case (to get married – for women only): Она́ **выходи́ла за́муж** три ра́за. (She **got married** three times.) Note, the verb **жени́ться** на + a noun/pronoun in the instrumental case is used to convey the same idea for a man: Он то́лько что **жени́лся**. (He **has** just **got married**.)
- **Выходи́ть/вы́йти из себя́** (to lose one's temper): Он **вы́шел из себя́** и на́чал крича́ть. (He **lost his temper** and started shouting.)
- **Выводи́ть/вы́вести** (кого́-ли́бо) **из себя́** (to drive someone mad): Свои́м поведе́нием она́ **выво́дит меня́ из себя́**. (She drives me mad because of her behaviour.)
- **Выноси́ть/вы́нести сор из избы́** (to reveal unpleasant secrets to the public): На заседа́нии парла́ментской коми́ссии бы́ло решено́ **не выноси́ть со́ра из избы́**. (At the meeting of the parliamentary committee they decided **not to go public**.)

Verbs of motion with the prefix **с-**:

- **Сходи́ть/сойти́ с ума́** (to go mad): Как ты мо́жешь тако́е говори́ть! Ты **сошла́ с ума́**! (How can you say such things! Have you **gone mad**!) The adjective сумасше́дший (mad) derived from the verb is often used in popular speech.
- **Своди́ть/свести́** (кого́-ли́бо) **с ума́** (to drive someone mad, often out of love): «Твои́ глаза́ зелёные **свели́ меня́ с ума́**» (Ру́сский рома́нс). (Your green eyes have driven me mad.)
- **Своди́ть/свести́** (с кем -ли́бо) **счёты** (to take revenge): В конце́ концо́в, ма́фия **свела́ с ним счёты**. (Finally, the Mafia has got him.)

- **Своди́ть/свести́ концы́ с конца́ми** (to make ends meet): По́сле ро́ста инфля́ции мно́гие се́мьи не мо́гут **свести́ концы́ с конца́ми**. (After inflation shot up a lot of families cannot make ends meet.)

Verbs of motion with the prefix **об-**:

- **Обводи́ть/обвести́** (кого́-ли́бо) **вокру́г па́льца** (to deceive/to cheat): Обвиня́емый **обвёл вокру́г па́льца** сле́дователей и судью́. (The accused **deceived** the detectives and the judge.)
- **Обходи́ть/обойти́** что́-то (to avoid something): В своём докла́де он **обошёл все о́стрые вопро́сы**. (In his paper, he avoided all difficult points.)

The verbs of motion **уходи́ть/уйти́** are used in the following idioms:

- **По́езд ушёл** (to be too late/to miss the boat): Извини́, я не могу́ тебе́ помо́чь, **по́езд ушёл**. (I am sorry, I cannot help you, it is too late.)
- **Уйти́ в себя́** (to keep oneself to oneself): Она́ **ушла́ в себя́** и переста́ла обща́ться с друзья́ми. (She **kept herself to herself** and stopped talking to her friends.)
- **Душа́ ушла́ в пя́тки** (to be scared): Моя́ **душа́ ушла́ в пя́тки** при одно́й мы́сли о встре́че с но́вым нача́льником. (I **got scared** just thinking about a meeting with my new boss.)

The verbs of motion **проходи́ть/пройти́** (to take place) and **проводи́ть/провести́** (to conduct/to hold) are often used when talking about events and activities in the present, past and future tenses. For example:

- Конфере́нция **прошла́** о́чень успе́шно. (The conference **was** a success.) В Петербу́рге ежего́дно **прохо́дит** фестива́ль «Бе́лые но́чи». (Every year in St Petersburg the festival 'White Nights' **takes place**.)
- Популя́рная поп-гру́ппа **провела́** благотвори́тельный конце́рт. (The popular pop-group **conducted** a charity concert.)

To describe a fast-going process the idioms of time with the verbs **проходи́ть/пройти́** (to pass); **пробега́ть/пробежа́ть** (to pass); **пролета́ть/пролете́ть** (to pass) are used. For example:

- Вре́мя пройдёт/**пробежи́т/пролети́т**. (The time **will fly** by.)
- Го́ды/дни/часы́ **пробега́ют /прохо́дят/пролета́ют**. (The years/days/hours **are flying** by.) Вот и день **прошёл.** (The day is over.)

Упражне́ния

1. Complete the sentences, choosing between the perfective and imperfective verbs of motion given in brackets:

1. «К вам (приходи́ть/прийти́) деловы́е партнёры. Они́ ждут Вас в кабине́те», – сообщи́ла секрета́рь своему́ нача́льнику.
2. Изве́стная фотомоде́ль (приезжа́ть/прие́хать) в наш клуб всего́ на не́сколько часо́в. По́сле встре́чи с покло́нниками она́ уе́хала в Москву́.
3. Как па́хнет ро́зами, но где же цветы́? Наве́рное, кто́-то (входи́ть/войти́) сюда́ с буке́том.
4. Про́шлым ле́том аспира́нт (прилета́ть/прилете́ть) в Ирку́тск на два дня.
5. Почтальо́н почему́-то не (приноси́ть/принести́) мне посы́лку.
6. Я (уезжа́ть/уе́хать) в командиро́вку за́втра.
7. Мы пригласи́ли на́ших друзе́й (приезжа́ть/прие́хать) к нам в го́сти на неде́лю.
8. Ско́лько коро́бок и чемода́нов. Вы, что (переезжа́ть/перее́хать)?
9. Наш друг всегда́ (заходи́ть/зайти́) к нам по суббо́там и (приноси́ть/принести́) торт. А сего́дня он (приноси́ть/принести́) шампа́нское.

2. Translate into Russian, using verbs of motion in the figurative sense as appropriate:

1. When I think of the forthcoming operation, I get very scared.
2. My friend (f) got married three times.
3. They could not help us. It was too late.
4. The swindler easily defrauded the trustful people.
5. After the accident the patient kept himself to himself.

25.7 Prepositions used after verbs of motion and other verbs describing movement

25.7.1 Prepositions used after verbs of motion and other verbs describing a directed movement: в, из; на, с; к and от

The fourteen verbs of motion and any other verbs describing movement have something in common. All verbs that describe a single or repeated directed movement to a precise destination (movement to a point) commonly take the prepositions **на** (to) or **в** (to) and the noun in the accusative case: Бизнесмéн **идёт в** бáнк. (The businessman **is going to** the bank.) Кот **пры́гнул на** пóлку. (The cat **has jumped on to** a shelf.) Вúктор **положúл** словáрь **в** портфéль. (Victor **put** the dictionary **in** his brief case.)

If the verb describes a straightforward movement from a precise place (movement from a point), it usually takes the prepositions **из** (from) or **с** (from) and the noun is in the genitive case: Бизнесмéн **идёт из** бáнка. (The businessman **is coming from** the bank.) Кот **пры́гнул с** пóлки. (The cat **has jumped off** the shelf.) Вúктор **вы́нул** словáрь **из** портфéля. (Victor **took** a dictionary **out from** his briefcase.)

If the verb conveys the meaning of 'visiting someone', the preposition **к** (to) and the noun in the dative case is used after the verb: Я **éду к родúтелям**. (I **am visiting** my **parents**.)

If the verb conveys the meaning of 'coming from someone', the verb takes the preposition **от** (from) and the noun in the genitive case: Я **éду от родúтелей**. (I am **coming from** my **parents' (home)**.)

The preposition **к** can also mean *towards*. The preposition **от** (from) is used as the prepositional pair of **к** in this context: Мáльчик **подошёл к** окнý. (The boy **moved towards** the window.) Мáльчик **отошёл от** окнá. (The boy **moved away from** the window.)

The choice between **в** and **на** (to) and **из** and **с** (from) depends on the meaning of the noun. For **в** and **на**, ☞ 6.3.1.1 and 10.2.1; for **из** and **с**, ☞ 7.3.2.2.

Summary Table 25.VI

Где? Where? в бáнке (в + prepositional): in the bank	Кудá? Where to? в банк (в + accusative): to the bank	Откýда? Where from? из бáнка (из + genitive): from the bank
Где? Where? на рабóте (на + prepositional): at work	Кудá? Where to? на рабóту (в + accusative): to work	Откýда? Where from? с рабóты (с + genitive): from work
Где? Where? у дрýга/у окнá (у + genitive): at a friend's place/ at a window	Кудá? Where to? к дрýгу/к окнý (к + dative): to visit a friend/ towards the window	Откýда? Where from? от дрýга/от окнá (от + genitive): from a friend/from the window

25.7.2 Other prepositions used after verbs of motion and other verbs describing movement: за, из-за, под, из-под, над, че́рез, сквозь, по, вдоль, ми́мо, от and до

The fourteen verbs of motion and other verbs that describe a single or repeated directed movement to a point and from a point take the following prepositions: за, из-за, под, из-под, че́рез, сквозь, вдоль, ми́мо, от and до. Summary Table 25.VII below shows that the prepositions за and из-за; под and из-под, до and от form pairs and can be used to describe a directed movement.

Summary Table 25.VII

Где? Where?	Куда́? Where to?	Отку́да? Where from?
де́вочка **за** столо́м/маши́на **за** угло́м (за + instrumental): the girl is at (behind) the table/the car is round the corner	сади́ться **за** стол/е́хать **за́** угол (за + accusative): to take a seat at (behind) the table/to go round the corner	встава́ть **из-за** стола́/выезжа́ть из-за угла́ (из + genitive): to get up from the table/to get out from round the corner
Где? Where? кот **под** дива́ном (под + instrumental): the cat is under the sofa	Куда́? Where to? лезть **под** дива́н (под + accusative): to get under the sofa	Отку́да? Where from? вылеза́ть **из-под** дива́на (с + genitive): to get out from under the sofa
N/A	Куда́? Where to? дойти́ **до** две́ри (до + genitive): to reach as far as the door	Отку́да? Where from? отойти́ **от** две́ри (от + genitive): to move away from the door

The prepositions над, че́рез, сквозь, вдоль, по and ми́мо are also used to describe a single or repeated directed movement. They do not form pairs:

че́рез (through/across) + accusative: перепры́гнуть **че́рез барье́р** (to jump over a barrier); перейти́ **че́рез по́ле** (to cross a field)

сквозь (through) + accusative: пройти́/прони́кнуть **сквозь стекло́** (to come through the glass)

вдоль (along) + genitive: идти́/гуля́ть **вдоль бе́рега** (to go/to stroll along the shore)

по (along/by) + dative: е́хать **по проспе́кту** (to go along the avenue); плыть **по мо́рю** (to sail on the sea); лете́ть **по не́бу** (to fly in the sky)

ми́мо (past) + genitive: пройти́ **ми́мо ларька́** (to go past the kiosk)

над (above) + instrumental: пролете́ть **над о́зером** (to fly above the lake, unidirectional sense)

25.7.3 Prepositions used after verbs of motion and other verbs describing non-directed movement: по, вокру́г, над

If the fourteen verbs of motion and any other verbs describe a non-directed movement, for example 'wandering around' etc., the prepositions по and вокру́г are usually used.

вокру́г (around): ча́йки лета́ют **вокру́г корабля́** (the seagulls are flying around a ship)

по (around): расстро́енный челове́к без це́ли **броди́л по го́роду** (an unhappy person was wandering around the city aimlessly)

над (above) + instrumental: пролете́ть **над о́зером** (to fly above the lake, unidirectional sense); кружи́ть **над о́зером** (to circle above the lake)

The prepositions **по**, **над** and **под** can be used to describe both directed and undirected movement. ☞ above.

The verbs of motion or any other verb can indicate the location where an undirected movement takes place:

Где бе́гают де́ти?	Where are the children running?
Де́ти бе́гают в па́рке/на у́лице/ря́дом с до́мом.	The children are running in a park/on a street/next to a house.

For the use of cases with the meaning of location, ☞ 7.3.2.1, 8.3, 9.3, 10.2.1.

25.7.4 Adverbs used after verbs of motion and other verbs describing movement

All verbs that describe straightforward movement to and from a precise destination are commonly used with adverbs that indicate movement. Summary Table 25.VIII lists adverbs of location and movement.

Summary Table 25.VIII

Meaning: location, no movement is involved	Meaning: moving towards	Meaning: moving from
Question word: Где? (where?)	Question word: Куда́? (where to?)	Question word: Отку́да? (where from?)
здесь/тут (here)	сюда́ (moving here)	отсю́да (moving from here)
там (there)	туда́ (moving there)	отту́да (moving from there)
сле́ва (on the left)	нале́во (moving to the left)	сле́ва (moving from the left)
спра́ва (on the right)	напра́во (moving to the right)	спра́ва (moving from the right)
наверху́ (above)	наве́рх (moving up)	све́рху (moving from the top)
внизу́ (below)	вниз (moving down)	сни́зу (moving from the bottom)

Упражне́ние

Level 2, 3

1. Insert the appropriate preposition:

1. Подсне́жники с трудо́м пробива́лись ... замёрзшую зе́млю.
2. Мы гуля́ем ... па́рку.
3. Ви́ктор пове́сил ку́ртку ... ве́шалку, поста́вил чемода́н ... шкаф, положи́л де́ньги ... сейф и с удово́льствием сел ... мя́гкое кре́сло.
4. Вы́скочив ... угла́, маши́на прое́хала ... до́ма и въе́хала ... откры́тые воро́та.
5. Незнако́мец легко́ перепры́гнул ... забо́р, пробежа́л ... огра́ды и скры́лся ... до́мом.

Level 2, 3

Обобща́ющее упражне́ние

2. Complete the text by using a verb of motion (listed below) in the required form. Add a suitable prefix to the verb as appropriate:

е́здить, е́хать, вози́ть, идти́, ходи́ь нести́, плыть

Пое́здка в Петербу́рг

1. В про́шлые выходны́е господи́н Смирно́в .... в Петербу́рг. 2. Он .... туда́ свои́х ро́дственников из А́нглии, кото́рые в пе́рвый раз .... в Росси́ю. 3. Они́ реши́ли .... в Петербу́рг на ночно́м по́езде. 4. Снача́ла они́ .... до вокза́ла на маршру́тке (private minibus). 5. У зда́ния вокза́ла они́ .... из авто́буса, нашли́ ну́жную платфо́рму и ....

в вагóн пóезда. 6. Пóезд .... от платфóрмы тóчно по расписáнию. 7. Гостя́м господи́на Смирнóва понрáвился ночнóй пóезд. Пóезд .... до Петербу́рга всю ночь. 8. Они́ хорошó вы́спались, а у́тром проводни́ца .... в купé зáвтрак. 9. Пóезд .... в Петербу́рг рáно у́тром. 10. С вокзáла они́ .... в гости́ницу в сáмом цéнтре гóрода. 11. Немнóжко отдохну́в, они́ .... гуля́ть по Нéвскому проспéкту – глáвной у́лице гóрода. 12. Они́ .... чéрез нéсколько мáленьких мóстиков, ... ми́мо Казáнского собóра, ... в магази́н за сувени́рами, и наконéц, ... до Дворцóвой плóщади, на котóрой нахóдится знамени́тый Эрмитáж. 13. Нéсколько раз они́ .... вокру́г плóщади, ... на Дворцóвую нáбережную и реши́ли покатáться по Невé на теплохóде. 14. Они́ купи́ли билéты на экску́рсию по рéкам и канáлам гóрода, сéли на теплохóд и .... вдоль нáбережной. 15. Как хорошó, что у них впереди́ цéлых два дня. Мóжно бу́дет .... в нéсколько музéев, а éсли остáнется врéмя, ... в Петергóф. 16. Рóдственникам господи́на Смирнóва так понрáвился гóрод, что они́ обязáтельно реши́ли ....сюдá ещё раз.

26 Participles

The participle (or verbal adjective) is a verbal form that combines characteristics of verb and adjective. Participles are most common in writing.

As with adjectives (11), participles can have a long and a short form. In a sentence, long-form participles function like long-form adjectives and can qualify any noun in a sentence. They usually describe qualities linked to some activity: **летя́щий** (flying), **влюблённый** (someone in love), **потеря́вшийся** (someone/thing who got lost) etc. In Russian, the following types of long-form participles are frequently used: present imperfective active participle, past imperfective active participle, past perfective active participle, present imperfective passive participle and past perfective passive participle. The English equivalents of Russian long-form participles are as follows:

Russian long-form participle	English equivalent
present imperfective active: **де́лающий**; **говоря́щий**	verbal form ending in -ing: do**ing**; speak**ing**
past imperfective and perfective active: **де́лавший**; **говори́вший** (impf); **сде́лавший**; **сказа́вший** (pf)	verb in the past tense: (who) did/was doing/has done; spoke/was speaking/has spoken
present imperfective passive: **опи́сываемый**; **производи́мый**	passive verbal forms 'is being done': 'is being described', 'is being produced'
past perfective passive: **сде́ланный**; **пригото́вленный**; **вы́питый**	passive verbal forms 'done': done/made; cooked; drunk

Only passive participles can have a short form. A short-form participle is the predicate to the subject of a sentence. Short-form passive participles function like passive verbs (21.3); they are translated into English using the passive verbal form (e.g. 'done'). The passive verbal form is connected to the subject of the sentence by **быть** (to be): 'is done/was done/has been done/had been done/will be done'. The short form can be used in the present, past and future: Фи́льм **снят**. (The film **is shot**.) Фильм **был снят**. (The film **was/has been shot**.) Фильм **бу́дет снят**. (The film will be shot.)

26.1 The long-form participles

26.1.1 Grammatical characteristics of long-form participles

Long-form participles combine the grammatical characteristics of verbs and long-form adjectives. A participle takes tense, aspect and voice from the verb from which it is derived, and agrees in gender, number and case with the noun it qualifies. Long-form active participles decline like adjectives with a stem ending in -**ш**/-**щ**; long-form passive participles decline like adjectives with a hard stem (11.1):

Essential verbal characteristics of long-form participles:

- **Tense:** present and past; participles do not have the future tense (for tenses and verb conjugation, 17, 18).
- **Aspect:** perfective or imperfective (for verbal aspect, 20). In the present tense, only imperfective participles can be used, because the perfective present tense of verbs does not exist in Russian. In the past tense perfective and imperfective participles are used.
- **Voice:** active and passive (for voice, 21.3–4). Active participles can be formed from transitive and intransitive verbs. Passive participles can be formed only from transitive verbs (for transitive and intransitive verbs, 21.1–2).

Essential adjectival characteristics of long-form participles:

- **Gender:** masculine, feminine or neuter (for genders, 2.3)
- **Number:** singular or plural (for number, 3)
- **Case:** all six cases (for cases, 4–10)

26.1.2 Formation of long-form participles

26.1.2.1 Formation of present active participles

Both transitive and intransitive verbs can form active participles. However, only imperfective participles can be formed in the present tense.

To form the present active participle:

- Take the present tense, 3rd person plural form of the verb, for example де́ла**ют** (they do), ид**у́т** (they go), у́ч**ат** (they study), ку́р**ят** (they smoke).
- Drop the ending: де́ла-, ид-, уч-, кур-.
- Add the suffix **-ущ/-ющ** for first-conjugation verbs. The suffix **-ущ** is used if the stem ends in a consonant: иду́щ-. The suffix **-ющ** is used if the stem ends in a vowel: де́лаю́щ-. For verb conjugations, 17.1–2.
- Add the suffix **-ащ/-ящ** for second-conjugation verbs. The suffix **-ащ** is used if the stem ends in any consonant affected by spelling rule 1: уча́щ- (for spelling rule 1, 1.3.1). The suffix **-ящ** is used if the stem ends in any other consonant: куря́щ-. Note, a second-conjugation verb stem never ends with a vowel.
- Add the appropriate adjective ending; a participle must agree in gender, number and case with the noun it qualifies.
- If a participle is formed from a reflexive verb, the particle **-ся** is added to the ending of the participle, after either a consonant or a vowel; for example, смею́щ**ийся** ма́льчик (laughing boy), улыба́ющ**аяся** де́вочка (smiling girl).

26.1.2.2 Formation of past active participles

Both transitive and intransitive verbs can form active participles. Both perfective and imperfective participles can be formed in the past tense.

To form the past active participle:

- Take the masculine form of the past tense verb; for example, рабо́тал (he worked). Some irregular verbs in the masculine past tense do not have the suffix -л: принёс (brought).
- Drop the suffix -л to get the appropriate stem: рабо́та-. Drop nothing, if the masculine past tense does not have -л: принёс-.
- Add the suffix **-вш/-ш**. The suffix **-вш** is used if the stem ends in a vowel: рабо́та**вш**-. The suffix **-ш** is used if the stem ends in a consonant: принёс**ш**-.
- Add the appropriate adjective ending; a participle must agree in gender, number and case with the noun it qualifies.

- If a participle is formed from a reflexive verb, the particle -**ся** is added to the ending of a participle, after either a consonant or a vowel. For example, смея́вший**ся** ма́льчик (boy who laughed), улыба́вша**яся** де́вочка (girl who smiled).

26.1.2.3 Formation of present passive participles

_evel 2, 3

Only transitive verbs can form passive participles. Therefore, reflexive verbs, some verbs of motion and any other intransitive verbs do not have passive participles. In the present tense, only imperfective participles are used.

To form the present passive participle:

- Take the present-tense, 1st person plural form of the verb; for example, отправля́**ем** (we send), несём (we carry).
- Drop the ending: отправля́-, нес-.
- Add the suffix -**ем** for first-conjugation verbs: отправля́ем-. If the 1st person plural ends in -**ём** (несём, везём, идём) add the suffix -**ом.**
- Add the suffix -**им** for second-conjugation verbs: ви́дим-
- Add the appropriate adjective ending. A participle must agree in gender, number and case with the noun it qualifies.

Exceptions

Note the following irregularity in the present passive participles:

- If a participle is formed from an infinitive that ends with -**авать**, keep the suffix -**ава**- in a participle: дава́ть (to give) – дава́емый (-ая, -ое, -ые).

Some transitive verbs do not have a present passive participle:

- Some monosyllabic verbs: пить (to drink); есть (to eat); быть (to be); бить (to beat), знать (to know) etc.
- Some first-conjugation verbs; for example, писа́ть (to write).
- Many second-conjugation verbs without prefixes: гото́вить (to cook, to prepare); держа́ть (to hold); плати́ть (to pay); смотре́ть (to watch, to look after); ста́вить (to put); стро́ить (to build) etc.

Present passive participles are mainly used in formal documents or scientific research; for example: С това́ров, **деклари́руемых** на грани́це, не взима́ется по́шлина. (The tax is not put on goods that **are declared** at customs.) Present passive participles are rare in spoken language unless they have changes to their function and are used as adjectives (☞ 26.1.3.2).

26.1.2.4 Formation of past passive participles

Only perfective participles are used in the past tense. They are formed from perfective transitive verbs.

To form the past passive participle:

- Use the stem of the past tense masculine form; for example, сде́лал (did), изучи́л (studied), унёс (took away), изогну́л (bend), вы́пил (drunk). Some irregular verbs in the masculine past tense do not have the suffix -л: унёс (took away).
- Drop the suffix -**л**: сде́ла-, изучи́-, унёс, изогну́-, вы́пи-. Drop nothing, if the masculine past tense does not have -л: унёс-
- Add the suffix -**нн** if the stem ends with a vowel other than **и**: сде́ланн-.
- Add the suffix -**енн** if the stem ends with the vowel **и** or a consonant and the stress does not fall on the suffix: изу́ченн-.
- Add the suffix -**ённ** if the stem ends with the vowel **и** or a consonant and the stress falls on the suffix: унесённ-. See comments below.
- Add the suffix -**т** if the stem ends with -**ну**, -**ер** or -**оло**-: изогну́-.

- Most monosyllabic verbs, with and without prefixes, will also have the suffix -т: вы́пит- (вы́пит- is formed from пить–вы́пить).
- Add the appropriate adjective ending. A participle must agree in gender, number and case with the noun it qualifies.

Comments:

The past participle formation of verbs ending in **-ить** can be complicated by the following consonant changes in the stem:

Consonant changes	Example	
	Verb	**Participle**
б–бл в–вл м–мл п–пл ф–фл	погуби́ть (to destroy) пригото́вить (to cook/prepare) сломи́ть (to break) затопи́ть (to flood) разграфи́ть (to rule paper)	погу́бленный пригото́вленный сло́мленный зато́пленный разграфлённый
т–ч т–щ	встре́тить (to meet) возврати́ть (to return)	встре́ченный возвращённый
д–жд д–ж	возбуди́ть (to excite) разбуди́ть (to wake up)	возбуждённый разбу́женный
с–ш	допроси́ть (to interrogate)	допро́шенный
ст–щ	подласти́ть (to sweeten)	подслащённый
з–ж	преобрази́ть (to transform)	преображённый

Level 2, 3

26.1.3 Using the long-form participles

26.1.3.1 Replacement of a relative clause

In writing, constructions with a long-form a participle are frequently used to replace a relative clause introduced by the relative pronoun **кото́рый** (which, that, who, whom). This can only be done if **кото́рый** is used in the nominative or accusative cases.

For relative clauses introduced by **кото́рый**, ☞ 14.8.1.

To replace a relative clause by a construction using a long-form participle:

- Omit **кото́рый** (which, that, who, whom) and the predicate in the relative clause.
- Replace **кото́рый** used in the nominative case, and the predicate (a verb), with the appropriate active participle. The participle is based on the verb it replaces.
- Replace **кото́рый** used in the accusative case, and the predicate (a verb), with the appropriate passive participle. The participle is based on the verb it replaces.
- The participle must agree in gender, number and case with the noun it qualifies.
- The standard position of the participle in a sentence is after the noun it qualifies.
- The participle and the noun it qualifies are separated by a comma.

For example:

Я зна́ю пожило́го мужчи́ну, **кото́рый** (nominative) **чита́ет газе́ту и ку́рит тру́бку** (a relative clause introduced by **кото́рый**).	I know the old man **who is reading the newspaper and smoking a pipe.**
Я зна́ю пожило́го мужчи́ну, **чита́ющего** (active participle) газе́ту и **куря́щего** (active participle) тру́бку.	I know the old man **reading the newspaper and smoking a pipe.**

| Óколо стола гуля́ла ку́рочка, **кото́рую** (accusative) **привяза́ли за́ ногу** (a relative clause introduced by **кото́рый**). | A hen, **which was tied by its leg**, was wandering around near a table. |
| Óколо стола гуля́ла **привя́занная** (passive participle) **за́ ногу ку́рочка.** (Толсто́й) | A hen, **tied by its leg**, was wandering around near a table. |

26.1.3.2 Other uses and functions of long-form participles

A participle can function:

- As a noun; for example, уча́щиеся (pupils; original participle 'studying'). **Уча́щиеся** сдаю́т экза́мены. (The pupils are sitting their exams.)
- As an adjective; for example, люби́мый (favourite, original participle 'being loved'). Хоккéй – **люби́мый** вид спо́рта мно́гих россия́н. (Ice hockey is the favourite sport of many Russians.)

26.2 Short-form participles

26.2.1 Formation and essential characteristics of the short-form participles

Only passive participles have a short-form participle. The short-form participle is formed by dropping the ending of the long-form participle. If the long-form participle has two letters **н** in the suffix, one **н** must also be dropped; for example, сде́лан**ный** (long form) – сде́лан (short form); унесён**ный** (long form) – унесён (short form); вы́пи**тый** (long form) – вы́пит (short-form).

The short-form participle retains all the verbal characteristics of the long-form participle, such as tense, aspect and voice (☞ 26.1.1). However, unlike the long-form participle, the short-form participle has the adjectival characteristics of a short-form adjective (for short-form adjectives, ☞ 12.5). This means that a short-form participle has number and gender, but cannot express case; for example, сде́лан (done; masculine singular); сде́лана (done; feminine singular); сде́лано (done; neuter singular); сде́ланы (done; plural): Рабо́та **сде́лана**. (The work is done.)

26.2.2 Using short-form participles

In a sentence, the short-form participle functions as a predicative passive verb. It must agree with the subject of the sentence in number and gender. The participle is connected to the subject of the sentence by the verbal link – **быть** (to be). In the Russian present tense, **быть** (to be) is omitted: Вы́ставка **откры́та**. (The exhibition **is opened**.) In the past and future tenses, **быть** (to be) is present in sentences. In the past tense, a short-form participle must agree with **быть** in number and gender: Вы́ставка **была́ откры́та**. (The exhibition **was open**.) In the future tense, a short-form participle must agree with **быть** in person and number: Вы́ставки **бу́дут откры́ты**. (The exhibitions **will be opened**.)

The imperfective past and present short-form participles are used extremely rarely: Целе́бные исто́чники всегда́ **бы́ли почита́емы** (passive present participle) в наро́де. (Healing springs **were** always **worshipped** by ordinary people.) Где э́то **ви́дано** (impf. passive past participle)? Где э́то **слы́хано** (impf. passive past participle)? (Драгу́нский). (Where **was** it **heard** about? Where **was** it **seen**?)

Conversely, the perfective past short-form participles are frequently used in both written and spoken Russian: Чёрным по белому **написано**. (It **is written** in black and white.) Извините, э́тот сто́лик **за́нят**? (Excuse me, is this table occupied?)

👁 Both the long and short forms of participles can be translated into English in a similar way by using a passive verbal form, for example 'done', except that the long form implies 'which was':

На столе́ лежи́т кни́га, **напи́санная** (long-form participle) Толсты́м.	The book, which was **written** by Tolstoy, is (lying) on the table.
Кни́га **напи́сана** (short-form participle) Толсты́м.	The book **is written** by Tolstoy.

However, long and short forms of the past passive participle function in the sentence in two different ways. The long form of the past passive participle functions as an adjective that is not the core part of the sentence and that could be omitted without destroying the sentence. The short form of the past passive participle functions as a predicate: it is the core part of the sentence and cannot be omitted without destroying the sentence.

Упражне́ния

Level 2, 3

1. Give the infinitive form of the verb from which these participles are formed:

1. напи́санный
2. несу́щий
3. привы́кший
4. танцу́ющий
5. живу́щий
6. взя́вший
7. е́дущий
8. унесённый
9. ку́пленный
10. вы́питый

Level 2, 3

2. A. Form the active present tense participle of the following verbs:

1. пить
2. бере́чь
3. класть
4. иска́ть
5. смея́ться
6. испо́льзовать

B. Form the active past tense participle of the following verbs:

1. прийти́
2. съесть
3. интересова́ться
4. встреча́ться
5. присе́сть
6. отдохну́ть

Level 2, 3

3. A. Form the passive present tense passive participle of the following verbs:

1. экспорти́ровать
2. люби́ть
3. изуча́ть
4. нести́

B. Form the passive past tense participle of the following verbs:

1. сказа́ть
2. изучи́ть
3. пригласи́ть
4. расста́вить
5. запрети́ть
6. откры́ть

Level 2, 3

4. Replace the participles with relative clauses introduced by **кото́рый**. Rephrase the sentence as appropriate:

1. Не ве́рьте дана́йцам дары́ принося́щим (idiom: Beware of Greeks bearing gifts).
2. Тури́сты купи́ли все понра́вившиеся им сувени́ры.
3. Лю́ди, прожи́вшие всю жизнь в дере́вне, не лю́бят городско́й суеты́.
4. При Ста́лине деся́тки ты́сяч несправедли́во осуждённых и приговорённых к ра́зным сро́кам сове́тских люде́й, пребыва́ли наказа́ние в ГУЛаге.
5. Кни́ги, напи́санные В. Пеле́виным и переведённые на мно́гие языки́ ми́ра, по́льзуются большо́й популя́рностью.
6. Мы купи́ли жаропонижа́ющие табле́тки.

Level
2, 3
5. Replace the relative clauses introduced by **кото́рый** by constructions with participles:

1. Иностра́нные студе́нты, кото́рые приезжа́ют из ра́зных стран, должны́ сдать экза́мен по ру́сскому языку́.

2. Мы нашли́ докла́д, кото́рый потеря́л рассе́янный профе́ссор.

3. Тури́сты купа́ются в горя́чих исто́чниках, кото́рые никогда́ не замерза́ют.

4. Па́пку, кото́рую оста́вил на сто́лике пассажи́р, переда́ли в «Бюро́ нахо́док».

5. Мы рабо́таем в компа́нии, кото́рую основа́л изве́стный бизнесме́н 10 лет наза́д.

6. Начало́сь восстановле́ние зда́ний, кото́рые разру́шил урага́н.

Level
2, 3
6. Choose between the short and long form of the participles given in brackets. Put the participle in the correct form:

1. Мы прочита́ли статью́ (опублико́ванный/опублико́ван) на са́йте.

2. Иссле́дователь (заинтересо́ванный/заинтересо́ван) в получе́нии то́чных результа́тов.

3. Отдыха́ющие (разочаро́ванный/разочаро́ван) круи́зом.

4. Нам привезли́ (отремонти́рованный/отремонти́рован) компью́тер.

5. Ви́ктор съел пирожо́к (ку́пленный/ку́плен) в кио́ске.

27 Gerunds

Level 2, 3 The gerund (or verbal adverb) is an unchangeable verbal form that combines characteristics of verbs and adverbs. Gerunds are common in writing. In Russian, there are only two types of gerund: imperfective and perfective, formed from imperfective and perfective verbs respectively (☞ 20). The Russian imperfective gerund is the equivalent of the English verbal form in *-ing*: де́лая (**doing**), рабо́тая (**working**). The perfective gerund is the equivalent of the English verbal form '*having done*': написа́в (**having written**); отпра́вив (**having sent**).

In Russian, gerunds can be used only in sentences with **one subject and more than one verb.** In this type of sentence, the verb always describes the main action. Imperfective gerunds can clarify a background action/actions that occur at the same time as the main action. Perfective gerunds can clarify an action/actions that occurred before the main action:

Слу́шая (impf gerund) му́зыку и гро́мко разгова́ривая (impf gerund), студе́нты (subject) гото́вят (principal action described by the verb) у́жин.	**While listening to** music and **chatting** loudly, the students **are preparing** dinner.
Пло́тно поу́жинав (pf gerund), тури́сты (subject) пошли́ (principal action described by the verb) в ночно́й клуб.	**Having had** a big meal, the tourists went to a nightclub.

Level 2, 3 ## 27.1 Essential characteristics of gerunds

All gerunds take their aspect from the verbs from which they are derived. However, gerunds have neither tense nor the voice. Like adverbs, gerunds are unchangeable and can clarify the time, place and manner in which the main action is carried out.

Level 2, 3 ### 27.1.1 Gerund formation

27.1.1.1 Imperfective gerund formation

To form the imperfective gerund:

- Take the present tense, 3rd person plural form of the verb; for example, де́лают (they do), молча́т (they study), говоря́т (to speak).
- Drop the ending: де́ла-; **молч-**; **говор-**.
- Add the gerund suffix **-a** after consonants affected by spelling rule 1 (☞ 1.3.1); for example, мо́лча.
- Add the gerund suffix **-я** after any other vowels or consonants: де́лая, говоря́.
- If the gerund is formed from a reflexive verb, add **-сь** after the gerund suffix: смея́ться (to laugh) – сме́ясь; занима́ться (to be occupied) – занима́ясь.

Exceptions

Note the following irregularities in the formation of the imperfective gerund:

- If a verb's imperfective infinitive ends with **-авать** keep the suffix **-ава-** in the imperfective gerund: **дава́ть** (to give) – **дава́я**; **продава́ть** (to sell) – **продава́я**.
- The verb **быть** (to be) forms an irregular imperfective gerund: **бу́дучи** (being)
- In folklore, poetry and popular speech some imperfective verbs retain old forms with the suffix **-учи/-ючи**: игра́**ючи** (playing); припева́**ючи** (singing; sense is 'living in clover'); жале́**ючи** (feeling sorry for); **йдучи** (going): Они́ живу́т **припева́ючи**. (They are **living in clover**.)

Some verbs do not have an imperfective gerund:

- Many monosyllabic verbs: пить (to drink); есть (to eat); петь (to sing).
- Verbs ending with **-чь**: мочь (to be able to); печь (to bake); бере́чь (to take care of); жечь (to burn).
- Verbs ending with **-нуть**: га́снуть (to go out); тону́ть (to drown).
- Verbs ending with **-ереть**: тере́ть (to rub/to grate).
- Verbs with **с–ш, х–ш, з–ж** stem consonant changes: писа́ть – пишу́ (to write), паха́ть – пашу́ (to plough); вяза́ть (to knit/to tie) – вяжу́.
- Some verbs of motion: е́хать (to go); бежа́ть (to run); лете́ть (to fly); гнать (to drive).

27.1.1.2 Perfective gerund formation

To form the perfective gerund:

- Take the perfective infinitive; for example, сде́лать (to do).
- Drop the ending **-ть: сде́ла-**
- Add the imperfective gerund suffix **-в**: сде́лав (having done).
- To form the perfective gerund from reflexive verbs, drop the ending **-ться** and add the suffix **-вшись**: засмея́ться (to laugh) – засмея́вшись (having laughed).

Exceptions

Note the following irregularities in the perfective gerund:

- If a perfective gerund is formed from a perfective infinitive that ends with **-ти**, it has the suffix **-я**: довезти́ (to deliver) – довезя́ (having delivered); унести́ (to take away) – унеся́ (having taking away) etc. Unlike the other perfective gerunds, gerunds formed from perfective infinitives ending in **-ти**, follow the rules of formation of imperfective gerunds (☞ 27.1.1.1). They are formed from the future perfective stems and not from the past tense stems. Compare: идти́ (to go) – иду́т (3rd person plural present) – **-ид-** (present tense stem) – идя́ (imperfective gerund); зайти́ (to call on) – зайду́т (3rd person plural future perfective) – **-зайд-** (future perfective stem) – зайдя́ (perfective gerund).
- If a perfective gerund is formed from a perfective infinitive that ends with **- сти, -чь** or **-зть**, it has the prefix **-ши**: вы́расти – вы́росши, зацвести́ – зацве́тши, спечь – спёкши. Formation of these gerunds may be complicated by various internal changes in the stem.

27.2 Using the gerund

27.2.1 Using the imperfective gerund

The imperfective gerund can be used **only in a sentence with one subject** and more than one verb and where all actions occur simultaneously. Imperfective gerunds usually describe background action/actions. Imperfective gerunds are frequently used to replace:

- A subordinate clause of time introduced by conjunctions **когда́** (when); **пока́** (while/meanwhile); **в то вре́мя как** (when/meanwhile); **та́к как** (since/because); **потому́ что** (because). When replacing a subordinate clause by a gerund, the conjunction is omitted:

Complex sentence with subordinate clause	Sentence with gerund
Когда́ он **обе́дал** (subordinate clause), он слу́шал му́зыку. (While he was having his lunch, he was listening to music.)	**Обе́дая** (impf gerund), он слу́шал му́зыку. (**While having lunch**, he was listening to music.)

- One of multiple verbs in a simple sentence with one subject. Often, in a sentence with multiple verbs, the choice of principal verb depends on the speaker's interpretation:

Студе́нты **отдыха́ют** (verb), **развлека́ются** (verb), **и танцу́ют** (verb). (The students relax, have fun and dance.)	Студенты **отдыха́ют** (principal verb), **развлека́ясь** **и танцу́я** (gerunds). (The students relax, **having fun and dancing**.)	Студе́нты **развлека́ются** (principal verb), **отдыха́я** **и танцу́я** (gerunds). (The students have fun, **relaxing and dancing**.)

The gerund is an unchangeable verbal form. Therefore, in a sentence, it is the principal verb which expresses the idea of present, past or future:

Present	Past	Future
Рабо́тая (gerund) в ба́нке, Мари́я **обслу́живае**т ру́сских клие́нтов. (**Working** in the bank, Maria **is serving/serves** Russian customers.)	**Рабо́тая** (gerund) в ба́нке, Мари́я **обслу́живала** ру́сских клие́нтов. (**Working** in the bank, Maria **was serving/served** Russian customers.)	**Рабо́тая** (gerund) в ба́нке, Мари́я бу́дет **обслу́живать** ру́сских клие́нтов. (**Working** in the bank, Maria **will be serving/will serve** Russian customers.)

27.2.2 Using the perfective gerund

The perfective gerund can be used in a sentence **with one subject** and more than one verb, where all actions occur as a sequence of events. The perfective gerund usually describes the action/actions that occur before the principal event.

Perfective gerunds are frequently used to replace a subordinate clause introduced by conjunctions **когда́/как то́лько** (when/immediately when); **по́сле того́ как** (after); **до того́ как** (before); **снача́ла ... пото́м ...** (at first ... then ...), **та́к как** (because of):

Complex sentence with subordinate clause	Sentence with gerund
Когда́ **он пообе́дал** (subordinate clause), он вы́мыл посу́ду. (**When he had had his lunch**, he washed the dishes.)	**Пообе́дав** (pf gerund), он вы́мыл посу́ду. (**Having had** his lunch, he washed the dishes.)

◐ When replacing a subordinate clause by the gerund, the following changes to the structure of the sentence need to be made:

- Drop the conjunction that introduces the subordinate clause.
- Drop the subject of the main clause, if applicable.
- The perfective gerund/gerunds replace the verb/verbs that describe the first action/actions in the sequence of action/s.
- The gerund usually opens the rephrased sentence, although it can appear after a time or location description.

For example:

Complex sentence with subordinate clause	Sentence with gerund
Когда́ (conjunction) **Викто́рия приготовила** обе́д и **вы́мыла** посу́ду, она́ (subject of main clause) позвони́ла подру́ге. (**When Victoria had cooked** the dinner and **washed up** the dishes, she called her friend.)	**Пригото́вив** обе́д и **вы́мыв** посу́ду, Викто́рия позвони́ла подру́ге. (**Having cooked** the dinner and **washed up** the dishes, Victoria called her friend.)

The gerund is an unchangeable verbal form. Therefore, in a sentence, it is the principal verb that expresses the idea of present, past or future.

Present	Past	Future
Опра́вив сообще́ние, Ви́ктор **звони́т дру́гу**. (Having sent an e-mail, Victor rings his friend.)	Опра́вив сообще́ние, Ви́ктор **позвони́л дру́гу**. (Having sent an e-mail, Victor rang his friend.)	Опра́вив сообще́ние, Ви́ктор **позвони́т дру́гу**. (Having sent an e-mail, Victor will ring his friend.)

27.3 Use of gerunds in idioms; as prepositions; adverbs that are derived from gerunds

In Russian, some gerunds have become essential parts of idioms. For example:

- рабо́тать **спустя́ рукава́** – to work in a slipshod manner
- труди́ться/рабо́тать **не поклада́я рук** – to work tirelessly (literally: to work without giving one's hands a rest)
- сиде́ть **сложа́ ру́ки** – to sit doing nothing (twiddling one's thumbs)
- уйти́ несо́лона **нахлеба́вшись** – to leave without achieving the goal (literally: to leave having had an unsalted meal)
- нести́сь **сломя́** го́лову – to run too fast (literally: to run risking breaking one's head)
- пе́сенка **спе́та** – someone's goose is cooked (literally: one's song is sung)
- открове́нно **говоря́** – frankly speaking

Some frequently occurring prepositions are derived from gerunds. For example:

- спустя́ – after/later; два́дцать лет **спустя́** (twenty years later)
- благодаря́ – thanks to/because of, followed by the dative case: **благодаря́** его́ самоотве́рженным де́йствиям (thanks to his selfless actions)
- включа́я – including, followed by the accusative case: **все, включа́я** президе́нта (everyone, including the president)
- исключа́я – excluding, followed by the accusative case: **все, исключа́я** президе́нта (everyone, excluding the president)

Some gerunds have similar meanings to adverbs ending in -**юще**. These adverbs are formed from the present active participles.

- умоля́я (pleading for) – умоля́**юще**: смотре́ть умоля́юще (to look with pleading in one's eyes)
- ожида́я (expecting) – ожида́**юще**: смотре́ть ожида́юще (to look with expectation in one's eyes)
- негоду́я (to be indignant) – негоду́**юще**: крича́ть негоду́юще (to shout with indignation)

Упражне́ния

1. A. Give the infinite forms of the verbs from which these gerunds are formed.

1. зако́нчив
2. существу́я
3. интересу́ясь
4. попроща́вшись
5. вы́росши

6. боя́сь
7. дава́я
8. переда́в
9. бу́дучи
10. унеся́

B. Form the gerunds of the following verbs.

1. прийти́
2. пога́снуть
3. брать
4. рисова́ть
5. зацвести́

6. иска́ть
7. улыбну́ться
8. найти́
9. жить
10. спечь

2. A. Replace the gerunds in the following sentences with the appropriate verbs. Rephrase the sentences if appropriate:

1. «Блестя́ на со́лнце, снег лежи́т». (Пу́шкин)
2. Учёные бу́дут рабо́тать над но́вой вакци́ной, испо́льзуя специа́льное обору́дование.
3. «Он про́жил в Пари́же четы́ре го́да, рабо́тая с утра́ до ве́чера, почти́ ничего́ не чита́я и ниче́м осо́бенным не интересу́ясь». (Бу́нин)
4. В 1994-м году́, прожи́в мно́го лет в Аме́рике, А. Солжени́цын верну́лся на ро́дину.
5. Придя́ домо́й, она́ тут же включи́ла компью́тер и прове́рила свои́ сообще́ния.
6. Официа́нт оступи́лся и упа́л, не донеся́ подно́с до на́шего сто́лика.
7. Услы́шав печа́льные но́вости о боле́зни де́душки, семья́ пригото́вилась к ху́дшему.

B. Replace the verbs in bold by gerunds. Rephrase the sentences if appropriate:

1. Де́ти **бе́гают** по двору́, они́ игра́ют и шумя́т.
2. Когда́ наш гость расска́зывал о своём путеше́ствии, он **шути́л** и **пока́зывал** смешны́е фотогра́фии.
3. Когда́ мы **поднима́лись** на холм, мы наслажда́лись прекра́сным ви́дом го́рода.
4. Урага́ны нано́сят большо́й уще́рб, та́к как они́ **разруша́ют** дома́, **лома́ют** дере́вья, **перевора́чивают** маши́ны и **оставля́ют** жи́телей без электри́чества.
5. «Когда́ я **верну́сь**, я пойду́ в тот еди́нственный дом ...». (Га́лич)
6. «Андре́й Андре́евич Си́доров **получи́л** в насле́дство четы́ре ты́сячи рубле́й и реши́л откры́ть на э́ти де́ньги кни́жный магази́н». (Че́хов)
7. Иностра́нные тури́сты снача́ла **запо́лнили** тамо́женные деклара́ции, пото́м **прошли́** па́спортный контро́ль и пошли́ получа́ть бага́ж.
8. Когда́ Пётр **зако́нчит** университе́т, он бу́дет иска́ть рабо́ту за грани́цей.

3. Replace the phrases in bold by suitable idioms that use a gerund.

1. Он был настоя́щим трудого́ликом и не мог **сиде́ть без де́ла**.
2. Опа́здывая на по́езд, они́ **с огро́мной ско́ростью бежа́ли по** перро́ну, раста́лкивая пассажи́ров и перепры́гивая че́рез чемода́ны.
3. В то вре́мя, когда́ студе́нт писа́л диссерта́цию, он **рабо́тал без выходны́х**.
4. Должно́ же мне хоть раз повезти́! Я **не теря́ю наде́жды** ...

Обобща́ющее упражне́ние

4. Replace the gerunds in the following sentences with verbs. Rephrase the sentences if appropriate:

Господи́н Смирно́в рабо́тает над но́вым прое́ктом

1. Господи́н Смирно́в рабо́тает не поклада́я рук, без выходны́х. 2. Занима́ясь но́вым прое́ктом, он в то же са́мое вре́мя пи́шет отчёт о свое́й рабо́те. 3. У него́ нет вре́мени сиде́ть, сложа́ ру́ки. 4. Открове́нно говоря́, у него́ сейча́с нет вре́мени да́же на его́ люби́мые кроссво́рды. 5. Наприме́р, вчера́ господи́н Смирно́в встав ра́но, приня́в

холо́дный душ, оде́вшись и вы́пив ча́шку ча́я, побежа́л к свое́й маши́не. 6. Сев в маши́ну и включи́в мото́р, он заме́тил, что в ба́ке нет бензи́на. Про́сто кошма́р! 7. Оста́вив маши́ну во дворе́, он побежа́л на стоя́нку такси́. 8. Добра́вшись, наконе́ц, до о́фиса, сев за свой стол и прове́рив все электро́нные сообще́ния (e-mails), он приня́лся за де́ло. 9. Он рабо́тал усе́рдно, сердя́сь ка́ждый раз, когда́ ему́ приходи́лось отвеча́ть на вопро́сы колле́г. 10. В два часа́, на́спех перекуси́в в кафе́ «Ёлки-па́лки», он верну́лся на рабо́ту. 11. Господи́н Смирно́в писа́л отчёт, ду́мая о прое́кте и о́чень беспоко́ясь, что не успе́ет зако́нчить рабо́ту в срок. И так ка́ждый день! Что за жизнь!

28 Prepositions

Prepositions clarify the various relationships between a noun, pronoun or a noun phrase and other words in a sentence. Prepositions are mainly used when talking about time, location, start and end points of movement, when indicating ownership, reasons and consequences of an action. Prepositions play an important role in governing nouns or pronouns (see noun declension ☞ 4, see pronoun declension (☞ 14)). Some prepositions can be used in several cases and their use depends on the context.

☉ Prepositions in Russian and English rarely match. The examples below show the use/ absence of prepositions in the two languages:

На ýжин мы купи́ли **буты́лку вина́**.	**For** dinner, we bought a bottle **of wine**.
Мы идём **на** ле́кцию.	We are going **to** the lecture.
Внук пи́шет письмо́ **ба́бушке**.	The grandchild is writing a letter **to** his **grandmother**.

Prepositions can be divided into two groups according to their origin:

- **Primary** prepositions that are not derived from other words.
- **Secondary** prepositions that are derived from adverbs, nouns, verbs or gerunds.

28.1 Primary prepositions

Primary prepositions form the largest and most frequently used group of prepositions. Most primary prepositions consist of just one letter or syllable: **к, у, на, про**. A few are formed by using two prepositions joined together with a hyphen: **из-за, из-под**. Many primary prepositions can appear with more than one case. The use and meaning of prepositions depends on the context. Summary Table 28.I gives the most common primary prepositions, along with the cases with which the preposition can be used and a translation. The chapters in this book on cases all have sections on prepositions. Numbers in brackets indicate where information can be found on using each preposition.

Summary Table 28.I: Primary prepositions

Preposition's meaning	Cases with which the preposition can be used				
	Accusative	**Genitive**	**Dative**	**Instrumental**	**Prepositional**
without		без (7.3)			
in/into/to/at/on	в (6.3)				в (10.2, 10.3)
on/on to/to/at/for/by	на (6.3)				на (10.2, 10.3, 10.3.2)
for		для (7.3)			

Preposition's meaning	Cases with which the preposition can be used				
	Accusative	Genitive	Dative	Instrumental	Prepositional
up to/to/until		до (7.3)			
for/behind/beyond/ during/in order to/at	за (6.3)			за (9.3)	
out of/from		из (7.3)			
except/besides		кро́ме (7.3)			
towards/*no translation; used in the construction 'visiting a friend'*			к (8.3)		
between				ме́жду (9.3)	
above				над (9.3)	
about/against	о (6.3)				о (10.3.2)
from/against		от (7.3)			
in front of/before				пе́ред (9.3)	
under/underneath	под (6.3)			под (9.3)	
up to/along/around/ on/by	по (6.3)		по (8.3)		
in the time of					при (10.3.1)
about	про (6.3)				
for the sake of		ра́ди (7.3)			
with/from		с (7.3)		с (9.3)	
through	сквозь (6.3)				
at/at one's place/ *no translation; used in the possessive construction*		у (7.3)			
across/over/through/ within/every other (day)/by some means	че́рез (6.3)				
from behind/beyond/ because of		из-за (7.3)			
from under/*no translation; used to indicate purpose of container*		из-под (7.3)			
against		про́тив (7.3)			

Preposition's meaning	Cases with which the preposition can be used				
	Accusative	Genitive	Dative	Instrumental	Prepositional
from ... to		с ... до (7.3)			
next to				рядом с (9.3)	

28.2 Secondary prepositions

Level 2, 3

Secondary prepositions are derived from adverbs, nouns, verbs or gerunds. The secondary preposition looks identical to the word from which the preposition is derived, but has a different function. For example:

Наш дом совсём ужé **близко** (adverb), мы почти дошли.	Our home is **very near;** we are almost there.
Наш дом нахóдится **близко от** (preposition) реки.	Our home **is near by** the river.
Дирéктор óчень сердился, **исключáя** (gerund) ученикá из школы́.	The head-teacher was furious **whilst he was excluding** the pupil from the school.
Все нáши гóсти, **исключáя** (preposition, takes the genitive case) детéй, сидéли за столóм.	All our guests, except the children, were sitting at the table.

Secondary prepositions are common in writing. Unlike primary prepositions, secondary prepositions are usually used with one particular case. Secondary prepositions may consist of only one word: **спустя** (after), **впереди** (in front of). They can also appear in a compound form accompanied by a primary preposition: **далекó от** (far away from), **несмотря на** (despite) etc. Summary Table 28.II gives an overview of the most common secondary prepositions. The table indicates the cases with which the prepositions can be used and provides a translation of the prepositions. Numbers in brackets indicate where information can be found on using each preposition. Examples of less common prepositions are given below the table.

Summary Table 28.II: Prepositions derived from adverbs, nouns and gerunds

Preposition's meaning	Case with which the preposition can be used				
	Accusative	Genitive	Dative	Instrumental	Prepositional
near/near by		близко/вблизи от (7.3.2)			
instead of		вмéсто (7.3.2)			
along		вдоль (7.3.2, 7.3.2)			
beyond/outside of		вне (7.3.2)			
inside		внутри (7.3.2, 7.3.2.1)			
close to		вóзле (7.3.2, 7.3.2.1)			

Preposition's meaning	Case with which the preposition can be used				
	Accusative	Genitive	Dative	Instrumental	Prepositional
around		вокру́г (7.3.2, 7.3.2.1)			
despite			вопреки́ (8.3)		
in front of		впереди́ (7.3.2)			
past/by		ми́мо (7.3.2)			
towards			навстре́чу (8.3)		
on the eve of		накану́не			
opposite		напро́тив (7.3.2)			
near		о́коло (7.3.2, 7.3.2.1)			
behind		позади́/сза́ди (7.3.2, 7.3.2.1)			
after		по́сле (7.3.2)			
against		про́тив (7.3.2)			
more than/ above		свы́ше / сверх			
in the middle of		посреди́/среди́ (7.3.2)			
among		среди́			
through	сквозь (6.3)				
according to			согла́сно (8.3)		
together with				вме́сте с (9.3)	
next to				ря́дом с (9.3)	
thanks to			благодаря́		
in connection with				в связи́ с	
after	спустя́ (27.3)				
in view of		ввиду́			
during		во вре́мя/в тече́ние			
alongside				наряду́ с	

Examples of some less frequently used prepositions:

Накану́не вы́боров все па́ртии должны́ прекрати́ть агита́цию.	On the eve of the elections all parties must stop campaigning.
Это **свы́ше мои́х сил**.	It is beyond my abilities.
Свы́ше ты́сячи челове́к пришло́ на ми́тинг.	More than a thousand people arrived for the meeting.
Среди́ студе́нтов на́шего университе́та мно́го иностра́нцев.	Among the students at our university there are a lot of foreigners.
Наряду́ с есте́ственными нау́ками здесь то́же преподаю́т гуманита́рные предме́ты.	Alongside the natural sciences, they also teach the humanities here.
Вам на́до обрати́ться к адвока́ту **в связи́ с э́тим де́лом**.	You need to consult a solicitor to discuss this matter.
Благодаря́ уси́лиям журнали́стов всё та́йное ста́ло я́вным.	Thanks to the journalists' efforts all the secrets became known.
Во вре́мя проведе́ния демонстра́ции движе́ние тра́нспорта бу́дет приостано́влено.	During the demonstration transport will be stopped.

Упражне́ния

Level 1, 2

1. Complete the sentences with an appropriate primary preposition:

1. Де́ти выхо́дят ... шко́лы.
2. ... Ива́на есть соба́ка.
3. Маши́на стои́т ... у́лице ... угло́м.
4. Инжене́р рабо́тает ... заво́де.
5. Ве́ра игра́ет ... те́ннис ... друзья́ми.
6. Ви́ктор е́дет ... Ита́лию.
7. Музе́й закры́т ... понеде́льник.
8. Магази́н рабо́тает ... шести́ ... десяти́.
9. ... вокза́ле есть кио́ск.
10. Ни́на лю́бит чай ... са́хара, но ... молоко́м.

Level 2, 3

2. Complete the sentences with an appropriate primary preposition:

1. ... сожале́нию, я не могу́ Вам помо́чь.
2. Сотру́дника отстрани́ли ... рабо́ты.
3. Депута́ты проголосова́ли ... приня́тие зако́на.
4. ... слеза́ми ... глаза́х ребёнок смотре́л на мать.
5. Аспира́нты выполня́ют рабо́ту ... руково́дством профе́ссора.
6. Мари́не прихо́дится подраба́тывать в кафе́ ... суббо́там.
7. Предприя́тие произво́дит това́ры ... э́кспорт.
8. Мать беспоко́илась ... здоро́вье дете́й.
9. ... заво́де ... сотру́дников мно́го специали́стов ... вы́сшем образова́нием.
10. Друзья́ встреча́ются ... клу́бе ... пя́тницам.

29 Conjunctions and particles

Conjunctions are indeclinable link words. They can link individual words within the sentence or clauses in compound and complex sentences (on types of sentence, ☞ 31.1). Conjunctions can govern neither a noun nor a pronoun nor have a role in their declension.

Conjunctions can be divided into two large groups depending on the type of the connections they support:

- Co-ordinating conjunctions (☞ 29.1).
- Subordinating conjunctions (☞ 29.2).

Some conjunctions can appear in either category depending on use.

29.1 Co-ordinating conjunctions

Co-ordinating conjunctions can connect either words that have a similar role within one sentence or independent clauses in compound sentences.

- Я люблю́ слу́шать му́зыку **и** петь пе́сни. (I like listening to music **and** singing songs.) **И** (and) connects two verbs within a sentence.
- Я живу́ в Великобрита́нии, **а** она́ в Росси́и. (I live in Great Britain **and** she lives in Russia.) **А** (and) connects two independent clauses in the compound sentence.

Different types of conjunction support different types of connection between words and clauses.

29.1.1 Conjunctions that link words or clauses that have similar meanings

These include:

и (and)   и ... и (both ... and)
a (and/but)   **как ... так и** (and)
да (also)   **ни ... ни** (neither ... nor)
та́кже/то́же (also)   да и (too, also)
не то́лько ... но и (not only ... but also)

Examples:

Ребёнок не лю́бит **ни** мя́со, **ни** ры́бу.   The child likes neither meat nor fish.
Щи **да** ка́ша – пи́ща на́ша. (Посло́вица)   Cabbage soup and porridge are our food.
                                             (Proverb)

29.1.2 Conjunctions that link words or clauses with opposite meanings

These include:

но/а/да (but)   одна́ко (however, though)
зато́ (but/on the other hand)

Examples:

Он уже неплóхо понимáет по-рýсски, **но** ещё плóхо говори́т.	He already understands Russian well, but is not able to speak.
Они́ хотéли приéхать в гóсти, **однáко** передýмали в послéдний момéнт.	They wanted to come and visit us; however, they changed their mind at the last moment.

29.1.3 Conjunctions that express the idea of choice

These include:

и́ли (or)	**и́ли ... и́ли** (either ... or)
ли́бо (or)	**ли́бо ... ли́бо** (either...or)
то ... то (translation may vary; indicates some change)	**не тó ... не тó** (neither ... nor)
тó ли ... тó ли (maybe)	

Examples:

Что бýдете пить? Винó **и́ли** вóдку?	What would you like to drink? Wine **or** vodka?
Тó тут, **то** там.	Now here, now there.

29.1.4 Explanatory conjunctions

Explanatory conjunctions explain a sentence further and include:

то есть (that means, that is), abbreviated to **т.е.** (i.e.)   **а и́менно** (namely).

Example: Учéбная прогрáмма рассчи́тана на 2 семéстра, **т.е.** на 22 учéбных недéли. (The programme consists of 2 semesters, i.e. 22 teaching weeks.)

29.2 Subordinating conjunctions

Subordinating conjunctions link the main clause of a complex sentence to a subordinate clause or clauses. The subordinate clause(s) clarifies the complete idea expressed by the main clause: Егó нет сегóдня на рабóте, **потомý что он заболéл.** (He is not at work today, because he is ill.)

29.2.1 Conjunctions that show cause and consequence

These conjunctions link to a subordinate clause explaining the reason for action in the main clause and include:

потомý что/тáк как/поскóльку (because)	**вслéдствие тогó что** (in consequence of)
в си́лу тогó что (on the strength of)	**ввидý тогó что** (in view of)

Examples:

Он записáлся на кýрсы, **потомý что** хотéл научи́ться води́ть маши́ну.	He enrolled for the course because he wanted to learn to drive.
В си́лу тогó что сократи́ли бюджéт, городскóй Совéт закры́л библиотéку.	Because of the funding cuts, the City Council closed the library.

29.2.2 Concessive conjunctions

These conjunctions link to a clause that 'concedes' the point in the main clause and puts forward a contrasting point; they include:

Хотя (although/even if)   **Несмотря на то́ что** (in spite of)

Examples:

Хотя́ врачи́ сде́лали всё возмо́жное,   Although the doctors did their best, they
больно́го не удало́сь спасти́.   could not save the patient.
Несмотря́ на все госуда́рственные   In spite of all the government subsidies,
дота́ции, заво́д обанкро́тился.   the factory closed.

29.2.3 Conjunctions showing comparison

These conjunctions link a clause that shows comparison.

как (as)   **бу́дто/как бу́дто/бу́дто бы/сло́вно** (as if)
чем (than)

Examples:

Они́ одева́ются **как близнецы́**.   They dress like twins.
Он оказа́лся намно́го умне́е,   He appeared to be cleverer than
чем все ду́мали.   everybody thought.

Чем is common in constructions with comparative adjectives and adverbs
(☞ 12.3 and 13.3.3).

29.2.4 Time conjunctions

These conjunctions link to a clause that gives an indication of time:

когда́/как (when)   **как то́лько/лишь то́лько** (as soon as)
едва́ (just)   **пока́** (while)
пока́ не (until)   **в то вре́мя как** (while)
тогда́ как (when/while)   **по́сле того́ как** (after)
пре́жде чём (before)   **перед тём как** (before)
до того́ как (before)   **с тех по́р как** (since)

Example: Пока́ ма́ма гото́вила обе́д, де́ти игра́ли в саду́. (While their mother was cooking, the children were playing in the garden.)

👁 The Russian equivalent of *before* and *after* translate in two different ways:

- The prepositions **до/пе́ред** (before), and **по́сле** (after) when a noun follows: до обе́да (before lunch), по́сле у́жина (after dinner).
- The conjunctions **до того́ как** (before), **перед тём как** (before), **пре́жде чём как** (before) and **по́сле того́ как** (after) when a verbal phrase follows: до того́ как мы пообе́дали (before we had our lunch), по́сле того́ как мы пообе́дали (after we had our lunch).

29.2.5 Conjunctions indicating purpose or result

что́бы/для того́ что́бы/зате́м   **что́бы** (not translated when
что́бы/с тём что́бы (in order to)   indicating an instruction or a wish)

Что́бы can be used in two different contexts:

- A subordinate clause introduced by **что́бы** can be used to make a request or express desire. The English equivalent of this type of construction is '*I want you to do it*': Посети́телям музе́я **сказа́ли, что́бы они́ вы́ключили** свои́ моби́льники. (The visitors in the museum *were told to* switch off their mobiles.) (On sentence structure and the use of verbal tenses, ☞ 22.4.2.)

● A subordinate clause introduced by **чтобы** can clarify the purpose or reason for the action described in the main clause. In this type of sentence, **чтобы** is followed by an infinitive. All actions described in both clauses are related to the same subject: Студенты должны много заниматься, **чтобы свободно говорить** по-русски. (Students must work hard *in order to* speak Russian well.) Я выключила мобильник, чтобы не мешать другим посетителям музея. (I switched off my mobile *in order not to* disturb the other visitors in the museum.)

29.2.6 Conjunctions of reason

These conjunctions link the clause that clarifies the reason for the action described in the main clause and include:

поэтому (therefore)   **так что** (so/so that)

Example: Я устал, поэтому не пошёл в бар. (I got tired and therefore did not go to a bar.)

29.2.7 Explanatory conjunctions

These conjunctions link a clause that clarifies the action in the main clause and include:

что (that)   **как** (not translated)

Example: Я слышу, **как** кто-то поёт. (I can hear someone singing.)

Что frequently introduces the subordinate clause clarifying the verbs **говорить, писать, думать, знать** when they appear in the main clause; for example:

Я думаю, **что** они не придут.	I think (that) they are not coming.
Говорят, **что** погода изменится к лучшему.	They say (that) the weather will change for the better.

29.2.8 Conditional conjunctions

These conjunctions link to the clause that determines conditions for an action described in the main clause. ☞ Conditional constructions are explained in section 22.3.

Level
3

29.3 Particles

Particles are indeclinable words that do not have a meaning of their own; they are common in informal speech. Their main role is to bring emotional emphasis to the word, phrase or sentence (☞ 29.3.1). Additionally, particles are used in negative constructions, conditional sentences and some verbal forms (☞ 29.3.3). Particles are derived from conjunctions, verbs or adverbs; some look identical to the words of their origin.

29.3.1 Particles that bring emotional emphasis to a word, phrase or sentence

Use of particles is determined by context and often by the speaker's intonation. Compare:

Neutral information	Message with emotional emphasis on the quality of the story
Он написал рассказ. (He wrote a story.)	**Ну уж и** рассказ он написал! (He wrote a story (of poor quality).)
Он написал рассказ. (He wrote a story.)	Он написал **такой** рассказ! (He wrote a story (of high quality).)

Particles are frequently used to:

- **Point out** someone or something: **вот/вон, а вот/а вон**:

Где туалéт? **Вот** он!	Where is the toilet? There it is!
А вон там! Смотри!	Over there! Look!

- **Intensify the original meaning** of a word, phrase or sentence: **ведь** (surely/you must know), **дáже/дáже и** (even), **прóсто** (simply), **ужé/уж** (already), **ещё** (yet), **же** (but), **всё-таки** (and yet):

«И **всё-таки** онá вéртится!» (Галилéй)	**'And yet it moves!'** (Galileo)
Тебé **ведь** сто раз говорили!	**You've** been told a hundred times!
Дáже дурáк смóжет это сдéлать!	**Even** an idiot can do it!
Ты **прóсто** прелéсть!	You are **so** charming!
Ужé стемнéло.	It is **already** dark
Ещё не стемнéло.	It is **not yet** dark
Óн **же** всё всегдá знáет!	**But** he always knows everything!

- **Emphasise the limitation** of a person's ability, quantity or time: **лишь/тóлько/лишь тóлько** (only/just), **единственно/исключительно** (only, exceptionally), **почти/чуть ли не** (almost):

Лишь тóлько подснéжник распýстится в срок ... (Матусóвский)	When one snowdrop will bloom **just** in time ...
И всё это – **исключительно** для Вас!	This is all **only** for you!
Кóшка съéла **почти** все сосиски!	The cat has eaten **almost** all the sausages!

- **Express doubts**: **авóсь/пожáлуй** (probably, perhaps), **вряд ли** (hardly, I wish), **едвá ли** (hardly). **Авóсь** is a favourite Russian word and is often used in idioms as a synonym for **удáча** (luck):

Авóсь повезёт!	**I hope** I will be lucky!
Надéяться **на авóсь**.	**To rely on luck.**
Это, **пожáлуй**, óстрая проблéма.	This is **probably** a serious problem
Поéдешь домóй? **Вряд ли.**	Are you going home? **Hardly.**

- **Defining** something: **именно** (even, namely, exactly), **тóчно** (exactly), **рóвно** (exactly), **приблизительно** (approximately), **почти** (nearly), **точь-в-тóчь** (exact in likeness). These particles are often used in time expressions:

Пóезд пришёл **тóчно** в 3 часá.	The train arrived at 3 **exactly**.
Гóсти пришли **рóвно** в вóсемь.	The guests arrived **exactly** at 8.

- **Confirm** a fact: **да/так** (yes), **тóчно/конéчно** (yes, of course/sure):

Встрéтимся пóсле рабóты? **Конéчно!**	Are we going to meet up after work? **Sure!**

- **Exclamations**: **Как/что за** (what/such), **вот это да!** (wow!). In contemporary Russian, the Anglicism **вáу!** is becoming popular in the spoken language: **Вáу!** Такóго не ждал никтó! (Wow! No one expected this!)

- **Questions**, to emphasise the information that is important for a speaker: **ли** (whether/if), **рáзве** (really), **неужéли** (really, is it possible):

Рáзве Вы не слышали?	Haven't you heard, then?
Неужéли это прáвда?	So it is really true then?

Note that **ли** always follows the word to which the question refers:

Знáете ли вы истóрию своéй страны?	Do you know the history of your country?
Ты не знáешь, **здорóва ли** онá сегóдня?	Do you know whether or not she is well today?

29.3.2 Other particles

- **Бы́ло** is used to emphasise an unsuccessful attempt to complete an action:

Он побежа́л, **бы́ло**, но споткну́лся и упа́л.	He started running, but tripped and fell down.

- **Быва́ло** is used to emphasise habitual action in the past:.

Быва́ло, Пу́шкина чита́л всю ночь до зорь ... (Высо́цкий)	I used to read Pushkin all night until daybreak ...

- **-ка**, **-то** and **-с** (old-fashioned) are added to a word, following a hyphen. They express friendly encouragement:

А **ну́-ка** пе́сню нам пропо́й, Весёлый ве́тер ... (Ле́бедев-Кума́ч)	**Come on**, cheerful wind, sing a song for us ...

29.3.3 Particles used in formation of constructions and word forms

Several particles are used in forming conditional sentences and negative verbal forms.

29.3.3.1 The following particles are used in negative constructions

- **не** (not) always precedes the word to which it is referring:

Мы ещё **не** е́ли.	We have not eaten.
Э́то **не** совсе́м то́чный отве́т.	It is not quite the correct answer.

- **ни** is used in negative constructions to reinforce negativity. Usually, **ни** precedes any word other than the verb:

На не́бе не́ было **ни** звёздочки.	There was not a single star in the sky.

- However, **ни** can replace **не** and precede the verb in complex sentences, when several verbs in each subordinate clause express similar meanings. This type of negative construction is common in writing:

Как **ни** стара́лись лю́ди ... изуро́довать ... зе́млю, как **ни** обре́зывали дере́вья и **ни** выгоня́ли всех живо́тных и птиц, – весна́ была́ весно́ю да́же и в го́роде. (Толсто́й)	However much people tried ... to disfigure ... the land ..., however much they cut down trees and carted off all the animals and birds, spring was really spring, even in the city.

29.3.3.2

The particle **бы** (cannot be translated into English) is used to form conditional constructions (☞ 22.3).

29.3.3.3

The particles **пусть/пуска́й/дава́й/да** (let) are used as alternative ways of forming the imperative (☞ 22.2.3).

Упражне́ния

Level 2, 3

1. Translate into Russian, using complex sentences with subordinate clauses:

1. The businessman has asked his secretary to cancel a meeting.
2. The housewife went to a market to get food.
3. Although the foreign students had not been in Russia long, they had already started to feel at home.
4. We did not have enough money and therefore we decided not to eat out.
5. Victor was as tired as if he had run a marathon.

6. The students were awarded first-class marks because they were working really hard.
7. Do you understand the Russian proverb: 'The further into the forest, the more woods'?
8. They wanted to go to the party, but turned down the invitation.

Обобща́ющее упражне́ние

2. Insert the appropriate conjunctions:

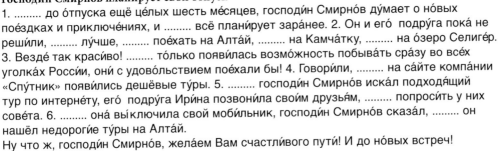

Господи́н Смирно́в плани́рует свой о́тпуск

1. .... до о́тпуска ещё це́лых шесть ме́сяцев, господи́н Смирно́в ду́мает о но́вых пое́здках и приключе́ниях, и .... всё плани́рует зара́нее. 2. Он и его́ подру́га пока́ не реши́ли, ... лу́чше, ... пое́хать на Алта́й, ... на Камча́тку, ... на о́зеро Селиге́р. 3. Везде́ так краси́во! .... то́лько появи́лась возмо́жность побыва́ть сра́зу во всех уголка́х Росси́и, они́ с удово́льствием пое́хали бы! 4. Говори́ли, ... на са́йте компа́нии «Спу́тник» появи́лись дешёвые ту́ры. 5. .... господи́н Смирно́в иска́л подходя́щий тур по интерне́ту, его́ подру́га Ири́на позвони́ла свои́м друзья́м, ... попроси́ть у них сове́та. 6. .... она́ вы́ключила свой моби́льник, господи́н Смирно́в сказа́л, ... он нашёл недороги́е ту́ры на Алта́й.

Ну что ж, господи́н Смирно́в, жела́ем Вам счастли́вого пути́! И до но́вых встреч!

30 Impersonal sentences

Level 2, 3 👁️ Unlike English, Russian sentences can have only one core element, a subject or a predicate. In Russian, a large number of sentences have neither actual subject in the nominative case nor an implied subject. Unlike in English, in Russian the formal subject 'it' is not used to replace an absent subject. Sentences without a subject are called *impersonal*. The predicate that remains the core element of an impersonal sentence clarifies a state or action that occurs as if without external forces. Impersonal sentences are used to describe natural phenomena, weather conditions, physical or emotional states, rules and customs etc. Russian impersonal sentences are short and expressive and are therefore very common in popular speech, literature and poetry.

👁️ Russian impersonal sentences do not fully correspond to English sentences that convey similar ideas. Usually, a Russian impersonal sentence describing natural phenomena or the weather is translated into English using sentences starting with the formal subject *it* and the verbs *to be* (is) or *to get* (is getting) in the present, past or future continuous tense: Темно́. (**It is** dark.) Темне́ет. (**It is getting** dark.) If a Russian impersonal sentence refers to a person, it is commonly translated into English using a personal sentence with a noun or pronoun as a subject: **Мне** нездоро́вится. (**I am** unwell.) **Больно́го** зноби́т. (**A sick person feels** shivery.) If the context of an impersonal sentences requires explaining who experiences a certain condition, this information is usually conveyed by a noun or personal pronoun in the dative case: **Студе́нту** ску́чно на ле́кции. (The **student** is bored at the lecture (literally, it is boring to a student at the lecture).)

The predicate of an impersonal sentence has no subject in the nominative case to agree with. Therefore, it is usually expressed by indeclinable words with a verbal link (☞ 30.1) or the neuter form of the verb (☞ 30.4).

30.1 Using adverbs, modal words, participles or nouns in impersonal sentences

Level 2, 3

The following indeclinable words can function as the predicate in an impersonal sentence:

- Adverbs ending in -o that describe quality, conditions or manner: хо́лодно (cold), тепло́ (warm), светло́ (light), интере́сно (interesting), ску́чно (boring), пло́хо (bad), до́рого (expensive), дёшево (cheap).
- The modal words на́до (need), ну́жно (need), необходи́мо (necessary), мо́жно (may/permitted), нельзя́ (forbidden), возмо́жно (possible), невозмо́жно (impossible).
- Comparative adjectives or adverbs that describe quality, conditions or manner: ху́же (worse), лу́чше (better) etc.

The following words can function as the predicate in an impersonal sentence, if they describe quality, conditions or manner:

- Short form of participle in neuter singular form: наку́рено (smoky), при́нято (customary), решено́ (decided) etc.
- Nouns: жаль (pity), лень (laziness), охо́та (desire), неохо́та (no desire), пора́ (it is time), грех (sin) etc.

The link-verbs **быть** (to be) or **станови́ться/стать** (to become) are used in this type of sentence to indicate the timing of an event: present, past or future. The verb **быть** (to be) is omitted in the present tense. The imperfective verb **станови́ться** (to become) is often used in the present or past tenses to emphasise a process. All link-verbs can be used in the neuter singular form in the present and past tenses, if applicable, and in the 3rd person singular in the future tense. **Быть** can precede or follow a predicate. **Станови́ться/стать** precede the predicate. For example:

Хо́лодно.	**It is** cold.
Бы́ло хо́лодно.	**It was** cold.
Бу́дет хо́лодно.	**It will be** cold.
Ста́ло ти́хо.	**It became** quiet.
Стано́вится ти́хо.	**It is getting** quiet.
Станови́лось ти́хо.	**It was getting** quiet.
Бы́ло на́до написа́ть or **На́до бы́ло** написа́ть.	**It was necessary** to write down.

If the context of an impersonal sentence requires explaining who experiences a certain condition, this information is usually conveyed by a noun or personal pronoun in the dative case. The predicate of the sentence is often followed by an infinitive:

Та́не (кому́? dative case) хо́лодно (adverb)   It is too cold for Tanya to walk.
гуля́ть (что де́лать? infinitive).

Им (кому́? dative case) на́до (modal word)   They need to speak Russian.
говори́ть по-ру́сски (что де́лать? infinitive).

30.1.1 Expressing necessity and obligation

Impersonal sentences are often used to convey necessity and obligation. The following indeclinable modal words (☞ 30.1) and impersonal verbs (☞ 30.4) commonly appear in this context (☞ 20.6 on the use of the verbal aspect with an infinitive):

Russian modal words/short-form adjectives/impersonal verbs	Examples
на́до/ну́жно (не на́до/не ну́жно) - need (no need) - indeclinable modal words followed by an infinitive *also see comments below*	Мне на́до/ну́жно позвони́ть. I need to make a call. Мне не на́до/не ну́жно звони́ть. I do no need to make a call.
необходи́мо - necessary/need - indeclinable modal words followed by an infinitive	Вам необходи́мо обрати́ться к врачу́. You need to see a doctor.
(не) приходи́ться/прийти́сь – to have to, impersonal verb followed by an infinitive; note that in different contexts the verb can have the meanings **to be/to happen**	Нам пришло́сь уе́хать. We had to leave. Other meanings: Мне приходи́лось быва́ть за грани́цей. I have been abroad (Literally: I happened to be abroad).
(не) сле́довать – ought to/should - impersonal verb followed by an infinitive	Студе́нту сле́дует посове́товаться с профе́ссором. A student ought to seek a professor's advice.

The predicative short-form adjectives до́лжен, -а, -о, -ы (must); обя́зан, -а, -о, -ы (obliged) and ну́жен, -а, -о, -ы (need) are also used to convey necessity and obligation. They can appear only in a sentence that has a subject in the nominative case and must agree with the subject in gender and number (☞ 12.5-6).

👂 Russian impersonal sentences with the adverbs **на́до, ну́жно, необходи́мо** (need, necessary) are often replaced by using a sentence with the subject in the nominative case and a short-form adjective **до́лжен** (must) as the predicate:

Ему́ (dative) **на́до** (adverb) позвони́ть.	He **needs to/must** call.
Он (nominative) **до́лжен** (short-form adjective) позвони́ть.	

👂 The English verb *to need* is translated into Russian by two different types of sentence depending on what a speaker needs:

- If a speaker needs 'a material or abstract object' that is expressed by a noun, the word *need* is translated by using the short-form adjective **ну́жен** (-**a**, -**o**, -**ы**) followed by a noun or pronoun in the nominative case. An adjective must agree with a noun or pronoun in gender and number. The person who is 'in need' is in the dative case.

Ви́ктору (dative) **нужна́ кни́га** (both words nominative, feminine, singular).	Victor **needs a book.**
Ви́ктору (dative) **ну́жен** Ваш **сове́т** (both words nominative, masculine, singular).	Victor **needs** your **advice.**

- When describing the *need* to 'do something', the word *need* is translated by an adverb (**на́до, ну́жно, необходи́мо**) followed by an infinitive. The person who is in need is an indirect object in the dative case:

Ви́ктору **на́до купи́ть** кни́гу.	Victor **needs to buy** a book.

Level 3

30.2 Using an infinitive in impersonal sentences

For more information on the infinitive, ☞ 16.1–16.1.2, 20.6–20.6.1.3.

Impersonal sentences can have an infinitive as their core element. Adverbs, modal words, participles and other verbs that are usually used with the infinitive need not be in the sentence, but can be implied. The infinitive can be used in perfective and imperfective aspects and in negative or affirmative forms. If the context requires explaining who experiences a certain condition, this information is usually conveyed by a noun or personal pronoun in the dative case. For example:

Мо́жет быть, (на́до/сле́дует/сто́ит) **позвони́ть** ему́?	Maybe we should give him a ring?
Мне **не реши́ть** э́той зада́чи (Мне невозмо́жно реши́ть э́ту зада́чу).	I cannot solve this problem.

30.2.1 Using an infinitive with the particle ли

In a question, the infinitive is often followed by the particle **ли** (if/whether) to emphasise the meaning of the question:

Не заня́ться ли нам ремо́нтом кварти́ры?	**Shall we do** some renovation work in the flat?

If **ли** follows the noun or personal pronoun in the dative case and is placed before the negative infinitive, the sentences emphasises a speaker's certainty about the described action:

Им **ли не вы́играть** э́тот матч?	**Sure, they will win** the match.
Вам **ли не знать** отве́та на э́тот вопро́с?	**Sure, you know** the answer to this question.

30.2.2 Using an infinitive in the subjunctive mood

Impersonal infinitive sentences are common in the subjunctive mood. They can express a speaker's wishful thought:

Покататься бы на слоне!	**I wish I could ride** an elephant!
Слетать бы на Луну!	I wish I could fly to the Moon.

Level 3

30.3 Using negative pronouns and adverbs in an impersonal sentence

Negative pronouns and adverbs with the particle **не**- attached to them can be used as an essential part of the predicate along with an infinitive in a Russian impersonal sentence. Negative pronouns and adverbs convey an idea of absence of someone or something. They can indicate lack of time, of reason or of course of action, absence of place where one can go, absence of an object, a person etc.; for example:

Мне **некуда** пойти.	There is **nowhere** for me **to go.**
Ему **нечего** делать.	He has **nothing to do.**
Извини, мне **некогда**.	I am sorry, I **have no time.**

This type of sentence is very common in popular speech as it can convey the idea of an absence of someone or something by using a limited number of words and a simple and clear sentence structure. A complex sentence with the relative pronoun **который** (who, whose, that, which) can convey the same idea as the impersonal sentence and can, therefore, replace it in writing;

for example:

Complex sentence with **который**	В фирме **нет сотрудников**, **которые могут работать** с новой компьютерной программой.	**Нет человека, с которым** Виктор **может общаться.**
Impersonal sentence with negative pronoun or adverb	В фирме **некому работать** с новыми программами.	Виктору **не с кем общаться.**
Translation	In the company, there are **no staff who can work with** the new computer program.	There is **no person with whom** Victor **can communicate.**

30.3.1 Characteristics of impersonal sentences with negative pronouns or adverbs

There are some important characteristics of impersonal sentences with negative pronouns or adverbs:

- There is no subject in an impersonal sentence with a negative pronoun or adverb. However, if the context requires explaining who experiences a certain condition, this information is expressed by using a noun or personal pronoun in the dative case:

Ему (dative) некогда.	He does not have any time.
Марии (dative) некуда пойти.	Maria has no place to go.

- If the context requires describing an action, this is done by using an infinitive in the affirmative form. Both perfective and imperfective infinitives can be used, depending on the meaning of the sentence (for the infinitive, ☞ 16.1 and 20.6). An infinitive usually follows the negative pronoun or adverb:

Ей **не с кем поделиться.**	She has no one to share with.
Им **нечего** делать.	They have nothing to do.

- Both negative pronoun and adverb retain their grammatical characteristics; for example, all negative pronouns decline and adverbs are indeclinable. For personal pronouns, ☞ 14; for adverbs and negative adverbs, ☞ 13; for declension of negative pronouns, ☞ 30.3.2.
- The particle **не-** always takes the stress.

30.3.2 Negative adverbs and pronouns with particle Не-

The negative adverbs that use the particle **не-** are **не́куда** (nowhere), **не́где** (nowhere), **не́откуда** (from nowhere), **не́когда** (no time) and **не́зачем** (no reason). The negative pronouns that use the particle **не-** are **не́кого** (no one) and **не́чего** (nothing).

Не́кого and **не́чего** do not have a nominative case form. The indefinite pronouns **не́кто** (someone) and **не́что** (something) may look like negative pronouns, but they have different meanings and use. Negative pronouns decline in the same way as **кто?** and **что?** If a preposition is used with any case, it is inserted between the particle **не-** and the pronoun (see Table 30.I). Most of the prepositions that can be used with a case can appear with a negative pronoun.

Table 30.I: Declension of negative pronouns with the particle *не-*

Nominative	–	–
Accusative	не́кого/не́ (за) кого	не́чего/не́ (на) что
Genitive	не́кого/не́ (у) кого	не́чего/не́ (у) чего
Dative	не́кому/не́ (к) кому	не́чему/не́ (к) чему
Instrumental	не́кем/не́ (с) кем	не́чем/не́ (с) чем
Prepositional	не́ (о) ком	не́ (о) чем

30.3.3 Personal and impersonal sentences with negative pronouns and adverbs

👁 Negative pronouns and adverbs using the particle **не-** must not be confused with negative pronouns and adverbs using the particle **ни-**. They are translated in the same way into English, but they have different function, use and meaning in Russian (for the pronouns, ☞ 14).

Comparison of negative pronouns and adverbs using the particles *ни-* and *не-*	
ни-	*не-*
Used in personal sentences with the negative verb in personal form (preceded by the particle **не**) that agrees with the subject of the sentence (noun or pronoun in the nominative case).	**Used in impersonal sentences** with no subject. The action is described by an infinitive.
Function: non-core element of a sentence, can describe an object, place, time etc.	**Function: core element** of a sentence, an essential part of the predicate; along with an infinitive forms a compound predicate.
Meaning: indication of absence of an action	**Meaning: indication of absence of something or someone.** The action is described by an infinitive.
Я **ничего́** не вы́учил. (I learned nothing.)	Мне **не́чего** учи́ть. (I have nothing to learn.)

Comparison of negative pronouns and adverbs using the particles *ни-* and *не-*	
ни-	**не-**
Я **ни о ко́м** не хочу́ говори́ть. (I don't want to talk about anyone.)	Мне **не́ о ком** говори́ть. (There is no one to talk about.)
Я **никого́** не люблю́. (I love nobody.)	Мне **не́кого** люби́ть. (I have no one to love.)
Я **никуда́** не пойду́ сего́дня ве́чером. (I will not go out anywhere tonight.)	Мне **не́куда** пойти́ сего́дня ве́чером. (I have nowhere to go tonight.)

The negative adverbs are indeclinable. As with negative pronouns with **не-**, negative pronouns with **ни-** decline in the same way as **кто? что? како́й?** and **чей?**

For negative pronouns with the particle **ни-**, ☞ 14.10.1; for negative adverbs with the particle **ни-**, ☞ 13.2.8.

30.4 Using impersonal verbs in impersonal sentences

Level 3 So-called *impersonal* verbs can be used only in impersonal sentences. Impersonal verbs have a limited number of verbal forms: the 3rd person singular in the present and future tenses and neuter singular form in the past tense. Many impersonal verbs have imperfective and perfective aspects; some have only imperfective. Impersonal verbs are most frequently used to describe natural phenomena and physical/emotional conditions.

Natural phenomena with no reference to a person: вечере́ть (impf, to grow dark), света́ть (impf, to get light), смерка́ться (to get dark), холода́ть (impf, to turn cold)/похолода́ть (pf), моро́зить (impf, to freeze)/подморо́зить (pf), тепле́ть (impf, to get warm)/потепле́ть (pf), тяну́ть (impf, to blow (of wind))/потяну́ть (pf), ве́ять (impf, to blow (of wind))/пове́ять (pf) etc. Ско́ро ли **рассветёт**? (**Will it get light** soon?)

Physical and emotional conditions: in this context impersonal verbs usually refer to the animate object that experiences these conditions. The object can be used in the dative or genitive case.

- The following verbs take an animate object in the genitive case:

  тошни́ть (impf)/затошни́ть (pf) – to feel sick
  мути́ть (impf)/замути́ть (pf) – to feel sick
  зноби́ть (impf)/зазноби́ть (pf) – to feel shivery
  лихора́дить (impf)/залихора́дить (pf) – to feel feverish

- The following verbs take an animate object in the dative case:

  сто́ить (impf) – to be worth
  хвата́ть (impf)/хвати́ть (pf) – to have enough
  недостава́ть (impf) – to be short of
  надоеда́ть (impf)/надое́сть (pf) – to be fed up
  везти́ (impf)/повезти́ (pf) – to be lucky
  удава́ться (impf)/уда́ться (pf) – to manage
  сле́довать (impf) – ought to/should
  приходи́ться (impf)/прийти́сь (pf) – to be obliged to, to have to
  остава́ться (impf)/оста́ться (pf) – to be left with
  хоте́ться (impf)/захоте́ться (pf) – to feel like
  каза́ться (impf)/показа́ться (pf) – to seem
  нездоро́виться (impf) – to feel unwell

For example:

Пацие́нта (genitive) знобит.   The patient feels shivery.

Нам (dative) пришло́сь поменя́ть биле́т.   We had to change our ticket.

30.4.1 Using verbs that can that can appear in either impersonal or personal sentences

Some verbs can can appear in either impersonal or personal sentences, depending on the context. Compare:

Impersonal	Personal
В до́ме вку́сно **па́хнет** пиро́гами. (**It smells** (nicely) of pies in the house.)	Пироги́ **па́хнут** вку́сно. (**The pies smell** good.)
Водо́й **зали́ло** окре́стные луга́. (**It flooded** (with water) over the neighbouring meadows.)	Вода́ **зали́ла** окре́стные луга́. (**The water flooded** over the neighbouring meadows.)
👁 (see comments below) Бизнесме́нам **понра́вилось у́жинать** в ру́сском рестора́не. (The businessmen **liked dining** in the Russian restaurant.)	Бизнесме́нам **понра́вился у́жин** в ру́сском рестора́не. (The businessmen **liked the dinner** in the Russian restaurant (literally: **The dinner pleased** ...).)

👁 Note the use of the verb **нра́виться** (impf)/**понра́виться** (pf) (to like) in the last example. In a Russian sentence, the person who 'likes' or 'dislikes' always appears in the dative case (☞ 8.2.3). Then, if **нра́виться/понра́виться** is followed by an infinitive, it functions as an impersonal verb with a limited number of forms. However, **нра́виться/понра́виться** can appear in a personal sentence that has a noun or pronoun in the nominative case (☞ 5.1.2). In a personal sentence **нра́виться/понра́виться** must agree with the subject in person and number in the present and future tenses and in gender and number in the past tense.

Level
2

30.5 Impersonal negative genitive sentences

For the use of the genitive case, ☞ 7.

Russian negative sentences that convey the idea of absence of an object or a person from a place, or absence of a possession, are impersonal. These Russian sentences are equivalent to the English constructions '*there are no/there is no someone/something somewhere*'.

In Russian negative constructions, the noun that indicates the absent object is in the genitive case. It can be used with both singular and plural numbers.

As negative genitive constructions have no subject, the predicate of the sentence (the verb) does not have a subject with which to agree. Therefore, unchangeable verbal forms express the predicate of the sentence. They are the negative word **нет** (there is no/there are no) in the present tense and the negative forms **быть** (to be) in the past and the future tenses. In the past tense, the singular neuter form **не́ было** (there was no/there were no) is used. In the future tense the 3rd person singular form **не бу́дет** (there will be no) is used. Note that **нет**, **не́ было** and **не бу́дет** are the Russian equivalents of the English expressions *there is no/there are no* in the present, past and future tenses respectively; for example:

На све́те **сча́стья** (genitive) **нет**, но есть   There **is no happiness** in this world,
поко́й и во́ля. (Пу́шкин)   but there is peace and freedom.

У него́ (genitive) **не́ было де́нег** (genitive).   He **did not have** any money.

| Level 3 |

Additional comments:

- The negative particles **ни** (none) or **ни... ни** (neither) intensify the negativity. In the present tense, **нет, не́ было, не бу́дет** are often omitted; for example:

И **ни** души́ в степи́, **ни** ку́стика, **ни** деревца́. (Бу́нин)	There is **not** a soul in the steppe, **nor** a bush, **nor** a tree.
В за́ле садя́тся за́втракать, а в гости́ной **ни** души́. (Че́хов)	They are about to start their breakfast in the hall; and **there is no one** in the sitting room.

- The idea of a person being absent can be conveyed by a personal or an impersonal sentence with a slightly different implication. Compare:

Студе́нты не́ были на ле́кции.	Студе́нтов не́ было на ле́кции.
Students were not at the lecture.	Students were absent from the lecture.

- Russian negative sentences have as many negative terms as are necessary to the logic of the sentence:

Мы никогда́ никого́ ни о чём не проси́ли.	We never asked anyone for anything.
Нам никогда́ никого́ ни о чём не приходи́лось проси́ть.	We did not have to ask anyone for anything.

| Level 2, 3 |

Упражне́ния

1. Translate into Russian using impersonal sentences:

1. It is getting stuffy.
2. They did not feel like working.
3. We have to hurry.
4. It is forbidden to smoke here.
5. I'd love to fly to the Moon.
6. There was no one with me in the woods. I got scared.
7. I don't have time.
8. I need your advice.
9. I like your hair-do!
10. Sorry, I need to go.
11. Most of all I like walking in the woods at dawn.

| Level 2, 3 |

2. Replace the negative pronouns or adverbs using the particle **ни-** with negative pronouns or adverbs using the particle **не-**. Rephrase the sentences as appropriate:

1. Ни́на никуда́ не е́здила э́тим ле́том.
2. Они́ ничему́ не удивля́ются.
3. Ма́льчик ни с ке́м не игра́ет сего́дня.
4. Коме́дия была́ глу́пой. Мы ни над че́м не смея́лись.
5. Ви́ктор никуда́ не спеши́т.

31 Essentials of syntax

Level 3
This section covers basic information on Russian sentence structure, types of sentence, word order and punctuation.

31.1 Types of Russian sentence

Russian and English sentence structures have much in common. Russian sentences fall into several categories depending on the number of clauses and the relationship between them. All Russian sentences fall into one of the following categories:

- **Simple sentences** that contain just one independent clause and one complete idea: У меня есть друг. (I have a friend.)
- **Compound sentences** that can have two or more simple sentences joined together by co-ordinating conjunctions: all parts of a compound sentence are equal and can exist independently. Compound sentences may contain several complete ideas:

В комнатах было душно, **а** (co-ordinating conjunction) на улицах вихрем носилась пыль ... (Чехов)	The rooms were stuffy, and the streets swirled with dust.

- **Complex sentences** that usually have one main clause and one or more subordinate clauses connected by subordinate conjunctions or conjunction words. The main clause contains the complete idea. Subordinate clauses clarify or expand on information provided in the main clause and cannot exist independently:

Чтобы сделать что-нибудь великое (subordinate clause), нужно все силы души устремлять в одну точку. (Толстой)	**To do something great**, you need all the power of the soul to strive to one point.

- **Compound-complex sentences** that contain independent and subordinate clauses:

Каждый должен был рассказывать что-нибудь фантастическое из своей жизни (independent clause), а так как умение рассказывать даётся не всякому (independent clause), то к рассказам с художественной стороны не придирались (subordinate clause).	Everybody has to tell some fantastical story from their life, and because not everyone can have a storyteller's ability, the literary worth of the stories was not judged harshly.

For conjunctions, ☞ 29.

However, there are some **important differences** between English and Russian sentences:

- Unlike English, Russian sentences **can only have one core element**, either a subject or a predicate. **Дом** (subject). (It is a **house** (☞ 5.1.3).) **Стало холодно** (predicate). (It **(has) got cold** (☞ 30.1).)
- Unlike in English, in Russian the absent subject is not replaced by the '*formal*' subject '*it*':

Трудно изучать русский язык.	**It** is difficult to study Russian.
На солнце стало слишком жарко.	**It** got too hot under the sun (☞ 30–30.1).

- The Russian equivalent of English indefinite-personal sentences (such as 'They say ...', 'They reported ...') does not have a subject. The pronoun 'they' is always omitted from Russian indefinite-personal sentences:

  Говоря́т, сего́дня бу́дет жа́рко.   **They** say it is going to be hot today.

  Что сего́дня **обсужда́ли** на собра́нии?   What did **they** discuss at the meeting today? (☞ 21.5).

- Russian does not have an equivalent of the English pronoun '*one*'. The pronoun 'one' translates into Russian in many different ways depending on the context. If 'one' is the subject of the English sentence, it is often translated into Russian by using an impersonal sentence with an adverb (☞ 30–30.1):

  One must not drink and drive a car.   **Нельзя́ пить** за рулём/когда́ ведёте

  One can never tell.   маши́ну. **Тру́дно** сказа́ть.

  If 'one' is the object of the English sentence, it is often omitted when translating into Russian:

  There are ten different sorts of cake on   Сего́дня в прода́же де́сять сорто́в

  sale today. **Which one** do you want?   пиро́жных. **Како́й** Вы хоти́те?

- Unlike in English, in Russian the verb **быть** (to be) (☞ 16.2) is not used in the present tense: Окно́ закры́то. (The window **is** closed.)

31.2 Word order

In Russian sentences, word order is **flexible** owing to the concepts of declension (☞ 4) and agreement between different elements of a sentence (☞ 11, 14.4–14.6, 15.2). However, word order plays an important role in determining the style of spoken or written speech, such as formal style, informal style or slang. The basic principles of word order can be summarised as follows:

- If a simple neutral message contains a subject, verb and object, it follows the order '*Subject – Verb – Object*':

  Весёлая стару́ха (subject) пойма́ла (verb)   The merry old woman caught a goldfish.
  золоту́ю ры́бку (object).

- Often a simple message is limited to just the subject and verb.

- Any changes to word order are made for a reason. The word that contains the most important or unknown information usually occupies the last position in the sentence. If the above example is rephrased, it can convey modified meanings. Note that words that qualify a noun or verb are not usually separated from them:

  Пойма́ла (verb) весёлая стару́ха (subject)   The sentence emphasises **what** the old
  золоту́ю ры́бку (object).   woman caught.

  Золоту́ю ры́бку (object) пойма́ла (verb)   The sentence emphasises **who** caught the
  весёлая стару́ха (subject).   goldfish.

  Золоту́ю ры́бку (object) весёлая стару́ха   The sentence emphasises **how** the old
  (subject) **пойма́ла** (verb).   woman got the goldfish.

In impersonal sentences (☞ 30), the person who experiences a certain condition is in the dative or genitive case and usually starts the sentence:

Ма́льчика зноби́ло.   **The boy** had fever.

Де́тям ве́село.   **The children** are joyful.

Informal speech, poetry, folklore and idioms are more expressive and have more flexibility in their word order. For example, one of the distinctive features of informal style is when the verb precedes the subject:

| Жи́ли-бы́ли дед да ба́ба. (Ска́зочный зачи́н) | Once upon a time there lived an old man and an old woman. (Traditional fairy-tale opening) |
| Над мра́чной Эльбо́ю **носи́лась** тишина́. (Пу́шкин) | Over the dark Elbe the silence **spread**. |

31.3 Punctuation

Russian and English punctuation have much in common. In Russian, the use of full stop, question and exclamation marks corresponds to their use in English. However, the use of the comma in Russian is highly formalised.

In a simple sentence or clause, the comma is used:

- In lists of words with a similar function in a sentence. For example:

Да́ма сдава́ла в бага́ж:	A lady was handing over her luggage:
Дива́н, чемода́н, саквоя́ж,	**A sofa, a suitcase, a bag,**
Карти́ну, корзи́ну, карто́нку	**A picture, a basket, a hat-box**
И ма́ленькую собачо́нку. (Марша́к)	**And a little dog.**

- To separate words with a similar function that are linked by conjunctions such as *и́ли ... и́ли* (either), *но* (but), *а* (but), *ни ... ни* (neither ... nor):

| **Ни** ры́ба, **ни** мя́со. (Посло́вица) | Neither fish, nor meat. (Proverb; meaning someone who lacks personality) |

- To separate parenthetical words and expressions from other words in a sentence, such as: ка́жется (it seems) , наприме́р (for example), пожа́луйста (please), коне́чно (of course), к сожале́нию (unfortunately), мо́жет быть (perhaps), по-мо́ему (in my opinion), наве́рное (probably), с одно́й/с друго́й стороны́ (on the one/on the other hand), допу́стим (let's assume) Переда́йте, **пожа́луйста**, соль.

- To separate the main and any type of subordinate clauses in a complex sentence:

| Мы не зна́ли (main clause), что тако́е квас (subordinate clause). | We did not know what 'kvas' was. |

- To separate independent clauses in compound sentences linked by conjunctions:

| Соба́ки ла́ют, а карава́н идёт. (Ру́сский вариа́нт ара́бской посло́вицы) | Though the dog may bark, the caravan moves on. (Russian variant of Arabic proverb) |

The colon is used in a similar way as in English, including introduction of direct speech or a quotation.

The dash is used:

- To indicate the omitted predicate: Сего́дня тури́сты ката́ются на лы́жах, за́втра – на конька́х. (Today the tourists are skiing, tomorrow they are skating.)
- To replace the omitted present tense verbal link **быть** (to be) between two nouns in the nominative case:

| **Но́вгород** – дре́вний **го́род**. | Novgorod **is** an old city. |

- To replace the omitted present-tense verbal link **быть** (to be) before the words э́то (this), зна́чит (means), вот (here), if it is part of the explanatory comment:

| Прича́стие – **э́то одна́ из глаго́льных форм.** | The participle is one of the verbal forms. |

- To indicate direct speech, if it is presented in the form of the dialogue:

| – Когда́ ты прие́дешь? | When are you coming? |
| – За́втра. | Tomorrow. |

The guillemets « » are used:

- As quotation marks:

  «Тяжело́ в уче́нии, легко́ в бою́.» (Суво́ров)   'It's hard to learn, easy in battle.'
- To indicate direct speech, if it is part of continuous text. Note that the colon precedes the guillemets; for example,

  Сестра́ спроси́ла: «Когда ты прие́дешь?»   My sister asked, 'When are you coming?'
- When naming literary works, newspapers, magazines, organisations: рома́н «Лоли́та» (the novel 'Lolita'), па́ртия «Зелёных» (Green party).

Bibliography

Dictionaries and reference books

Даль, В. И. 1996. *Пословицы русского народа.* Санкт-Петербург: Диамант.

Ожегов, С. И. 1989. *Словарь русского языка,* 20-ое изд. Москва: Русский язык.

Wheeler, M. 2000. *The Oxford Russian Dictionary,* 3rd edn. Oxford: Oxford University Press.

Grammars

Dunn, J., Khairov, Sh. 2009. *Modern Russian Grammar.* Oxford: Routledge.

Levine, J. 2009. *Schaum's Outline of Russian Grammar,* 2nd edn. New York: The McGraw-Hill Companies.

Offord, D., Gogolitsyna, N. 2005. *Using Russian: A Guide to Contemporary Usage,* 2nd ed. Cambridge: Cambridge University Press.

Pekhlivanova K. L., Lebedeva, M. N. 1994. *Russian Grammar in Illustrations.* Москва: Русский язык.

Пулькина, И. М., Захава-Некрасова, Е. В. 1994. *Русский язык: Практическая грамматика с упражнениями.* Москва: Русский язык.

Wade, T. 1998. *A Comprehensive Russian Grammar.* Oxford: Blackwell.

Валгина, Н. С., Розенталь, Д. Е. 2002. *Современный русский язык.* Москва: Логос.

Other books on the Russian language

Murav'eva, L. S. 1986. *Verbs of Motion in Russian.* Москва: Русский язык.

Одинцова, И. В., Малашенко, Н. М., Бахкударова Е. Л. 2008. *Русская грамматика в упражнениях,* Москва: Русский язык.

Розенталь, Д. Е. 2004. *Пособие по русскому языку.* Москва: Оникс.

Хавронина, С. А., Широченская, А. И. 1993. *Русский язык в упражнениях.* Москва: Русский язык.

Literary sources

Бунин, И. А. 1983. *Рассказы.* Москва: Правда.

Высоцкий, В., Галич, А., Окуджава, Б. 1990. *Я выбираю свободу: стихи, песни.* Кемерово: Книжное издательство.

Гоголь, Н. В. 1985. *Избранные произведения.* Кишинёв: Лит-артистикэ.

Горький, М. 1982. *Избранное.* Москва: Детская литература.

Довлатов, С. Д. 1995. *Собрание прозы.* Санкт-Петербург: Лимбус-пресс.

Драгунский В. Ю. 1998. *Избранное.* Москва: Детская литература

Лермонтов, М. Ю. 1998. *Сочинения в 2-х т.* Москва: Правда.

Лесков, Н. С. 1997. *Повести и рассказы.* Москва: Олимп.

Маршак, С. Я. 1999. *Стихи.* Москва: Малыш.

Народные песни. 1999. Москва: Олма-Пресс.

Пушкин, А. С. 1986. *Сочинения в 3-х томах.* Москва: Художественная литература.

Русские советские песни. 1977. Москва: Художественная литература.

Толстой, Л. Н. 1997. *Собрание сочинений в 20-ти томах,* Т. 4–5. Москва: Терра.

Тургенев, И. С. 1998. *Избранное*. Магнитогорск: ПМП.

Чехов, А. П. 2000. *Избранное*. Москва: ЭКСМО-Пресс.

Internet sources

www.newsru.com

Links to news on current affairs, sport, photos and celebrities from across Russia and the world.

www.sovsport.ru

Links to sports newspaper *Sovetsky Sport*, which publishes news on football, tennis, ice hockey, athletics, volleyball, formula 1, swimming, skiing and other sports tournaments.

The internet is a great resource for learners of Russian. Simply search for keywords in your area of interest, in either English or Russian. Be aware that websites are ephemeral and sometimes contain inappropriate or offensive material.

Key to exercises

Chapter 1

1.1. кни́ги 2. сле́дующем 3. лежа́т игру́шки 4. испа́нцы 5. Большо́м
2.

I	II
стул	слова́рь
окно́	Австра́лия
пого́да	собра́ние
	чай
	врач
	психоло́гия
	пло́щадь

Chapter 2

1. A, I, A, I, A, I, I, A, A, I, A, A
2.

Masculine	Feminine	Neuter
Ура́л	Москва́	окно́
чай	ко́мната	упражне́ние
челове́к	я́рмарка	вре́мя
план	пло́щадь	де́ло
янва́рь		живо́тное

3. **A**. молодо́й ю́ноша (m), молода́я де́вушка (f), молодо́й маэ́стро (m), молодо́е млекопита́ющее (n), молодо́й водопрово́дчик (m) **B**. большо́е Онта́рио (n), большо́е такси́ (n), больша́я ООН (f) **C**. интере́сное хо́бби (n), интере́сный конце́рт (m), интере́сное заявле́ние (n)

Chapter 3

1. ло́шади, сады́, кни́ги, сёстры, бра́тья, маши́ны, соба́ки, преподава́тели, моря́, о́кна, карандаши́, англича́не, города́, упражне́ния, края́.
2. **A**. дома́, глаза́, у́ши, я́блоки, де́ти, гра́ждане, щеня́та/щенки́, ма́тери, времена́.
B. друг, су́дно, анлича́нин, поросёнок, па́спорт, дочь, плечо́, учи́тель, де́рево, и́мя.
3. 1. роди́тели, дя́ди, тёти, близнецы́-племя́нники 2. котя́та 3. племя́нницы 4. двою́родные сёстры 5. мужья́ 6. англича́не, имена́ 7. бра́тья, жёны 8. колле́ги, друзья́.

Chapter 4

1. S N, S P; 2. S N, S P; 3. S I, Pl D, S A; 4. S **A**, S I, S G; 5. S N, Pl D, S A, S G; 6. S N, S I, Pl P, S G, Pl G; 7. S D, S N, S I, S G; 8. S G, S P, Pl G; 9. S D, Pl G; 10. Pl N, S G, S I, S I, Pl A, S G; 11. S D; 12. S I, S G, S P, S N, S I, S I, S G, Pl A, S A.

Chapter 5

1. 1. Ве́ра – учи́тельница. 2. «Га́рри По́ттер» – кни́га. 3. Газе́та на столе́. 4. Отца́ зову́т Са́ша. 5. Аэропо́рт называ́ется Пу́лково.

2. 1. Два́дцать одно́ окно́, сто одна́ кварти́ра. 2. Компью́теры доро́же книг/чем кни́ги. 3. Таки́е живо́тные, как ти́гры и леопа́рды, нахо́дятся под угро́зой вымира́ния. 4. Мы смотре́ли о́перу «То́ска».

3. 1–3, 2–5, 3–8, 4–6, 5–9, 6–4, 7–1, 8–7, 9–2.

Chapter 6

Sections 6.1–6.2

1. 1. о́перу 2. ры́бу, хлеб, фру́кты 3. дру́га 4. тури́стов 5. соба́ку

2. 1. ка́ждый день 2. неде́лю наза́д 3. весь ме́сяц 4. це́лое у́тро

Sections 6.3–6.5

1. 1. на, на 2. в 3. на 4. в 5. в

2. 1. за́ 2. за 3. на 4. за 5. сквозь 6. че́рез 7. на 8. в 9. в 10. в

3. 1. обе́д, приготовле́ние 2. реце́пты 3. говя́дину, свини́ну, карто́шку 4. свёклу, морко́вь, капу́сту, лук 5. па́сту, соль, пе́рец 6. карто́фель, морко́вь, я́йца 7. огурцы́, лук 8. горо́шек 9. ингредие́нты, майоне́з, соль

Chapter 7

Sections 7.1–7.2

1. 1. Ната́ши 2. бра́та 3. попуга́я 4. подру́ги 5. мо́ря

2. 1. нет ли́фта 2. нет апте́ки 3. нет компью́тера 4. нет подру́ги 5. нет телеви́зора

3. 1. челове́к 2. га́за, не́фти, угля́ 3. па́рка, музе́я, гости́ницы. 4. рубле́й, копе́ек 5. сигаре́т, конфе́т, мёду/мёда 6. ча́ю/ча́я 7. са́хара, молока́, хле́ба.

4. A. a. тре́тье октября́ две ты́сячи оди́ннадцатого го́да **b.** пе́рвое декабря́ ты́сяча девятьсо́т во́семьдесят четвёртого го́да **B. a.** три́дцать пе́рвого февраля́ ты́сяча девятьсо́т се́мьдесят восьмо́го го́да **b.** трина́дцатого ию́ня двухты́сячного го́да C. **a.** че́тверть оди́ннадцатого. **b.** пять мину́т деся́того **c.** полови́на седьмо́го. **d.** два́дцать пять мину́т пя́того.

5. Счастли́вого пути́! Споко́йной но́чи! Мя́гкой поса́дки! Прия́тного аппети́та! Счастли́вого Рождества́! Всего́ хоро́шего! Всего́ до́брого!

Section 7.3

1. 1. нет кани́кул 2. нет рабо́ты 3. нет вре́мени 4. нет до́мика 5. нет при́были 6. нет вну́ков

2. 1. не бу́дет ма́тча 2. не появи́лось при́знаков 3. нет бу́дущего 4. нет сюже́та 5. небу́дем зака́зов

3. 1. – 2. есть. 3. – 4. – 5. – 6 –

4. 1. от 2. от 3. от 4. от 5. до, по́сле 6. с, до 7. про́тив 8. от, до 9. от, из-за

5. 1. господи́на Смирно́ва 2. из-за боле́зни, подру́ги Ири́ны 3. у Ири́ны 4. у Ири́ны 5. у Ири́ны 6. от ка́шля и на́сморка 7. для Ири́ны 8. ча́ю/ча́я без са́хара и молока́, два я́блока 10. до обе́да. 11. от температу́ры, у Ири́ны 12. до конца́ неде́ли

Chapter 8

Sections 8.1–8.2

1. 1. Ната́ше 2. студе́нтам 3. бра́ту 4. друзья́м 5. Ю́рию Гага́рину 6. преподава́телю 7. Ребёнку

2. 1. го́рю 2. свиде́телям 3. ро́дственникам 4. покло́нникам 5. по́мощи 6. иссле́дователям

Section 8.3

1. 1. по лингви́стике 2. к языка́м 3. к прия́телю 3. к сча́стью 5. к сожале́нию 6. по пя́тницам 7. по де́лу 8 по утра́м, по пля́жу

2. 1. к пра́здникам, по магази́нам 2. господи́ну Смирно́ву, роди́телям, дя́дям, тётям, племя́нникам-близнеца́м, племя́нницам, сёстрам, мужья́м, бра́тьям, жёнам 3. семье́ 4. племя́нницам, племя́нникам 5. игру́шкам 6. к сча́стью, по ра́дио, по исто́рии, по иску́сству 7. бра́тьям и сёстрам 8. ро́дственникам 9. господи́ну Смирно́ву 10. сове́ту

Chapter 9

Sections 9.1–9.2

1. 1. ножо́м 2. па́лочками 3. карандашо́м 4. по́ездом 5. стрело́й 6. кре́мом 7. зимо́й 8. весно́й 9. у́тром

2. a. высото́й оди́н метр во́семьдесят сантиме́тров; b. ширино́й оди́н метр пятьдеся́т сантиме́тров; c. глубино́й три́дцать пять сантиме́тров

3. 1. же́нщиной-космона́втом 2. столи́цей 3. те́мпами 4. фло́том 5. музе́ями, моста́ми, дворца́ми. 6. прия́телями 7. жи́знью 8. поп-му́зыкой, пла́ванием, го́льфом

Section 9.3

1. 1. Ме́жду Ло́ндоном и Москво́й 2. за овоща́ми 3. пе́ред едо́й 4. С го́рдостью 5. Пе́ред университе́том 6. с пра́здниками 7. под откры́тым не́бом 8. над статьёй 9. с колле́гами 10. со льдом, с то́ником

2. познако́миться с сосе́дом 2. ко́фе со сли́вками 3. пиро́г с гриба́ми 4. смея́ться над шу́тками 5. развести́сь с жено́й 6. спря́таться за угло́м

3. 1. с колле́гами 2. с удово́льствием, с тради́циями и обы́чаями 3. гостеприи́мством, красото́й 4. с господи́ном Смирно́вым 5. с любопы́тством, ве́ником 6. вхо́дом, полоте́нцем, ве́ником 7. ве́ником 8. со здоро́вьем, па́ром 9. с лимо́ном, мёдом, варе́ньем 10. с гриба́ми, ры́бой, мя́сом, я́блоками, я́годами

Chapter 10

1. 1. в шкафу́. 2. в о́фисе 3. на ле́кции 4. в саду́ 5. на се́вере 6. в Аме́рике

2. A. 1. о ко́смосе 2. об общежи́тии **B.** 1. о ма́тери 2. о царе́ **C.** 1. на самолёте 2. на велосипе́де

3. 1. При Горбачёве 2. В 1945-ом году́ 3. в октябре́ 4. о ме́рах 5. в креди́те 6. в подде́ржке 7. о любви́ 8. о заседа́нии

4. на у́лицах, «О чём»

1. о семье́, до́ме, де́тях, роди́телях, ро́дственниках	6. здоро́вье
2. пробле́мах, стра́хах, фо́биях	7. путеше́ствиях, приро́де
3. бога́тстве, сла́ве, почёте, уваже́нии, поку́пке	8. поли́тике и поли́тиках
4. повыше́нии	9. пого́де
5. инопланетя́нах	10. встре́чах

Chapter 11

1. 1. но́вых 2. ва́жными 3. спорти́вную 4. зубно́му 5. кита́йском 6. серьёзных 7. ру́сские наро́дные

2. 1. худо́жественной гимна́стикой, де́тской спорти́вной шко́ле 2. ма́ленькой дере́вне, стари́нного ру́сского го́рода 3. огро́мная кварти́ра, больши́ми о́кнами, многоэта́жном зда́нии 4. совреме́нную оде́жду 5. бли́зкие ро́дственники, мо́дный дорого́й айпо́д 6. вече́рнем конце́рте, популя́рной рок-гру́ппы, свобо́дных мест.

3. 1. ру́сских семе́й, ма́ленькой дере́вне 2. ста́рый дереве́нский дом, родовы́м гнездо́м 3. небольшо́м ую́тном двухэта́жном до́ме, резны́м деревя́нным крыльцо́м,

огро́мным све́тлым чердако́м, тёмным холо́дным по́гребом 4. про́шлого ве́ка 5. бе́лой
сире́ни, чёрной сморо́ды, садо́вой мали́ны 6. скрипу́чим ступе́нькам, дли́нный у́зкий
7. просто́рную ко́мнату, настоя́щей ру́сской пе́чью 8. вку́сные обе́ды, румя́ные пироги́.
9. ру́сской печи́ 10. ру́сской печи, большо́й деревя́нный стол, бе́лой льняно́й ска́тертью
11. ста́рый ме́дный самова́р 12 больши́м столо́м, тёплыми ле́тними и холо́дными зи́мними
вечера́ми, горя́чими вку́сными пирога́ми

Chapter 12

1. 1. трудне́е 2. деше́вле 3. доро́же 4. кре́пче
2. 1. са́мое глубо́кое 2. са́мая дли́нная 3. са́мые высо́кие 4. са́мый тру́дный
3. 1. тяжеле́е 2. моло́же 3. ху́же 4. доро́же 5. мла́дше
4. 1. са́мый глубо́кий, глубоча́йший, глу́бже всех 2. са́мый густонаселённый 3. са́мая
коро́ткая, кратча́йшая, коро́че всех 4. са́мое ядови́тое и опа́сное, опа́снейшее,
ядови́тее и опа́снее всех

Chapter 13

1. 1. по-англи́йски 2. интере́сно 3. ме́дленно 4. по-соба́чьи 5. и́скренне 6. дру́жески/
по-дру́жески.
2. 1. ду́шно 2. ску́чно 3. домо́й 4. неда́вно 5. отовсю́ду 6. туда́, за́втра
3. 1. нигде́ 2. никогда́ 3. не́куда 4. не́где 5. не́ от куда 6. ниотку́да
4. 1. интере́снее/увлека́тельнее, увлека́тельнее 2. бо́льше 3. я́рче, гро́мче 4. быстре́е,
бо́льше 5. прово́рнее, бли́же, бли́же 6. гро́мче 7. сильне́е 8. ча́ще 9. лу́чше 10. ре́же,
интере́снее/увлека́тельнее/оживлённее, интере́снее/увлека́тельнее/оживлённее
11. са́мый интере́сный

Chapter 14

Sections 14.1–14.7

1. 1. мне 2. Вам 3. нам 4. нём 5. тобо́й 6. их
2. 1. мое́й сестре́ 2. на́шему сосе́ду 3. Ва́шему бра́ту 4. их у́лице 5. э́тому челове́ку 6. э́ту
откры́тку, тот слова́рь 7. таки́ми ве́рными слова́ми
3. 1. свои́м го́лосом 2. свою́ рабо́ту 3. мое́й ко́мнате 4. свои́х стиха́х 5. его́ жена́, свою́
рабо́ту.

Sections 14.8–14.11

1. (a) кото́рый (b) кото́рая (c) кото́рый (d) кото́рый (e) кото́рый (f) кото́рая (g) кото́рая
(h) кото́рый 2. кото́ром 3. кото́рую 4. кото́рого 5. кото́рого
2. 1. Его́, тако́го 2. всю свою́, э́том са́мом 3. Она́, её 4. всех, э́то 5. Никто́, э́тот 6. Все,
свой, свои́ 7. Всем 8. Кто́-то, кому́-то, что́-то 9. кем-то, чем-то 10. никако́го, каки́е-то
11. самого́, така́я 12. Его́, никако́е 13. Сам, свое́й 14. Ему́, себе́ 15. Его́, его́, тако́го
16. все 17. все́ми свои́ми, свою́, э́тот

Chapter 15

1. 1. кра́сные ро́зы 2. но́вую маши́ну 3. жёлтую ды́ню, сла́дких я́блока 4. молоды́х
актёров 5. интере́сных встре́ч
2. 1. к семи́ часа́м 2. с оди́ннадцати утра́ до десяти́ ве́чера 3. без че́тверти де́вять, в
полови́не шесто́го 4. с ча́су до двух 5. в час
3. 1. Пе́рвого сентября́ ты́сяча девятьсо́т три́дцать девя́того го́да 2. Двадца́того
ноября́ ты́сяча девятьсо́т деся́того го́да 3. В ты́сяча четы́реста девяно́сто
второ́м году́ 4. В ты́сяча пятьсо́т шестьдеся́т четвёртом году́ – в ты́сяча шестьсо́т
шестна́дцатом году́ 5. В деся́том ве́ке 6. Два́дцать пе́рвое ию́ня

Chapter 16

1. 1. была́ 2. бу́дет 3. бу́дем 4 бу́ду 5. бы́ли
2. 1. явля́ется 2. бу́дет быва́ть 3. наступа́ет, стано́вится 4. счита́лся 5. нахо́дится

Chapter 17

1. 1. отдыха́ет, собира́ют, игра́ют, разгова́ривают, обсужда́ют 2. танцу́ет 3. рису́ет, пи́шет, печёт, продаёт

2. 1. зову́т 2. и́щет 3. беру́т 4. пью, ем 5. ждут 6. лжёте 7. мо́жете 8. пла́чет.

3. 1. провожа́ют 2. конча́ет, начина́ет 3. разруша́ет 4. погиба́ет 5. боле́ет

4. Встаёт, принима́ет, бре́ется, одева́ется, занима́ется, купа́ется, лежи́т, загора́ет, ката́ется, игра́ет, расслабля́ется, танцу́ет, поёт, пьёт, е́здит, ест, устаёт, спит, ви́дит

Chapter 18

1. 1. ходи́ла 2. чита́л 3. не рабо́тала 4. интересова́лся 5. спа́ли

2. 1. тёр 2. пекла́ 3. нёс 4. выра́щивал 5. везла́ 6. е́ли 7. пры́гдл 8. привы́кли 9. танцева́л, рисова́л 10. текла́ 11. шли, разгова́ривали, смея́лись

3. Встава́л, ложи́лся, мы́лся, бри́лся, принима́л, одева́лся, занима́лся, пла́вал, ката́лся, расслабля́лся, танцева́л, пел, игра́л, обе́дал, пил, е́здил, ел, торопи́лся, ходи́л, у́жинал, устава́л, смотре́л, спал

Chapter 19

1. 1. бу́дем изуча́ть 2. бу́дет рабо́тать 3. бу́ду есть 4. бу́дут пла́вать 5. бу́дете обе́дать

2. Вста́ну, вы́зову, поза́втракаю, вы́пью, прие́ду, вскочу́, расположу́сь, познако́млюсь, пообе́даю, прие́ду, переночу́ю, отпра́влюсь, пойма́ю, искупа́юсь, верну́сь, расскажу́

Chapter 20

Sections 20.1–20.5

1. 1. вы́учили 2. узнава́ли/узнаём 3. обе́дал/обе́дает 4. вы́пили, съе́ли

2. 1. сдава́л, не сда́л 2. научи́л, учи́лся 3. проводи́ть 4. позвони́л(а) 5. зако́нчит, поступи́т 6. снял

3. 1. за час 2. 10 лет 3. на 2 дня 4. на 25 лет 5. че́рез полчаса́

Sections 20.6–20.7

1. 1. слу́шать 2. встава́ть 3. выгу́ливать 4. пить 5. встава́ть 6. кури́ть 7. занима́ться 8. чита́ть 9. обсужда́ть

2. 1. веди́, не груби́, слу́шай 2. ешь(те), пей(те) 3. не расска́зывай, не проговори́сь 4. говори́(те) 5. заходи́(те), принеси́(те) 6. не упади́(те)

Chapter 21

1. 1. Сли́шком мно́го де́нег бы́ло потра́чено на сва́дьбу. Мно́го госте́й бы́ло приглашено́, мно́го бы́ло съе́дено и мно́го вина́ вы́пито. 2. Москва́ не сра́зу стро́илась. 3. Статья́ должна́ быть перепи́сана. 4. Вор бу́дет по́йман и отпра́влен в тюрьму́. 5. Ря́дом с о́фисами стро́ится но́вая парко́вка. 6. Осторо́жно! Две́ри закрыва́ются.

2. 1. Вам звони́ли два́жды. 2. Принесли́ для Вас паке́т и оста́вили на столе́. 3. Заходи́ли, спра́шивали, когда́ Вы бу́дете? 4. Вы́ставку открыва́ют за́втра. 5. В газе́тах писа́ли о Ва́шем докла́де.

Chapter 22

Sections 22.1–22.2

1. 1. уходи́(те) 2. пригото́вь(те) 3. критику́й(те) 4. ешь(те) 5. пе́й(те) 6. сади́сь(тесь)

2. А. «И́ра, будь добра́, позвони́ ма́тери. Поздра́вь её с днём рожде́ния. Купи́ ей цветы́. Жди меня́ у вхо́да в рестора́н.» **В.** «А́нна Ива́новна! Бу́дьте добры́, пошли́те факс г. Сми́ту. Закажи́те сто́лик на четверы́х в рестора́не.»

Sections 22.3–22.4

1. А. 1. съе́здил бы 2. купи́л бы 3. помо́г бы 4. провёл бы **В.** 1. съе́здит 2. ку́пит 3. помо́жет 4. проведёт

Chapter 23

1. 1. у́читесь / учи́лись 2. расслабля́ются / рассла́блялись 3. занима́ется / занима́лся
4. купа́ются / купа́лись / 5. бои́тся / боя́лся
2. 1. начнётся 2. продаю́тся 3. куса́ется 4. спря́чутся 5. разбива́ются

Chapter 24

1. 1. е́здили/ката́лись на верблю́дах 2. пое́дет в Москву́ 3. лета́ть на самолёте 4. хо́дят
5. е́здили/ката́лись на велосипе́де
2. А. 1. хо́дит 2. ла́зит 3. во́зит 4. во́дит **В.** 1. лети́т 2. иду́т, несу́т 3. е́дем 4. везёт **С.**
1. лета́ли 2. вози́ла 3. ходи́ли 4. е́здили **D.** 1. пое́дет 2. пойдёт 3. полетя́т 4. повезёт
3. 1. е́дет/е́здит, е́хала 2. пла́вать 3. шёл 4. бу́дем ходи́ть 5. ходи́л/броди́л 6. ла́зил
7. по́лзают 8. лета́ли
4. 1. идёшь 2. иду́, хожу́, идёшь 3. иду́, е́здить, е́зжу, пла́ваешь 4. пла́ваю 5. бе́гаю, идти́

Chapter 25

Sections 25.1–25.4

1. 1. выво́зит, ввози́т 2. выво́дит 3. войти́, входи́ 4. ухо́дит/отхо́дит 5. приходи́/заходи́
6. прихо́дит, ухо́дит 7. довезёте 8. отвезти́ 9. подхо́дит/подошла́ спета́ет 10. слети́т/
слете́ла подойдёт 11. взлета́ет
2. 1. перебега́ют/перебежа́ли/перебегу́т 2. переходи́ть 3. прошёл 4. объе́хать 5. зае́хал(а)
6. залете́ла 7. переплы́ть 8. дое́хать, дойти́
3. 1. пое́хать 2. пошёл 3. пое́дете 4. пое́хали 5. пошли́, пошли́ 6. пое́хала
4. 1. проходи́ли 2. сходи́ть 3. побе́гала 4. заходи́ла

Sections 25.5–25.6

1. 1. пришли́ 2. приезжа́ла 3. входи́л 4. прилета́л 5. не принёс 6. уе́ду/уезжа́ю 7. прие́хать
8. переезжа́ете 9. захо́дит, прино́сит, принёс
2. 1. Моя́ душа́ ухбднт в пя́тки при одно́й мы́сли о предстоя́щей опера́ции. 2. Моя́ подру́га
выходи́ла за́муж три ра́за. 3. Они́ не смогли́ нам помо́чь, по́езд ушёл. 4. Моше́нник
с лёгкостью обвёл вокру́г па́льца дове́рчивых люде́й. 5. По́сле несча́стного слу́чая
пацие́нт ушёл в себя́.

Section 25.7

1. 1. сквозь 2. по 3. на, в, в, в 4. из-за, ми́мо, в 5. че́рез, ми́мо, за
2. 1. е́здил 2. вози́л, прие́хали 3. пое́хать 4. дое́хали 5. вы́шли, вошли́ 6. отошёл 7. шёл
8. принесла́ 9. пришёл 10. пое́хали 11. пошли́ 12. перешли́, прошли́, зашли́, дошли́
13. обошли́, вы́шли 14. поплы́ли 15. сходи́ть/зайти́, съе́здить/пое́хать 16. прие́хать

Chapter 26

1. 1. написа́ть 2. нести́ 3. привы́кнуть 4. танцева́ть 5. жить 6. взять 7. е́хать 8. унести́
9. купи́ть 10. вы́пить
2. А. 1. пью́щий 2. берегу́щий 3. кладу́щий 4. и́щущий 5. смею́щийся 6. испо́льзующий
В. 1. прише́дший 2. съе́вший 3. интересова́вшийся 4. встреча́вшийся 5. присе́вший
6. отдохну́вший
3. А. 1. экспорти́руемый 2. люби́мый 3. изуча́емый 4. несо́мый **В.** 1. ска́занный
2. изу́ченный 3. приглашённый 4. расста́вленный 5. запрещённый 6. откры́тый
4. 1. кото́рые прино́сят 2. кото́рые им понра́вились 3. кото́рые прожи́ли 4. кото́рых
осуди́ли и приговори́ли 5. кото́рые написа́л В. Пеле́вин и кото́рые перевёл 6. кото́рые
понижа́ют жар.
5. 1. приезжа́ющие 2. поте́рянный рассе́янным профе́ссором 3. в не замерза́ющих
исто́чниках 4. па́пку, оста́вленную пассажи́ром 5. осно́ванной изве́стным бизнесме́ном
6. разру́шенных урага́ном
6. 1. опублико́ванную 2. заинтересо́ван 3. разочаро́ваны 4. отремонти́рованный
5. ку́пленный

Chapter 27

1. A. 1. закóнчить 2. существовáть 3. интересовáться 4. попрощáться 5. вы́расти
6. боя́ться 7. давáть 8. передáть 9. быть 10. унести́ **B.** 1. придя́ 2. погáснув 3. беря́
4. рисýя 5. зацвéсши 6. ищá 7. улыбнýвшись 8. найдя́ 9. живя́ 10. спёкши

2. A. 1. лежи́т и блести́т 2. бýдут рабóтать и испóльзовать 3. прóжил, рабóтал, не читáл,
не интересовáлся 4. Пóсле тогó как Солжени́цын прóжил 5. Пóсле тогó как онá пришлá
домóй 6. оступи́лся, упáл и не донёс 7. Когдá семья́ услы́шала, онá приготóвилась
B. 1. бéгая 2. шутя́, покáзывая 3. поднимáясь 4. разрушáя, ломáя, перевёрáчивая,
оставля́я 5. вернýвшись 6. получи́в 7. запóлнив, пройдя́ 8. закóнчив

3. 1. сидéть сложá рýки 2. несли́сь сломá гóлову 3. не поклáдая рук 4. Моя́ пéсенка до
концá не спéта

4. 1. рабóтает мнóго 2. занимáется 3. ничегó не дéлать 4. éсли говори́ть откровéнно
5. встал, при́нял, одéлся, вы́пил 6. сел, включи́л 7. остáвил 8. добрáлся, сел, провéрил
9. серди́лся 10. перекуси́л 11. дýмал, беспокóился

Chapter 28

1. 1. из 2. у 3. на, за 4. на 5. в, с 6. в 7. в 8. с, до 9. на 10. без, с
2. 1. к 2. от 3. за 4. со, на 5. под 6. по 7. на 8. о 9. на, среди́, с 10. в, по.

Chapter 29

1. 1. Бизнесмéн попроси́л секретаря́, чтóбы онá отмени́ла встрéчу. 2. Домохозя́йка пошлá
на ры́нок, чтóбы купи́ть продýкты. 3. Хотя́ инострáнные студéнты прóбыли в Росси́и
недóлго, они́ ужé нáчали чýвствовать себя́ как дóма. 4. У нас нé было достáточно
дéнег и поэ́тому мы реши́ли поéсть дóма. 5. Ви́ктор устáл так, как бýдто он пробежáл
марафóн. 6. Студéнты получи́ли пятёрки, потомý что они́ мнóго рабóтали 7. Вы
понимáете рýсскую послóвицу «Чем дáльше в лес, тем бóльше дров?» 8. Они́ хотéли
пойти́ на вечери́нку, однáко отказáлись от приглашéния.
2. 1. хотя́/несмотря́ на то что, поэ́тому 2 что, и́ли, и́ли, и́ли 3. éсли бы 4. как бýдто 5. в то
врéмя как/покá, чтóбы 6. едвá, что

Chapter 30

1. 1. Становится дýшно. 2. Им не хотéлось рабóтать. 3. Нам нáдо спеши́ть. 4. Здесь
нельзя́ кури́ть. 5. Полетéть бы на Лунý. 6. Никогó нé было в лесý со мной. Я испугáлся/
лась. 7. Мне нéкогда. 8. Мне нýжен ваш совéт. 9. Мне нрáвится Вáша причёска.
10. Извини́те, мне нáдо идти́. 11. Бóльше всегó я люблю́ гуля́ть по лéсу, когдá рассветáет.
2. 1. Ни́не нéкуда бы́ло поéхать. 2. Им нéчему удивля́ться. 3. Мáльчику нé с кем
игрáть. 4. Нам нé над чем бы́ло смея́ться. 5. Ви́ктору нéкуда спеши́ть.

Grammatical Index